TO

EDWARD

CW00926793

FROM TEAM MASERATI

MASERATI
AT
HEART

Ermanno Cozza

MASERATI AT HEART

GIORGIO NADA EDITORE

Giorgio Nada Editore Srl

Editorial manager
Leonardo Acerbi

Editorial
Giorgio Nada Editore

Cover and layout
Giorgio Nada Editore

Translation
Neil Davenport

Photographs
Ermanno Cozza
Giorgio Nada Editore/Fondo Franco Villani
Adolfo Orsi
Archivio Maserati

Cover photo (top) Renato Zacchia

Translator's note

A feature of Ermanno Cozza's writing is his use of professional and honorary titles such as Ingegner (Engineer), Avvocato (Lawyer), Signor (Mr.), Commendatore (Knight Commander) and so one. We have decided to retain these titles in the original Italian to reflect Signor Cozza's very formal and respectful attitude to the various people he encountered during his remarkable career.

Giorgio Nada Editore - Via Claudio Treves, 15/17
I – 20090 VIMODRONE MI
T + 39 02 27301126 - F + 39 02 27301454
E-mail: info@giorgionadaeditore.it
http://www.giorgionadaeditore.it

Allo stesso indirizzo può essere richiesto il catalogo di tutte le opere pubblicate dalla Casa Editrice.

The catalogue of Giorgio Nada Editore publications is available on request at the above address.

Distribuzione:
Giunti Editore Spa
via Bolognese 165
I – 50139 FIRENZE
www.giunti.it

Maserati at heart
ISBN: 978-88-7911-716-6

Summary

PREFACE

Business history is composed of the men involved, with the automotive sector being no exception to the rule. Ermanno Cozza is the living proof. Having joined Maserati in 1951, 66 years later, he still passes through the gates on Viale Ciro Menotti with all the enthusiasm and dedication he displayed on his first day.

The company has known various ownerships and enjoyed alternate fortunes, but Ermanno has always been there to defend the fortress from attack and attempts to modify the DNA of design excellence, attention to detail and client service that has characterised Maserati from the heroic times of Bologna onwards. I often find myself leafing through correspondence with early Maserati collectors who contacted the factory for information about their car. It is always a pleasure to read the replies, some written in Ermanno's idiosyncratic "broken" English, that tried to provide every possible assistance. That there are still so many classic Maseratis around the world is in part down to Ermanno, their "guardian angel".

After having made his practical contribution to the engine testing room, where he had "Tonino" Reggiani as his guide, and to the Technical Office, he donned the hat of the "senator" and became, by example, a point of reference for the younger generations of Maserati employees.

Reading the first drafts of his story, I relived the magical atmosphere of the Fifties and Sixties, I read the names and saw once again the faces of the numerous employees who contributed to the history of Maserati, alongside the managers, the engineers, the drivers and the designers. Without their effort and support, the Maserati story could never have been written.

This book is a tribute to their labours.

Adolfo Orsi

INTRODUCTION

I decided that I would begin writing about the years I spent at Maserati given that at meetings, lunches and dinners I would inevitably be invited to recount a few anecdotes, recall a race or a driver or perhaps explain the genesis of new engines or cars or talk about a Maserati character. In the end there would always be someone who suggested I should write something about those years. On countless occasions I was told that I had what amounted to a moral duty to leave a written testimony, otherwise nothing would be left of those who experienced those 60 years at Maserati at first hand. On Saturday the 23rd of August 2014, at dinner at the Sankt Moritz meeting, I was sitting at the same table as Signor Venanzio Fonte, a Maserati collector who, after having brought back numerous memories, took me by the hand and looking into my eyes made me promise that I would sit down to write my memoirs. Being a man of his word, I am determined to keep that promise; I have no idea what will come of it, but I will try jotting something down.

Ermanno Cozza

THE "MASERATI VIRUS"

1943. I was 10 years old and while I was helping a neighbour by holding pliers and spanners as he unscrewed nuts and bolts to dismantle a Moto Guzzi, hiding it away from wartime requisitioning, he taught me about the functioning of internal combustion engines. I told him that a few days earlier, I'd been riding my bike to my Uncle Achille's, who had a trattoria in Via Ciro Menotti, on the corner of Via Usiglio, when I'd seen through an open doorway where they built racing cars on Via Trento Trieste, before the Pradella bridge. According to Signor Vito those were Alfa Romeos, built in Milan, and that in that garage they only repaired them after they had raced. The real racing car factory was at the end of Via Ciro Menotti, before the level crossing; he told me that the Maserati brothers had come from to Modena from Bologna a few years earlier, that they were exceptional people and had already won many races, one of which was very important and had been run in America. Signor Vito explained that they built everything themselves, they didn't employ engineers, but they had such talent, passion and enterprise that they managed to win with their own cars at the expense of other marques with far larger and more famous factories. Within two or three days I had heard so many stories about the Maserati brothers and their Officine Alfieri Maserati that they'd become engraved in my mind. I think that it was actually then that I contracted the "Maserati virus" that over time was to develop into full-blown "Tridentitis"!

CHILDHOOD MEMORIES

I was born in the August of 1933 at Collegarola, a village five kilometres from the centre of Modena, in a small house close to the elementary school. Signora Elena, who brought me into the world, was a retired midwife living in the neighbouring villa with her husband Signor Gaudenzio, a retired Carabinieri marshal. My mother always talked to me about those years and I have retained wonderful memories: my father was a carpenter at Americano in Collegara and built wooden wheels for agricultural machinery and carts for the Zucchi company.

On my third birthday he brought home a tricycle, a gift from Signora Elena. It had been sent from Modena and left at the "bottega", the trattoria-cum-tobacconist's-cum-grocer's run by my paternal grandparents and uncles, with my father having agreed to pick it up. As soon as I had that tricycle in my hands I shot off to show it to my "nanny" (none other than Signora Elena of course); at the first corner I overturned and burst into tears. Signor Gaudenzio dusted me down and told me there was no need to rush because the "tata" already knew about the tricycle as she had actually bought it.

I remember the summer evenings: Signor Peppino Froia would bring ice cream and we would all hop around the table on one foot (we were doing what we called the "*piè zupàt*", or lame foot). The one who could stay on one foot longest won; the prize consisted of being allowed to lick out the ice cream container. Of course, they always let me win.

These were the war years and I remember that on certain evenings Signor Gaudenzio would bring out large rolled up maps and all the men would talk amongst themselves, looking at those maps. On my fifth birthday, Signora Elena gave me the uniform of the "Figli della Lupa" (the Children of the She-Wolf, a Fascist organization for young children) and my father would stand me on the table to put on the white belt and braces crossing over my chest. Like most people in those years, Signora Elena was a fan of Mussolini and in the summer she would spend a few weeks by the sea at Riccione, in a *pensione* directly opposite the Duce's villa. One year my parents and I went to visit her and I stayed on with her for a few days. She took me to the beach where I played with other children including Romano, the Duce's son, who was a few years older than me. I remember a red open-top car, a spider, parked on the driveway alongside the villa and later learned that it belonged to Bruno, Romano's elder brother.

We moved when I was six because the house at Collegarola was very old and very damp; we went to live at number 956 in Via Vignolese, the first house after the bridge over the Grizzaga torrent, where five other families were already living.

I went to the elementary school at Collegarola through to the third year; when I came out of school I always went to Signora Elena's for lunch and to do my homework; I would go home between four and five in the afternoon. When I saw my friends around that time they would tease me thinking I had been kept back in detention at school. Signora Elena also moved into town in the same period, in Via della Pace, because she and Signor Gaudenzio, both ageing by then, could no longer cope in the winters in that large house with no central heating. This meant that I spent the fourth and fifth years of elementary school at the Istituto Casa e Famiglia in Via Tamburini in Modena, so that my mother could go and take care of the "nanny".

I was in Signora Elena's room when she died. She was holding my hands and I felt a strong shaking and then realised she was no longer breathing. I cried for the passing of one of the key figures of my childhood.

In 1939, my father passed the exam and was accepted as a carpenter at the Military Academy; in those years many civilians were working there, builders, electricians and so on; he stayed there through to retirement in 1964. Naturally, in order to be able to take the exam he was obliged to sign up to the Fascist party, as so many were in those years. I remember one Sunday afternoon that year when I went with my father to Portile, to the home of the lawyer Enrico Vezzalini, a well-known Fascist party official from Modena, from whom he hoped to gain a reference to find a stable job and therefore maintain his family. Even before the American bombing of Modena I had seen a toing and froing of Maserati electric delivery trucks that would go down to the end of the lane immediately after the Grizzaga bridge. There, there was a large villa and then the Corradinis' house, an agricultural family numbering around 15 people who had a huge farm. I often went there because two of the Corradini brothers were the same age as me and we were friends. Machine tools and other things were taken there because of concerns about possible bombing. I later learnt that the tooling and so on was from the Officine Alfieri Maserati, the farm and the villa in fact being the property of Commendatore Adolfo Orsi. I also met and played with Gianfranco Giacomazzi, the son of a sister of the Commendatore whose family had been evacuated to the villa for some time between 1944 and 1945.

THE NEW BICYCLE
AND THE WATCH

When I was between six and twelve years of age I had a
bicycle that was smaller than normal (a 20" model), it was
a present from Signora Elena and I had great fun roaming
the city and the countryside on it. I remember that when I
went to the Vignolese, the grocer's-cum-restaurant run by
my aunts, they would always send me on errands. Back
then the streets of Modena were child-friendly. I'd go to the
Industria del Gelo to get a stick of ice. Signor Sergio would
break it into two pieces and put them in two bags, one either
side of the handlebars. The ice was for the cooler, because
at that time we were still waiting for the refrigerator to be
invented. Or I'd go to fill two syphons with *seltz* in Via
Sant'Agostino, at Dr Testi's store. I've wonderful memories
of the trips on that bike. Many of my friends envied me
because there were few children of that age who owned
their own bicycle suitable for their height. When I started
at the Corni school I was given a new 26" man's bicycle
with gears, a Wander painted beige. Together with the bicycle I was also given a watch as having to go to different
places at set times meant a watch was indispensible. I've
no idea how many kilometres I covered in seven years on
that bike: from Collegarola to school in Modena twice a
day and in the summer sometimes as far as Serramazzoni
or Pavullo. Via Giardini, in the stretch known as "the cut",
was a particularly hard climb. I'd learnt to repair punctures
and my father always told me to keep it clean well-oiled.

ISTITUTO TECNICO
FERMO CORNI

My father had a fully equipped carpenter's workshop in our cellar as in order to top up his wages he would do jobs at home on Saturdays and Sundays; he'd inherited many of the tools from his Uncle Achille, the brother of his mother, my grandmother Carmelina. I'd therefore become confident using those tools to build elastic guns, go-karts and other toys. But how many dressings down from Father because I never put away the tools I used! He'd always be telling me: "I'm please you're learning to do a few things, but you've got to learn to be tidy and always keep the workbench in order". All that grumbling did pay off in the long run in my scholastic and working life.

When I finished elementary school I registered at the Istituto Tecnico Fermo Corni in Modena (in October 1945), an industrial school for mechanics, electricians and radio technicians. As early as the late 19th century, Fermo Corni had realised that for the embryonic industry of Modena to grow and flourish it needed workers with at least a basic technical training. He had himself founded a small toolmaking firm in Modena and struggled to find suitable staff; in 1917 he overcame numerous obstacles to open the first technical school in the town. Over time, thanks to donations, including personal gifts from Corni himself and from other bodies, the school developed into professional school for the arts and trades and in 1922 it was designated as an Istituto Professionale Statale or State Professional

Institute. The Istituto Corni turned out the best technicians that industrial firms in Modena and elsewhere could
hope to find. It was inevitable that numerous mechanical
engineering firms were established in Modena as the art
of the "*Ferarii*" (a dialect term for metalworkers), who
were already contributing to the construction of Modena
cathedral (1099), gave rise to the Corporazione dei Ferarii
e Magnanti (a corporation of itinerant sheet metal and tin
workers). Their statutes are among the earliest documented
in Modena. These smiths worked iron and in Italy their
corporation was already placed between the 15th and 20th
position in the standings of the various trade consortia. The
industrial wealth and the specialisations in numerous pro-
ductive sectors which the city of Modena boasts is therefore
the result of multiple concomitant causes: the talent, the
professionalism, the passion displayed, the sacrifices made
and above all the courage shown in the face of innumerable
obstacles encountered during this long historical and social
development. During the last war, the Istituto Corni was
bombed and only the building housing the girls' course
was left standing. When school restarted in the October of
1945 therefore, many classes were placed in other schools
around the city or in buildings formerly occupied by the
fascist authorities.

OCTOBER 1945,
FIRST DAY OF SCHOOL
AT THE CORNI

I was in the first year Initiation Section C class that had been relocated to the former Scientific High School in Via Servi after the destruction of the school premises during the bombing. For the practical lessons in metalworking we'd go to the workshops at the main site. There were around 30 boys in my class, many of whom came from out of town. I made a lot of friends, in particular Cottafavi who came from Campogalliano. I have always been very shy and a little introverted, although as I got older I did start to open up. The first few days were particularly tough as there were so many new subjects, all with different teachers. We had lessons morning and afternoon. A couple of weeks after the start of school, one afternoon after the first hour of French, in the break before the maths lesson, many of my classmates were moving around out of their desks making a lot of noise. I was sitting at my desk with my back to the door, chatting quietly to my friend and while the others were slipping back into their seats, I didn't see Professor Venturi coming in. All hell broke loose, the dressing down even mentioning the American soldiers still present in Modena: what if they had heard and seen our behaviour! I was identified as the most undisciplined and was given a two-day suspension. I was distraught, above all because I hadn't been causing trouble; I hadn't even left my desk, just turned round. I was also worried about going home and having to tell my parents about the suspension. When I told my mother what had happened, she asked me for every last detail and then told me not to worry because she would be going to talk to Professor Venturi. When my father got back I told him everything; as I sobbed he too consoled me. The following morning I went to school, even though I was suspended, accompanied by my mother who knew the Italian teacher, Signora Carla Camurri who had been evacuated to San Donnino during the war, and together they went to talk to Professor Venturi. The prof was adamant that he had to set an example for the class as a whole. My mother, an energetic, resolute woman, refused to bow down and threatened Professor Venturi that she would report him to the headmaster for an abuse of power; in short, she kicked up such a fuss that my two-day suspension was lifted.

BACK TO THE OLD SCHOOL

In 1948, at the end of the three-year Initiation course, my class, now designated 1st year Technical, section B Mechanics, went back to the old school premises, with other classes being transferred to the other side of the road, in the former 26 Settembre premises that housed the benchwork classrooms and the technology workshop. On the first day of the school year, the headmaster, Ingegner Malagodi, gave an inaugural speech and among his various pieces of advice I remember the following: "When you need to telephone, always first say your name and who you want to speak to." Malagodi was an extremely important figure for the Istituto Corni, which over the years had continued to evolve thanks to exceptional teachers, in particular those of the technical subjects. It is worth remembering in fact, that many of the RAI TV technicians of the Fifties graduated from the Corni, the only Radio Communications School in Italy. Malagodi was also the president of the Modena Municipal Electric Company. He therefore had a direct understanding of the need to firstly train and find specialist workers and technicians, the kind of staff that industry was crying out for. An example of his illuminated management came in 1955; having witnessed the growth in the number of cars on Italian roads, he established the Motorista (power unit engineer) course. Heading the practical course was Signor Sergio Scapinelli, a former Ferrari mechanic and Nuvolari's co-driver in the last Mille Miglia disputed by the "Flying Mantuan".

THE AERAUTODROMO

The Modena motor racing circuit was inaugurated on the 7th of May 1950, but had been in use from early March. One day, as we were coming out of the Corni around lunchtime, we could here the sound of racing cars on the track. A couple of my friends and I decided to go and watch; the Autodromo was less than a kilometre from the school. We climbed onto the outside wall and sat and watched as two Maseratis lapped the track. I was more attracted by the roar of the engines than the cars themselves. I closed my eyes and imagined all those mechanical moving parts that Signor Vito had taught be about years earlier. I didn't notice that it was gone one o'clock and the three-hour technical applications lesson started at half-past; I wouldn't have time to go home for lunch. My two friends, who lived out of town, had sandwiches and gave me one each. My mother, concerned that I hadn't come back for lunch, came to the Corni to make sure nothing had happened to me. I can't remember ever seeing my father as angry as that evening as he tore into me for having left them worrying. Nonetheless, it was from that day that I decided I would go to work for Maserati and above all that I would make the moving parts in the engines of those cars.

One afternoon a few Sundays later, I was at the home of my friends, the Corradini boys, on the Orsi property. While we were playing football I overheard two men talking to the farmers; when I realised that one of them was Commendatore Orsi I picked up the ball, approached them and said: "Signor Commendatore, I would like to come and work for Maserati." Smiling, he asked me how old I was and what I did, to which I replied, "I'm 16 and I'm in the last year at the Istituto Corni." He told that I should come to Maserati then once I had finished school.

VISITING THE OFFICINE ALFIERI MASERATI

During the summer holiday, together with a group of school friends, I frequented the Istituto Corni's workshop and under the supervision of Professor Rino Fochi dismantled machine tools in order to draw details to reconstruct; above all, it was an excuse to stay in contact with the school and with Signor Fochi, because we knew that he would have helped us find a job after we had graduated. Having heard that a few boys older than me had left the Corni and gone to work at the Officine Maserati, I began to get anxious and to ask my mother to look for "references". Those were turbulent years from a socio-political and trade union point of view and many businessmen were very careful about who they would employ.

One afternoon after school had finished, Signor Fochi, the head of all the Corni's technical applications courses, asked me to go with him to Maserati because he'd been called by the workshop foreman Ingegner Bellentani, a friend of his. I could hardly wait, I was so excited! When we arrived in Via Ciro Menotti we entered the front door of the factory and I remember a polished brass plaque that read "Officina A. Maserati - Uffici". The doorman went to call Bellentani who arrived a few minutes later. He greeted Fochi very warmly, confirmation that they were great friends. I followed them as Bellentani took Fochi on a tour of the various departments. I was amazed by the cleanliness and sense of order that reigned in the workshop. A few of the workers greeted Signor Fochi with great familiarity and I later learnt that they were all the same age and had attended the Corni together. You could hear the sound of an engine they were probably testing... how I would have liked to have visited that department too! Instead, Bellentani turned in a completely different direction. While I followed on behind, I could hear they were talking about work, about increasing the labour force, but I was so busy looking at everything left and right that I didn't really catch what it was they were saying. I later learnt that it was Bellentani's custom to ask his teacher friend to recommend any particularly talented pupils. In the meantime, my mother had also been active: she had gained a reference via a friend of Signora Idina, the daughter of Commendatore Orsi, while one of my old teachers, a friend of Signora Carla, wife of Omer Orsi, obtained another. I was therefore anxiously waiting for my job application at Officine A. Maserati to be accepted. As I mentioned previously, given the union problems, the company was unwilling to employ anyone associated with or supporting a certain party and therefore gathered information from the parish council, from the Carabineri and so on, about the individual in question, his family and his acquaintances. Despite all the references some time inevitably passed following the presentation of my application given that all these company regulations had to be observed.

23 OCTOBER 1951

On Wednesday 18 October a man on a bicycle came to my home in Collegarola with the news that I was to report to Maserati on Monday 23 October. The next five days were interminable; I could hardly wait for Monday and was all but jumping out of my skin with excitement. At 7:30 on Monday morning I was already outside the employees' entrance. The man who had come to my home was the delivery man, Signor Mantovani. When he saw me, he told me to follow him and we passed through a deserted workshop with the workers still to arrive. We met Commendatore Orsi who told Signor Mantovani to remember that he had to take him to the bank at 9 o'clock. Mantovani replied: "I'll just take this lad to the personnel office and then I'll go and get the car ready." I still remember the thrill when I said to Commendatore Orsi "I'm that boy from Collegarola" and the memory of his reply accompanied by two pats on the back is even more vivid, "Yes, yes, I remember; work hard and you'll see you'll be happy here." At the personnel office, Signorina Xella had me sign a series of papers and told I would be employed as an apprentice engine fitter with a year's contract. She gave me a coupon to exchange at the store for the tokens I would use to withdraw tools and so on and my time card to be stamped on entering and leaving the factory. Time card No. 36, the same number was impressed on the tokens for tools and the hook where I could hang my bicycle under the canopy; that same number also corresponded to my locker in the changing room. I was taken to the Quality Control Centre and entrusted to the foreman, Signor Ardilio Manfredini. He was only a little older than me and seeing me a little bewildered he immediately tried to put me at my ease. He explained what it was that went on at the Quality Control Centre and introduced me to the other four workers: Alberto Godeas, Nello Poltrini, Enzo Vincenzi and Franco Bellettini were all from the Corni and had joined Maserati a few years earlier.

The Quality Control Centre was a space of around 100 square metres fenced off within the Auto machine tool production department. It was composed of two surface plates, equipment for checking the hardness of steels and all the instruments, micrometers, dial gauges, comparators and so on that served to check the worked pieces for both the milling machines and the cars. Signor Manfredini explained that I'd be replacing Godeas who was to go to the Auto Production office. It was in fact the workshop foreman Bellentani's policy to place all new employees coming from the Corni in the Quality Control Centre. This immediately provided them with an overview of everything that was being manufactured for both the milling machine and car divisions. The midday bell rang, but I was so caught up in it all that I mistook it for the eight o'clock start. In any case, I went home for lunch while many colleagues from out of town had brought their lunch with them. There was no canteen at that time, but next to the changing room there was a hall with tables and benches and a large stainless steel tank about 20 cm high, full of water, that a worker would switch on at 11:30 so that it would act as a bain-marie to heat the numerous pans left by the workers as they made their way to their departments. At 13:15 I was back at work where I was told to check the dimensions and threads of a box of ring nuts for the milling machine shelf; half-past five came around in the blink of an eye. The Quality Control Centre personnel were also expected to go and check the part-finished pieces in the various departments, in particular the milling machine uprights and the engine crankshafts and cylinder blocks. The next day, Signor Manfredini took me round the various departments, introducing me to the various foremen so that they would recognise me should we meet during the working day.

The two divisions of the factory (milling machines and cars) organized along similar lines. The Milling Machine section was composed of a machine shop for the various components headed by Signor Bianchini, who was also responsible for the gear cutting group for the machining of all gears including those for the Auto division. Then came the milling machine assembly department headed by Signor Barbieri, who was also responsible for the planing group and the and preparation of the uprights (massive components in cast iron that formed the structural frame of the Maserati milling machines). The same department also housed the group of markers for castings for both the milling machines and the engine cylinder head and block castings. At the centre of the two sections was the tooling department headed by Signor Baracca; the best workers were to be found here, turners, millers and fitters, as it was here that all the tooling was made for the various production phases. The department also housed the Genevoise (or Ginevrina), an extremely precise boring machine that worked according to movements made by coordinates, which the operator Candini calculated with trigonometry.

The Car section was composed of the component production department headed by Signor Barani, which also housed the Quality Control Centre. The chassis and welding department, headed by Signor Boni, was where the various chassis of the cars were constructed along with all the pipework for the engines. Beyond this department was the paint shop for milling machine uprights. Finally came the engine assembly department headed by Signor Gino Bertocchi and the racing department and testing room controlled by Signor Guerino Bertocchi.

There were also two general stores: one for the Car section, run by Signor Zani and the other for the Milling Machine section run by Signor Martini. These two answered to Signor Tommasini who was responsible for deliveries and shipping. Two small stores were located in the Milling Machine and Car divisions where the workers would hand over one of the 10 tokens they were issued with and receive in return the small tools needed for particular job and which had to be returned at the end of the day in exchange for the token. On the other side of the courtyard, in a still unfinished building, were the heat treatment department under Signor Montipò (aka Monti), the bar cutter and the store for all the various types of steel needed to fabricate the various components headed by Signor Parreschi. Signor Fantuzzi occupied part of this building where the bodies for the racing cars were built. Lastly, there was a bunker containing the many types of oil and above all the drums of benzol and methyl alcohol used to mix the fuel for the racing cars. The blacksmith's shop with the drop hammer and forge were housed in a building in the field behind the factory.

Running what might be considered either a small or a large concern (depending on one's point of view) were two production offices managing the workflows of the two divisions and two technical offices for the design work. Signor Cavaberra headed the Milling Machine technical office while Ingegner Massimino was his counterpart for the Car division. The purchasing department and the personnel office completed the administrative area, while the factory as a whole was run by Ingegner Bellentani who had tweaked and improved the entire organization.

The employees were mainly veterans (for us boys a man of 40 was already old), while the youngsters of between 18 and 20 (around 30 of us) had been taken on between 1950 and 1953 when Maserati was reinforcing and preparing the Car division. The emotions of those first days at Maserati and then a lifetime spent in that workshop are for me unforgettable. Despite my shyness and perhaps in part because of the very deferential way in which I always behave, I immediately felt accepted by my colleagues and soon struck up friendships with many of them. There was a strong family feeling about the place. Only after a few months did I notice a certain ideological attitude rather than any union activity; then again, we should not forget the historical context of those early post-war years and Modena's role in the notorious "red triangle", but I'll talk more about these things later. I performed my tasks with passion, every day was always more interesting and thanks to my colleagues I learnt new things and the use of the department's various tools.

UNFORGETTABLE
CHARACTERS

Among the many "veterans" from whom I was lucky enough to learn and who enriched my professional life, of particular note was Signor Montipò, the foreman of the heat treatment shop. He had a depth of experience in the treatment of steels, cast-irons and light alloys; he was a shrewd person, smiling and laughing, always in shirt sleeves, summer and winter. In the Quality Control Centre we would often use lead mallets to extract certain mechanical parts and one of these was so deformed as to be virtually unusable. Signor Manfredini suggested that we should go to Montipò to have it reformed.

When I entered the heat treatment department, the tempering and annealing furnaces were giving off a fierce heat and as they were closing the door of one of those furnaces I caught a glimpse of its fiery interior. I asked one of the workers for Signor Montipò and smiling he replied: *"Mo che sgnòr e sgnòr mè a soun sol Montipò... c'sa vòt e chi tà mandèe?"* ("Less of the Signor, I'm Montipò and that's it... Who would you be and who sent you?") Face with this fire-eater, I timidly replied that I had a lead mallet to be reformed. He grabbed the tool, snapped off the handle in a vice and put the lead part in a receptacle that he placed in a small incandescent furnace. A few minutes later he picked up two long tongs and extracted the receptacle containing the molten lead which he mixed with a finger saying, *"L'hè bèle àbasta liquid"* ("It's already nice and liquid.") So shocked was I by this operation that I hardly dared look at Montipò's hand for fear of seeing less than the usual five fingers! Instead, he asked me for a box that was sitting on a shelf (it was of course the mould), inserted the handle and using a ladle poured in the molten lead until it was full. He then quenched the whole lot in the water bath and said as he handed me the mallet, «*Tò mò al too màrtel l'è bèle fat*» ("Here's your hammer, good as new.") When I got back to my department I told Signor Manfredini the story and learnt that Monti was well known for impressing the novices and having fun with similar tricks.

A few days later I had the chance to visit the racing department and see at first hand the A6GCM single-seater racing car that Signor Fantuzzi assisted by two fitters was finishing to body. Fantuzzi, a Bolognese through and through, was a true master, an artist in the hand-beating of aluminium panels to the required shape. Seeing me arrive he asked, *"Dèm bein so fansein... chi serchet?"* ("Tell me lad, who're you looking for?") I timidly replied that I was looking for Signor Guerino Bertocchi so that he could advise me on five odometer cables for GT cars; Fantuzzi then told me I'd have to come back because Guerino was out testing. Signor Manfredini once told me a propos of Fantuzzi that a few years earlier the single-headlight A6GCS had cycle wings that could be attached or removed according to the use the car was to be put. Manfredini pointed out to Fantuzzi that if you touched these wings they flexed and there might be a risk of them falling off; on hearing this Fantuzzi wittily replied in his Bolognese dialect, *"Dem bein so fantesma, a scosa anch la cavà d'un èsen, ma l'an sèlta mengha via!"* ("A donkey's tail also twitches but it never falls off!")

Another character was Signor Abele Botti who it was said talked to the distributors and magnetos as he bench tested them. An expert motor vehicle electrician, he was a giant of a man who spoke very slowly, a trait those closest to him would tease him about.

At times life in the workshop, with all its distractions and jokes, could become dangerous, like the time we heard a deafening bang and saw a cloud of dust billowing from the chassis and tube bending area. In that era, when aluminium or steel tubes needed to be bent, a method as old as it was safe was used to ensure that the tubes did not "wrinkle" with required curvatures remaining smooth. That method consisted of closing one end of the tube with a welded plate and then filling it with very fine and perfectly dry sand, tamping it down repeatedly to make sure it was perfectly full. The other end was then sealed with a plug in very dry wood, after which the area to be curved was heated with a blowtorch. On this occasion during the operation the wooden plug exploded with a bang leading to an indescribable dust cloud. The episode earned the worker involved, Enzo Bonfiglioli, the nickname *"Spùlvràz"* (Dust cloud) which stuck with him.

When in mid-morning we saw Bianchini, an extremely talented turner from the tool works, going past, we didn't need to look at our watches to know it was 11 o'clock. He was as precise at work as he was in life and that was the time Bianchini went to the toilet; he was a veteran and for us youngsters he too in his own way was guru of life and work.

Philosophy combined with practicality can occasionally be the root of misunderstandings. There was a young engineer called Vecchi who had joined Maserati early in 1953. He was said to be a genius and soon gave proof of his talent by recalculating the lobes of the camshafts for the twin-cam A6GCS engine that immediately produced more power. This engineer had been installed in a small room alongside the technical office and the story went that one morning Ingegner Bellentani, hearing strange noises from Vecchi's office, opened the door and to his great surprise found him bouncing a tennis ball with great precision off the walls, ceiling and floor. This is the dialogue between the two engineers as reported by those present. Ingegner Bellentani: *"Inzgnèr al dèga so mò csà fàl?"* ("Ingegnere, what on earth are you doing?"); the reply of a genius could only have been in Italian rather than dialect: "In my moments of reflection I turn my thoughts to technological innovations." It took little to rile Ingegner Bellentani: *"Mè an nò capì gnìnta ed cùsa al vlìva dir, però l'è propria vera quii chi gàn una gran tèsta i ein àanch un po' màt"* ("I didn't understand a word you said, but it's true those with a great brain are always a little off their heads"). A few months later Vecchi resigned and went to work for a multi-national and we never heard from again.

SIGNOR BINDO MASERATI

Three or four months had passed since I joined the company and I had settled in well. Given my willing and respectful nature I got on with everyone and in the Quality Control Centre I even undertook jobs of a certain importance and professionalism. One afternoon Signor Tommasini came to Quality Control with another man in overalls, below which however he wore a shirt and tie; they were talking with Manfredini. The gentleman had a crankshaft to be balanced, but it wasn't from one of our engines, it was a fairly small four-cylinder shaft. I was entrusted with the job and as Tommasini and the gentleman left I noticed a degree of familiarity between the two. I set to work with the Trebel, the balancing machine, trying to be as precise as possible: I found the heavy spot and used a punch to make two marks for the 6 mm holes to be drilled to a depth of 5 mm; I then completed the report and the time card for the job and took everything to the deliveries and shipping section. Signor Manfredini later told me that the gentleman was Bindo Maserati, one of the famous brothers, who had remained in Modena around 10 years after selling their factory to the Orsi family. That was why, he told me, he seemed so at home, greeting here and there many of the older workers.

A few days later I saw him again and after he had spoken to Manfredini, they came towards me and he asked me to balance the crankshaft again; I was very surprised that I hadn't done a good job the first time round. Signor

Bindo soon put my mind, however, at rest by explaining that this time he would like the crankshaft balanced so as to simulate, with rings applied to the con-rod stems, the full con-rod, piston and crank weight; this meant that the entire crank mechanism would be balanced. He stayed with me throughout the operation which made me rather uncomfortable; I realised he must have noticed when, to put me at my ease, he began talking about their new OSCA four-cylinder, 1500 cc MT4 engine. He asked me how long I had been working at Maserati, congratulating me on my work and the way I kept my tools tidy; the crankshaft needed no further modification, the balancing proved to be perfect. He told me that they intended to acquire their own balancing machine because the driveshafts required careful balancing to eliminate certain vibrations. He shook my hand as he left and wished me success in my job. It was a source of great pride for me to have met and talked to one of the famous brothers about whom I'd heard so much since I was a child.

Signor Benetti, head of the production office, a former Maserati brothers employee who had come with them from Bologna together with Bertocchi, Tommasini, Fantuzzi, Ferri and Parenti, had taken a shine to me and took me with him to Imola to the Cogne workshop where they did work for Maserati, in particular for the milling machines and where I would have to perform certain quality control procedures on some of the products. Signor Benetti also complimented me for how I'd worked with Signor Bindo: the two had talked about me, something that gave me great pleasure and further reinforced my attachment to the company.

THE POST-WAR LEGACY OF
THE MASERATI BROTHERS

Commendatore Adolfo Orsi, a Modense businessman, acquired the Maserati firm in 1937, moving it in the autumn of 1939 from Bologna to Modena in Via Ciro Menotti, where it is still located today. The Commendatore was assisted in the running of the company by his son Omer. It was said of the Commendatore that he could see things "in three dimensions", trusting his colleagues and allowing a degree of initiative in organization and above all technical matters. His business mind undoubtedly led him to consider racing as a means of publicising his other industrial activities and the construction and sale of road-going cars built in limited numbers. Signor Omer, who grew up and developed within Maserati, proved to have a great talent for running the firm in the immediate post-war years, a period in which conflicts with the unions were making life very difficult. Blessed with a kindly, relaxed nature, he always managed to maintain a cordial, respectful and above all constructive dialogue with everyone. Leaving aside what went on, there was always a deeply rooted human substrate in the workshop, something difficult to find in other firms. Merit for this undoubtedly lies with all the Maserati brothers, and to those who had the good fortune and honour to work with them, for having succeeded in transmitting that *humus* of passion and dedication throughout the firm. It might seem strange, but despite the fact that after the brothers had left Maserati had been industrialised, with the machine tool production division having been added (horizontal and vertical milling machines; the production of machine tools had actually begun in 1940 when the Maserati brothers were still playing active roles in the factory), which financed the racing department, many of the men who grown up alongside the brothers had followed them to Modena and around 10 of them had even stayed on after 1947. These people, whom I met and remember very well, were able in their turn to transmit to the many youngsters who had just joined the company that attitude, that approach to the work. Their ingenuity was surpassed only by their self-sacrifice and dedication to the company. The socio-economic and political situation was also having an enormous influence on the world of works, especially in the factories, and Maserati was by no means immune to these changes. There were the union men, almost all "reds", who tried to convert the newcomers, many of us only having just left the Corni.

Ingegner Bellentani, the workshop foreman, was intent on creating a team of young engineers, which was gradually taking shape. In fact, all of us youngsters, after having spent at least a few months in the Quality Control Centre to get an overview of everything that was made in the factory, both parts for engines and cars and components for the milling machines, were then put on other jobs, with this rotation being completed after just over a year. At the end of the cycle, according to the aptitudes of the individual as evaluated by Bellentani, we were allocated to a definitive position. If we consider the legacy of the Maserati brothers, therefore, in my opinion what they left on the human level and in terms of working methods was even more important than the technical side as following the stagnation of the war years and the immediate post-war period, many technical issues were seeing rapid changes. Just think of the introduction of Vandervell bearings and the amount of fitting work they saved for the engine builders! The 4CLT/48 single-seaters were giving up their primary role in racing to the A6GCS equipped with a single-cam natural aspirated two-litre engine: this unit was based on an Ernesto Maserati design which Ingegnere Massimino was gradually modifying to the point where it was completely transformed into a twin-cam F2 engine for the A6GCM. Of the A6 1500 GT engine designed in the war year by Ernesto only the six-cylinder architecture remained. From 1950 it may be said that the Maserati brothers influence on Maserati cars was restricted to the front suspension, a masterful design by Ernesto, used on all our sports cars, with the exception of the 150S and the 200S and even on the 250F through to 1958, while the rear end was still an antiquated design. The pool of design engineers was radically revised in 1952. Ingegner Massimino was succeeded by Ingegner Gioacchino Colombo who arrived from Alfa Romeo, but only stayed for six or seven months. Bellentani, the workshop foreman, had already begun to restructure the technical office, which from three draughtsmen had expanded to accommodate eight, with the production office staff similarly being increased from one to three persons. Ingegnere Giulio Alfieri arrived in August 1953 and the following year took over as technical director, a position he occupied through to June 1975. Following the completion of the offices, Bellentani, with the unwavering support of Signor Omer who concurred with his initiatives, had a Research and Testing Department organized with two Schenck engine test benches and a torque dynamometer, a true laboratory. It was to be run by two elder statesmen and two youngsters, one of whom was me.

Bellentani was keen to break the hegemonies that were created within the factory around certain figures and this policy was determinant in terms of the new organizational structure. In general terms, the phases in the construction of a new car hardly varied from one manufacturer to the next: the differences concerned the people working there and the way they did so. The new technical concepts were focussed on making progress in racing while allowing new drivers to emerge who, along with the designer and mechanic, would contribute to achieving better performance. More than any other firm, Maserati has always taken into account these multiple issues and the production of each new model was always an opportunity for the discovery and launch of new drivers. The most striking example was without doubt the launch of the A6GCS/53, which debuted in that year's Mille Miglia, winning its class with Emilio Giletti. The engine was a version of the A6GCM unit revised by Gioacchino Colombo, while the bodywork, built by Fantuzzi, was also fruit of an idea by Colombo. This was to say the least a revolutionary car so easy was it to drive, with a powerful and very reliable engine. In fact it was the sports model that was produced in the greatest numbers between 1953 and 1955 (58 examples). It launched the career of numerous young drivers who eventually made it into Formula 1 including Luigi Musso, Sergio Mantovani, Cesare Perdisa, Sergio Scarlatti and Maria Teresa de Filippis.

THE 250F

The masterpiece of the team assembled by Bellentani was, however, the 250F single-seater, defined by Formula 1 historians as "immortal". From its victorious debut in the Argentine Grand Prix in January 1954 through to 1958, only minor modifications were made. Ingegner Colombo was responsible for the engine, while the gearbox, final drive, rear suspension and chassis were the work of Valerio Colotti. In November 1953, five cars were sent by sea to Argentina fitted with the 2500 cc engine required by the new formula; in effect the cars were still the A6GCM with the gearbox in-unit with the engine.

Unfortunately, the new Colotti transaxle was not yet ready, despite the technical office having worked 12-hour days and shifts had been organized in the factory to manufacture all the parts. For the first all-new car, the engine was entrusted to Signor Antonio Reggiani (known as the "professor" such was his skill), with me as his assistant. We signed off the engine at 11 o'clock on the 25th of December (that's right, Christmas day). That the afternoon it was installed in the new car, which was tested on the 26th of December at the Modena Autodromo.

Bertocchi came in after just a few laps and sat silently, prompting Commendatore Orsi to ask, "So, Guerino?" Bertocchi eventually admitted that yes, we had a car that went very well indeed. It arrived in Buenos Aires by plane together with Ing. Alfieri and all the mechanics. Giulio Borsari had already arrived by ship with all the equipment and the six A6GCM's updated with the 250F engine. On the day of the race it was 40° C, while we had tested at Modena with temperatures of 2 or 3°C. Alfieri was naturally concerned about overheating, a problem he hoped to overcome by opening vents in various parts of the bodywork. A providential downpour then helped Juan Manuel Fangio to win the first round of the World Championship.

In the meantime, Reggiani and I had begun testing the fuel injection system for the 250F engine, while Signor Leoni (the other "professor") and Giulio Cavazzuti (the other "boy") were working on desmodromic valvegear to be applied to the 250F in the future. For this job, an Ernesto Maserati design from 1942-1943 was dusted off, together with another by Ingegner Massimino from 1945. In the end, an intermediate version of the two designs was adopted, although as encouraging results had yet to come, priority was given to the introduction of fuel injection that took the power output from 260 to 280 hp.

A month or two before the Belgian Grand Prix, Alfieri brought Fangio to the testing room to see this fuel injected engine, but the great driver, in his affable way, put a hand on Alfieri's arm and in his thin voice said, "Ingegnere, I prefer the more reliable carburettors and I'll make up the extra 10 or 15 horsepower". He went on to win at Spa with the 250F before moving to Mercedes. Bellentani in the meantime encouraged the technical office to design a four-cylinder engine for the 150S, from which he later derived the 200S. Signor Tadeucci, the engine designer, derived the 200S from the 250F and launched the 450S V8 project. In the meantime, Ingegnere Bellentani had left Maserati, to the great disappointment of we youngsters who owned him so much. He was replaced by Cav. Galetto, who arrived from Ferrari but was without doubt less experienced and less professional than Bellentani.

In the spring of 1956, the technical office modified the spur gears of the differential from module 4 to module 7 as with the arrival of Stirling Moss, we had had certain problems, especially on the 300S, probably due to the his different driving style with respect to that of Fangio.

The fuel-injected 250F engine had won a few races and with Reggiani we were looking at power additives for the fuel mixes that Alfieri had prepared every so often, including some with percentages of nitromethane. We had moved on from MS1 to MS14. On the 250F for 1956 the engine was skewed to allow the driveshaft to pass alongside the lowered driver's seat to permit a lower centre of gravity.

Early in 1957, the experimental department was put under pressure with the development of the new 60°, 1500 cc V12 engine. From initial testing it was producing 320 hp at 12,000 rpm, with rivals going as far as suggesting the figures had been manipulated (news leaked even back then). Unfortunately, Maserati's withdrawal from racing interrupted development of this engine although 10 years later in 1966, it did win the South African GP in a Cooper and the 1967 Monaco GP. In 1958, Alfieri introduced the 3500 GT and with it a new conception of a way of constructing cars in limited series.

THE A6GCM VALVE
CONTROL FINGER

Late one morning in mid-June 1952, Ingegner Bellentani rushed breathlessly into the Quality Control Centre with two A6GCM valve control fingers that had broken at around 7000 rpm during a race. He called together all six members of the department staff, showed us the two broken components, asked for a modified job order so that the finger would not break again and then left. After exchanging worried glances, each of us grabbed a piece of paper and started to write. Before starting, I picked up one of the fingers and examined the point in which it had failed. The breakage had occurred between the radius where the camshaft lobe worked and the connecting radius of the fulcrum (the hole where the fingers were attached to the spindle). I used a magnifying glass to observe the depth of the case hardening and deduced that at that point the finger was too fragile and shouldn't be hardened.

Given that I had lost too much time in checking these things, instead of writing I drew a sketch, using a dotted line to indicate the area to be protected during the case hardening at the point of the breakage. When Bellentani came back he said in his customary rough manner, *"Alòra siiv dvintee tòt scribachein?"* ("So, have you all become scribblers?"). As I was closest to him I passed him my sketch saying, "Ingegnere, I'd do it like this". He picked up the sketch, looked at it and said, *"Pròpria axè bisègna fèr!"* ("Now that's what we've got to do!"). *"Uciàlein* [as he called Manfredini because he wore glasses, *AN]* do some tests with Montipò like this lad says and find a way to stop them breaking".

Turning to me he said, *"Adèsa che tè avu l'idea giòsta tem fe dò serie ed linguàti!"*("Now you've come up with the right idea, make me two sets of fingers"). To which I replied, "But Ingegnere, how?". *"Arangèt!"* ("Work it out!"), and off he went, winking at Manfredini. Clearly, he already had an idea of how to avoid the failures, but wanted to hear from us whether we were ready to tackle certain issues. Up until then, these fingers had been milled, two holes were bored, one with a diameter of 12 millimetres where it pivoted, and a smaller one of 2 millimetres for lubrication. They were then tempered, case hardened and lastly polished one by one by hand.

When I got back from lunch I went straight to Signor Benetti in the production office to pass on Ingegner Bellentani's new job order for the production of 24 fingers, part 30 38 / 41246. In the milling of the two radii I left 3 tenths of tempered and case hardened machining allowance stock, protecting the radius close to the hole and lastly ground the two radii. I then went to Signor Baracca in the tool store to pick up a tool to lock the 12 fingers into position on the surface grinder as the one used by the milling machine operator was the wrong type. During the week necessary for the delivery of the 24 fingers ready for grinding, I was also entrusted with the verification of two 15 TM twin-cylinder engine blocks. This was a 550 cc two-stroke engine for an urban goods delivery vehicle of which around 51 examples were built between 1949 and 1956. I went to Montipò a number of times to keep tabs on the heat treatment and was then present with Manfredini when Montipò locked into a vice a finger that had previously been heat-treated with a new procedure. He unsuccessfully tried twisting the finger to see if it would break. The test was passed and they told me that the following day they would have delivered the 24 fingers for grinding. I had already made arrangements with Signor Bruini, the chargehand of the grinding team, so that he would prepare the surface grinder for me and set up the grinding wheel for the two radii. Ingegner Massimino also helped me with the 10:1 scale drawing of the two radii that I would use in the projector to check precisely the grinding work. I began after having positioned and fixed the tool on the surface grinder plate, I made a few passes but the grinding wheel had to be spotted with the diamond at various points.

Bruini had only rough shaped the piece. I had to check numerous times, after having taken the first finger off the tool, whether the shape matched. When I felt that the job was ready, I made a few passes, trying to remove as little material as possible; in so doing I obtained two perfectly filleted radii and no sign of incipient breakage. I also ground the other 12 fingers after having checked their case hardened radius one by one with the appropriate instrument: they all had a hardness of 60 Rockwell, the optimum degree of case hardening.

My Quality Control colleagues slipped the 24 fingers onto a wire and jokingly placed them on my head, crowning me King of the Fingers. From then on there was not a single failure of this small but important component of our racing engine.

THE 4CF2 ENGINE

This was a four-cylinder, 1998 cc Formula 2 engine designed by Ingegner Massimino to replace the six-cylinder A6GCM. It should be noted that the A6 code, followed by other letters, had been used on our engines since 1944. This was down to Ernesto Maserati who, when he designed his first engine for a road car, called it the A6. The letter A was to commemorate Alfieri, the founder of the marque with 6 the number of cylinders: it was a 1500 cc unit with a bore and stroke of 66x72.5 mm. It then became the A66G, a 1954 cc, 72x80 unit. The G stood for *ghisa*, or cast-iron, the material of which the cylinder block was to be made.

Two or three units were produced with this material before the firm went back to aluminium for the cylinder blocks with pressed-in liners because it was easier to work with, but the letter G appeared on so many drawings it was left. When it was decided to adapt it to a racing car, the engine was given the A6GCS designation, with the last two letters defining a Corsa Sport or Sports Racing car. A 1978 cc, 72x81 mm six-cylinder, again with a single overhead camshaft.

The car was generally known as the *monofaro* because it had a single headlight in the middle of the radiator grille; it was fitted with cycle wings that were removed for circuit races. The letter G remained, even when Ingegner Massimino introduced the A6GCM engine, a twin-cam six-cylinder, 1985.5 cc, 76x72 mm unit, with the CM standing for Corsa Monoposto or Racing Single-seater. This engine was fuelled with a mixture of butyl alcohol and benzole and ran a compression ratio of 12:1 or even 13:1. Diverse versions were built with different bore and stroke dimensions (75x75 for 1988 cc; 72.8x80 for 1998 cc), but we never managed to do better than 180 hp at 8000 rpm.

The best configuration proved to be 76x72 mm producing 190 hp. Massimino favoured a short stroke, while Bellentani preferred a long stroke unit. Bellentani was an industrial engineer who had attended the Corni before graduating in Freiburg because in Italy a technical institute diploma was not sufficient for access to the university. He had worked with Signor Guerzoni who built the Mignon motorcycles and was a very practical man and a great organizer of the factory. Ingegner Massimino, who had followed the same academic path, qualifying as an engineer in Freiburg, was an excellent draughtsman; as he was from Piedmont he had worked for Fiat in the aviation division before joining Commendatore Ferrari's Auto Avio Costruzioni at Modena before the war and after a spell at Alfa Romeo.

He was the technical director at Maserati from 1939 through to 1952. During the war years he produced numerous designs for engines and cars. I have found a number of his painstaking drawings for projects that were never built. He was inspired by Auto Union and had designed a rear-engined car and worked with Ernesto Maserati on the desmodromic valve system. Wanting to give our A6G-CM single-seater a more powerful and lighter engine, he designed the 4CF2, with a bore and stroke of 88x82 mm (1994 cc), a compression ratio of 12:1 and an assembled crankshaft using roller bearings on the connecting rods as Ernesto Maserati had done on the 4CL in 1938.

This crankshaft was the cause of my first and only serious work-related injury. I was marking out the position of the lubrication holes in a crank mechanism that I had positioned on a *coulisse* (an ICS tool 10 cm deep and 20 high) that I had to move to adjust the position of the piece. As I struggled the coulisse fell on the middle finger of my right hand. The pain made me see the proverbial stars. They were about to take me to the hospital when Ingegner Bellentani arrived, "If you go to the hospital they'll take the nail off and it'll be even more painful, but if you listen to me we'll make a small hole of a couple of millimetres to let the blood out and then you won't feel a thing."

The blood was coagulating, I was almost screaming with pain and I could hardly understand what was going on. Manfredini and someone else held me up and took me to a drill where Bussi, the specialist in taking swarf out of eyes and who went by the nickname the "Nurse", was waiting. I remember them taking my hand and Bussi telling me to bear with him and not move. All of sudden I felt as if I had been reborn, the pain had vanished. They had drilled a hole in the nail, allowing the blood to spray out. An hour later, a plaster on my finger, I was back at work.

The 4CF2 engine was completed, but testing failed to provide satisfactory results, with the power output lower than expected.

I don't remember the exact month, but towards the end of 1952, Ingegner Massimino left Maserati, for what reason I can only imagine. He was replaced by Ingegner Gioacchino Colombo as a consultant and technical director. He arrived from Alfa Romeo and had also worked at Ferrari. His first move was to reduce the piston stroke and modify the timing of the A6GCM, obtaining a power output of 197 hp at 8000 rpm. He reinforced the chassis and the front running gear, improved the rear suspension and lightened the car by 25 kg. The "Colombo cure" bore fruit, thanks to the competitiveness of his technical team and leading drivers such as Fangio, González and Marimón. Colombo modified the A6GCM engine for a new two-seater A6GCS sports car and also designed the shape of the bodywork.

SPECIALIZED WORKER

At the end of my one-year fixed term contract I was given a permanent contract as a specialized worker. I was earning 33,000 Lire a month. My father, a state employee, was earning 31,000. Given that my salary meant I could afford it, my parents convinced me to buy a scooter, a Lambretta 125 that was then considered a luxury for a 19-year-old. I was called up for the national service medical and from the Modena district I was sent to Bologna because I was almost 180 cm tall but terribly thin with it, weighing less than 60 kilos. At Bologna I was exempted from military service for *insufficienza toracica* or a weak chest. The reason was also that the classes of 1932 and 1933 were particularly numerous and the selection process had therefore been more rigorous than usual. In any case, I was delighted despite the saying "those not good enough for the king aren't good enough for the queen". I had in fact a girlfriend who would occasionally meet me out of work between five and five-thirty and regular as clockwork there would be some colleague or other who had noticed and would tease me by saying she'd got be on a leash.

It didn't last long and after a year we split up: perhaps I wasn't so in love after all and in any case her parents were very strict and would never let her go out with me on the Lambretta. That was how it worked back then with girls. They were allowed out if a party was organized on a Sunday afternoon at someone's home, but if an evening they were always accompanied by their mothers. Bygone times!

Honour first and foremost! Even at that time there were a few girls who broke the rules, but earned a bad reputation often simply because they had more freedom than others.

On Saturday afternoons we would go dancing at the Eden, at the student's tea dance. I used to go when I was at school and then for the first few years I was working. However, once I began to have more responsibility and motor races were more frequent, I'd be working on Saturday afternoons too. There were three or four dance halls open in Modena on Saturdays and Sundays and in the summer there were open-air dances, especially at Cognento or Salvarola where I could go on the Lambretta and there was always one friend or another asking for a lift. The Sirenella was an open-air dance hall a short distance from Maserati that occasionally my colleagues working shifts on the machine tools from 6 AM to 2 PM and from 2 to 10 PM would visit; when they came out they'd stop even for just a chat, still in their overalls (albeit clean and pressed), and always did well with the girls because Maserati workers were privileged and well thought of!

My family and I came into Modena every day for work, a distance of five kilometres from Collegarola. My father worked at the Military Academy, my mother for Professor Domeniconi (the doctor who had treated my nanny, Signora Elena, in the Forties). My brother, six years younger than me, was at the Corni where he was doing very well, while I of course was at Maserati where I would frequently work late. As I was exempt from military service and wouldn't have lost around two years' wages, at home we talked about moving closer to town. My mother and I wanted a small detached house with a garden and a vegetable patch. My father was more naturally thrifty and would have preferred to buy an apartment given that our finances were limited and he was reluctant to bite off more than he could chew.

My mother was always an enterprising woman, my father more down to earth. After days of discussions and comparisons of costs, my mother and I got our way and it was decided that we would look for a piece of land on which to build a house. Naturally, we didn't have all the money required, but with my wages, those of my father and a loan we could manage, while my mother's wages would allow us to get by. My father was set against going into debt! What if we weren't able to repay the loan? But the decision had been taken and all that remained was to find the loan. As we had nothing to act as collateral the banks wouldn't lend anything and I was undecided whether to ask at the firm; I'd heard that Signor Orsi had helped some of his employees, but in the end there was no need because my mother had found a friend of her father's, Grandfather Enrico, who had a cheese factory at San Donnino and who said to her, "Your father is a gentleman, I hope you are too." And with that he lent us two million Lire at 7% interest for 10 years. I had however calculated that we would be able to settle the debt much earlier. At work I made myself available for more overtime and never turned down the chance to work on Saturday afternoon; certainly, I needed to work to earn more, but it was above all my passion for and attachment to the firm that kept me in the factory. I was by now well-established and popular; the working environment was excellent and we were all part of a family with a degree of togetherness found in few other companies. Even though the internal organization was comparable to that of a large firm, we were actually more of a craft-based operation with a team of highly skilled workers.

A WORD OF EXPLANATION

Maserati was not of course immune to the socio-political changes that from the immediate post-war years influenced the working class world. The strongest union was inevitably the CGIL, given that Modena was one of the "reddest" cities in Italy, followed by the FIOM, the engineering workers union that had strong links to the PCI, the Italian Communist Party.

What went on in certain factories was unimaginable. At Maserati, there were two union delegates from the FIOM, one in the Milling Machines division and one in the Auto sector: Gibertini and Facchini. There was also a representative of the CISL but he had no influence given that there were no members among the workforce.

There had been political strikes in which I had chosen not to be involved, but as I had still been on a fixed term contract I had gone unnoticed. However, once I had signed a definitive contract, Facchini became increasingly insistent that I should join the union, but as my ideas were very different to his I refused.

A four-hour strike was called against a visit to Italy by a NATO general. Like a number of my colleagues, I did not agree with the motives and declined to participate. When we went into the factory there was a lot of shouting, pushing and shoving, while a CGIL union official from Modena, Eliseo Ferrari, was waving boxes of Krumiri biscuits [*Krumiro* being the equivalent Italian word for blackleg or scab, AN], nothing out of the ordinary in short.

In the afternoon, Facchini came to Quality Control with the excuse of checking a piece and then approached me with what was obviously a prepared speech: "As the union representative I seriously deplore your behaviour, your lack of solidarity with the union and the workers' struggle" and so on and so forth. He went on and on, but I remember that all I said was "I'm working at the moment, but a five-thirty in the changing room I've a few words to say to you too". In fact, he was waiting for me and I took him by the arm and said, "Listen Franco, about your fine speech and your insistence on me joining your union. Please cut it out because politically we're miles apart and I'll be joining neither your union nor the CISL if that's what you're thinking. The unions, red or white as they may be, share a political ideology and for me this is enough for me to steer clear. And as for the strikes, you can be sure that if they are not economic but purely political, I'll be going to work and none of you can stop me. Because you'd be arrogantly interfering with my freedom of expression and movement, in contrast with the flaunted democracy you're so keen to say that you've conquered. In 1939, my father, in order to be able to go to work at the Military Academy in Modena, had to join the Fascist Party. He was obliged to; there was no democracy then. He joined the resistance movement, he smuggled arms out of the Academy, took them out in under stacks of wooden planks; had the RSI have found out he would have certainly been shot. He was given a Diploma of Garibaldine Valour, so my father contributed, in his own small way, to the liberation of Italy from the dictatorship. And now you are trying to force me to do what your ideology forces you to do. Think about it; what you're doing flies in the face of what your party is supposed to be all about. Look, in your Russia, the workers are worse off than in Italy. In Russia, those who don't join the Communist Party are sent to Siberia, and you say that there's democracy in Russia! Listen Facchini, I'm passionate about Maserati, I like my job, I'm a sociable person and would like to be friends with everyone, even you and your faithful, so don't come preaching to me like you did this morning." Since then I've never suffered any pressure from the unions.

THE MILLING MACHINE SPINDLE

Following the worm screw that moves the milling machine table, the spindle is the most important moving part of the entire machine tool. Seven finished spindles arrived at Quality Control to be checked. Signor Manfredini entrusted me with the job that required painstaking attention. The part is a shaft around 70 cm in length and weighing around 18 kilos, with bearing holder diameters of between 40 and 100 mm: at the end of the larger diameter is a #4 Morse taper that holds the chuck.

After having checked with the micrometer the various diameters on each of the seven shafts to make sure that they complied with the design tolerances, I set two coulisses on the surface plate to carry the spindle and allow it to be rotated to check that the 300 mm-long tip inserted into the Morse taper turned with a tolerance of $1/100^{th}$ of a millimetre. On the third spindle that I was checking I found an error of over nine hundredths and therefore removed the piece, cleaned it thoroughly, rechecked and again found an error of over nine hundredths.

I checked all the other spindles which were fine. I called Manfredini and told him the Morse taper on one spindle did not meet the tolerance. He asked me to show him the error and after having verified the piece asked me to go and called Nasi, the fitter from Signor Bianchini's department. I was a little embarrassed because this was the worker with the reputation for being the best fitter in the factory. Having informed his foreman that Nasi would have to come to my department I went and told him about the problem and he replied, "Impossible! Did you clean it well? Did you check again? I'll come and see for myself!"

After he had checked the piece too, he removed it and cleaned the inside of the taper by hand as gently as if he was caressing the face of a baby, replaced the spindle, rechecked and said, "You're right". He shouldered the spindle saying he'd be back in half an hour and so he was. I checked the taper again that found that it fell within the 0.01 mm tolerance. He apologised and told me that in future if I found something off in the pieces he'd worked I was to come to him without hesitation.

In the workshop there were certain workers who could on occasion correct errors that the machine tool on which they were working would otherwise have introduced. A typical example was that of the reamer Martinelli: when I went to check a part-finished cylinder block while he was reaming the crankshaft bearing supports he said, "Wait a moment while I make a finishing pass and then check and you'll see that all the other supports meet the tolerance." He zeroed the gauge on the micrometer with an inside caliper and I checked with the dial gauge: I could see the hundredths on the instrument dial. After a few times that I heard him say "wait while I make the last pass", I noticed that after the third support he pushed the milling machines with his right leg and I asked him why. He replied that the after the third support the milling machine made an error of 3/100 of a millimetre. If I hadn't personally checked each of the six supports I would never have believed what he was saying. Another worker who knew all the defects of his machine tools was Ezio Medici, the gear-cutting foreman, who was capable of producing the gearing for the timing system for our engines and gearboxes to such incredibly tight tolerances that we would joke that he made rubber gears so silent were they when running.

ERMANNO COZZA
AND THE MILLE MIGLIA

In the Fifties, it was company policy that the young-sters who had only recently joined Maserati were sent to cut their teeth for at least a year in various departments before being assigned a definitive position. There was also the possibility of joining the racing department staff at the service and refuelling stops during the world's greatest race. The Mille Miglia.

The various teams, composed of three or four expert mechanics and one or two of us novices, were recruited by the sporting director. As well as the start teams, there were those despatched to the four stations at Ravenna, Pescara, Rome and Florence. Those at Ravenna, which the cars passed through in the morning, would then move on to Bologna. In 1953, I was assigned to the Florence refuelling station with Giovanni Leoni, Giulio Borsari and Fausto Bietolini, three talented mechanics from the racing department. I was absolutely thrilled with the job I had been given. Giving drinks to the crew and cleaning the headlights and the Plexi-glas windscreen were important and necessary tasks and the adrenaline flowed as the clocked ticked to the time the first of our Maseratis were due in for refuelling.

These were the new A6GCS, numbers 503, 511, 512 and 525; the race number could help determine the position of a car with respect to the others. No. 525 was the first to pass through Florence, driven by Emilio Giletti, and finished 1st in class and 6th overall. No. 512 driven by Mantovani finished 10th and the other two retired after passing through Rome. I was not a member of the service team in the 1954 Mille Miglia as these duties had been assigned to the new Experimental Department and the engine testing room.

However, an extraordinary thing happened: at around 12:15 the day before the start of the Mille Miglia that year I was about to go home from lunch when I met Ingegner Bellentani, the factory manager: "Where are you going?" he asked. "Ingegnere, it's gone 12 o'clock and I'm going home to eat." "Yes, yes, go home, eat in a hurry, get a clean pair of overalls and come straight back to the factory as you're going to Brescia with Ingegner Mantovani, we're finishing off his car, the prototype 250S." If I think about that moment I still get goose bumps! Home and back, around five + five kilometres for which I think I broke the all-time record. I ate standing up while telling my mother what to pack in my bag for two days away and by 1 o'clock I was already back at work. Car No. 537 was almost ready, Ingegner Sergio Mantovani arrived at two o'clock with Ingegner Bellentani and said, "I'm sending this boy with you, if you need anything, he'll give you a hand". I was so excited that I got into the car without my bag.

After a slow few kilometres, Ingegnere Mantovani gave the car its head a few times at over 6000 rpm, explaining that he had to complete the running in of the engine. I took notes on the things that would need to be done when we reached Brescia, as to all intents and purposes this was actually the car's shakedown test. I remember that we stopped halfway to Brescia at a bar to get something to drink. Everybody gathered around the car to wish us luck in the race; I was ecstatic and in their eyes I was incredibly lucky as I was participating in a race which the next day kids and adults alike would be watching, lining the roads and cheering on the various competitors. At Brescia, the Maserati team had been installed in a garage on the outskirts of town. On our arrival we were warmly greeted by my colleagues, all happy to have an extra pair of hands to help them. They were in fact extremely busy with the last minute fettling of no less than 15 Maseratis.

When Guerino Bertocchi, the boss, came back, I reported the things that had been dictated to me by Ingegner Mantovani; he told me he had already spoken to the racer and would have taking the car out for a test drive straight away to get an idea of what needed to be done. Car number 500, Luigi Musso's A6GCS, was the car that was attracting most attention, as among our drivers he was the one with the greatest chance of success. We worked into the small hours and as our last car was Mantovani-Palazzi's No. 537 we went to sleep from 6 AM to 2 PM. We were all exhausted but at the same time anxious to get to the finish: the Mille Miglia was the race that kept Italy awake. From the radio we knew that Musso had placed well at Rome and Florence and we were hopeful that he could win the race. We were all on tenterhooks in Viale Rebuffone and after Ascari came in with his Lancia we hoped to see the nose of the A6GCS, instead it was Marzotto who arrived just 9 seconds ahead of Musso.

In 1955 and 1956, I placed no part in the Mille Miglia service teams as both Antonio Reggiani and I had plenty to keep us busy in the Experimental Department. We were studying and testing new mixtures with flame additives for the development of the 250F. We had the new 4500 cc V8 engine to develop and 12-hour days were the norm.

However, I made sure not to miss the Mille Miglia passing through the War Memorial park area of Modena where a bugler (from the Istituto Figli del Popolo) announced the arrival of the cars and the loudspeaker informed us that car XXX had passed the Cavazzona, a straight before Castelfranco. Those who have never had the opportunity to see this race can hardly imagine the participation and the enthusiasm of the local people.

In 1957, Maserati had the car to challenge for overall victory and had entrusted it to Stirling Moss, the holder of the outright record set in 1955 with Mercedes: 10 hours 7 minutes and 48 seconds. I was assigned to the Ravenna checkpoint and was then due to move on to the Bologna refuelling stop in the afternoon. That year we had 20 Maseratis in the race, from the A6G/54 berlinetta through all the models to the 450S with race number 537 driven by Moss and Denis Jenkinson. Our first car started at 3:10 and the last at 5:37. After reaching Ravenna in the late afternoon, we set up our equipment in the area assigned to us and went to dinner; sleeping was impossible though. There were seven of us and Ingegner Alfieri, Bonacini and I went to see the sights of Ravenna. The other four with friends from Ferrari for a game of billiards. We had agreed to meet at 3:30 to wait for the passage of our first car, expected at around 4:30. Moss was due to arrive at around 6:00; I was holding a 6-millimeter wrench to adjust the dampers if necessary and I was gripping it so hard it left an impression on the palm of my hand. It was gone 7:00 and the 17th Maserati had gone though but not the 18th (back then communications were still very hit and miss); Ingegnere Alfieri then learned via a telephone call that the crew had retired around 20 km from the start with a broken brake pedal.

A pity, from 1927 to 1957 Maserati had secured around a dozen class wins but had always missed out on overall victory, which we had hoped would come that year. We consoled ourselves with Giorgio Scarlatti's fourth overall and third in class with the 300S, despite the fact that at the Bologna checkpoint he had been ready to abandon the car due to brake problems. Ingegner Alfieri slapped him on the helmet saying, "Stay there, it's all flat now and you'll not need the brakes, keep the throttle flat to the floor." Tragically, at Guidizzolo, close to Mantua, around 40 kilometres from the finish in Brescia, Alfonso de Portago had suffered a blown tyre and ploughed into the crowd at over 250 kph in his Ferrari. He was killed instantly together with his navigator and nine spectators.

Three days later, the Italian government banned all racing on open roads. Attempts by the founders Signor Castagneto and Ingegner Canestrini to save this wonderful race were in vain and a glorious chapter in motorsport history drew to a definitive close.

It was decided to celebrate the 50th anniversary of the birth of the Freccia Rossa in 1977. A group of young enthusiasts of the legend of the Mille Miglia were determined to revive it. The obstacles were seemingly endless, despite numerous supporters eagerly supporting the organization of a regularity trial. They succeeded in overcoming all the logistical and organizational difficulties. Around a hundred cars took part in the first Mille Miglia revival. The organization proved to be so efficient that the number of entrants continued to double until a thousand applications were being received. However, no more than 380 cars could be accepted.

In the 1980s, on the return leg from Rome, the Mille Miglia called in to Modena for a checkpoint and a timed stage on the plaza behind the Scaglietti works. Along with a number of colleagues, I had obtained permission to set up a kind of service station for the Maseratis, of which around 20 were always entered.

One year, one of our American collectors driving the A6G/54 Zagato berlinetta had indulged a little too long at the buffet organized by the Neri firm, which was always well supplied with *gnocco fritto*. He restarted in such a hurry that he had to brake so hard before passing over the track of the sliding gate that he grounded and left his sump plug behind along with a stream of oil. Fortunately he stopped immediately; when he got out of the car and realised quite how serious the damage such was his desperation he was on the point of tears. After a brief discussion with my colleagues we towed him to Maserati; while the damage was in fact serious and the sump had to be removed and dismantled to be welded, he insisted that he wanted to finish the race and reach Brescia. We therefore made an emergency repair with four screws, a piece of rubber and an aluminium plate. With the oil topped up he was on his way three quarters of an hour later, but not before embracing all of us.

The organizers of the Mille Miglia have always presented the event in March at the Geneva Motor Show. In 1986 I was as usual organizing the Maserati stand and was able to see the presentation and pick up the folder with all participants, the timings, the stages and so on… While I was in our office talking to Signora Maria Teresa de Filippis, the former Maserati driver, Alejandro de Tomaso arrived, looked at the Mille Miglia folder, saw that there were 25 Maseratis and said to me, "Cozza, I'd like you and Sala to follow the Mille Miglia, take a van with sandwiches and drinks and…". I added, "Signor de Tomaso, the sandwiches and drinks are provided by the organizers at the refreshment points, the cars need spares, batteries, spark plugs and so on". He then came back, "Fine, get yourselves organized as you see fit". So for around 10 years we followed the Freccia Rossa in our Quattroporte.

The Maseratisti called us their "guardian angels" because we helped out so many of them when they were side-lined by various problems, which we always managed to solve and allow them to go on their way. One year in Rome, ahead of the start of the last leg at 6:30 in the morning, while we were talking to Franco Meloni, the Maserati service representative in Rome since 1948 who had come to give us a hand, we didn't notice that behind us was Avvocato Gianni Agnelli who was watching as we worked on one Maserati or another so that they were ready for the start. He said to us, "The Maseratis are always the most attractive!" As he smiled at us he made me blush because I remembered that at Anzio I had marked his trousers with an oil pipe on Ultima Dea, his boat powered by three Maserati engines.

The years passed and many things inevitably changed at Maserati too, the Register was struggling and was replaced by the Maserati Club. Year after year, the Mille Miglia has continued to attract enthusiasts and is a true touring museum of cars of numerous marques built between 1927 and 1957 and is frequented above all by foreigners. Our Maserati Register member, Signor Antonio Alberoni, is the owner of various Maseratis including a Sport 200S. We assisted in its restoration and he drove it in the 1990 Mille Miglia. Subsequently, as a result of an argument with the ASI, it no was no longer accepted. Having finally obtained a homologation certificate, he informed me at the annual Maserati Club dinner in late 2006 that he had sent in his entry form for the following year with my name as co-driver! Despite my protests that I was too old for this kind of thing, he wouldn't take no for an answer and I had to accept to take part. At this point it has to be pointed out that following the Mille Miglia to provide servicing is one thing, participating aboard a racing barchetta is quite another!

A very meticulous person, Albertoni had organized everything perfectly. From the helmet with a visor in the case of rain, to waterproof capes (that from the trailer parking spot to the service car we fortunately never had to use). The competitors were all already excited at dinner organized ahead of the start because while the event is a revival, it is still a regularity trial with a series of timed stages; everyone knows that at eight o'clock in the evening the first car will be pulling away from the start in Viale Rebuffone. 1600 kilometres are covered in three legs taking in much of Italy. All the cars were lined up waiting for their turn to start. We had race number 358 and started at 10:30 that evening. We put our Maserati caps on backwards as during the crawls through the various towns before reaching Ferrara, there was always a chance they would be flipped off and pinched by the various groups of young lads specialised in the harvesting of this kind of trophy. The city of Ferrara is always hospitable and so it was even at one o'clock in the morning when we arrived, with a large crowd of onlookers and enthusiasts. With the car left well-guarded, various minibuses took the competitors to the designated hotel. In the morning, well before the start, everyone was tending to their cars, wiping down the dew, checking the oil and water levels and chatting to neighbours. It's great because there is such an atmosphere of friendship, of cordiality, chamois leathers are swapped to dry off the cars, advice is sought and given on how to tackle the San Marino climbs for those with old-school, non-sintered clutches and then its *arrivederci* at the refreshment stop around at around one o'clock. My driver, who was not aiming at a placing in the final standings, tackled the various timed stages without actually considering the stopwatch.

The arrival in Rome is always tricky for the last cars in as they no longer benefit from the assistance of the police once they get left behind due to the traffic lights and big city congestion. In any case, the self-service lunch was plentiful and the hotel equally comfortable, even though given our physical condition we could hardly appreciate it to the full! There was no need for an alarm clock, there was enough light to look out of the window and see that various mechanics employed to prepare their clients' cars were up and about at work. A full breakfast as insurance against missing a meal and we were away to prepare our 200S for the third and final leg from Rome to Brescia. The longest and the most beautiful in terms of the landscapes. The weather was kind to us, as unusually for the Mille Miglia it didn't rain that year. The passages through the historic town centres were lined with enthusiastic crowds, even the kids at school were allowed out to wave to this fantastic caravan. We were all greeted warmly and welcomed with gifts of local products.

We reached the refreshment stop, as well organized as ever, at half past one and were back on the road by two o'clock. We had Bologna and Modena ahead of us with the latter being the town where the most Maserati fans congregated. At the Scaglietti coachworks there was no longer that enticing smell of *gnocco fritto* from the Neri firm, instead there were those of the Ferrari Classiche who offered us a taster. The next time we stopped we were on the avenues in the park, waiting our turn for the timed stage organized by the ACI and the Circolo della Biella; among the many acquaintances who stopped by were my two grandsons, Emanuele and Cesare, 4 and 7 years old who stared in surprise at their grandfather and Alberoni, many years later, still reminds me of the wonder he saw on their faces.

A further four or five historic town centres awaited us. As dusk falls it is not as much fun as during daylight, but the crowds were still numerous and people were lining the route as we drove into Brescia and onto the podium. The adventure was over and it had been wonderful, the car ran faultlessly, my driver drove extremely well, but a fifties barchetta is not the most comfortable of cars and the fatigue sets in at a certain age! Signor Alberoni and I said, "Never again... until the next time!"

On the Sunday morning in the theatre at Brescia, in the presence of the authorities, each competitor was presented with the timings of the various stages and the leaders received their prizes. For us what was important was to have taken part and we were happy to finish in the middle of the standings. Various photographers exhibit their work in the piazza to try and sell the shots they have taken during the event and many are tempted by a souvenir of their participation. We then went on to the former convent that now houses the Museum of the Mille Miglia for the official lunch and final farewell. Following this experience I thought my Mille Miglia days were over, but in 2010 Signor Alberoni insisted on involving me again. For some years, the organization of the event has been in new hands and the route and the various passages have been changed. Our application was accepted but unfortunately we were assigned number 374 out of the 380 starters. It's a disadvantage to start so late in part because of the timing, but also because you tend to lose touch with the cars in front of you. Nonetheless, we were lucky to be able to take part as over half of the applications had to be turned down.

That year Signor Alberoni organized things even better. We had a support car with a mechanic following on behind. Unfortunately, given the season there is always a risk of rain and in open car it's not much fun even with waterproofs. However, the enthusiasm of the spectators is unchanged even if rains and there are always big crowds. Not on the Terminillo though, where we passed between banks of snow two metres high. Between one downpour and another we reached Maranello, passed through the Ferrari factory and in front of the Gallery where my Maserati colleagues were waiting with a huge banner. We completed a lap of the Fiorano track and then headed straight for Brescia. It was already nine o'clock and it was too dark to see the signs for the passage through the town centres and as we were among the tail-enders we had lost contact with the others. Signor Alberoni was tired and handed over the wheel to his mechanic, Signor Ugo Tommasini, an excellent and very attentive driver. We were together therefore, on the podium, having arrived after midnight, to receive the congratulations of the organizers for having finished the race.

A NEW JOB

Ingegner Bellentani was always very attentive to us youngsters and at times would have no hesitation in giving us a righteous tongue-lashing. Like the time he surprised me leaning a hammer on the part-finished milling machine table after I had been to conduct the Poldi hardness test.

Signor Manfredini often sent me to the engine assembly department to check the cylinder blocks: it was the department where I would have liked to work. There were extremely talented engine builders whom I frequently asked for explanations and who took me under their wings thanks to my curiosity, especially Gino Bertocchi, the foreman, who had grown up professionally with the Maserati brothers.

Late in 1952, the tooling department took delivery of a new German machine tool, a Linder grinder for screw threads, for the grub screws for steering mechanisms and above all the grub screws used to move the milling machine tables which required ever greater precision. Ingegner Bellentani assigned Ermanno Nasi to operate the new machine, the most skilful and one of his pupils, the one of the out of tolerance mandrel that I had noted a few months earlier.

One day I went to the tooling department with five steering box screws of which I had tested the case hardening and Signor Baracca, the department foreman, told me to take them to Nasi who would decide when to work on them.

While I was talking to Nasi, curious about how the Linder worked, the calculations required for fitting the gears and for adjusting the movement of the carriage to suit the pitch of the piece to be ground, Ingenger Bellentani turned up. Thinking that he had caught me lingering where I wasn't supposed to be, I explained that I had brought the pieces I'd checked the hardness of and was just asking Nasi about the functioning of this magnificent machine tool.

Very politely, which surprised me given that I had always seen him grouchy, he said, "Well, well, you'd like to know how this machine works? From tomorrow, you'll spend a week or two with Nasi and when you've learnt the necessary Nasi will move on to engine assembly because the new 250F engines are arriving for the new 1954 Formula 1 car."

I went back to Quality Control and told Manfredini what had happened and he said he was sorry to lose me and then told me to stay on my toes because I wouldn't be spending long in the tooling department as a Linder operator because Ingegner Bellentani would have moved me to different jobs.

Newcomers from the Corni had arrived to replace me when I went to tooling and Pultrini who was destined for the production office. At the start of 1953, Maserati's car sector was being drastically transformed. Ingegner Bellentani was reorganizing and reinforcing all areas, including the production departments but above all the technical office. Ingegner Gioacchino Colombo came in to replace Ingegner Massimino and, as mentioned previously, was asked to make certain modifications to the A6GCM. He created the A6GCS engine and set to work on the power unit for the new Formula 1 car for the Championship about to get underway in January 1954.

Ingegner Bellentani therefore firstly tackled the design sector and Ascari, Molinari, Rebecchi and Golinelli went to assist Ingegner Colombo, who shortly afterwards left

Maserati to move to Bugatti. The office was taken on its own identity and creating three groups of specialists: engines, transmissions and chassis. At the Quality Control Centre instead, new faces from the Corni were arriving such as my classmates Bonettini and Boccolari.

The most numerous reinforcements were destined for the production departments. Andrea Cavani and Arturo Brancolini, former Ferrari concessionaire employees, went to the engine and gearbox assembly department, while Ermanno Nasi and Ciccio Montanari from the machining sector went provisionally to the milling machine assembly department, while another two of my Istituto Corni classmates, my great friend Ivo Tavoni and Luciano Luppi, were placed respectively with the cylinder head and engine block specialist, Sacchetti, and the chassis department. Five workers from the Officine Reggiane also arrived, including three for the chassis department and two with Guerino Bertocchi in the testing room. Giorgio Neri, Mazzetti (formerly with Ferrari), Beppe Consoli, Emore Manni, Luciano Brandoli and my friend Carlo Morandi also joined Guerino Bertocchi's racing department.

While in just less than two weeks in the tooling department, Nasi instructed me on the complicated use of the Linder, the foreman Signor Baracca frequently came to check my progress and ask me about what I was doing. Within a few weeks I knew I had gained his trust as he stopped dropping by to check up on me and we even became good friends. Personally I felt flattered to work in the department that was considered to employ the cream of the factory. Both the fitters working at the benches and the operators of the various machine tools were the best in professional terms. When you could here the noise of an engine being tested Bianchini, the old lathe operator who knew about my passion for engines, would say as he went by, "Listen to that beast roaring!"

A PLEASANT SURPRISE

When I picked up my wage packet for June I found note that read "Given your performance, your willingness and your dedication to the tasks entrusted to you, we are happy to inform you that you are to receive a pay rise of 500 Lire per month". I was so happy that tears actually started flowing, above all due to the firm's recognition of my work. I was 20 years old, I was working for an important firm, I was happy there, I was well liked and above all it was a wonderful working environment. One that I had always dreamt of being part of.

I saw that my parents were proud, especially my mother whom I'd always given cause for concern regarding food as I have to admit I was always a fussy, picky eater. Following the purchase of a small plot of land, we as a family had begun to construct a new house in the Sant'Agnese area, in Via Ciro Bisi, immediately after the Via Vignolese railway crossing coming away from the city centre. I didn't have a great deal of time to devote to the project; I'd worked on the plans and then Mother brought in the surveyor Mundici, the husband of one of my old teachers of Italian, a very good man who gave us a great deal of help with advice and all kinds of suggestions on how to proceed with the work, where to purchase the materials and even how to obtain discounts as if the various materials were being purchase by him.

THE DOCTOR'S HERE

Jokingly, those who had known Antonio Reggiani (Tonino) for some time had nicknamed him the "Doctor". Born in 1915, he was what was known as a *patronatino* as he had been orphaned at a very young age and had grown up in the Patronato dei Figli del Popolo, the orphanage in Corso Canalgrande. At 14 years of age he was already working for the Scuderia Ferrari in Viale Trento Trieste and later followed Ferrari to Maranello where he became a skilled engineer and carburettor specialist.

When he was tuning an engine he had the habit of placing his ear on a screwdriver handle and touching the engine with the tip at various point to listen to the vibrations or the tremors, hence the nickname "Doctor" given to him by his closest colleagues.

In December 1952, he was in New York visiting Luigi Chinetti, the Ferrari concessionaire in the USA, working on a number of Ferrari cars. He had arrived from Mexico and was then due to return to Italy. On Christmas Eve, while Mr Momo, one of Chinetti's men, was giving him a lift to the hotel in which he was living, they crashed at fairly high speed into a metal traffic divider. Reggiani's forehead slammed into the windscreen leaving him with numerous fragments of glass in his head. He was hospitalised for a couple of months but once he had recovered he was able to come home. However, he came back to work at Maranello to the bitter surprise that his insurance policy had been neglected; he slammed the door on the way out and told the Commendatore Ferrari where he could go. Ingegner Bellentani who knew him well, brought him to Maserati and installed him in Gino Bertocchi's engine assembly department. In late September he was moved to the new Experimental Department. Reggiani was my "guru" at work, but above all my "guru" in life. Even though it is but a gesture compared with what Reggiani gave me, I would like to remember and revive an article written about him by Giovanni Canestrini and published in the weekly *Europeo* in December 1952.

A BEARING
FROM THE SKIES

by Giovanni Canestrini

"It was Vandelli, Villoresi's mechanic, who calmed the Mexican fans by quickly adjusting the carburettors of Ibarra's car. Certainly, in the race, Ibarra's car, which finished comfortably, performed better than its fiery but inexperienced driver. The Ferrari mechanics found themselves with more serious problems to resolve once everyone had recognised that there were serious defects in the transmissions. A needle bearing had to be replaced and reworked and it was impossible to find appropriate machine tooling in Tuxtla. It was therefore decided to send a plane with the mechanic Reggiani, fresh out of New York. Reggiani was to travel to Oaxaca, the closest city in which it was hoped he could fabricate the required bearing. However, when the mechanic, who left at dawn in the company of the pilot Vinega, reached Oaxaca, he found that it was impossible to make the bearing locally and that he would have to go as far as Mexico City, 1300 kilometres from Tuxtla. Reggiani found the tooling and everything else he needed in the workshops at the airport, but once he had finished his bearing, the pilot Vinega said that it was not possible to set off for Tuxtla because it would have involved over five hours flying time. As all Tuxtla had to offer was a small airfield unequipped for night flights, travelling in the hours of darkness really did seem to be reckless.

Nonetheless, Reggiani insisted as he knew that the without the part he had fabricated, one of the Ferrari 4100's would not be able to start the race. The young Navion pilot then relented and agreed to fly Reggiani to Tuxtla even at night.

However, the airport authorities then refused permission for them to take off. In the meantime, back in Tuxtla, we were waiting for the plane to arrive. It was eight o'clock, night had already fallen and there was still no news of the Navion. By then we were losing all hope of repairing Ascari's car. Shortly after eight o'clock, however, a single-engine plane appeared low in the sky above Tuxtla and there could be no doubt: it was the Navion bringing Reggiani. We rushed to the airfield by car, and arranged lights, torches and lanterns in the runway, but even before we had finished installing this improvised illumination the Navion had touched down successfully and Reggiani was running towards with the new bearing in his hand. There were hugs and kisses. But Vinega was now in trouble with the Mexican aviation authorities, accused of having taken off without permission from the airport at Mexico City."

A NEW COMPANY STRUCTURE

In late 1952, the revision of the shareholdings of the Orsi brother and sisters led to Officine Alfieri Maserati SpA becoming the exclusive property of Commendator Adolfo, who was also its CEO. His son, Signor Omer, the general manager, assisted by Ingegner Bellentani, was intent on focusing the company's attention on the automotive sector, and in particular on motor racing. 1953 began with magnificent results in various competitions, both with Sports cars and the single-seater A6GCM that closed its cycle with Juan Manuel Fangio's triumph on 13 September in the Italian Grand Prix at Monza and seven days later in the Modena Grand Prix. Ingegner Colombo's work was bearing fruit.

For 1954, the new international regulations specified naturally aspirated 2500 cc or supercharged 750 cc engines for Formula 1 Grands Prix. Before leaving Maserati, Ingegner Colombo had already configured and designed a straight-six 2495 cc engine (with a bore and stroke of 84x75 mm), with Taddeucci being entrusted with its completion. Running on a mixture of alcohol and benzole, the manufacture of at least 10 units had been launched so as to be ready for the first race in Argentina in the January of 1954.

INGEGNER
GIULIO ALFIERI

Avvocato Camillo Donati, Commendatore Orsi's manager and right-hand man, was also president of the Modena Autodromo. One morning in late June, while he was attending with Signor Omer a series of tests of Maserati cars, he saw a van arrive that unloaded in the pits area a faired motorcycle, an Innocenti Lambretta scooter that was due to undertake tests in the afternoon as previously agreed with the circuit managers. Directing operations with this faired Lambretta, that was subsequently to break various records, was a 29-year-old engineer who presented himself as Giulio Alfieri, a designer with Innocenti. The conversation that unfolded left Donati and Signor Omer with a very positive impression of the young engineer, to the extent that the two were convinced they needed an engineer, even a young one, to add to Maserati's technical staff. After a series of further contacts, therefore, Ingegner Giulio Alfieri joined Maserati on the 1st of August 1953. He was given an office alongside that of the draughtsmen and day by day he explored the factory, got to know the various department foremen and, as always accompanied by Ingegner Bellentani, came to the tooling department too He spent some time with the Genovoise where the operator Candini was working on the first cylinder blocks for the 250F engine. The following day he returned to Signor Baracca and then stopped to talk to me, asking me questions about the Linder. He asked me my name and how old I was, then he introduced himself and gave me the impression of someone who was very polite and eager to get to known everything about everyone.

THE NEW 250F

The first six 2.5-litre Formula 1 engines were machined, assembled and then tested on Guerino Bertocchi's bench. He also tested the A6GCM cars fitted with the engine at the Autodromo as they were assembled. I therefore came to know from those who were well informed that these cars were due to be despatched by sea, with all the support materials, at the end of October and that my friend Giulio Borsari from the racing department would be accompanying them, as requested by the insurance company. The cars that were shipped out were effectively *interim* 250F's, while we waited for the true 250F with its new gearbox, rear suspension and chassis. I leave the honour of commemorating the birth of the legendary 250F to the Maserati designer Valerio Colotti.

THE OLD FLAME

by Valerio Luca Colotti

I've read, and I continue to read, various articles, books and publications regarding classic cars, in particular the Maserati 250F, a celebrated F1 machine from the Fifties. All of them feature the name of a person who, at the time, had nothing to do with the design and production of the car in question. I've therefore decided to redress this error, describing how the Maserati 250F truly came into being. Many will ask, "Why now, after so many years?" For the sake of truth. I'd therefore like to dedicate this article to Commendator Adolfo Orsi, to Omer Orsi, to Ingegner Vittorio Bellentani, to Guerino Bertocchi and to all those who contributed to the creation of a car that in one of his books Denis Jenkinson defined as an "immortal single-seater".

In the first decade of the month of September 1953, I started work in the Technical Office at Officine Maserati. I'd been given a very exciting job: designing the new Formula 1 car on the basis of the regulations established by International Federation for the 1954 season. This is what I was told by Ingegner Vittorio Bellentani who, after having presented the project to the Orsi family, Commendatore Adolfo and his son Omer, and having been given the green light, gave me in turn *carte blanche*. I was so euphoric that I never gave a thought to the possibility that the difficulties I was bound to encounter might, given my youth, have compromised my future in the case of a *fiasco*. After a number of years in which I had elsewhere demonstrated the achievement of a good technical proficiency, excellent, in fact, according to the department head, I began to think about how far I could go and to consider the possibility of an independent technical office. At worst, I thought, I will have enjoyed illusions, if that is what they are, destined to disappear. I contacted various companies, including Maserati, in person or through a letter of presentation. Maserati was the first to get in touch, via a messenger sent by Ingegner Bellentani. It is not hard to guess the outcome of this contact. I was introduced to the technical office staff by Ingegner Vittorio Bellentani, whom I would like to sincerely thank for his trust, just as I would like to thank Adolfo and Omer Orsi for their perhaps reckless courage in entrusting me with a project that was undoubtedly going to cost a great deal of money. He presented me the staff of the Technical Office: Guido Taddeucci, the engine designer, the draughtsmen Giancarlo Rebecchi, Ennio Ascari, Giulio Malavolti, Domenico Nicola and the archivist Albano Guerzoni. I was also introduced to Ingegner Gioacchino Colombo, whom I had already met, and who some time later was to leave the firm, but not before giving me an excellent piece of advice for which I still thank him warmly today. Excited more by the anxiety and fear of getting down to work rather than the introduction to the Orsis, with whom I had a brief conversation in which they encouraged me to produce a new and effective design, I hardly noticed that it was already midday. At home during the lunch break, my enthusiasm outweighed the controversy caused by my having abandoned months earlier the company whose technical office I was working in (Ferrari). That afternoon I toured the factory and met the racing team mechanics and above all the chief test driver Guerino Bertocchi. We were close to the 1953 Italian Grand Prix at Monza and before I

started work on the new project, Ingegner Vittorio Bellentani asked me to look at the rear suspension of the A6GCM
(the M standing for *monoposto* or single-seater), the rigid
axle of which was decidedly anachronistic for an F1 car
and was suspended on two cantilevered quarter-elliptic
springs that were tasked with both springing and acting
as reaction struts together with radius rods that were fixed
with a ball head to the lower part of the axle casing, with
the other ends attached to the chassis. What was in truth
a modest project was completed in record time and two
cars were prepared. At Monza, the thrilling race I watched
from the stands was encapsulated in a famous photograph
immortalising a monster with four heads and 16 wheels, so
close were the cars to one another, two Maseratis driven
by Fangio and Marimón and two Ferraris in the hands
of Ascari and Farina. I never liked being in the pits. On
the last lap, like many of the others before it, when the
cars appeared from the porphyry curve, everyone in the
stand, which was crammed with people, rose to their feet,
meaning that because I am short I could only see the cars
as the crossed the finishing line. On the last lap I saw a
(British) green car go past followed by a red one; the Race
Director Restelli kept the chequered flag raised. The red
car that had crossed the line was Fangio's Maserati: I had
recognised him from his unmistakeable chocolate brown
helmet. One more lap and finally the chequered flag came
down to consecrate Juan Manuel Fangio's victory. We later learnt that on that porphyry curve all hell had broken
loose, with Farina leaving the track, Ascari going sideways
and Marimón being blocked on one side by Fangio, who
miraculously or perhaps skilfully succeeded in passing, and
crashing into Ascari who was occupying the remaining

space with his Ferrari. The victory and the drivers' declarations about the decidedly improved car, in particular its rear suspension, encouraged me to give the new project my very best. A blank page, as large as a drawing board, was the battleground on which I would have to go for broke. A multitude of thoughts and ideas whirled around in my head without giving me the impression of any concrete validity. With a pencil in hand, I stared at the paper on the board but it remained stubbornly white. Patience was needed to consider which of a number of apparently acceptable solutions best responded to the very precises brief given to me: new and effective!

It's just a word! Fortunately, the unexpected happened, an episode that was unusual to say the least and which distracted me.

Ingegner Bellentani asked me to go to Monza. A new Mercedes sports car (the 300 SL) was lapping. "You must go and see how it's put together." I objected that it would be difficult for me to get into the circuit and even if I could it would be impossible to reach the pits. "Ingegner Bottasso will be at the entrance to the autodromo. Everything's arranged, there'll be no problems." The following day I took the train to Milan and then the tram to Monza. A car was waiting for me; I got in and as we headed towards the circuit I was handed a pair of overalls and a "Pirelli" cap. I quickly put on the overalls and cap and at a stroke my disguise was complete. Mercedes, with their driver Karl Kling at the wheel, were testing various brands of tyre. The mechanics answered to Neubauer's orders. The various test sessions followed one after another, with of course different tyres being fitted each time. During the brief stops in the pits to change them I was unable to get close until, on the main straight, the left rear tyre disintegrated and the car stopped just past the pits, right in front of me. The Mercedes mechanics came running up, lifted one side of the car, removed the wheel, handed it to me and told me to take it to Neubauer. The brake had made the wheel rim to hot too hold and as I didn't have thick gloves like the rest of the Pirelli mechanics I soon realised it would be better to roll the wheel. Everyone had gone to check on the problem. The car without the wheel, lifted on one side of course, offered itself to my inspection. I slowly made my way back, picking up pieces of rubber from the track as I went so as not to draw attention to myself. I was therefore able to see what I was interested in. After a while, a Mercedes mechanic noticed me and used a wheel to try to protect the team's secrets. Too late! The Pirelli tyres proved to be the best. Neubauer invited all the company's technicians and mechanics to lunch. Naturally, I was included in the party. We ate in the restaurant under the grandstand. At the end Neubauer thanked us all and shook the bosses' hands. I got back in the car and drove away from the circuit. During the trip I changed back into my own clothes, thanked Ingegner Bottasso for his invaluable help and then headed back to Modena. The following day I was back in the office. Ingegner Bellentani came in and when he saw me he confronted me a little surprised and somewhat (to use a euphemism) menacingly, "You're supposed to be still at Monza to see the Mercedes!" I updated him with a concise report. A smile, a pat on the back and a "well done". My first mission had gone well. That blank sheet was still desolately white, however. On the way back on the train, no longer gripped by the anxiety and fear I had been suffering as I headed to Monza, I had sketched out an idea that was, albeit vaguely, worthy of consideration. Back at my desk, I began to sketch the general layout of the various mechanical assemblies on the pages of a notebook. A few days later, I finally had a well-defined idea that in technical terms would satisfy the brief I had been given with respect to functionality. The original idea was firmed up on that previously blank sheet in a 1:3 scale drawing of the basic structure, the chassis and the mechanical organs, the engine, the gearbox and so on in their various locations. I also began to consider the aerodynamic problem, even though at the time this was virtually an unknown science in the automotive field. By inclining the engine 6° longitudinally to the left from the driver's point of view, the drive shaft could pass below the driver's left knee (rear-mounted engines were still some way in the future), allowing me to sit him virtually on the floor of the car. This had the effect of significantly reducing the car's frontal area and consequently the drag it created. The shape of jet aircraft inspired me when sketching the lines of the bodywork. Ingegner Vittorio Bellentani who was following the development of the project step by step, albeit with admirable discretion, suggested that I should leave the front suspension of the old A6GCM unchanged. This proved to be invaluable advice for which I am still very grateful; during the course of my career, it enabled me to solve a major technical problem and to design other cars of which everyone, Guerino Bertocchi and his fellow test driver Umberto Stradi in particular, declared themselves to be very satisfied as were were easy to drive and boasted excellent roadholding. In racing jargon they were, and still are as classic racers, "forgiving" and "sincere" cars. With the outline study of the configuration of the car completed, the process of the design and the relative calculations regarding the transmission system began. Its principal characteristic, revolutionary for the time, was that thanks to the inclined installation of the engine it could be located transversally behind the driver's seat. A bevel gear pair transformed the motion from longitudinal to transversal and led to the gearbox offering four speeds and reverse (later fitted with five speeds). The spur gear final drive transmitted torque to the half-shafts via a ZF-type limited-slip differential.

This type of differential had already been used, and with remarkable success, by Mercedes and Auto Union in the years leading up to the Second World War. The technology of the time had nothing better to offer. The dimensioning of the gearing (the profile of the involutes, the modules, the width of the cogs, the radii at the base of the teeth) involved long and complicated calculations. Firstly because in that period we had neither calculators not computers. We had to use slide rules, while for the calculations requiring extreme precision we had no alternative to logarithms, adding and subtracting sums with pencil and paper. Those who know the methods will understand! I used the same system to verify the hardness of the bearings, the flexural-torsional stress on the shafts and their elastic deflection in order to correctly dimension the gearbox casing while taking into account the weight factor, which in this type of car had to be as low as possible. Back then, the restrictions imposed on current cars did not exist. With the gearbox casing mounts on the chassis positioned and two steel slides fitted at the front of the same to act as guides for the De Dion axle anchors, Nicola began to develop the various detail drawings. In the meantime, I continued with my design work and attempted to create a De Dion-type rear suspension. This configuration comprises a tube of relatively large diameter that links the rear wheels. Two cylinders are welded at either end to contain the bearings supporting the wheel hubs. The extremities of the tube also carry two pieces of sheet steel welded at 90° to the principal axis to carry the pins for the struts, one above and the other below the tube axis. There was also room for the pins for the links securing the transverse leaf spring. This last was mounted on the upper part of the tubular chassis, with the mounts in the form of four Duralumin cylinders, set at carefully calculated distances from one another to allow the leaf spring to act as both the springing medium and the anti-roll bar. At the rear of the underside of the aforementioned sheet steel elements were the arms controlling the Houdaille shock absorbers attached to the rear lower extremity of the chassis. I was somewhat perplexed and concerned when I realised that as soon as a drawing of a gearbox component had been completed a number of copies were made and the piece was immediately put into production, virtually without any checks. What if something was not right? What if, given the hurry, the calculations were wrong, leading to the under- or over-dimensioning of a component?

I took my concerns to Ingegner Bellentani who reassured me by saying that those like me who pay such attention to both the calculations and the design work would not make mistakes. While this did cheer me up, it could hardly eliminate the worry that errors might creep in. This led me to slow down so that I could check the calculations made earlier. I effectively interrupted the work of Domenico Nicola, aka "Nicolino". Ingegner Bellentani quickly stepped in to get me to pick up the pace again. I was just as quick and just as firm to repeat my sacrosanct concerns and also took the opportunity to add that with the current workforce it would be impossible to do more. A response was not slow in coming: a young high-school graduate, Giorgio Molinari, was moved from the testing department and soon became my right-hand man. This accelerated productivity with the detail drawings. The addition of Molinari gave me an idea: I asked Molinari and Nicola to pass the drawings to one another so that there was at least a rudimentary verification of all the engineering data. With this system in place, I went back to the assemblies that I still had to calculate, design and dimension. I have listed them here so that readers can get an idea of what a small technical team is capable of:

• drive shaft
•clutch and bell housing
• front brakes with two leading shoes and self-venti-lating drums
• rear brakes with single leading shoes and self-venti-lating drums
• pedalbox and relative appendages for the brake pumps, the accelerator and the clutch control
• water and oil radiators
• fuel and oil tanks
• gear lever and relative linkages
• adjustable steering wheel and seat
• last but one, but certainly not in terms of importance, the dimensional redefinition of the chassis that in the outline design phase I had intended to construct as a space frame in small-diameter, thin-wall tubes
• lastly, an outline configuration for the bodywork.

The absence of a precise deadline, something which no one had yet mentioned, allowed me to programme the phases in the development of the various project on the basis of the limited time available to my two colleagues.

I had to avoid overloading them so as not to make them worry about not keeping up, or in an attempt to keep up and save time to avoid exchanging the drawings for the final verification. The system adopted was working and everything was proceeding fairly smoothly when the foreman on the gearbox assembly line called having come across a serious problem. I was very surprised when I saw that the gearboxes were already being assembled in the department and that a number of units had already been completed. I hardly had time to ask about the whys and wherefores of such rapid progress when the engineer Bellentani emerged, evidently satisfied with what had been achieved so far and ironically happy to see the surprise on my face, surprise which soon changed to disappointment, when the foreman showed me the rods that through the forks they are attached to, were reversed with respect to their correct position. The hunt for the guilty party did not take long as there were of course only two draughtsmen working up the drawings. The incorrect interpretation of the design was found to be the responsibility of Nicola who was the recipient of a few choice words from Ingegner Bellentani after having inverted by 180° the lugs into which the fork selecting the various gears was inserted. The drawings were rapidly revised. A few days later the gearboxes were ready to use. A visit to the technical office by Omer Orsi was a fairly rare event given his many commitments and on this occasion Ingegner Bellentani had little cause for concern as everything was proceeding well and the first concrete results could already be seen. The usual pleasantries and then mention of the Grand Prix of Argentina where, it was said, it would be nice (a beaming smile spreads across his face) to debut the new car, if everything was ready of course. A few more questions about the progress of the on-going projects and then with best wishes and an *arrivederci* he left with Bellentani. That mention of the Argentine race was left hanging in the air. What was the date of the race? I'd like to point out that we were already in mid-October! The next day, Taddeucci told me that the Grand Prix of Argentina would be held on the last Sunday of January 1954. Ingegner Bellentani called me into his office, asked me to speed things up and added one of Taddeucci's draughtsmen to the team. I objected that even with this help, it was unlikely we'd be ready in time. I was immediately authorised to take any necessary decisions. "We need to do this, you've got to it everything. Signor Omer has expressed a wish shared by Commendator Adolfo too." After a rapid consultation with the members of my group (the aforementioned, Domenico Nicola, Giorgio Molinari and, added from on high, Giancarlo Rebecchi) the decision was taken: new working hours 8-12, 14-19, 20:30-24, with the exception of Saturday when the 20:30-24 shift was eliminated. The work took on a hellish pace both in the technical office and in the workshop where the various components were manufactured in real time. My rapid incursions into the various departments had shown me that our commitment was mirrored by the efforts the workers were making to guarantee the realisation of what we designed, with the proviso "if everything works out". Despite my youth and the energy that went with it, towards the end of November I started to fall apart. My head was spinning, I couldn't eat, in short everything was just a little off kilter.

As well as drastic treatments, the doctor prescribed a few days' rest. All the designs and relative drawings of the parts had been completed, the pieces manufactured:

nonetheless, there were concerns at Maserati. Confirmation came in the form of visits by both Ingegner Bellentani and emissaries from the Orsis, enquiring after the state of my health but fortunately there was nothing seriously wrong. I was back at work by early December, delighted to find that the car was in a very advanced state of preparation. Boxing day afternoon had been earmarked for testing the new car designated as the 250F. Guerino Bertocchi and a group of mechanics were on track at the Aerautodromo. It was a grey day of fine drizzle or condensed fog. Without doubt, I thought, the worst possible day to test a new car. Aware how much was riding on the outcome, this thought was preying on my mind. I would have liked to smoke, but it was prohibited in the garage and probably would have made me worse in any case. The Orsis, Commendator Adolfo and his son Omer, Ingegner Bellentani, "Giangi" Moncalieri and others I don't remember, tried to distract themselves by chatting. You could see in their faces they shared my anxiety, and I could understand them, especially the Orsis given how much they had invested. Finally the roar of the engine announced the return of the car. Guerino climbed out and calmly took off his right glove and then his left, without saying a word. He pushed his goggles over his helmet and undid the chin-strap. He took off his helmet and placed it on the seat. My heart was thumping and felt like it was bursting out of my chest. Everyone was showing signs of impatience and irritation. Commendator Adolfo could hardly contain himself and took a few steps towards Guerino saying, "So... Guerino?" I felt like I was in court with the judge about to pronounce his sentence. "Gentlemen, finally we have a car worthy of the name", he said. With a shout and a leap with arms held high, I expressed all my uncontainable joy. I had won the battle I had begun 110 days earlier in front of that haunting sheet of white paper on the drawing board. It still seems incredible that in such a short time we were able to design, calculate, draw and construct a Formula 1 car. I received congratulations, handshakes, moral recognition and a material reward to conclude one of the most memorable days of my life to that point. The car left for Argentina where, with the great Juan Manuel Fangio at the wheel, it won the Grand Prix in Buenos Aires. I'm sure you can imagine how I felt. Thank you. The success of the 250F, which Fangio also drove to victory in the Belgian Grand Prix at Spa-Francorchamps, encouraged Ingegner Bellentani, in agreement with the Orsis, to enter sports car races too. I subsequently designed the rolling chassis of the 300S, which was derived from the 250F, then the rolling chassis, gearbox transaxle and brakes for the 150S, the 200S and finally the rolling chassis, transmission, suspension and brakes of the imposing 450S. In that same period, I also designed the first Touring Superleggera GT car and before leaving Maserati, in 1958, the Eldorado, a single-seater for the Monza-Indianapolis races (of which only one was held). I would like to thank once again those who put so much trust in me and I hope I managed to repay them.

The birth of the 250F is also recalled here by Ingegner Giulio Alfieri, Maserati's technical director through to 1975.

"Remembering a car that was much loved is always a great pleasure and writing something about experiences that left a mark on a great period in automotive history is virtually obligatory. It is in this spirit that I am responding to the invitation I was given. The 250F was, without a shadow of a doubt, the car that stole a march in the 2500 cc Formula 1 era. It raced for over five years and throughout that period was never modified.

The components of the car all had the same origin and satisfied the demands of the time in a very simple fashion. Efficiently, we would say today. I can make this observation because when I arrived at Maserati on the 1st of August 1953 the engine had only just been designed by a team composed, among others, of Ingegner Bellentani, Ingegner Gioacchino Colombo and Nicola.

The differential was designed by Valerio Colotti who was also responsible for the design of the chassis and the brakes. In the months that followed I attended the car's first race which took place in January in Argentina. I took part in the construction and fine tuning of the first examples and then took over as head of the project in May 1954. The characteristics of the car can be easily summarized: a car created to exploit the available power, with roadholding worthy of the best tyres of the time."

THE NEW EXPERIMENTAL
DEPARTMENT

It was well known that Ingegner Bellentani and Guerino Bertocchi, the head of the racing car assembly department and the testing room (the "prince" as his workers called him), did not get along. Guerino had grown up with the Maserati brothers, had raced as a mechanic and handled all our drivers at the time and therefore was very close to them. Bellentani understandably felt somewhat excluded and furthermore was never kept sufficiently up to date by the testing room regarding the development and the true power outputs of the engines; finally, there was also an element of hegemony in that Gino, Guerino's brother, was or was about to become the head of engine assembly, creating a situation that did not sit well with Ingegner Bellentani at all. As soon as he had the opportunity, Bellentani obtained from the powers that be permission to establish a new research and development department working on new features for the new engines. Within a few months the new Experimental Department was inaugurated in which he placed two of the firm's best engineers and two youngsters under the direction of Ingegner Alfieri, another who struggled to bond with the people mentioned previously.

One morning in late October, I saw Signor Barani and Guido Veratti, a lad from the Corni who had joined Maserati before I did, come into the toolroom. Barani went to talk to the foreman, Signor Baracca; he then came over to me with his customary gruff approach and told me that he had been ordered by Ingegner Bellentani to leave Veratti with me so that I could show him how to work the Linder. A little surprised by this, I thought to myself, "Either I'm being moved again or they want some one new who knows how to use this machine and the new internal grinder that has just arrived". Given that Veratti worked with Barani in the grinding group, I was convinced that this second hypothesis was more likely, especially as there was an external grinder in the toolroom but no operator. A few weeks later, in mid-November, Ingegner Bellentani visited the toolroom, called Signor Baracca and, coming towards me, said to him, "This lad's coming with me, I need him more than you and you've already got a replacement."

I was stunned; the Ingegnere then added in dialect, "*Vin meg!*"(Come with me!), I followed him anxiously, thinking, "who knows where he'll take me?" We crossed through various departments and after the chassis sector we took the corridor leading towards the exit and then entered the second door on the left. I knew what was in that little department that had been operational for just a few days, but I still didn't know what Ingegner Bellentani had taken me there for. I remember seeing Giulio Leoni first, an old, extremely skilful engineer, along with Giulio Cavazzuti, a lad from the Corni who until the day before had been in the Control Centre but was now working on a set of tubes. At the back was another worker bent over a frame who when he saw Ingegner Bellentani arrive stood up and came over to us.

"*Vè Tonino a to purtè al to aiutànt, cerca ed tirerel só bein e dinsgnergèl tót*" ("Look Tonino, I've brought you your assistant, make sure you bring him up right and teach him everything he needs to know"), then turning to me he said, "*E te guerda èd derg a meint*" ("And you make sure you listen to him"). Turning to Leoni, he asked him when he thought he would have finished that little derrick he was building and then left.

I was speechless such was my surprise, but then Giulio helped me out by saying, "Just think how lucky we are to work with these two; you know what I mean?" In fact, I was so happy that I could hardly take in what was happening. While asking me my name, how old I was, how long I'd been at Maserati, where I lived and so one, Reggiani took me over to the project he was working on and so began that morning my first lesson. He was building a frame with four feet that held a 20-litre drum of oil with an oil pump, which I immediately identified as belonging to the A6GCM engine. The pump was set above the frame and had been modified so that it could be turned with a small crank; Reggiani in fact intended to use the device to charge the engines with oil before starting them up on the test bench. Even though the engine builders were careful to lubricate the various components before they assembled the engines, when they were first started they would complete a few revolutions with little oil pressure, something which might have caused problems. Reggiani told me that he would be adding four casters that he had ordered via Norma, the lady in the Purchasing Department. This new department was at the back of the last shed on the left looking at Maserati from Viale Ciro Menotti, so as well the small doorway onto the corridor it had a large glazed door and two windows that overlooked the internal courtyard.

One of the windows was in the area of the torque meters, two alternating current electric motors controlled by a transformer that served to measure the power absorbed by the various ancillary components such as the oil and water pumps and the gearbox. The second window was above the two workbenches while another was located in the area of the two Schenck test benches, one rated at 500 hp and the other at 1000 hp at 10,000 rpm, that were due to arrive in a matter of days. A large extractor fan had been installed on the back wall, along with the exhaust pipes and the two cabins with the control instruments. When I went home for lunch at midday, I told my mother and father what had happened and they insisted telling me to be polite and helpful and that if this Signor Reggiani was so good, to pay attention and learn from him. That afternoon we were joined by Ingegner Alfieri, who as the head of the design department and having already met me in the toolroom, told me about what he had in mind: as soon as we had finished equipping and completing the department the two Schenck test benches would be delivered and Reggiani and I would test a 250F engine that Bietolini was finishing with new fuel mixtures the Ingegnere was having prepared. In the meantime, Leoni and Cavazzuti would start work on a cylinder head for the desmodromic valvegear. He had also brought a drafting table so Cavazzuti and I could produce the necessary drawings as he didn't want to interfere with the Technical Office, which was extremely busy with the design for the new transaxle. I immediately got on well with Reggiani; I'd told him I was building a house with my parents and he was doing the same thing with his in-laws, just a kilometres away. Tonino as he wanted me to call him rather than Signor Reggiani as I occasionally addressed him, had married late; he was around 40 years old and had yet to have children, something he was very much looking forward to. It was the beginning of a friendship that rather than fraternal was more like that between father and son. Moreover, I benefitted from the friendship and admiration of the many admirers Reggiani had attracted as soon as he joined Maserati, something I suspect may have aroused a little envy on the part of my contemporaries given the fame the "doctor" enjoyed.

THE FIRST TRIALS ON THE SCHENK TEST BENCH

Mid-November saw the arrival of the two dynamometers; they were accompanied by the firm's Italian representative and a German technician of the same age as me, Klaus Dambacker, with whom I immediately struck a chord. We became great friends and over the years whenever he was in Italy for inspections at Weber, Ferrari or with us in Maserati, he would always visit me at home and I remember he had a taste for Lambrusco. As everything had already been prepared, it took just a few hours to install the equipment consisting of the hydraulic unit with a turbine whereby you could manually open or close the flow of water. The 50-cm dial provided readings down to the tenths of a kilo. The ratio was 1:1 therefore the value indicated on the dial, multiplied by the number of revs gave the horsepower delivered by the engine. In order to achieve greater precision, it was essential to take into account the ambient temperature and the barometric pressure with an abacus indicating the correction to add or remove to have the true value of the power delivered.

The second dynamometer was then tested, with Dambacker making all the necessary adjustments and providing Tonino and Leoni with all they needed to know for future adjustments and maintenance. The representative, who also acted as our interpreter, informed us that while he was always available regarding any problem with the two test benches, they were now so reliable that the technician would only need to call once every two years. The following day, Reggiani and I began to conduct the tests with the various fuel mixtures Ingegnere Alfieri had had prepared by Palermo, the technician in charge of the oil, petrol, alcohol and other flammable liquids store, housed in a bunker at the end of the courtyard. Reggiani's first instruction was that, before starting up an engine for any reason it was essential that we opened the register and recorded date, time, temperature, barometric pressure, the internal engine number and the name of the engine builder, along with any timing and advance adjustment data. Ingegner Alfieri would therefore have the opportunity to draw his diagrams on the basis of the recorded data. All the more important was that by recording in this way every change that was made a trace remained of what we were doing.

This was all new for me; every day it was like being back at school, learning new things. Reggiani was a fount of wisdom; whenever we tackled a new subject he would explain all the whys and wherefores.

Once, when we were conducting a test at full power before moving on to the second with the MS3 mixture, Reggiani took his hands off the carburettor control levers and said to me, "There's something up with cylinder number 3"; I asked him how he knew as everything seemed fine to me. He explained that he'd noticed that cylinder 3's exhaust manifold was a different colour to the others. After a painstaking examination we discovered the throttle valve feeding that cylinder was not opening fully like the others. Reggiani always said, "Don't worry, you'll see that within a year you'll have learnt so much you'll have overtaken me because you've studied whereas I left school after five years." Reggiani was always a surprise even for Alfieri whom he would advise on certain tricks regarding the play and the tolerances between pistons and cylinder liners and in particular the carburetion of the engines. He understood the functioning of a carburettor in every minimal detail.

He asked me to draw an aluminium syringe containing around 100/150 cc, male and female, with external milling to stop it slipping out of the hand, and went to the toolroom himself to have the two pieces turned. I couldn't work out why we needed a syringe, but then the day after I was introduced to its importance. While the engine was running at a certain speed, at over 5000 rpm, Reggiani fanned a spray from the syringe over the intake trumpets while checking whether the needle on the dial rose or dropped, thus determining the precise carburetion. If it rose then we would adjust the high speed jets by a maximum of 5/10 or even 1/10 of a millimetre until we determined the exact diameter required. The spark plugs were subjected to a similar process; we had a certain number of various heat ratings. After accelerating to full revs, the engine would be stopped, we would remove a plug and from the colour of the ceramic Reggiani would be able to tell whether the rating was correct; the colour was also determinant for fine-tuning the carburetion.

The days, the weeks passed in a flash, I was so caught up in my work that I didn't even have time to keep up to date with progress on the new house. My father had bought the wood from the lumberyard he used for the Academy, all the timber necessary for make the doors and windows. He would do the work himself in a neighbouring carpenter's workshop, in the evenings after work and on Saturday afternoons.

Every two or three days Ingegner Bellentani would visit our department to find out how things were progressing. He wasn't entirely happy with the tests Leoni and Cavazzuti had conducted with the desmodromic valve cylinder head. In simplifying the two projects (the first by Ernesto Maserati from 1942-1943 and the second by Ingegner Massimino from 1945-1946) an intermediate design had been chosen that theoretically, and under the supervision of Ingegner Alfieri, should have been more efficient. The work required time, especially the building of the camshafts with two lobes, one to actuate the opening of the valve and the other to actuate and guide the closure. When he spent time with Reggiani, who would show him the register with the tests we had done with the new mixtures and the new carburettor tunings, he was delighted, above all because he now had the opportunity to see the true power output figures for the new engine. Previously instead, in Bertocchi's testing room the dynamometer was an obsolete model with a manual balance that at best could recognise half a kilo and was unable to register those tenths of a kilo that could make all the difference in tuning the engine. Moreover, Ingegner Bellentani was satisfied with the solution Reggiani had had prepared to avoid coolant leaks, creating a 2 mm^2 groove around the full perimeter of the engine block and inserting a 3 mm rubber strip which the cylinder head then compressed when tightened, while the pressed in sleeves, protruding by 0.15 mm, were perfectly aligned with the head, thus creating an excellent seal that had never been guaranteed by the previous designs.

THE ASTORIA PLAYS ITS PART

The Astoria was a dancehall located behind the former Albergo Reale in Piazza Garibaldi. There was also an open air dance floor in the internal garden for the summer months; it was Modena's most fashionable venue and frequented by a fairly high social class. One Saturday evening, together with my friend Ivo Tavoni, I decided to go to the Astoria after having heard other friends who went there often talking about it. We bumped into them as soon as we got in and were invited to sit at their table. When the band started to play again, I stood up to go and look for a girl to dance with, as we used to do back then. Not far away I caught the eye of a girl I thought I had already met; she smiled at me and I asked her to dance. After we had exchanged a few words I found out in fact that it was the girl who, when I was in my last year at the Corni, I often saw because she lived at Punta di Sant'Agnese and took the same route as me by bicycle as far as Viale Vittorio Veneto. One morning I had caught her up and had said something, "How you pedal fast, Miss!" We were very formal back then and we would speak to girls with a degree of circumspection, not like now. I remember that on that occasion she didn't even look at me. I tried to meet her on other mornings and always very politely tried to talk to her. I gradually came to know that she was called Giordana and that she kept her bicycle at the mechanic's at the start of Calle di Luca and together with other girls she went to the house in front to work for the seamstress

Sernicoli. She was always very elegant, I liked her, but she was serious and measured her words. One morning I dared invite her to a party one Sunday afternoon, as we used to do back then, and she very politely declined. School then finished, I had exams and I never had the chance to see her again. That evening, over two years later, she seemed even prettier, certainly more loquacious, or at least she smiled as we looked into one another's eyes. She was with her sister and had been accompanied to the dance by an aunt, another custom of the time. We almost always danced together that evening and I was very pleased to see that she refused to dance with others as she waited for me to invite her again. She was still working for the seamstress Sernicoli, according to her the best in Modena and who dressed the high society women of the city and the local area.

Having learnt what her hours were, I asked her if some evening I could meet her at 7 o'clock and ride home with her. She accepted with pleasure and so one evening I asked Reggiani if I could leave at 6:30, an hour earlier than usual. That afternoon I went to work by bicycle and at 7 o'clock I was waiting for her at the place where she kept her bike. Pedalling slowly, we reached the Punta, we stopped in front of her house to chat. Shortly afterwards a gentleman passed us, staring at me as he went. "Hello Dad, I'll be right in", she said to that gentleman. I caught on and said to her, "He glared at me; I hope I haven't caused you any problems." She reassured me by saying that she had already told her parents about our friendship, who I was, where I lived and where I worked. Her father, having learnt my name, told her that he had done his military service in Turin with my father. All this because the sister and the aunt had blabbed that Giordana and I had decided to go steady that evening at the Astoria. We met up on other Saturdays and she introduced me to her mother and her sister with her boyfriend-almost-fiancée and, around a month after we had been seeing each other, she accepted an invitation to the cinema. It was late November and as we came out of the cinema at around 6 o'clock it was already fairly dark (there was no daylight saving time then). Hand in hand we crossed the city centre and when we reached the park we passionately exchanged our first kisses. She had to be home by 7 o'clock so we had to rush to avoid upsetting her parents the first time we had gone out on a date together.

I had told her about the house I was building with my parents and the hours I was working which meant that I would be unable to meet her out of work very often. Moreover, I would have to save given all the expenses that we were facing and I still remember her reply today. "Ermanno, don't worry, your job and the house you're building are very important; if we love each other we have a lifetime in front of us", showing me that she was a sensible girl with her head on her shoulders as they say. She then told me she would be off work for a week because they were moving to Via Sabbatini: her family had in fact bought an apartment in a new building, she and her sister would be taking care of the furnishings and they were trying to convince their parents to celebrate New Year's Eve in the new apartment, taking the opportunity to present me and her sister Marisa's fiancée to them. Naturally, other friends would also be invited.

25 DECEMBER 1953

This was the date recorded by Ingegner Giulio Alfieri on the register and the diagram relating to the testing of 250F engine number 5, signed off at 11:00 AM on Christmas Day. This was an engine with which we had conducted numerous tests with new fuel mixtures and, having learnt that a new engine would not be available for some time, Alfieri agreed to a partial overhaul to check and where necessary replace the big- and little-end bearings only to permit the assembly of a 250F with the new chassis and rear suspension and the new transmission that was being completed. While Reggiani explained to me how to proceed systematically, we worked quickly to replace all the bearings, without removing the pistons, reassemble all the parts with painstaking care and fit the sump, with Ingegner Alfieri looking on. Reggiani had told him the operation was delicate and he shouldn't hurry us. We remounted the engine on the dynamometer at around five o'clock and ran it at 2000-3000 rpm until seven, with a little brake so that it would be ready the next morning for the power test. The engine was started up again at quarter past eight and Ingegner Alfieri arrived at nine o'clock anxious for us to start the power test straight away. Reggiani very politely advised him to keep the engine running in for another hour. After having replaced the plugs with ones with a colder rating we then began to bring it up to full power. We stopped a number of times to check the advance on the two magnetos we had marked and moved while the engine was running at 7000 rpm. The plugs we checked confirmed that the carburetion was correct and therefore Ingegner Alfieri gave the order to take the unit off the test bench and hand it over to the racing department.

In the meantime, Signor Omer, the lawyer Donati and Ingegner Bellentani had arrived in the department and Alfieri himself confirmed that the engine was giving over 240 hp at 8000 rpm. While Manfredini was helping us Ingegner Bellentani called him over, "*Veè uciàlein* [a nickname referring to his glasses, AN] *al vaga a cà ed Manni e Brancolini a direg che incò i vegnen a mùnter al mùtor com d'acord*" ("Hey, specs, go and call Manni and Brancolini at home and tell them to come and fit the engine to the car as we agreed"). At that time, very few people, especially workers had a telephone at home and so Manfredini had to cycle firstly to Manni's home and then to Arturo Brancolini who was not best pleased to be called in to work at noon on Christmas day; the very polite and discreet Manfredini never told us what it was Arturo said that morning. The engine was fitted to the new car and on Boxing Day morning, as Colotti has described, it was tested to the satisfaction of all at the Autodromo with temperatures of around 2-3° C.

The car reached Buenos Aires by air early in January, along with Ingegner Alfieri and all the mechanics. There they found a temperature of 40° C in the shade, the castor oil was so fluid it was unable to maintain the normal pressure in the engine. This was Ingegner Alfieri's debut and naturally he was keen to make a good impression; they tried adjusting the valves on the oil filter casing and cut apertures in the front of the bodywork but to little effect and when Commendator Orsi arrived he found everyone downhearted, including Fangio, the best driver we were fortunate to have. Orsi reassured Ingegner Alfieri saying that if they had done their best they should have faith and hope. Fangio held back in the early laps, keeping one eye on the oil pressure gauge, trying to conserve his engine, something he was a master at. Midway through the race, a storm blew up with a downpour that lowered the ambient temperature by a number of degrees, allowing Fangio to drive the 250F to its first victory in the Driver's World Championship.

100 HP/LITRE AND ANOTHER PLEASANT SURPRISE

To my great surprise, I found in my pay packet for the month of December a note like the one from the previous year informing me of a monthly pay rise of 1300 Lire; this was the second time my hard work been rewarded and I was over the moon and encouraged to give my utmost for the company. Ingegner Bellentani had sent us a new 250F engine and while our foreman Alfieri was in Argentina we went ahead with tests with other fuel mixtures, eventually achieving the sought after target of 250 hp at 7500 rpm.

When Ingegner Alfieri got back we were informed about a problem with the lubrication circuit and concentrated our efforts on finding a solution to this potentially serious issue. Giulio Cavazzuti was free as Leoni was seriously ill and off work and he helped us prepare the dynamometer room to conduct tests on the oil pump performance that, on the basis of Ingegner Alfieri's calculations should have been adequate, while Reggiani had worked on the engine to modify the internal oil flow. Substantial modifications were made to the location and the structure of the oil cooler and all the pipework within the car. Moreover, Ingegner Alfieri had the combustion chambers modified with an increase in valve dimensions that had the effect of increasing the power output to over 260 hp.

Having been informed that Mercedes would soon be competing in Formula 1, the specialist press gave ample coverage to the new car that was to be fitted with a new six-cylinder engine featuring Bosch fuel injection and developing over 300 hp. Ingegner Alfieri saw that the desmodromic valvegear still required lengthy testing and fine-tuning and that it had yet to show any great promise. He therefore told us that he intended to explore the fuel injection path. He had already contacted Bosch by post regarding the supply of a pump so as to be able to begin work on its application and adaptation to our engine to start testing, firstly with an indirect injection system and later the more complicated and demanding direct system. One morning in mid-February, Ingegner Bellentani came into the department with a letter for Ingegner Alfieri who on reading it exclaimed, "Impossible! I don't believe it!" Bosch had replied explaining that they had an exclusive contract with Mercedes for their injection pump and were sorry that they would be unable to satisfy Maserati's request.

THE ENGAGEMENT

I was invited to Giordana's home for New Year's Eve as together with her sister Marisa, she had been given permission by her parents to organize a party in the new apartment. In reality, it was just an excuse to introduce Angelo, Marisa's fiancée, and me to their father in that we had already met their mother at the Astoria, and to make things official so that we would be able in the future to visit them at home. Giordana's father, who that evening when he had surprised us together in front of their old place had seemed so strict and austere, instead proved to be very sociable. He told me that he worked at Fiat Trattori, that he knew my aunt Iride, my mother's sister who worked in the gatehouse at Fiat, and that he had done his military service with my father. Three friends of the sisters with their respective fiancées had also been invited to the party. We danced to the music from the record player and at midnight opened a few bottles of spumante and ate the delicacies the girls had prepared for us. We finally left at two o'clock in the morning. Even though the apartment was spacious and Giordana's parents' room was some way away, we didn't want to create too much trouble; the party had been fun with friendly, open people. The other lads were all older than me but I knew them by sight because they were all frequented the Timekeepers's club.

They were all Seniors, had obtained their license and were already members of the Federation. I was instead still a Junior, not having had time to attend the lessons and I had all but decided to give it up as work and the house we were building left little time for anything else. I had learnt that Angelo, Marisa's fiancée, worked at Ferrari, in the technical office at Maranello, while one of the others was a clerk in a distillery, another had just started teaching at the Corni and the third worked in a bank. One of their girl-friends worked as a hairdresser like Marisa, while another, who was from Sassuolo, had a small workshop making quilts. Giordana and I were the youngest of the group. I had arranged with her to meet up at four o'clock the next afternoon to go for a coffee and a walk in the town centre. It had snowed that night, but it wasn't particularly cold. I was lovely walking arm-in-arm through the snow-covered park. I was in love with and loved in turn by a wonderful girl and had the sensation that I had been accepted by her parents (naturally after the usual enquiries had been made about my family, with my mother telling me questions had been asked of shared acquaintances). That was how things were done at that time. I was happy and could hardly have hoped for more from my life.

FUEL INJECTION

Ingegner Bellentani tried to console Alfieri who that morning had seemed demoralised on learning that Bosch could not supply us with a pump. Ingegner Bellentani did not see the problem as being so serious and suggested that we could get round the obstacle by procuring a diesel injection pump like those used on lorries and adapt it to our purposes. He smiled at Ingegner Alfieri saying he was sure we would be able to resolve the problem. Work in what for the Italian technology of the time was an unknown field, began with the fitting of a pump manufactured in Brescia by OM to an A6GCM engine. This was in late March 1954, before Mercedes had entered the Formula 1 Championship. We should not forget that the German firm with the support of Bosch was the leader in this sector for many years. We were starting from scratch, armed with a wealth of enthusiasm and the various suggestions that Ingegner Alfieri had managed to pick up from Bosch. We were undecided as to the direct system (with the fuel mixture injected into the combustion chamber) or the indirect version (with the injectors mounted on the intake manifold, upstream of the valves). Unfortunately, with no support from Bosch we were only too well aware of the difficulties facing us.

For Ingegner Alfieri, the fuel injection path potentially provided for increased power and was therefore the only one to follow. It was not particularly difficult to fit the pump to the engine as we fabricated a support from welded sheet steel to be mounted to the block, beneath the exhaust manifolds as in that position we had the point for the pump drive. We were now faced with the problem of timing and Ingegner Alfieri and Reggiani pondered issues regarding the valve timings, until now suitable for carburettors, that would work with fuel injection too. Given the enormous quantity of work required to get the fuel injected engine running and to begin testing required the support of all the various departments. From the technical office for the drawings of the gate valve, to the lathe and milling machine operators for the fabrication, in just under a week we were ready for the first test – which proved to be extremely disappointing. I suggested to Reggiani that we could remove the flywheel from the test bench and have it graduated with grooves so that we could mark it with chalk. The idea was accepted. The toolroom quickly performed the modification so that we were able to establish the precise degree of injection.

We had made the pipe to the first cylinder of such a length that, equipped with its injector, it was close to the flywheel on which, marked in chalk, we could see and note by turning over the engine for a few revolutions the angle of injection and that of the closure of the valve. With the original first cylinder tube replaced, we conducted a rapid test noting the power outputs at the various engine speeds. We began with an injection angle of 50 degrees and, by retarding the injection by 5 degrees for in 15 for every test we obtained the exact angle. These were empirical tests, made during working days of 10 or 12 hours. We were so busy we lost track of time. Comforted by the partial results obtained with the A6GCM engine, the tests continued with a 250F engine in order to confirm that the research would bring the sought-after results. From the

250 hp of the carburettor engine we managed to obtain 280 hp with indirect fuel injection. Ingegner Alfieri was enthusiastic, even though power at low revs was still not satisfactory. One morning in early May, Ingegner Alfieri came into the department with Fangio and Signor Omer to see the results we had obtained. In fact he suggested to Fangio that for the race in the 6th of June at Spa we could equip his car with the fuel injected engine that would 18 horsepower more than the carburettor version. In his usual low voice, Fangio very politely placed his hand on Ingegner Alfieri's arm saying that he would prefer the more reliable carburettors and that he would see to finding the extra 18 horsepower himself.

In fact, he won at Spa with the 250F before moving to Mercedes and winning the 1954 World Championship, a feat he repeated with the German car in 1955. The work we had done had provided sufficient data for us to take a stab at direct fuel injection, even though the system presented particular difficulty in the passage from the crankcase to the cylinder liner; we had the circulation of the cooling water to overcome in order to screw the injector to the suitably modified sleeve. We worked around this last obstacle with a specific bush with external and internal threads and relative O-ring seals. In the final tests of the direct injection system we did not see any clear improvements in the power output, but rather a worsening of the low revs delivery. Ingegner Alfieri therefore decided to proceed with direct injection experiments with a comparative purpose on a 4CF2 engine, naturally fitted with a different pump for the four-cylinder unit and on another 250F engine.

All these interminable tests did allow use to explore and get to understand the phenomena relating to the various fuel mixtures and additives in which Ingegner Alfieri was particularly interested. We had reached MS14 and MS16, with the addition of small doses of nitromethane, methyl alcohol and of course the major component, benzole. The engine was the focus of Ingegner Alfieri's attention, with the rest of the major assemblies (transmission, suspension and chassis) presenting only minor modifications. The tests aiming at obtaining ever greater power outputs continued with the 250F engines with carburettors too, new cylinder heads with innovative combustion chambers being developed and Weber 45 DCO carbs replacing the 42 DCOs, with over 270 hp being produced at 8000 rpm. A 250F with indirect fuel injection provided conclusive proof of the validity of our work by winning on its debut at Goodwood in the traditional Easter Monday Grand Prix. Despite this success, Moss complained to Ingegner Alfieri about the engine's lack of bottom end grunt.

A TERRIBLE TRAGEDY

The Association of Timekeepers, of which I was also a member, was organizing a coach trip to San Pellegrino Terme on Sunday the 20th of June 1954. Angelo Bellei, Marisa's boyfriend, invited Giordana and me to go with them. Personally, I wasn't keen because on Sundays I had time to work on my new house where the roof had just been completed. However, given that Giordana wanted to go, I agreed, above all because we didn't get to see each other very often and I didn't have much time to spend with her. We spent a very pleasant Sunday together. The group was composed mainly of young couples, but there were also some older people including Signor Gino Barbieri, the photographer from Via Farini with his wife, who nearly made us die laughing at his jokes and one-liners. Signor Crotti, the president of the Association, was no less amusing, recalling the various mistakes made by inexperienced timekeepers when recording the results of certain races. We got back home as planned at about 10 o'clock. After we had taken Giordana and her sister home, Angelo and I picked up our mopeds from their garage and went home and started chatting then before we knew it, it was eleven o'clock.

When I got home, I looked up and saw the light on in my parents' bedroom, and I immediately thought that my father was not feeling well, as he occasionally suffered from the aftermath of a pulmonary abscess. I was just putting the Lambretta away in the cellar when I heard steps coming towards me. I turned around and in amazement, in the half-light, I saw Uncle Zoello, my father's brother, who was crying and came and hugged me. I immediately shouted, "What's happened?" thinking it would be about my father, but he told me that Gianluigi, my brother, had drowned in the River Panaro. I ran into the house and I found my mother and father in a desperate state of mind. Professor Domeniconi was also there. He had been summoned urgently to give them medicine as they had been fainting repeatedly as a result of their grief. I went to our bedroom and couldn't find Gianni, as we called him, in the room. "Where's Gianni? Where's Gianni?" My Uncle Zoello hugged me again and told me that they had yet to find him and that my Uncle Vasco was with a number of other people, near the old Panaro heliotherapy centre, where Gianni had disappeared when he dived down into the river. I ran downstairs, got on my Lambretta and rode as fast as I could to the place where it had happened. It was dark. They realised who it was when they came towards me. I shook them off and went to the water's edge and pointed the beam from my headlight at the water to see if I could see anything. My Uncle Vasco tried to calm me down but it was no use, I was inconsolable. Why couldn't he be found?

I asked a lot of questions but they were all in vain. Nobody gave me any reasonable answers. Then my uncle told me that the firemen had been there for as long as it was possible to see anything and that they would be back as soon as it was light. I went back home to my parents who were dozing because they had taken tranquillizers. I wanted to know exactly how the tragedy had happened. My uncle calmly told me everything while we drank a cup of coffee that my aunt had made. Immediately after lunch, Gianni had been at home studying before leaving the house on his bicycle at about three o'clock to go and play football with some friends. He'd met one of his friends who persuaded him to go for a swim in the River Panaro. Gianni didn't want to go as he didn't have a swimming costume or a towel with him but Irmo managed to convince him and told him that he would lend him his costume. So when they got to the Panaro, near the former health centre where there was a wider stretch of river and a bend with very deep water, they jumped in for a swim. As soon as Gianni hit the water, he was paralysed, probably because he had not digested his lunch completely, and never came to the surface again. When his friend saw that he hadn't resurfaced, he began shouting at the top of his voice and two men who were fishing nearby ran towards him. Once they realised what had happened, they told Irmo to go and tell Gianni's family what had happened. When he got to our house, there was no one at home. My mother and father had gone to the new house, so Irmo went to tell Uncle Zoello who lived nearby and it was he who went to tell my parents what had happened.

By now, it was five o'clock in the morning and it was getting light. After making sure that someone stayed behind to look after my parents, I went back to the river where my Uncle Vasco had stayed all night without sleeping like me. At eight o'clock the fire brigade arrived, launched a rubber dinghy and started to drag the river in various places, thinking that Gianni's body had been trapped on the bottom of the river. For a whole hour they searched but couldn't find him. Then an old fisherman came along. He knew the river with its currents and eddies very well and began to tell the firemen where to look and in the end they found Gianni's body. After completing the necessary legal procedures with a coroner, the body was taken home. I'm sure you can imagine how distraught everyone was, especially our mother.

The funeral, attended by a great number of people, was held at three o'clock on the 22nd of June in the church in Collegarola. The chaplain from the Military Academy gave a very moving sermon, as is appropriate in these circumstances. Gianni was buried in the cemetery at San Donnino, where my maternal grandfather had bought a vault with four places, for him, my grandmother and their two daughters.

On Wednesday the 23rd, I went back to work where I was comforted by everyone's condolences. I was especially moved when Signor Omer and the engineers Bellentani and Alfieri, who had been informed of the tragedy by Reggiani, came to the department to speak to me. Gianni was six years younger than me, he had always been a well behaved, good-looking child, had been making very good progress at the Corni school and played football with the Saliceta Panaro team. He adored me and I returned his goodwill by taking him by Lambretta to see Modena play hockey every other Saturday evening. Even though he was only fourteen years old he too had blisters on his hands from digging the earth when we were laying the foundations for our new house.

Life goes on, you have to get over these things, but my mother found it impossible. Every Saturday, when I got home from work, she always asked me to take her to the cemetery. She had always been too scared to get on my Lambretta, but she was able to overcome this fear as long as she could go to San Donnino. My father asked the carpenter for help in making the new doors and windows, because we wanted to leave Collegarola and the unhappy memories that haunted us. In November, we moved into our new home even though my father had yet to finish the housings for the roller blinds. At last we had our own house but there was still a lot to do, including the perimeter fence and the floors on the ground floor. It was a beautiful little house that we had gradually completed while managing to pay off the two million Lire loan, as I had calculated, well before it became due. This was the result of having had to give up lots of things to save money such as rare visits to the cinema, no holidays or trips. Giordana, my fiancée, had consequently also had to lead a rather limited life. However she didn't mind because she knew that one day that house would be her house too. The arrival of television helped us out and on Thursdays and Saturdays we spent the evenings watching the programme "Lascia o Raddoppia?" or some film or other.

One of the tiles on the doorway of Modena Cathedral depicting a "ferraiolo" or metalworker, the corporation of which was already active in the 12th century.

The six-year-old Ermanno Cozza in his first year of elementary school in a photo dated 1939.

The current façade of the Istituto Tecnico Industriale Fermo Corni in Modena.

My brother Gianluigi (Modena 1939-1954), aka Gianni, who drowned in the Panaro River near the San Damaso Heliotherapy facility on 20 June 1954.

Me at 19 years of age in 1952, with my faithful Lambretta.

At 12, in 1945, at the time of my introduction to the Istituto Fermo Corni.

AERAUTODROMO DI MODENA

The Modena Aerautodromo, the "Little Indianapolis", built in record time between 1949 and 1950; it was inaugurated on 7 May that year with a race for Formula 2 cars.

1948, the A6GCS Monofaro with the new full-width bodywork by Fantuzzi. The car in the photo is the one Alberto Ascari and Guerino Bertocchi raced in that year's Mille Miglia.

1950, the Technical Applications and Fitting classroom at the Istituto Fermo Corni.

1954, me together with Antonio "Tonino" Reggiani working on a way to dampen the carburettors on the four-cylinder 150S engine.

1956, my master Antonio Reggiani had already given me permission to test and sign off the 2500 cc six-cylinder Formula 1 engines.

1955, the 90°, 4500 cc V8 engine just
delivered to the Testing Room.

The dynamometer room, a 1500 cc four-cylinder engine
and a cylinder head for the brake horsepower test.

Antonio Reggiani, Ardilio Manfredini the visiting Argentinian engineer Riccardo Bonen and me, around a 4500 cc V8 engine.

August 1955, here I am examining the 1500 cc, four-cylinder engine for the Maserati 150S with which Jean Behra was to win the Nürburgring 500 km on the 28th of the month.

Together with my fiancée
Giordana during an out
to Lake Iseo in June 1954.

1940, an advertising brochure for the Electric Delivery Truck, bodied in various forms and built in the war years.

1951, a brochure for the 15 TM Muletto delivery truck built through to 1954.

1952, a brochure for our milling machines.

NOTE DELLA SALA PROVA

Il motore ha effettuato un rodaggio di due ...
dopo la revisione.
Il motore gira leggermente duro dalla tenuta ...

OSSERVAZIONI

Viene montato sul telaio 2504.

OFF. A. MASERATI
MODENA   Dati e risultati del Motore N. 5

MOTORE TIPO 250 F   N. CILINDRI 6   CORSA 75   ALESAGGIO 84   CIL. TOT. 2498

MAGNETE O SPINTEROGENO TIPO St 25 OA3   ANTICIPO FISSO 6°   CANDELE Champion u. TIPO NA 49

VOLUME CAMERA SCOPPIO cc. 36   RAPPORTO DI COMPRESSIONE 1:12.5

CARBURATORE Weber TIPO 42 DCO3 N. 3 doppio corpo.
DIFFUSORE Ø 36   GETTO MAX 195   GETTO MIN. 70   VITE ARIA FRENO   TAPPO SPILLO

CARBURANTE M1   LUBRIFICANTE Racer 00/IV

DISTRIBUZIONE: ASPIRAZIONE 41034   SCARICO 41278
E. AA 40 CA 75 - AS 83 CS 30 GIOCO ASP. 0,25 GIOCO SCAR. 0,30
VALVOLE linea ASP. Ø int 40 SCAR. Ø int 34 MOLLE N. 3 CARICO TOT. 150 Kg

BIELLE 250 F PISTONI Borgo GIOCO 8/100 R.O.N. 1 SEGMENTI 3 Kit
BRONZINE DI BANCO Vandervell GIOCO 6/100 ALBERO A GOMITI mitrunato

TEMP. AMBIENTE 14   PRESS. ATM. 760 mm UMIDITÀ REL. 50   FATT. CORR.

	Kg	HP	P. Olio	T. Olio	T. Acqua	Consumi	Anticipo
4000	40,8	186	8	90	80		
5000	43	165	"	"	"		
6000	46	212	"	"	"		
6500	44,8	224	"	"	"		
7000	43	233	"	"	"		
	41	263					

OFF. A. MASERATI
MODENA   Dati e risultati del Motore N. 3

MOTORE TIPO 250 F   N. CILINDRI 6   CORSA 75   ALESAGGIO 84   CIL. TOT. 2498

MAGNETE O SPINTEROGENO TIPO St 25 OA3   ANTICIPO FISSO 6°   CANDELE Champion u. TIPO NA 49

VOLUME CAMERA SCOPPIO cc. 36   RAPPORTO DI COMPRESSIONE 1:12.5

CARBURATORE Weber TIPO 42 DCO3 N. 3 doppio corpo.
DIFFUSORE Ø 36   GETTO MAX 195   GETTO MIN. 70   VITE ARIA FRENO   TAPPO SPILLO

CARBURANTE M1   LUBRIFICANTE Racer 00/IV

DISTRIBUZIONE: ASPIRAZIONE 41034   SCARICO 41278
E. AA 40 CA 75 - AS 83 CS 30 GIOCO ASP. 0,25 GIOCO SCAR. 0,30
VALVOLE linea ASP. Ø int 40 SCAR. Ø int 34 MOLLE N. 3 CARICO TOT. 150 Kg

BIELLE 250 F PISTONI Borgo GIOCO 8/100 R.O.N. 1 SEGMENTI 3 Kit
BRONZINE DI BANCO Vandervell GIOCO 6/100 ALBERO A GOMITI mitrunato

TEMP. AMBIENTE 14   PRESS. ATM. 760 mm UMIDITÀ REL. 50   FATT. CORR.

	Kg	HP	P. Olio	T. Olio	T. Acqua	Consumi	Anticipo
4000	40,8	186	8	90	80		
5000	43	165	"	"	"		
6000	46	212	"	"	"		
6500	44,8	224	"	"	"		
7000	43	233	"	"	"		
7400	41	263	"	"	"		

25 December 1953, technical file for the 250F engine, signed off on Christmas day, for the car with which Fangio raced in and won the Argentinian Grand Prix on 22 January 1954.

25 April 1953, the start of the Mille Miglia for Luigi Musso and Oscar Donatello in the A6GCS. They later had to retire with mechanical troubles.

In that same edition of the Mille Miglia, Emilio Giletti and Guerino Bertocchi started in the A6GCS/53, finishing first in class and sixth overall.

13 September 1953, a truly historic photo for the Trident marque: Juan Manuel Fangio crosses the line as the winner at Monza with the A6GCM, following a thrilling finale, conquering Maserati's first World Championship title.

Maria Teresa de Filippis about to complete a few test laps with the A6GCS at the Modena Aerautodromo.

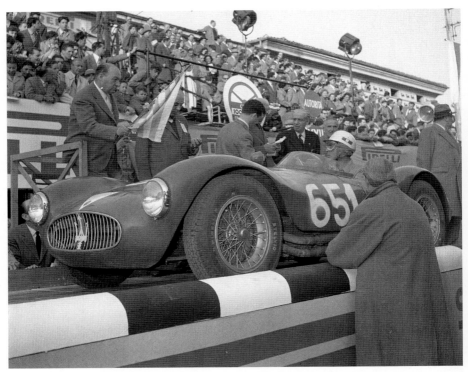

1955, Mille Miglia, Luigi Musso in the A6GCS seconds before descending the start ramp for the 22nd Mille Miglia. The talented Roman driver was then obliged to retire.

Also on the "starting blocks" for the same edition of the Mille Miglia was Cesare Perdisa with a Maserati 300S bodied by Fantuzzi, but he too failed to finish the race.

1957, Mille Miglia. Stirling Moss about to drive the Maserati 450S, which he was sharing with Denis Jenkinson, into Piazza della Vittoria in Brescia, ahead of the race. A broken brake pedal put an end to their race after just a few kilometres.

Juan Manuel Fangio conducts a few test laps at the wheel of the 2500 cc V12 Maserati 250F T2 ahead of the Pescara Grand Prix of 18 August 1957. Giorgio Scarlatti drove this car in the race, qualifying 10th and finishing 6th.

The cars lining up on the grid. Still in the pits can be seen the two 250Fs of Juan Manuel Fangio (No. 2) and Harry Schell (No. 6). The other 250F of "Chico" Godia (No. 10) is instead on its way to the fifth row from where it would start.

August 1960, me and
my first car, a FIAT 600,
bough second hand a few
days earlier.

The Officine A. Maserati in 1953,
seen from the steelworks tower
on the other side of Via Ciro
Menotti.

1958, the Car assembly department after the transfer of the car division to the new shed.
Bottom right, on the chassis builders' table can be seen the frame of the 420 Eldorado.

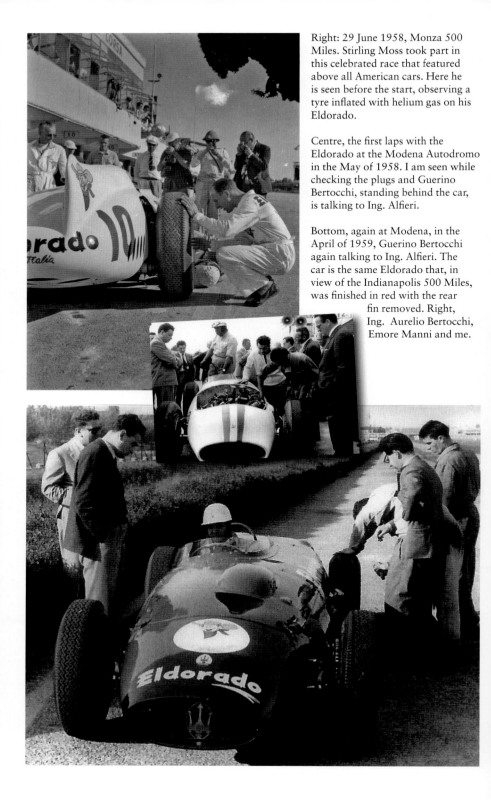

Right: 29 June 1958, Monza 500 Miles. Stirling Moss took part in this celebrated race that featured above all American cars. Here he is seen before the start, observing a tyre inflated with helium gas on his Eldorado.

Centre, the first laps with the Eldorado at the Modena Autodromo in the May of 1958. I am seen while checking the plugs and Guerino Bertocchi, standing behind the car, is talking to Ing. Alfieri.

Bottom, again at Modena, in the April of 1959, Guerino Bertocchi again talking to Ing. Alfieri. The car is the same Eldorado that, in view of the Indianapolis 500 Miles, was finished in red with the rear fin removed. Right, Ing. Aurelio Bertocchi, Emore Manni and me.

THE A6G/54 ENGINE

The massive commitment to design work that had been needed to prepare the A6GCS and 250F cars for racing, along with the enormous workload of the production department meant that we were unable to make similar progress on the Gran Turismo cars. In late 1954 Bellentani, with his forceful, practical personality, led the way and gave instructions to the technical office to overhaul and convert the fantastic A6GCS engine to make it suitable for use in touring cars. It would replace the single overhead camshaft A6G unit, with the new name being created, rather unimaginatively, by adding the number 54 to the old one. This gave rise to a new six-cylinder 2000 cc engine with a bore and stroke of 76.5x72 mm that developed 150 horsepower at 6000 rpm, with twin overhead camshafts driven by a triple row chain that did away with the gears and made it run quieter. The valves had 12 mm stems that were adjusted by means of a plate screwed onto the valve itself, twin spark ignition could be fitted to the cylinder head if requested by a customer, while a different sump with extensive finning and containing eight litres of oil meant that the scavenge pump could be done way with. There was also a range of options for the fuel supply, with carburettors of several different types.

The first engine was assembled by Enzo Torricelli, the senior engine specialist. It was delivered to us one November afternoon. We put it on the test bench and ran it at low revs with a little brake applied to the dynamometer for around ten hours, with an occasional increase in revs. The following day we started leak testing with special attention being given to the carburetion. We tested various different types of Weber carburettors, from the 36 DC04 to the 38 and the 40 DC03. Within two days we had gathered all the necessary data to pass on to Bertocchi in the Testing Room, as this sort of engine needed to be run-in and tested on a less demanding test bench more in line with the type of use that the engine would be subjected to. Bertocchi had two lads in the testing labs able to carry out the necessary work for the production department. Reggiani and I had plenty of other work to carry out on more demanding engines intended for competition use. Furthermore, Alfieri was certainly paying more attention to the development of the 250F engine and the new competition engines that people in the Technical Office were working on.

150S ENGINE:
NEW ARRIVALS AND
DEPARTURES

Following the experiment with the 4CF2 engine designed by Massimino in 1952, which failed to live up to our expectations, Bellentani decided to simplify the specifications and in 1953 started working on a four-cylinder 1500 cc unit, with bore and stroke dimensions of 81x72 mm, a double overhead camshafts, valvegear actuated by roller finger followers and needle valve springs, twin spark ignition with two distributors mounted at the front. There was a slight delay in production, caused by all the work needed to make improvements to the 250F engine and all the fuelling and ignition tests. It was only at the end of 1954 that we signed off the first engine. Fine-tuning was fairly straightforward because with Reggiani we had already worked out the correct settings for the two double-choke Weber 45 DCO carburettors. The only minor problem that we had come across was the slight vibration typical of four-cylinder engines and for this reason we had to find a solution that would prevent it affecting the carburettors. Reggiani was a genius; in a flash he explained to me what he intended to do – place a 30 mm thick rubber ring held in place by a 26 mm metal washer between the intake manifold and the carburettor and widen the mounting holes on the flanges of the two carburettors to allow rubber bushes to be fitted so that the carburettors would be dampened when fixed in place on the studs. This first engine was fitted to the inboard-engined "Maria Luisa IV" which belonged to Commendatore Guidotti with which he established a new world record for its class. On seeing the potential of this engine, in the spring of 1955 the Technical Office began working on the design of the car, something that proved to be very complex for various reasons.

At the start of the year the Ingegner Aurelio Bertocchi arrived. He had just graduated and was the son of Guerino, the chief test-driver and he was appointed to the Control Centre following a long-standing tradition initiated by Bellentani. Without doubt this was not a very rewarding post for the young graduate "Lelo" as he was known to his friends as he had spent a lot of time with his father and the racing team since he had been a small boy. In this case in particular, apart from the need to give new personnel a good grounding in basic training and make them familiar with all aspects of the company's business, Bellentani thought it was important to limit the sort of nepotism that is always present in family-run firms. On the 26th of March 1955, for reasons I have never understood, Bellentani left Maserati and was replaced by the workshop manager Cavalier Attilio Galetto, who had come from the competition.

Many of us younger employees were very upset by this. In fact, after a few weeks we were aware of significant differences in the way the new workshop manager related to his heads of department and how he paid little attention to us, the younger members of staff. And on a purely technical level too, we had clear evidence that he was not nearly as good at his job as Bellentani had been. Giulio Cavazzuti in our Experimental Department had gone off to do military service too, so Reggiani and I now answered directly to Alfieri who in the meantime had been appointed technical director. Reggiani was giving me more and more room to move and had greater trust in me. I followed his instructions to the letter. I had become familiar with the fine-tuning of the engines that were signed off by our section, to the extent that I was complimented by Alfieri for the car Jean Behra used in the Nürburgring 500 Kilometres, the 150S that I had prepared myself. Another engineer, Aurelio Polli had also arrived. He was older than Alfieri and he was given responsibility for administrative, organisational and secretarial tasks. Bertocchi had finished his training in the Control Centre, and had ended up in an office where for the time being he was responsible for Logistics regarding the various Formula 1 and sports car racing commitments.

THE 300S ENGINE

Before defining a new power unit that would replace the magnificent two-litre A6GCS, which had demonstrated a vitality exceeding all expectations, Ingegner Alfieri entrusted us with the task of transforming a 250F engine running on blended fuel to pure petrol to be used in sports cars, interest in which was growing thanks to the new championship organized for the category. The configuration of the 250S engine remained unchanged, we simply replaced the pistons to obtain a compression ratio of 9:1. We put the unit on the test bench and worked on the new carburettor tuning: we were unable to produce more than 230 hp at 7000 rpm. On this engine the flywheel was replaced with a geared version to allow starting via a starter motor mounted on the suitably modified crankcase. It was also fitted to the 250S that participated in the Supercortemaggiore Grand Prix in the hands of Fangio and Marimón. This idea of using a 2500 cc Formula 1 engine to produce a power unit for a sports car was reprised a year later to supply Talbot with two engines for cars conforming to the new Le Mans regulations that called for a maximum displacement of 2500 cc.

This experience provided Ingegner Alfieri with guidance in defining in detail the engineering of the new 300S engine. Guido Taddeucci, head engine builder in the Technical Office, had opted for the configuration dear to Ingegner Bellentani of a long stroke engine. The resulting bore and stroke dimensions of 84x90 mm gave a displacement of

2993 cc, with an increase in piston velocity that did give rise to certain doubts. The architecture of the new engine was similar to that of the six-cylinder 250F, the engineering of which was transferred to an engine to be used in sports cars. When the first example assembled by Fausto Bietolini was brought to us in the Experimental Department, Reggiani and I had no difficulty in tuning it, with only a modification of the two breather pipes located below the exhaust manifold giving us cause for concern regarding excess humidity. A power output of 250 hp at 7000 rpm satisfied Ingegner Alfieri who in the meantime had made contact with Milan Polytechnic, from where he had graduated and where he knew some of the people conducting the first experiments on the aerodynamics of the bodies built by the great Fantuzzi. The suggestions deriving from the tests conducted on scale models in wood led to the lengthening of the noses of both the 150S and the 300S. Their lines had appeared to be a little heavy from an aesthetic point of view and this modification rendered the Maserati Sports car sleeker and more attractive and provided Fantuzzi with guidelines for all the future bodies for the new sports models then being designed.

With the approval of the Orsis, having had confirmation of the great commercial potential of the 150S, early in 1956 Ingegner Alfieri decided that the time was ripe to increase the displacement of the four-cylinder engine to 2000 cc (92x75 mm). This engine used all the components of the 150S, with the exception of the crankshaft and the pistons, leading to a notable increase in power – 190 hp at 7500 rpm. Its fine-tuning was extremely easy and Reggiani was happy for me to take all the merit for the work. We were swamped with work in the Experimental Department with Reggiani and I being on our own and Ingegner Alfieri promised that he would have found us some help. I asked him to give us Alvaro Soli who had just joined the firm, one of the first to graduate from the Corni's car repair mechanics course. However, Soli was one of Gino Bertocchi's men and he did all he could to obstruct Ingegner Alfieri's request. Under Reggiani's tutelage, I had begun to understand those subtle internal rivalries deriving from differences in character and above all that hegemony that Ingegner Bellentani had always fought against.

THE 350S AND 450S ENGINES

The 350S engine project was begun in 1956 in a wholly unexpected form in that there was no way of expanding the 300S unit. This was an engine that Ingegner Alfieri was thinking about producing for a new Grand Touring car. The first Type 53 unit, as the project was designated, was delivered to our department early in February. It was an all-new design, although the architecture did derive from the six-cylinder range with twin-spark ignition; the twin overhead camshaft drive was replaced with a triple chain that was very quiet and economical compared to the gear train. The cams no longer acted on fingers but rather bucket tappets guided in the new cylinder head. Distributor ignition meant the elimination of the two magnetos, while the 45 DCO carburettors were retained although 48 DCO ones were also tested. The displacement of 3486 cc (derived from a bore and stroke of 86x10 mm) eventually allowed us to obtained 290 hp at 6000 rpm. The valve control system gave us a number of problems because the material used for the bucket tappets was inadequate. This delayed the testing programme, as we had to wait for new one in a different type of steel. Various solutions were approved and within a month we were able to deliver the engine to the Racing Department so that it could be fitted to the new chassis destined to receive the 450S engine (as for various reasons the 450S engine was not available the 350S momentarily replaced it).

At the Technical Office, with the arrival of Ingegner Colombo in 1953, the organization was revise and a rule was adopted for the designation of the various types of engine and car projects. It was decided that Formula 1 and single-seater cars would have a numbering from 1 to 50, the sports cars and engines from 51 to 100, the Grand Touring cars from 101 to 150 and the prototypes and special cars from 151 to 200.

The 450S engine was born in the Technical Office as the Type 54, the project for which suffered significant delays due to the firm's commitments on multiple fronts. The paternity of the design was divided equally between Taddeucci, head of the engine designers, and Colotti for the transmission and chassis. Ingegner Alfieri, heading what for the Orsis was a by no means simple project, devoted to it all his passion and determination, aware that the most difficult aspect was the engine, which had an unusual configuration with respect to those we already had in production. It was a 90° V8 with twin overhead camshafts per bank driven by a gear train; the valves were actuated using the system already tested with the 150S and the design cylinder head of the straight-four was also reprised. The V-conformation of the banks of cylinders facilitated the positioning of the four Weber 48 IDM vertical carburettors, while the exhausts were on the outside.

The two magnetos for the dual ignition were mounted on the front, below the intake camshafts; also at the front were the two centrifugal water pumps and an assembly with two supply and one scavenge pumps for the lubrication system. The starter motor and the dynamo were positioned on either side in case distributors were used instead of magnetos. The engine was assembled by Nemore Barbieri, a skilled engineer who had worked at Maserati for years with his two brothers: Gianfranco worked on the machine tools under Barani while Giorgio, the younger, was in the testing room with Guerino Bertocchi. Together with Reggiani we had prepared everything to position and install the new engine that was handed over to late one afternoon in the first few days of June. The first exhaust reports at around 7 o'clock were toasted with a bottle of gin that suddenly appeared from who knows where, in the presence of the Orsis, Ingegner Alfieri and Commendator Stanguellini.

After the engine had been idling for around 10 minutes, as soon as we tried to increase the revs to 1500-2000, we noted vibration severe enough to convince us to check and correct all the fairly complex carburettor control system. Reggiani was on one side and I was on the other to synchronise all the linkages and adjust the idle screws on the carburettors. While we were working we noticed a cracked exhaust manifold; we stopped the engine and I ran to get an electric welder to close the crack. While Reggiani was welding I whispered into his ear: "It seems to me it could be the firing order, the vibrations are strange". So as not to let Ingegner Alfieri overhear, Reggiani winked at me. We restarted the engine, increasing the revs a little without the loading of the dynamometer and after 10 minutes another exhaust manifold cracked. This time I made a rough repair and we restarted, but despite all our adjustments the vibrations remained. We had already agreed with Ingegner Alfieri that I would stay until 10.00 PM to keep the engine turning over so as to speed up the running in period and begin to start the bench testing and tuning. I had already had a sandwich sent in via the gatekeeper. It was 8:30 and while everyone else went home, I was left alone with

Reggiani and he said, "If another exhaust pipe breaks, turn everything off and go home, tomorrow someone will have to admit *mea culpa.*"

I knew there was something wrong, but I couldn't quite put my finger on it. As Reggiani had predicted, at around 9 o'clock, another pipe cracked, I repaired it and restarted by 10 minutes later another one broke. This time I did what Reggiani had told me, locked up and went home.

The next morning, I arrived quite early and as I was opening the large door onto the internal courtyard, I passed Taddeucci who, arriving from Reggio Emilia by train, was one of the first into the factory, well before 8 o'clock. We waved his hand at me as if to ask, "So?" I replied with a downturned thumb, he beamed at me, rubbed his hands and headed for his office. A moment later, Reggiani arrived and I told him how things had gone the previous evening and what had happened with Taddeucci. I also asked him to explain just what was going on. While indicating that we would have to take the engine off the test bench before the arrival of Ingegner Alfieri, Reggiani began to explain, taking a roundabout route at the start: "Let this be a lesson to you, one that you always remember, in life you should never act as if you're better than the others, you need the humility to listen to the opinion of others, even if they are your inferiors, never insist on doing things your way if you're not absolutely sure you're right and so on." He continued in this life lesson vein that I could hardly interrupt because I was eager to know what was behind the recent events. He went on to tell me sadly as if he were truly very upset. It was all to do with an argument between Ingegner Alfieri and Taddeucci: in the design of the crankshaft for the V8 engine, Taddeucci had chosen a well-known firing order used by other car manufacturers, while Ingegner Alfieri wanted a different one that no one had ever employed, with the results had experienced first hand. Reggiani had been informed by Taddeucci about the episode and had tried to persuade to Ingegner Alfieri to think again but had the opposite effect and had to listen as Alfieri declared that we had to experiment with things that others didn't do.

Once a new crankshaft and camshafts had been made for a firing order as specified by the designer, the engine was brought back to us three weeks later; when we fired it up we immediately had the sensation that the engine was good, the vibrations had disappeared, it ran smoothly and gave no sign of imbalanced as we increased the revs. We had had a series of new exhaust pipes made and after running in for around eight hours we changed the plugs and conducted the first dynamometer tests that showed just under 400 brake horsepower at 7000 rpm. We had to tune the carburetion, the magneto advance and also test the distributors. Ingegner Alfieri was always in the department; he was in a hurry to install the engine in the chassis and test the car.

However, Reggiani knew how to tackle him and explained that if we were to do the job well, it would take the necessary time. To the satisfaction of both, after three days' work, the power output was measured at 412 hp at 7000 rpm, the engine was fantastic, it would accelerate up to maximum revs incredibly quickly without the slightest hesitation. Ingegner Alfieri intended to have the car make its debut on the 12th of August in the Swedish Grand Prix. Given the great importance of the race, the sporting director Nello Ugolini managed to convince Ingegner Alfieri not to enter it officially, and in fact it was only used in practice. The bodywork differed with respect to that of the 300S thanks to the prominent and less than attractive bulge on the bonnet required to cover the four carburettors. Reggiani subsequently had the idea of inclining the carburettors towards the inside with new intake manifolds, searching for a carburetion compromise that would permit shorter intake trumpets. With this configuration the engine and carburettor assembly was much lower, making the bulge on the bonnet much more attractive and improving visibility for the driver.

A similar case of opinions trying to be imposed through authority occurred with the material used to construct the 450S driveshafts. Cavalier Galetto, the workshop foreman, in contrast with the views of Montipò, a wizard in the field of steels and treatments, wanted them fabricated in a certain type of steel with a particular heat treatment. In testing, however, they twisted, just as Montipò had predicted.

ALIVE BY A MIRACLE

All the A6G/54-type engines for the Grand Touring cars were run-in and tested in Guerino Bertocchi's Racing Department testing room. Two dynamometers were available, a 500 hp Froude, that had belonged to the Maserati brothers and which was used for the racing engines, and a smaller Ranzi-type 300 hp unit acquired in the immediate post-war years and used almost exclusively for the commercial vehicle engines. One November afternoon, Giorgio Barbieri, the lad in the testing room, came to call me because an A6G/54 engine that had finished its running-in had to be tested. The engine was needed urgently and Ingegner Bertocchi had promised to conduct the test in the absence of department head, his father, who was in Venezuela with the racing team for the Grand Prix and Barbieri had not yet been authorised to sign-off engines. When I arrived in the testing room, Ingegner "Lelo" Bertocchi asked me to give him a hand. He wanted to conduct two tests with revs rising to 6000 rpm and descending in 1000 rpms steps while Barbieri recorded the data on the register. The engineer operated the accelerator while I dealt with the brake; everything went smoothly and we stopped to examine the data. They fell within the parameters but were a little on the lean side. I suggested doing a test that Reggiani had taught me, blocking the brake at around 5000 rpm and loosening the distributor slightly so as to be able to rotate it and find the optimum advance point and thus gain a few horsepower.

Ingegner Bertocchi agreed, drew a reference mark between the distributor and the support and we restarted the engine. I went to lock the brake at 5000 rpm and returned close to Bertocchi to rotate the distributor; once we'd found the optimum position, I tightened the fixing nuts and at the same time heard a great bang like a cannon going off and something big flew into the air.

It bounced off the ceiling and kept spinning on the concrete floor, giving off sparks. The three of us were stunned for a few minutes, unable to comprehend what had happened. The accountant Moncalieri who had been passing on the way to his office, turned back and stuck his head into the testing room: "What's going on? Did something explode?" The test bench flywheel had stopped spinning and was lying on the floor, while we were white faced and just starting to get over the shock. What had happened was that the brake shaft had seized and, due to the inertia of the centrifugal force, had sheared the flywheel's attachment to the dynamometer allowing it to come off the coupling to the engine, fly up to ceiling and bounce down to the floor.

Had it happened 10 minutes earlier, while we were conducting the power scale and were much closer if not actually on the trajectory of the missile, I wouldn't be here now to tell the story. Moncalieri went to call Signor Omer, telling him there were three employees still alive thanks to a miracle. When I got home that evening I avoided say anything to my mother so as not to alarm her; she was unaware that on occasion I was in danger at work. Unfortunately, the grief over Gianni's death had changed her. She had become so possessive of me that she always insisted on knowing where I was going and when

I'd be back. My father had also changed, but he tried not to be as apprehensive about me as my mother. Having overcome some considerable doubts, my fiancée Giordana had decided to strike out on her own. After around 10 years working for the dressmaker Sernicoli, she felt she was ready to take the great step. She already had a number clients, one of whom owned a small villa that was to be demolished to make way for an apartment building. Knowing that I had just finished the house, she suggested that we should go and dig up a magnolia of over three metres tall from the garden, otherwise it would be chopped down. One Sunday morning, armed with shovel, spade and pickaxe, I went with Giordana to get the magnolia, not knowing that the job would be much more laborious and demanding than I'd thought. My father had advised me to leave as much earth around the roots as possible to give the plant a chance to survive the move. It was an exhausting job; Giordana tried to help as much as she could, passing me the shovel or the spade. I was accustomed to digging, having helped prepare the foundations of our house, but I'd never dug up a tree!

Having loaded the magnolia into a sidecar I'd borrowed, with the roots wrapped in sacking to keep the earth intact, we managed to get it back to my house, a couple of kilometres away. My father helped us unload it and plant it in the hole I had prepared the week before. My mother then arrived and it was on that occasion that I introduced them to Giordana who was covered in mud, albeit a little less than me. I would never have expected the welcome my parents gave Giordana. They wanted her to stay for lunch with us as it was already one o'clock, but red in the face she thanked them, apologised for the state she was in and explained that she wanted to go home for a bath. Our efforts were repaid the following spring when the magnolia produced a number of beautiful, perfumed white flowers. My wage packet for December 1956 again contained the pleasant surprise of a complementary note and the announcement of a small raise.

THE NEW CUSTOMER SERVICE DEPARTMENT

Behind the factory's internal courtyard a shed of around 5000 m² and double the usual height had been constructed some time previously. It had been intended to house a rolling mill, although the project was never followed through. The changing rooms had been located there and it had also provided a temporary home for Montipó's Heat Treatment Department. When the smaller cars like the A6GCS, the 150S and the 200S went into production, the number of clients increased and Guerino Bertocchi's Racing Department was unable to house all the cars that were beginning to obstruct day-to-day operations on the works cars. A space was therefore found at the back of the shed to house this new Customer Service Department. The administrative side was entrusted to Signor Siro Lemmi, who arrived with Cavalier Galetto, while Umberto Stradi, a Maserati employee since 1939,was appointed as foreman and test driver. Stradi had a team of around 10 young lads chosen from the factory to form the various engine, transmission, chassis and general groups. Along with the usual maintenance and repair work, they were to service and assist the clients in the various races held almost every Sunday in Italy and elsewhere in Europe.

Stradi had been given permission by Signor Omer and Ingegner Alfieri to take certain clients to the Experimental Department to see the new engines and the new projects we were working on. Firstly Reggiani and then Stradi had assisted Commendator Guidotti when he installed the first 150S engine in the motorboat Maria Luisa IV, arousing no little envy among those who saw their pre-eminence continually diminishing. Commendator Guidotti ordered a 3500 cc engine for an attempt on the speed record in the category for 500 kg hulls. He was provided with a 350S engine, the unit removed from the car in which the 450S was installed, and he had it fitted to a Timossi three-point hull for the record-breaking run. When Commendator Guidotti informed Maserati of the date and made a request for assistance at Sabaudia, it was immediately clear that in that period, from the 29th of April to the 2nd of May, Reggiani, Stradi and others were all committed to Sports and Formula 1 car races. The only one who could go to Sabaudia was me as I had tested the engine and had sufficient carburettor experience. Ingegner Alfieri introduced me to the Guidottis, father and son, whom I had already seen. They knew who I was too and told me they would pick me up from Maserati in the early afternoon of the 29th of April with their large off-roader towing a trailer for the boat.

On the 19th of April, as we had agreed, Commendator Guidotti, his son Flavio and one of their employees picked me up and headed for Sabaudia where the record breaking attempt was to be made on the 1st of May. It was a pleasant trip, Commendator Guidotti was very loquacious and told me all about his passion for nautical sports to which he would have liked to devote ever more time had his electrical components business permitted. He was transmitting this passion to his sons too: Flavio who travelled with us was the same age as me and had already raced, while his younger brother Giorgio, was impatiently waiting for a chance to beat him. Every 100/150 km we alternated at the wheel with Signor Mario, their factotum. When crossing Rome we took fairly central routes because the Commendator wanted to show us, at least from a distance, the Colosseum and the dome of St. Peter's, which neither I nor Mario had seen before. We reached Sabaudia at around eight o'clock in the evening and met up in the hotel restaurant at half past. After a first course of *rigatoni*, Commendator Guidotti ordered *mozzarella in carrozza*, a speciality I had never tasted before. He explained that this was the area of production of *buffalo mozzarella* and that they knew how to use it well. During the dinner we established the programme for the following day, which consisted of launching the boat and seeing if the engine could reach 6000 rpm, otherwise the propeller would have to be replaced with one with a different pitch.

By half past seven I had already had breakfast and when the Guidottis arrived they were surprised to find me ready to go. They were extremely kind and very considerate, confirming what Reggiani and Stradi had told me. At the port, the boat was hoisted into the air by a large crane and lowered gently into the water. Having started the engine and let it tick over so that it warmed up properly (I was wearing rubber-soled shoes to move around the wooden hull without scratching the paintwork, something the owners appreciated), I checked the oil and water lines, found no leaks and revved it a few times until I felt that the engine temperature was sufficient before replacing the spark plugs with others better suited to high revs. Commendator Guidotti went out and made two passes on the course that he would have followed the next day. He then came back in to report that while the engine was running well, he had been unable to get more than 5000 rpm. We therefore had to replace the propeller, a fairly straightforward operation, but I was worried because the engine was not supposed to exceed 6500 rpm. I was reassured when they showed me a box with various propellers with different pitch and told me they would proceed gradually.

With the boat lifted out of the water, Signor Mario replaced the propeller with a certain familiarity and we then hurried to start the engine to ensure it was up to temperature. The engine restarted a little reluctantly due to the cold plugs, but after 10 minutes of ticking over and occasional bursts of acceleration, it was warm enough. Commendator Guidotti lowered himself into the driver's seat and made a number of passes, raising his thumb after each. When he came back in he was very satisfied and at full throttle the engine had reached 6150 rpm. By this time it was already half past one and we went to lunch. In the afternoon, agreements had to be reached with the timekeepers and the other Powerboat Federation officials for the homologation of the record. At about five o'clock we visited Latina, the town built during the Fascist period when the Pontine marshes were being reclaimed. I found it all very interesting from a historic and political point of view. Dinner that evening was equally enjoyable and given that everyone had appreciated the *mozzarella in carrozza*, it made a reappearance. By eight o'clock the next day, the 1st of May, we were all ready to head to the port. Commendator Guidotti was rather tense and kept glancing at his watch, even though our appointment was for 10 o'clock and the timekeepers would not be ready before then.

He had plenty of time to prepare. I only had to start the engine and warm it thoroughly with the spark plugs I had used the previous morning in place of the harder, high speed ones. At half past nine, Commendator Guidotti was ready with his helmet in his hand. He gave me the signal to start the engine and I kept it running a little faster so it would get up to temperature quicker before I replaced the plugs again. When I reached the third, the plug came out with the aluminium thread attached, I blanched and when Commendator Guidotti saw the plug he began to curse: "What's happened? How can we be that unfortunate?" He told Flavio to go into the centre of Sabaudia and see if he could find a screw tap with a diameter of 14 by 1.5 mm while I finished replacing the others. As it was the 1st of May all the shops were shut and Flavio came back in a fluster not having found anything, not even the garage near the hotel having a suitable tool. I therefore finished to replace the hard plugs, fitting the third in its housing an with a punch I tried to beat as much material as possible around the plug, covered the attachment with insulating tape and explained to Commendatore that the cylinder would have operated with a single spark plug. It was 10 o'clock and time to got, but Guidotti was reluctant: "But will it hold? Will it hold?" he repeated fairly irritably and I shouted, "We'll only know if we try!".

The engine started without showing any sign of anything amiss; my heart was in my mouth even though I knew I wasn't to blame for what had happened. The first pass was interminable, the second too until Flavio leapt for joy while his father came back in to the port. He climbed out and without even taking his helmet off hugged me: "It held! It held!" He embraced Flavio and Signor Mario as the Federation officials arrived to offer their congratulations on the new record of 188 kph, no less than 6 kph faster than the previous mark. No one apart from us four had seen what had made us so anxious and at lunch with all the people that had been invited no mention was made of it. Only on the trip home, heading for Modena, did I bring the subject up, explaining that it was not the first time it had happened, that in aluminium castings porosity could be created that weakened the material. It had never happened to me personally, but there was always a first time. In these cases the thread is repaired by inserting a steel coil. We reached Modena fairly late, even though we had only stopped for a coffee after the large lunch. The Guidottis left the trailer with the boat with me at Maserati and set off immediately for Milan, saying that they would have spoken to Ingegner Alfieri by phone about the engine. Ingegner Alfieri and Reggiani only got back two days later having been attending a race. I couldn't wait to tell them what had happened and that nonetheless Commendator Guidotti had broken the record.

MASERATI'S FIRST
12-CYLINDER ENGINE

For around a year, following the birth of the 450S engine to be precise, Ingegner Alfieri had been seriously considering an engine to replace the 250F as other marques were preparing to enter Formula 1. In the near future, our six-cylinder would allow little room for further development. Initially, with Taddeucci, they were considering an engine with horizontally opposed engines. This solution, however, would also have required a new chassis and as an eye had to be kept on costs, Ingegner Alfieri opted for a 60° V configuration, which could be installed in the existing chassis with only minor modifications. With the help of Alvaro Soli, the engine fitter Fausto Bietolini had assembled the first 12-cylinder engine within a week. Extensive use of Elektron was made for the casting, while the bore and stroke dimensions were 68.7x56 mm. This reduction in stroke with respect to the bore immediately suggested the high maximum revs it would be capable of. The compression ratio of 12:1 was suitable for the MS12 fuel mixture. A complex gear train that after having driven the oil and fuel pumps rose to the water pump and finally the four camshafts actuating the valves. The famous fingers had been eliminated, while the return springs were of the needle type. Two special Marelli magnetos fed the 24 spark plugs with a small 10 mm thread, via a series of 24 small coils.

The individual fuelling system featured Dell'Orto carburettors mounted between the camshafts on each bank, while the exhausts were lateral. The engine was started one afternoon in mid-December 1956 in the presence of numerous people, including Avvocato Donati, who after the first few detonations burst into enthusiastic applause. After careful adjustment of the carburettor control linkages, Reggiani on the right and me on the left, we noticed that the engine ran smoothly with no problems and agreed with Ingegner Alfieri to run it in well for seven or eight hours and begin a few tests the following afternoon. The next morning, I restarted the V12 and left it running for four hours at between 2500 and 3000 rpm, gradually increasing the loading. In the afternoon, at around five o'clock, Ingegner Alfieri arrived, eager to know the result of the first test at full revs. We replaced the 24 spark plugs with a harder grade. Reggiani was always very cautious when conducting the initial tests of an engine whose behaviour we had yet to get to know and he warned me to look at him before operating the dynamometer controls as due to the noise I wouldn't be able to hear his words. We were now so close that we understood one another through looks and gestures.

With the first power curve we registered 320 hp at 12,000 rpm. Ingegner Alfieri could hardly contain himself. I was incredulous and initially we thought that the test bench rev counter and the balance instrumentation must have been faulty. Having checked that the dynamometer was working properly, we repeated the test and recorded with the Hassler manual rev counter 13,000 rpm, exactly the same as with the test bench, the power output being 322 hp, without considering the correction for barometric pressure which that day was 2%. In the acceleration sweep test we had noted that the engine came under load over 5000 rpm while it dropped off at the same speed when decelerating from maximum revs. In any case, our enthusiasm knew no bounds as we'd witnessed an unimaginable power output; what remained for us to do was to smooth out and lower the engine speed at which the power began to cut in. Reggiani had some doubts as to the functioning of the Dell'Orto carburettors as we had noted that they were not very sensitive to the injections of fuel Reggiani was giving them to establish the precise jet settings. Ingegner Alfieri told us to try something, to attempt to obtain an improvement, but he didn't really insist as Weber had promised him that within a few weeks they would have provided a set of six new carburettors specially made for our 12-cylinder engine.

Our Technical Office had some time previously supplied Weber with the dimensions for fixing the manifolds to our cylinder heads. Early in January Signor Daini arrived, a veteran Weber engineer with six 35 IDMs that Reggiani and I immediately fitted to our engine. The assembly of the control linkages was fairly demanding but in a couple of hours the engine was started and as soon as it was up to temperature we replaced the plugs and commenced a series of tests at intermediate speeds, just to check the carburetion, which proved to be too rich. With the main jets and the air screws replaced, we tried higher engine speeds, but then we had to increase the pump flow as the power delivery came in at too high a speed. In any case, the new Webers had immediately shown themselves to an improvement over the Dell'Ortos. We were now faced with a great quantity of work to be done. As well as perfecting the carburettor tuning, the most demanding problem was that of lowering engine speed of the excessively violent power delivery. Moreover, we also had a deadline to respect as Ingegner

Alfieri wanted to install the engine in the car and have it tested by Fangio when he returned from Argentina with the rest of the Racing Department.

With one test or another, we were finishing at eight or nine o'clock almost every evening and we even needed to enlarge the diffuser diameter by one or two millimetres. In the Machine Tool department there was always some one working the shifts from 6:00 AM to 2:00 PM and from 2:00 to 10:00 PM, which meant we always had the necessary support to get these jobs done quickly and repeat the test while the engine was still warm. It was therefore natural that we would respond to those contributing and asking about the new 320 hp engine. The news had spread around the factory and even in the local bars, among the Maserati and Ferrari fans the rumours were doing the rounds: "Right, those down the road (as our adversaries called us) have got a 320 horsepower engine. Rubbish!" The news had by now reached many enthusiasts and we were actually accused of being liars and of spreading fanciful stories. One afternoon, Ingegner Alfieri said to me, "Be at the station at 10:30 tomorrow to pick up Ingegner Canestrini (the doyen of sporting journalists, ed.) who'll be arriving from Milan. I've already told Erio Mezzetti to give you the 1100." Instead of 10:30, the train got in at 11 o'clock. I saw Ingegner Canestrini, whose face I recognised, get off and went to meet him. I was wearing overalls and he noticed the Trident badge; I introduced myself and took him to Maserati where Signor Omer and Ingegner Alfieri were waiting for him. They accompanied him to the Testing Room, where Reggiani had everything set up for a test. Our guest had the opportunity to see the engine produce 320 hp at 12,000 rpm no less than three times.

He was therefore able to write an article for *La Gazzetta dello Sport* confirming that Maserati was working on an extraordinary engine. After a month's testing we had succeeded, at the expense of around 10 horsepower, in bringing the power delivery down to 4500 rpm, with the band stretching from 4500 to 11,000 rpm for a maximum 310 hp. The engine was installed in the car for a series of track tests that left Bertocchi, Scarlatti and Behra hugely disappointed in that at the Campale corner, the engine speed fell off when changing down and the pick-up was sluggish. When it was Fangio's turn he took just a lap to work out what to do. He continued lapping, keeping the engine speed over 4500 rpm. When he came in to the pits he was tired but positive, noting that there was still a lot of work to be done as the engine required a completely different driving style but that on a very fast circuit there would be more opportunities to use all the power. Ingegner Alfieri was very satisfied with the Tipo 2 engine, the 2500 cc 12-cylinder Formula 1 unit, even though it was not immediately pressed into service. He had a 3.5-litre cc sports car unit developed using the same engine block. The bore and stroke dimensions of 73.8x68 mm corresponded to a displacement of 3490 cc, with a compression ratio of 10:1 for 100 octane petrol. The result of the tests: 335 hp at 9000 rpm.

JUAN MANUEL FANGIO'S MOST REMARKABLE VICTORY

The Nürburgring Grand Prix, the 4th of August 1957. Maserati was using Pirelli tyres that would not last the full distance of around 500 kilometres. Ferrari, instead, had Englebert covers that would last the entire race. The Grand Prix was disputed over 22 laps, with Fangio due to stop midway through to refuel and change the rear tyres. Taking advantage of the lower fuel load he was carrying with respect to the Ferraris, his intention was to build up within ten or so laps an advantage sufficient that he would still be in the lead after his pit stop. Mike Hawthorn and Peter Collins in the Ferraris shot away at the start, but within two laps Fangio had moved into the lead. As planned he pitted on the 12th lap with a lead that was large enough for him to restart still ahead of his rivals. The Maserati mechanics held the record of 22 seconds for changing tyres. On this occasion, however, the unexpected happened! While replacing the rear tyres, the spinner from the right-hand wheel was dropped and fell under the car. Once the wheel was back in place, Manni, the mechanic, was unable to find the spinner. Fortunately, from his spot on the pit wall, Giulio Borsari had seen it fall, but in the meantime the seconds were ticking away. Usually refuelling and changing the tyres would take 20/22 seconds using copper mallets. Borsari screamed at the top of his voice, "The spinner! The spinner!" In the midst of the confusion the spinner was found, but Fangio restarted after 55 seconds, almost 30 more than expected. At that point the race appeared to be in Ferrari's pocket, with its cars first and second, Maserati perhaps taking third. Fangio instead, after one relatively slow lap as he allowed the tyres time to get up to temperature, staged an incredible chase with 10 laps remaining and almost a minute to make up. As Fangio himself confessed on more than one occasion, this

GP. GERMANIA · NURBURGRING. · 4-AGOSTO-1957.

N° corsa	1	8	7	6	10
Pilota	FANGIO	HAWTHORN	COLLINS	MUSSO	MOSS
Vettura	Maserati	Ferrari	Ferrari	Ferrari	Vanwall
Giri					
1	9.46.8	9.42.5	9.43.4	9.56.6	10.02.5
2	9.34.6	9.37.9	9.37.6	9.44.9	9.51. 2
3	9.33.4	9.40.4	9.39.4	9.52.9	9.59. 9
4	9.33.5	9.35.2	9.36.7	9.50.0	9.51. 3
5	9.33.0	9.38.1	9.40.7	9.44.6	9.42. 9
6	9/32.5	9.39.2	9.39.4	9.44.7	9.43. 5
7	9.32.8	9.37.2	9.33.7	9.42.5	9.44. 3
8	9.30.8	9.33.9	9.34.1	9.42.9	9.44. 6
9	9.35.9	9.35.1	9.36.8	9.42.7	9.41. 0
10	9.29.5	9.31.6	9.32.7	9.41.5	9.36. 6
11	9.32.9	9.32.4	9.34.2	9.38.2	9.39.9
12	9.35.3	9.32.2	9.28.9	9.39.6	9.39.1
13	10.48.6	9.38.9	9.37.5	9.43.4	9.39.7
14	9.36.2	9.33.8	9.32.4	9.38.9	9.40.3
15	9.31.2	9.37.1	9.38.3	9.39.5	9.43.7
16	9.31.2	9.41.3	9.40.3	9.37.6	9.51.8
17	9.28.5	9.34.3	9.35.5	9.40.7	9.48.8
18	9.25.3	9.30.4	9.30.1	9.43.5	9.59.0
19	9.23.4	9.30?2	9.30.5	9.43.8	10.05.7 T.Q.
20	9.17.4	9.29.1	9.28.9	9.45.0	9.45.0
21	9.21.8	9.26.2	9.34.8	9?49.3	9.46.5
22	9.23.7	9?24.9	9.46.0	9.53.1	9.38.5
	3.30.38.3/3.30.41.9		3.31.13.9 /3.34.15.9		/3.35.15.8

was the race in which he ran most risks because making up 10/12 seconds a lap at the Nürburgring meant going well beyond the normal limits. The Argentinian ace confessed to feeling the 250F like a second skin, responding consistently and handling exactly as he asked it to. Four laps from the finish he passed Collins and, on the following lap, overtook Hawthorn too. The latter had been feeling fairly secure and had failed to check his mirrors. All of a sudden he found Fangio alongside him. As he swerved in surprise, the Maserati driver passed and went on to win by a whole three seconds. That was the most remarkable race of his career. At the Nürburgring, with our Maserati 250F, he had demonstrated that he was the greatest driver of the 1950s.

SEMISKILLED WORKER

To my great satisfaction, on the 1st of September, 1957, the Personnel Department managed by Miss Xella informed me of my promotion to semiskilled worker with a corresponding pay rise. Certainly, my dedication, willingness and, all modesty aside, my talent for the work had helped me make this step up. Without doubt, references from Reggiani and Alfieri tipped the balance. Reggiani's departure for the United States was in the air as he had to attend the trial regarding the accident he had had in 1952. I was worried because I would have been left on my own with Roberto Losi, a young lad who had been seconded to me.

There was al lot of work going on in the Experimental Department along with the testing of the 4500 V8 and the 12-cylinder engine (they could not be tested in the Testing Room because the dynamometers there were inadequate), with Reggiani we had begun developing the 3500 cc six-cylinder engine for a Grand Touring car, a demanding job in that as it was for a road car the engine had to be reliable enough to run faultlessly for thousands of kilometres. However, from the start there were issues with the breather pipe in the wet sump that we overcame with a new breather I designed and fabricated personally. We then had to deal with the gasket between the cylinder head and the block in that the rubber seal invented by Reggiani, which was so simple and convenient, was not appropriate or advisable for a road car. The question of the rubber gasket was causing us problems that Ingegner

Alfieri was also concerned about. The bucket tappets, the material of which had proved to be unsuitable on the first three 3500 cc engines fitted to sports cars, also presented scratching on the area that came into contact with the camshaft lobes after 1500/2000 kilometres.

FANGIO'S RANT

The 12-cylinder 250F T2 had been taken to various circuits, but it had never been raced. The most disparate reasons had prevented it being entrusted to any of the leading drivers. Perhaps the circuit was not suited to such a capricious engine given its high-revving nature, or perhaps it was the driver who preferred the six-cylinder version of the 250F. Ingegner Alfieri suspected, as he confessed to Reggiani, that there was also a degree of manipulation on the part of certain figures. It was finally decided to race the 12-cylinder 250F *2530* at Pescara on the 18th of August, entrusted to Giorgio Scarlatti.

It was Reggiani who assisted at all the races involving cars with special or experimental engines prepared by our department, but as he had flown to New York for his trial, Ingegner Alfieri told me that I would be leaving with him the following day with all the cars and the mechanics from the Racing Department. Personally, I didn't like attending the races, I preferred working a 12-hour shift in the Experimental Department. Some of my colleagues would instead have done anything to have been able to work in the Racing Department and play a part at all the races. In any case, it was quite the experience. Ingegner Alfieri, Colotti, Molinari and I left early on the Saturday morning in the 1100. Colotti and Molinari from the Technical Office had come along as a kind of prize (or so it was said), while I was to look after the engine of the T2. We reached Pescara at around 11 o'clock, just in time to get the car ready for qualifying. Scarlatti said that the car was running well but that it was very difficult to keep the engine speed up compared to the six-cylinder.

Maserati entered four works cars, captained by Fangio, and six privateers, Vanwall three and Ferrari just one, for Luigi Musso. A total of 16 cars participated. Fangio recorded the fastest qualifying time, followed by Stirling Moss in a Vanwall and Musso, while Jean Behra was fourth and started from the second row. Unusually, the race was held on the Sunday morning starting at 10 o'clock, on a street circuit that probably adopted in part the course used for the old Coppa Acerbo, a memorable race from the Thirties. At seven o'clock, I was working alongside the whole Racing Department and making the final preparations before the start. Shortly before nine o'clock I asked Bertocchi whether Giulio Borsari could give me a hand to start the T2 (the 12-cylinder engine). Not having a starter motor, the Formula 1 cars were started with a special piece of equipment, the shaft of which engaged with the nose of the crankshaft. In the meantime, all our drivers had arrived with the exception of Behra. After having allowed the engine to run and warm up I replaced the 24 spark plugs and again with the aid of Borsari, restarted the engine and pushed the car to its place on the grid. There were less than 10 minutes to go before the start when I heard Fangio asking Bertocchi: "Where's Behra?" To which Bertocchi replied, "Come on, it's almost time!" In the meantime, Behra had arrived with the air of a sleepwalker and Fangio went up to him shouting, "What time do you think this is? Look at you, you're a disgrace! You should be ashamed of yourself!" He continued in this vein for five minutes as the pair went to take their places in their cars. I was following Behra to his car and heard all of Fangio's rant. I would never have thought such a cool, calm, individual could become so aggressive. We subsequently learnt that Behra had spent the night partying with a blonde who was accompanying him, while the model professional Fangio was almost maniacal in his search for perfection in his race preparations. Neri and Borsari from the Racing Department told me that he would begin to think about the circuit a week before the race and would walk the track or occasionally take a moped round, depending on the length, observing the condition of the asphalt in the corners, looking at everything. He would not tolerate other drivers taking things lightly, as Behra had done at Pescara (the Frenchman later retiring halfway through the race with a broken transmission). Fangio finished second, with victory going to Moss in the Vanwall.

After the race we went to lunch and then immediately began loading up the cars, tyres and all the equipment. Back then there were no forklift trucks and it was all manual labour. I can still remember Rino Ragazzi, the transmission specialist, Luciano Bonacini and Andrea Cavani in their sweat soaked overalls. Ingegner Alfieri had left with Bertocchi and I went back to Modena on the Bartoletti transporter driven by Ciccio Montanari. It was about six o'clock and we were on the coast road, well out of the city and I asked if we could stop for 15/20 minutes for a swim given that the water hadn't reached the third floor in our hotel and there had been very little in the improvised pits at the circuit. I had brought my swimming trunks with me, with the idea of enjoying a dip in the sea. The cab of the Bartoletti housing my eight colleagues echoed with laughter as they told me I could bathe when I got home. We stopped for dinner past Ancona, in a restaurant recommended by Setti, the driver of the other lorry ahead of us.

THE XXVIII
ITALIAN GRAND PRIX

In view of the Italian Grand Prix at Monza on the 8th of September, the Maserati management decided to conduct a series of tests with the new 250F T2 *2531* with the engine offset as had been the case with the six-cylinder 250F the previous year. This intelligent configuration provided undoubted advantages as the offset engine allowed the driveshaft to pass alongside rather than between the legs of the driver, while the seat could be positioned lower in the chassis, improving the car's centre of gravity. Even though the six-cylinder 250F was an extremely reliable car that was still very competitive and particularly well liked by Fangio, the now five-time World Champion, it was time to think about the future, as Vanwall and BRM were arriving on the World Championship scene with very competitive machinery. The Monza circuit management had made the track available to us on the 25th of August and there was no better opportunity to test the new T2 (the Technical Office's internal designation) on a circuit that suited the characteristics of our 12-cylinder engine. I had tested and tuned the V12 myself and then passed it on to the Racing Department. The Monza test was conducted by Fangio and, above all, Behra who was to drive the car in the race. The drivers and engineers were left only partially satisfied, in particular due to the uncertainly over the durability of the tyres. Bertocchi, an open detractor, had said that we needed to adopt spark plugs with a 14-millimetre thread (as Ingegner Alfieri had told me). Who knows what benefit they would have brought compared to those with a 10 mm thread. In spite of the climate of familiarity and humanity, attachment and togetherness among the majority of the employees, there was also an evident rivalry, fortunately not noticed by everyone, between the Technical Director Ingegner Alfieri and the head of the Racing Department Guerino Bertocchi. In any case, the T2 lined up for the start of the Italian Grand Prix with Jean Behra at the wheel, flanked by Fangio with the six-cylinder 250F. The over 300 hp produced by the engine were finally able to express its full potential, allowing Behra to contest the moves of both Fangio and Moss in the Vanwall. After having led the race for a couple of laps Behra had to replace the rear tyres, as had been expected. Unfortunately he was later forced to retire due to a banal leak from an oil pipe. Ingegner Alfieri could be content with fact that Maserati had an extraordinary engine and a car with huge potential for development ahead of the next racing season. Monza also saw the launch of the 3500 GT Touring, the prototype presented at Geneva the previous spring, and was widely admired by the Grand Prix spectators.

MASERATI 3500 GT:
THE "DAMA BIANCA"

In the history of every car manufacturer there are moments and models that represent milestones and which have over time become legends. One of Maserati's magic moments cam in 1957, a year of fabulous sporting victories and the presentation of the 3500 GT at the Geneva Motor Show in March. The prototypes of the AM.101 model with two styling variants, one by Carrozzeria Touring in white with a blue leather interior and the other by Carrozzeria Allemano in blue and ivory with a white leather interior, exhibited at Geneva, were tasked with testing the waters of the market, gauging public opinion and allowing a choice between the two to be made. The response was very positive and the choice of Commendatore Adolfo Orsi, the CEO, his son Omer, the managing director, and the designer Giulio Alfieri, fell on the Touring prototype, a 2+2 coupé with all-aluminium bodywork, a true grand tourer, comfortable and elegant, which immediately took a deserved place among the restricted circle of great GTs thanks to its confident high performance and everyday practicality. The thinking behind Ingegner Alfieri's design was focussed on the rational assembly of a car in limited numbers, drawing heavily on Maserati's racing culture and basing production where possible on the sourcing of third-party suppliers, with Maserati providing the all-important technological heart of the car in the form of the engine and the chassis.

The mechanical configuration featured a spaceframe chassis composed of oval and round tubes derived from the 300S and 350S sports car design, while the engine, a light-alloy straight six with double overhead camshafts and twin-spark ignition also had a racing heritage: it combined high performance with absolute reliability; for example, the crankshaft was machined from billet and subjected to a series of heat treatments to obtain a depth of hardness of around 8 tenths of a millimetre that would allow the shaft to be ground up to three times. The bodywork designed and built by Touring was fitted directly to the chassis and arrived in Modena already painted and trimmed in fine leather. At the same time as the various assemblies sourced externally were being configured and organised, the various road tests of the prototype AM.101.001 began because together with the head tester Bertocchi we had to define the spring and damper ratings, the front suspension geometry and the steering ratio, devoting all our attention to obtaining maximum confort from a car that was designed to be driven hard on the first fast motorways of the period, in absolute safety. As these tests progressed, for a few months we saw a coming and going in the workshop of this elegant, austere white coupé that, emphasising the contrast with the racing cars finished in red, was given the particularly appropriate nickname "Dama Bianca" (all references to the great cyclist Fausto Coppi were purely casual).

Over the course of its long life, after the final signing off and throughout the homologation tests, the car continued to be known as the Dama Bianca and its present owner who, over fifty years later, began a thorough restoration, still calls it by this name. Alfieri's idea of using a gearbox supplied by ZF, suspension by Alford & Adler, brakes and dampers from Girling, a Borg and Beck clutch and a Salisbury rear axle brought enormous advantages in simplifying and configuring production as initially the cars were all assembled on trestles, as with the racing models, and only in the early Sixties was a raised assembly line constructed allowing work to go on above and below the car, shortening production times and raising output from two or three a week to three or four a day.

Maserati has always followed its own production philosophy, cultivating a broad category of clients and enthusiasts who prefer to race little less and travel more comfortably with a little more space available. This did not, however, prevent certain individuals exploiting their cars' potential to the full. Our Milan concessionaire, for example, Commendator Cornacchia, held the record from the Milan to the Modena North toll booths in 40 minutes, and when he visited Modena his sole desire was to be able to measure himself against the competition. 1980 examples of this model were constructed between 1958 and 1964 and subjected to a gradual evolution: firstly four light alloy drum brakes, then front discs in 1960, four discs and a five-speed gearbox and in 1961 the adoption of Lucas fuel injection which increased the power output from 220 to 230 hp at 5800 rpm. In concluding this chapter, a technical file illustrates the vital statistics of a model that was so important to the Maserati story.

Engine	vertical straight six
Bore, stroke and displacement	86x100 mm, 3486 cc
Brake horsepower	220 hp
Carburettors	3 x Weber 42 DCOE, from 1961 235 hp using Lucas fuel injection
Compression ratio	8.5:1
Valvegear	two valves per cylinder, two overhead camshafts, twin-spark ignition with distributor, pressurised lubrication with supply pump
Gearbox	ZF, four speeds + reverse, from 1960 five speeds
Chassis	tubular, front suspensions wishbones with coil springs and anti-roll bar telescopic dampers
Rear suspensions	semi-elliptical leaf springs and dampers, anti-roll bar
Brakes	drums, servo-assisted from 1959, front discs from 1960, four-wheel discs
Steering	recirculating ball
Wheelbase	2600 mm
Front track	1390 mm
Rear track	1360 mm
Wheels	500 x 16" discs, 6.5x16" tyres, optional wire wheels and limited slip differential
Bodywork	coupé 2+2
Dry weight	1300 kg
Maximum speed	230 kph, with fuel injected engine 240 kph

THE OFFICIAL WITHDRAWAL
FROM RACING

Like a thunderbolt from a clear sky, in mid-November 1957, I don't recall the exact date, the newspapers published an official press release from the Maserati board announcing the manufacturer's withdrawal from all direct involvement in Formula 1 and sports car racing. The service provided to clients competing with privately entered cars was to continue. This news perplexed the Maserati workforce and the automotive world in general as 1957 had been a remarkable year for Officine Alfieri Maserati. Juan Manuel Fangio's conquest of the World Championship for Drivers with the timeless 250F, the European Mountain Championship won by Peter Daetwyler with the 200S, the launch of the new 3500 GT road car and the new 12-cylinder engine all promised much for 1958. Instead, on the 3rd of November 1957, in the Grand Prix of Venezuela at Caracas disputed with sports cars and in which Maserati was about to conquer the World Championship for Marques too, a series of incidents during the race and the refuelling stops sidelined all of the Trident's cars. Moreover, almost all the drivers, including Bertocchi, had suffered burns, even though slight, and lastly the economic consequences were notable. Following the Caracas debacle, the decision to withdraw from racing, without doubt one that was agonizing and complex for the Orsi family, was further prompted by the numerous variations to the international regulations planned for 1958. Formula 1 cars would now be obliged to use commercial petrol rather than alcohol-based mixtures, sports cars would have a maximum displacement of three litres, while the displacement of cars participating in the European Mountain Championship would be reduced to 1500 cc.

However, the principal reason behind the decision is to be sought further afield. In 1955, with the fall of the Perón government in Argentina, Maserati had suffered a huge economic and commercial loss in terms of sales of our machine tools as the new government had imposed import duties that were so high as to put an end to any hope of doing business. The failure to reach an agreement on the organization of the Maserati Corporation of America also exacerbated the crisis the company suffering. At the end of November, almost all of the members of the Racing Department were sacked. Only Manni, Morandi and Ciccio Montanari were spared because they were manual workers, while the others who had reached the position *Equiparati* or foremen, were called in to the management offices where Commendator Orsi informed them of the decision he had had to take. Giulio Borsari told me that Arturo Brancolini, speaking for the group, had said, "Commendatore, look, if there are problems regarding wages, we can come in and work the same. You can pay us when you can." They could see the tears in the eyes of Signor Omer and Commendator Orsi, who replied, "Thank you lads, I know how attached you are to Maserati and how we have always been close. Don't worry because I've already sorted you out, you'll not miss a single day's work." In fact, four went to Ferrari, while Neri and Bonacini set themselves up on their own, opening a workshop.

Reggiani was still in America for the trial. I had written to him about the problems I had encountered with the 3500 GT engine and that I hoped to see him soon. When he returned early in December, he went straight to Signor Omer who gave him the sad news and his redundancy letter. When he came back to the department he said, "Look, you were so anxious for me to get back and instead I have to leave immediately and you'll have to do without me." I didn't know what to say. Reggiani was also an *Equiparato* (he clocked on with the administration staff and was paid monthly, while the manual workers were paid every 15 days, the first part on account and then the balance). Fortunately, the following day he too was taken on by Weber of Bologna, with the same qualification and the same pay. Sadly, Maserati also sold off its milling machine operation to Oerlikon, a large Swiss company that had a factory in Milan and that for a brief period was to have occupied the department at Modena. The building firm Scianti in fact quickly started work on the flooring of the large shed that had housed the Client Services Department and Montipò's Heat Treatment workshop and which within a month had been transferred to another shed alongside the existing one as the Car Division had to move and free up the old red brick buildings. The administrative and executive offices were also being moved to the upper floor of a small building alongside the railway where, on the ground floor, our changing rooms and the canteen for those living outside Modena were located.

RECEIVERSHIP

On the 1ˢᵗ of April 1958, Officine Alfieri Maserati went into receivership for a year at the behest of the Court of Modena, probably requested by a local bank that would undoubtedly have been waiting for unpaid loans to be repaid. In any case, the Orsi family, in particular the Commendatore, proved to be very sensitive to the future of Maserati and its employees. For six months our wages were paid by a bank and when Ingegner Alfieri needed supplies of third-party parts for the construction of the first examples of the 3500 GT he had to ask for permission and have the documents signed by the court lawyer who was a frequent visitor to the company. Nonetheless, Commendator Orsi made sure that the matter was concluded six months early.

The factory was working at full capacity, the move to the very high shed where the Commendatore had probably intended to create a rolling mill, had been completed very quickly. Looking at it from the front, to the right were all the machine tools from Barani's department, in the centre two dividing walls created the store while to the left was the Car Assembly Department with the Chassis Department to one side. Engine Assembly and the preparation of the castings were at the back of the shed. The Technical Office was to the right and the Production Office to the left of the spacious entrance. Remaining in the old buildings, in the last of the sheds yet to be occupied by Oerlikon, were Manni, Morandi and Consoli who were working in the former Racing Department to finish off a few racing cars before they were sold, and my Experimental Department that to all intents and purposes had become the 3500 GT engine testing room. While they were built and assembled on stands, like the racing cars, the GTs were produced at a rate of almost a car a day.

At the head of the Car Assembly Department was Ardilio Manfredini with whom I was good friends, although he did hound me for the engines I would pass on to him. One day he called me making a scene because when he had started the engine after finishing the assembly of a car it was leaking oil from the pipe linking the block and the head. As I saw it this was impossible, because when my two lads called me to conduct the final test of the tuning of an engine on the dynamometer, I always insisted, and set an example myself, that they should always check for leaks above and below. And so I repaid Manfredini in kind, insisting that the engine I had delivered had been fine. While we were arguing I saw that they were inserting an engine in a chassis. The engine was hoisted with a crossed line from the hook of a small crane and I noticed that the taut rope was touching the left-hand pipe and almost crushing it against the wall of the crankcase. I pointed out to Manfredini that the cause of the leak he was blaming me for was actually the disattention of his workers. He apologised and from then we became better friends than ever. As well as signing off the engines in the testing room, almost every day I would have to deal with calls from the Client Services Department asking me to check the carburetion of one car or another. One day Commendator Lamborghini arrived with his 3500 GT with which he had covered around 10,000 kilometres for a service and tuning of the carburetion, which I paid particular attention to given the character involved. He said to me, "*Vè cinó, al minim l'è un po' elt e in dal rilascii la scupiàta*" ("Look lad, the tick-over's a little high and it backfires when you lift off"). Having done everything required as well as possible, I let the client know that the problem had been resolved.

One morning Nava, the gatekeeper, came to tell me to go up to Signor Omer who needed me. I was immediately apprehensive, this was unusual, but knowing that I had done nothing wrong and went straight away to find out what he wanted. After knocking, I entered a little tentatively but he said, "Today or tomorrow Umberto Stradi will be bringing you a 250F, test it and bring me the results, without saying anything to anybody about what you find. If anyone asks you anything you're to say you know nothing about it." In fact, late that afternoon, Stradi arrived with the labourer from the Client Services Department and left me the engine with its trolley. I had a good relationship with Stradi and he let me know that Miss Maria Teresa de Filippis had complained because she was unable to achieve a qualifying time with her 250F on her debut as the first woman in a Formula 1 Grand Prix due to an under performing engine. Bertocchi and Mimmo Dei of the Scuderia Centro Sud, which ran the car, had instead assured her that her 250F was identical to those of the other Maserati drivers. I tested the engine without saying anything to my two assistants who were setting up a 3500 GT engine on the other test bench. After having warmed it up I ran it hard and noted the power output at 7000, 6000 and 5000 rpm: this was all I needed to establish that the engine was flat and that Miss de Filippis was right. I hurried to take the test results to Signor Omer who thanked me and asked me to send the engine back to Stradi.

A month later, Commendator Lamborghini came back with the 3500 GT and asked for me to adjust the carburetion while they were changing the oil and filters; I replaced the plugs and he came up to me and said, *"Adésa ag fag vadér mé al vòster pàdroun e a quàl là, ed Maranel, cóm as fà a fér di automobil!"* (Now I'm going to show your boss and him down there at Maranello how you build cars!"). And I replied, "Commendatore, you keep building tractors and boilers and leave the cars to those who have always built them." He smiled at me saying, "You'll see what I'm capable of doing!" He never came back to Maserati after that.

THE TIPO 420/58 ELDORADO

Even though the company found itself in receivership due to a temporary economic crisis, there was no lack of work in the factory. Ingegner Alfieri told me about the construction of a special new single-seater for the Monza 500 Miles race that was to be held on the 29th of June 1958. With the customary enthusiasm and enterprise that had always characterised Maserati, on the chassis builder's surface plate the spaceframe chassis was taking shape while the engine block was being prepared in the Engine Assembly Department. The power unit was a 4200 cc V8 conforming to the Indianapolis regulations. In late 1956, we had already built two 4200 cc V8s running on blended fuel for an American client, Mr. Tony Parravano who intended to use them in Offenhauser chassis. This Italo-American, something of a *Mafioso* it was said, who made his money in construction, also ran a racing team with a number of Maserati cars. On the occasion of the organization of the Trophy of the Two Worlds focussed on the Indianapolis 500 Miles at Monza, he had persuaded the industrialist Gino Zanetti, owner of the Eldorado ice cream factory, to sponsor the construction of a Maserati special to be put at the disposition of Stirling Moss. Guerino Bertocchi's brother, Gino, the head of engine assembly, delivered the engine to me one Friday afternoon; we had already prepared the dynamometer and were therefore able to get it running quickly. I had agreed with Ingegner Alfieri that the engine would have been run-in for around seven hours on the

Saturday morning and would then be ready for testing at full power. I already had parameters for the carburetion, the magneto advance and the type of spark plugs thanks to the register of the tests done with Reggiani almost two years earlier on similar engines ordered by Mr. Parravano.

Ingegner Alfieri had told me to wait for him because he would have liked to be present for the test. As soon as he arrived we conducted a first sweep test, noting that at every 1000 rpm increment the power output value was not far from the scalar value: the best result was 412 hp at 8000 rpm with the MS1 blend, the normal and least sophisticated fuel. Having also checked the magneto advance which had proved to be correct, we handed over the engine to be installed in the car. Fantuzzi, with his customary skill, had constructed a magnificent body with an air intake on the body that revealed the offset of the engine and a conspicuous rear stabilizing fin. The car was finished in white with large Eldorado and Italia scripts, the logo of the figure with hat and neckerchief, the air intake with the colours of the Italian flag along its length and finally the name of the driver Stirling Moss.

A week ahead of the race we took it to Monza for testing as there was no way of conducting a meaningful test on the Modena circuit. With a two-speed gearbox, one for the start and a direct drive, it was virtually impossible to lap at Modena. I left in the OM Leoncino with Setti early in the morning and we were met at Monza by Ingegner Alfieri and Bertocchi in the Dama Bianca, and by Commendator Zanetti who was anxious to witness the realisation of his dream. With the engine thoroughly warmed up, Bertocchi climbed in to complete a few laps in an anti-clockwise direction, as required by the race regulations, on the banked oval. We could hear that engine had lost its full, clear roar and after two or three laps Bertocchi came in saying, "It feels like the fuel feed cuts out." I exchanged glances with Ingegner Alfieri and suggested that we raise the level of the carburettor float chamber. Alfieri agreed with me as he felt that due to the high speed and the banked curves, centrifugal force was affecting the fuel level. I set to work straight away, but as I wasn't sure by how much I would have to raise the level, I had to work by degrees so as not to flood the engine, which would have been worse. Mindful of the teachings of Reggiani, who had always told me that "the distance from the level at the hole of the centre square should be between 3 and 3.5 millimetres, at most 4, depending on the carburettor." I removed the carburettor covers, emptied the float chambers with a syringe, adjusted the float travel by half a millimetre and refitted everything. Having had to blow into the jet chamber I had a foul taste in my mouth and worked rapidly to restart the engine and send Bertocchi out again. I then ran towards the pits where I'd seen an Eldorado van to see whether they had an ice cream. Having learnt who I was, the driver very kindly gave me what I asked for and while Bertocchi lapped I focused on getting rid of the taste of the fuel mixture! After around 10 laps, Bertocchi came in again saying that the carburetion was almost right; in fact, we had heard that the engine had a good strong sound. I asked Ingegner Alfieri what I should do, whether I should raise the level again with the risk of making things worse. Bertocchi wanted to raise the level again. I immediately set to work. Setti, the driver, did what he could to give me a hand and in half an hour the engine was running again and Bertocchi restarted. I then ran to get another two ice creams, one for Setti, as I again had to get rid of that foul taste. Bertocchi came in after another 10 laps, saying that he was satisfied, the engine was fine and everything else too. Once the bosses had left, I helped Setti load the car onto the Leoncino and we too left shortly after one o'clock. Setti wanted to stop to eat at a restaurant he often visited but which was some distance away. When I pointed out that we would get there too late and they wouldn't serve us Setti said, *"Té fidét ed mé et vedree che doo taiadèli i'sli dan anch' a doo ori"* ("Have faith in what I say and you'll see that they'll give a plate of tagliatelle even if it's two o'clock."). In fact, Setti and I were seated and served despite the unusual hour. On the day of the race, I was left out of the group of mechanics chosen by Bertocchi, who probably thought that my skinny frame would not have served when it came to pushing the Eldorado and our other two cars, a 12-cylinder 350S and a three-litre 250F. The European cars had little chance against the American machines, conceived and built exclusively for the 500 Miles. Our Eldorado finished the first and second heats in fourth and fifth place, but in the third, on the 40th lap, the steering linkage broke and Moss went off the track, finishing in 7th place overall. Commendator Zanetti, the Eldorado director, applied great pressure to try to ensure that the Eldorado could participate in the 1959 edition of the Indianapolis 500 Miles. Changes were made to the chassis and the bodywork of which Gentilini, a former Fantuzzi employee who had struck out on his own, modified the rear part, eliminating the stabilizing fin painted in Italian red. The car was entrusted to young and inexperienced American driver, Ralph Liguori, who failed to qualify. The brief Eldorado adventure thus drew to a close.

THE ENGINES FOR
THE SCUDERIA CENTRO SUD
AND POWERBOATS

In 1957-1958, Signor Mimmo Dei, our concessionaire in Rome from 1949-1950, moved to Modena with his new Scuderia Centro Sud to start a racing driver school and participate in motor racing, including Formula 1. He owned a number of Maseratis including four A6GCS's, two 300S's, two 200S's and two 250F's. He found premises right in front of the Autodromo, where previously the former Monaco-born driver Louis Chiron and then Ingegner Piero Taruffi had worked with a leading high-speed driving school that had led them to discover over the years important and talented drivers such as Masten Gregory, Lorenzo Bandini, Giancarlo Baghetti and many others. At least once a week, Mimmo Dei brought an engine in to Maserati to have it tested. Considering that Bertocchi's testing room had been dismembered, I was responsible, together with my two assistants, for the running in and signing off of these engines, generally overhauled by our former Racing Department mechanic Giulio Borsari, who had been appointed as the Scuderia Centro Sud's chief mechanic. Ever attentive to the foreign competition, Signor Dei had succeeded through one of his sponsors, BP, in having two Cooper chassis acquired for him, the first to be prepared and conceived with innovative technology for fitting the engine at the rear. He thus had two Maserati 2500 cc four-cylinder engines installed. The new international Formula 1 regulations called for the use of 1500 cc engine and ours were well suited to the task and provided the Scuderia Centro Sud with excellent results.

There was also a call for more powerful engines in power-boat racing: Signor Liborio Guidotti had ordered a 5000 cc unit for his Timossi KD 800 kg racing powerboat. Ingegner Alfieri who was present at the test was impressed by the engine's output of 450 hp at 7000 rpm. Ciccio Montanari instead encountered various difficulties when installing the unit in the boat and when Signor Guidotti conducted his first shakedown test they came up against a number of fuelling issues. When the hull lifted to plane at high speed the engine was inclined by around 10 degree, shifting the level of the fuel in the carburettor float chamber, leading to flooding and irregular fuel supply. This left Signor Guidotti very disappointed as he had hoped that the new boat and new engine would have allowed him to dominate powerboat events. Ingegner Alfieri assured him that he would have taken care of the problem and that, as soon as he had found the way to modify the carburettors, Ciccio Montanari would have returned to update his engine.

The other 5000 cc V8 powerboat engine had been ordered by Signor Spagnoli of Perugia, again for a Timossi KD 800 kg boat that Fausto Bietolini was finishing to assemble.

I talked to Ingegner Alfieri about the possibility of calling in Reggiani from Weber for a consultancy. I saw Reggiani every Sunday, we were neighbours and frequented one another. I knew that Weber had sent him to Rolls-Royce in England and Porsche in Germany. Ingegner Alfieri reached an agreement with the director at Weber whereby as soon as the engine was ready for testing, Reggiani would have come to Maserati. In the meantime, I had visited Reggiani at home and had explained to him the problem that had cropped up with the powerboat engine. He replied that within a couple of days he would have fashioned a series of floats of different shapes and would come over to test them. When Bietolini brought me Spagnoli's second 5000 cc V8, after a good six- or seven-hour running in period we disactivated the hydraulic brake so as to be able to incline it by around 10°, in the position in which it would me mounted in the boat. Fortunately, the engine mounting plate on the test bench was adjustable and had independent front and rear supports. Even though we were unable to measure the power output, we could start it with its starter motor and take it up to 5000/6000 rpm and work out how to improve the carburetion. When Reggiani arrived, a few mornings later, many of his former colleagues came to greet him, such was the respect he commanded. He had brought with him the modified floats and when Ingegner Alfieri arrived I explained to him the reasoning behind the different shape and how it would have prevented surge in the chamber. He had brought a series of four of one shape and four of another. The first test took a long time because, once the floats had been replaced, we had to adjust the levels as there hadn't been time at Weber as they had only finished the previous evening. One carburettor at a time, we filled the chamber with the electric pump, measured, emptied the chamber with the syringe and worked on the closing tongue of the needle valve to find the correct measurement. There was then only time to conduct one test because it was already midday. In the afternoon, we tested the other series of floats, finding a worsening with respect to the morning session. With those of the first test that worked better refitted, Reggiani wanted to test the engine horizontally and connected to the brake. It was already around seven o'clock and while we were checking the spark plugs, Commendatore Orsi entered from the wide door giving onto the courtyard, clearly after hearing the noise of the engine. "What are you doing lads?" Reggiani, "Commendatore, we're testing a powerboat engine, this 5000 cc unit with 400 domesticated horse would make the Americans happy fitted to their saloons with 200 hp." Commendator Orsi replied, "Who knows, perhaps one day we'll build a saloon." The Maserati Quattroporte saloon was built in 1963.

Having finished testing the engine, Reggiani went to say goodbye to Ingegner Alfieri, agreeing to have a series of the first type of float sent to us for Guidotti's engine and defining the order of delivery of the next 45 IDM carburettors for the powerboat engine with the latest modifications.

Frequently at the end of the day, with the factory almost empty, we'd stop and chat with Ingegner Alfieri, Ingegner Bertocchi, Ingegner Pollio, Manfredini, Barani, Renato Soli and someone from the technical office. Generally, the discussions revolved around our rivals' latest developments and our own future plans. We had had the opportunity of examining a Cooper chassis belonging to the Scuderia Centro Sud to which we supplied 2500 cc four-cylinder engines for Formula 1. Observing that very simple frame in narrow gauge tubes, Ingegner Alfieri posed the question of what could be done to counter the British technology. It was one evening in late October 1958 that the idea of building the lightest possible chassis that was equally robust and strong was born.

ABSURD BANS AND GRATUITOUS ARROGANCE

During a lunch break, a careless employee climbed into one of the now few sports cars remaining in the racing department, started the engine without noticing the car was in gear and consequently crashed into the opposite wall, slightly denting the nose. The song and dance Guerino Bertocchi made about the incident when he arrived was endless and he decreed that no one else would be allowed to get into a car and move it under its own power. All cars were to be pushed to move them around or transfer them from one department to another. There were only Manni, Morandi, Losi and I left in the old buildings. Even my Experimental Department had been dismembered. The test benches had been moved and set up in a new Testing Room at the back and to the side of the new Engine Assembly Department where the lads from Bertocchi's old testing room were now working. The dynamometers had also been moved provisionally, as at that time there was no need to use them. Together with Ingegner Alfieri, we had finally found the ideal solution to the problem of the 3500 GT cylinder head gasket. I was by then so well practised that with Losi's help I was able to replace the gaskets on the cars that came in for servicing in 35 or 40 minutes. In that period, I was working on the tuning of the carburetion of the new cars and for the Client Services Department.

One afternoon, after having finished working on a 3500 GT with various problems we had to take it to the atrium of the new shed. I refused to push it and said to Manni, "You get in, start it up in first and drive, Morandi and I will follow you." As we came out of the doorway I saw Signor Omer, Ingegner Alfieri and Guerino Bertocchi, their heads turning to follow us, startled to see two men pretending to push a car. I plucked up the courage to head over to them, saying, "Signor Omer, do you think it's right that three people with driving licences should push the cars when they could be moved by just one of us? The other two could be getting on with something else, it's not as if there's nothing to do." Signor Omer replied, "Well, I'd say that would be fine! What do you think Guerino?" Bertocchi, for his part, replied, "If you say so..." Ingegner Alfieri winked at me in understanding.

During Maserati's racing period in the 1950s, Guerino Bertocchi had been known as "the prince" by his team in the Racing Department. He was always very strict and was as bad tempered as he was skilled behind the wheel, having an innate feel for the behaviour of a car on road or track. He was not a bad man, quite the contrary, but he did exaggerate in making his authority felt.

One day I was working on the levels of the carburettors of a 5000 GT, No. 103.004. (No. 103.002 had already been delivered to the Shah of Persia). I had placed the car over the pit as Manfredini had to do some work on the exhaust pipes and Bertocchi and I, one on each side, placed pads on the front wings so as not to damage the paintwork and set to work removing the carburettor covers. Having tuned the four carbs and almost finished replacing the covers, we found that a brass washer was missing and Bertocchi said, "See, you don't pay attention, let's hope it burns off when we start the engine otherwise we'll have to take off the cylinder heads." I was sure that I hadn't made a mistake, but lacked the courage to reply. When the air filter had been replaced and all the pads removed, Bertocchi got in, started the engine and went out for a test drive. I called Manfredini and told him what had happened while we searched for the washer. We found it, in fact, all burnt up but recognisable, on the side where Bertocchi had been working. Fortunately, the exhausts were empty and the engine had spat it out. Had it remained caught between one valve and the other, we would have had to remove one or rather both of the cylinder heads given that Bertocchi had blamed me. This wasn't the first time I had come up against his attitude that was hardly based on respect and sincerity; perhaps I was still too accustomed to Reggiani, who had treated me more as a son, providing me with so many life and work lessons. When we met I told him about what had happened and he consoled by telling the story of what he had to go through when he first joined Maserati.

A few weeks later, Reggiani asked me whether I wanted to join him at Weber because they were looking for an experienced youngster to work on the construction of a fuel injection system Taddeucci and Rebecchi, two former engine designer colleagues, had been designing on paper for the past year. When I mentioned the opportunity at home, they knew I was bitter about what had happened and not as happy working at Maserati as I had once been, but they tried to convince me to be patient. My father said I should think twice before taking certain decisions, while my mother was instead irremovable and became very angry. She began by saying I should think of the impression I would give to Signora Laura and Signora Idina, the daughters of Commendator Orsi who had provided references for me years earlier. To which I replied that I had always worked hard and had never given anyone cause to regret employing me. They would hardly have given me those unexpected pay rises and relative compliments otherwise. To which my mother in turn replied, "Quite, and now you want to leave an excellent job where the owners respect and appreciate you. Before making a decision you should at least talk to Ingegner Alfieri, after all he is still your boss." In effect, I drifted between the Car Assembly and Client Services Departments and I was still waiting to be told to whom I should report and who my boss was. The new arrangement had created a certain upheaval and now the move was almost complete there was nothing left in the old buildings. The new owners of the milling machine business were having a prefabricated wall erected in the middle of the courtyard to separate the two factories.

Towards the end of November, I met Ingegner Alfieri one morning and asked him, "Ingegnere, I need to ask your advice, I've received an offer to got to work at Weber, Reggiani has been courting me and has already spoken to his director and they would take me immediately." "What? "What? What are you thinking, with all the work to be done at Maserati, now that we're actually relaunching? Listen, Ingegner Pollio in the Technical Office hardly knows which way to turn. What with homologations, instruction manuals, and the spare parts catalogue for the 3500 GT, who can do that if not some one like you who knows the car from top to toe?" I looked at him in surprise, almost regretting having said anything and asking for his advice. "Listen Cozza, from the 1st of December, you'll be working in the Technical Office, I've already discussed it with Signor Omer. So I'm sorry that you feel a little abandoned, but you have to understand the situation. And forget all about what you've been telling me." When I told my parents what Ingegner Alfieri had said, my mother was delighted, above all because it confirmed she had been right to suggest that I should speak to my boss before taking certain decisions.

IN THE TECHNICAL OFFICE

A few days before the end of November I began returning to the store all the tools I had been issued with, raising a few eyebrows in the process as this was what people usually did before leaving the company. I hadn't said anything to anybody about my move to the Technical Office. Ingegner Bertocchi, with whom I had an excellent relationship and who in those years, as well as dealing with post-sales and client relations, was also working with Renato Soli on the organization of the factory, heard from the storeman what I was doing, called me and asked for an explanation. At that point I had to tell him that from the 1st of December I would be working in the office. He said that he was disappointed as he had been counting on entrusting me, in a few years, with the new prototypes department that Maserati would need to create. I replied that I had been on the point of resigning because I wasn't getting on with the people had found myself working with recently and that only Ingegner Alfieri had kept me at Maserati. He knew who I was talking about and simply said, "Hmm!"

It was a Monday morning and I would never have expected to receive such a warm welcome from my new departmental colleagues who had been informed of my new position by Ingegner Alfieri. They had already prepared a desk for me and I had spoken to Ingegner Pollio about starting work straight away on the use and maintenance manual for the 3500 GT, updating it with speed tables. When Ingegner Alfieri arrived I asked him if I could also work on tidying up the outside of the 3500 GT engine, removing all those pipes that were vital to racing engines but unsuited and unsightly on a Grand Touring unit. He agreed and immediately sent me to talk to Ascari, the draughtsman to dealt with the engines. The Technical Office had been radically overhauled with Colotti, Rebecchi, Taddeucci and Nicola all leaving, but their disciples had remained and the organization of the work was still organized in the same way: Ascari for the engines with the addition of an assistant, Golinelli on transmissions and brakes and Molinari on chassis and suspension who would also be provided with an assistant. Lastly there was Ingegner Pollio with whom I was to work on homologation and technical documentation.

Renato Soli, formerly of the Tooling Department also had a drawing board in the office and dealt with all the tooling necessary for the production work. He was later to become the shop foreman. An extraordinary person in both technical and human terms. We were fairly cramped and as I would also need to use a drawing board and another two or three draughtsmen were on their way, while we were waiting for new buildings to be constructed we temporarily occupied the upper floor, accessible via a spiral staircase. It was on that occasion that I saw for the first time the chests containing all the drawings done in Bologna by the Maserati brothers and put them away in a corner of the general store while waiting for a better and definitive home for the archive. The ground floor of the Technical Office was occupied by Soli with Manzieri, Benatti and Vincenzi, the latest arrivals, Ingegner Pollio and I and, at the back, Menozzi with the photocopier.

When one day we started talking about the compilation of the spare parts catalogue I was worried because I had no idea how to organize the work and where to start. Gradually, as the days went by and I became more accustomed to the internal organization of the office and with correcting and modifying the itemized list of all the components making up the car, I realised that I had the solution right in front of me. The basic list was a book of numerous pages that of which three or four photocopies were made to be used in the production office, the store, the purchasing department and elsewhere. In the 1950s it was compiled with diagrams alongside the names of each part. There was a huge amount of work to be done, as Ingegner Alfieri had said, but he was more interested in thinking about new projects than about organization, which in my opinion was instead vitally important. He had had all the development work on the 5000 GT engine passed on to me by Ascari, so that I could make all the necessary updates, while the 3500 GT was continually subjected to improvements. The oil pump had been modified, now being located internally and front disc brakes had been adopted, along with a five-speed gearbox. I therefore suggested to Ingegner Alfieri that we should postpone the publication of the spare parts catalogue by a few months otherwise we would find ourselves with a manual that was already out of date. I also asked Ingegner Pollio if he could contact the numerous foreign component supply companies to get reference numbers for all the parts they supplied. The 3500 GT had become the guarantee of Maserati's future and its sales success had favoured production of the open-top spider version constructed by Vignale.

WEDDING PREPARATIONS

By the end of 1959, my parents and I had already re-paid ahead of schedule the loan we had taken out for the construction of our new house. It was now finished, all that was missing was the fence and a few finishing touches that we would have completed the following spring. I had realised a dream, that of having a house, as modest as it might be, that was all mine, with an allotment and a garden. We had had to make numerous sacrifices, including those Giordana had also had to make, but it had been worth it. My parents, in particular my mother, were slowly getting over the loss of my brother. When I hinted that towards mid-April Giordana and I were going to get married, my mother was overwhelmed by a euphoria I would never have expected.

The ground floor of the house had a cellar, garage and laundry room but also a bedroom and a small sitting room where Giordana would have worked. As she had been self-employed for a couple of years now, she had built up a clientele and had plenty of work. She also had two or three young girls giving her a hand. The fence with a low wall and a gate was completed by the end of March. While we were waiting for the furniture to be delivered, Giordana and my mother were busy with curtains and lightshades. There were now just a few days until the 23rd of April 1960. The week before we had been to the town hall for the civil wedding ceremony and unaware of the formalities we had turned up without witnesses. After a moment's embarrassment we found a clerk I knew because he lived near us and a colleague of his who kindly agreed to step in. Giordana had come to an arrange with an acquaintance who was getting married the following day and together they had decorated the church of Sant'Agnese with flowers, while I had decided that the wedding reception would be held at the Hotel Real Fini, in the Astoria Dance Hall where to all intents and purposes we had got engaged.

My mother did not want to accompany me to the altar, she couldn't get over the memory of my brother, and so my Aunt Pia, my father's sister and my godmother, did the honours. My witness was Professor Domeniconi while Giordana's witness was her brother-in-law Angelo. There were around guests including friends and relations. While Monsignor Santi was marrying us, the sacristan whispered something in his ear, at which point Don Roberto said we would have to hurry because an aircraft had taken off from the Aerautodromo to salute us as we left the church. In fact, as we got outside to a propitiatory shower of rice and a flock of doves, a light aircraft flew low overhead and dropped a bunch of flowers. I had absolutely no idea who that maniac could be. I later learnt, once I'd got back from my honeymoon, that my friend and colleague Alvaro Soli, who had recently earned his pilot's license, had decided to send his best wishes in this original way.

After the reception we dashed home to change and pick up our luggage before my uncle took us to the station. We had a train to Rome at two o'clock. We hadn't booked a hotel – travel agencies had yet to appear – but as soon as we got off the train (who knows how newlyweds are so easy to spot) a very distinguished gentleman approached us, offering to take us to the Hotel dell'Opera where he worked, together with another newly married couple from Genoa. We were a little suspicious but timidly accepted. Instead our minds were soon set at rest as while the hotel was hardly luxurious, it was welcoming and the food was excellent. We stayed five Rome, exploring the length and breadth of the city at the expense of more than a few blisters. We were also fortunate enough to be received, together with other couples, by Pope John XXIII. I still have the key ring with the souvenir medallion of that moment. From Rome we went to Naples and from there to Capri and the Amalfitana coast, on coaches organized by the hotel. It hardly seemed true, accustomed as we were to always working, in less than 10 days' holiday we had quickly got used the "bella vita"! It was nonetheless nice to get home and the warm welcome from our parents and above finding ourselves in our new home that we had dreamed of for so long filled us with joy.

EQUIPARATO

Intermedio or *Equiparato* were the terms used to describe those belonging to a category of employee who had certain responsibilities as a team or department foreman, who was paid monthly and who clocked on with administrative staff. I joined this category in September 1960 and I believe that the promotion was recognition for the completion of the first parts catalogue to be published by Maserati. I had worked hard on it for two or three months with Signor Giovanni Cavara, a highly skilled and well-respected freelance perspective draughtsman from Parma. He had visited Maserati on a number of occasions to draw complete cars for *Automobile Revue*, a Swiss magazine directed by Signor Adriano Cimarosti, whom I met years later. Giovanni Cavara had come to inspect the work in order to organize himself and above all to meet me and decide how best to proceed to make things easier for ourselves. I outlined what I intended to do, always asking for his opinion. There were around 36/38 plates be prepared, roughly divided like the itemized list into cylinder head, cylinder block and so on for all the major assemblies of the 3500 GT. I was to have sourced and provided him with all the various components and I also suggested how we might arrange and divide the various details. Signor Cavara was a lovely and very friendly person and we got on well from the outset. He said that within two weeks at most he would have produced pencil drawings for the 36-38 plates which he would then have inked, inserting the reference numbers, while I would produce the list of the various components for each plate before passing the completed catalogue on to the printer. Everything that went to print was inspected by the firm's lawyer Avvocato Donati, a rather haughty man, always elegant but nonetheless fairly friendly to me from the Experimental Department days. When the proofs for the spare parts catalogue arrived he called me into his office one afternoon to correct them. We each occupied a desk and were there until gone seven o'clock before we finished. He complimented me on the job done and said that from then on I was to be responsible for all the technical material printed by Maserati. Avvocato Donati was also president of the Aerautodromo and I had thought about asking him for a couple of tickets for the race that was due to be held the following Sunday but didn't dare. As I was about to leave with the work, he called me back saying, "I was forgetting, take two tickets for the grandstands for the race on Sunday". I thanked him warmly and a little awkwardly as the gesture had caught me unawares.

BECOMING A FATHER

At lunch one Sunday in July 1960, Giordana announced that she was pregnant. You can imagine the surprise; I was speechless, open-mouthed for a minute while my mother and father hugged one another. As usual, my father started saying we should do this, we should do that and was even more euphoric than me. In the afternoon we went to my in-laws' house to tell them the happy news at which they immediately burst into tears. By way of Professor Domeniconi, for whom she had worked, my mother organized the customary health checks at the clinic of Professor Barbanti, an excellent gynaecologist and a great friend of Professor Domeniconi.

The 7th of April 1961 saw the birth of Giovanna, a beautiful baby girl weighing three and a half kilos. We were all delighted because the birth had gone well and the baby was healthy; only my mother was a little disappointed because she would have liked a baby boy who could be named Giovanni and who would have filled the gap left in her heart by my poor brother. Giovanna, who has always been known as Gianna, grew rapidly. At home things changed and I could never have imagined the upheavals a baby would bring. Feeds at the right time and sleepless nights, actually few and far between I have to admit. Giordana went back to work and my mother would pull into the garden the cradle on wheels she herself had bought with a special mattress and a mosquito net. Gianna slept like the proverbial baby under that magnolia her mother and I had transplanted years earlier.

As all too frequently is the case, joy and happiness were short lived. My mother, whom I had never even seen with a slight headache, was increasingly listless, had no appetite and even stopped playing with Gianna, who was everything to her. Professor Domeniconi had diagnosed a terrible disease of the breast and said an operation was required as soon as possible. Naturally, this hit my mother hard as she had never previously needed doctors or medicines and things were very gloomy at home. She was operated on at the hospital by Professor Gibertini, a well-known surgeon and a childhood friend of my aunts Pia and Angela. Following the operation the professor called my father and I to one side to tell us that the operation had gone well, that he had tried to remove everything anomalous that he could, but that we should not delude ourselves because the tumour might already have taken hold elsewhere. The return home was joyous and my mother was anxious to see Gianna again, who was growing by the day. After a few chemotherapy sessions, my mother began to experience pain again just three months after the operation. She took to her bed and was never to get up again, suffering atrocious pain all over her body in the last few weeks. We had taken on a nurse as Gianna had commitments and couldn't abandon her work completely and then there was Gianna who took up a lot of her time. Mother left us on the 9th of January 1962 after weeks of terrible suffering. She had turned 53 just three days previously. We were all desperate, we had lost the person who kept the family together, always optimistic and full of ideas. For my father in particular it was a terrible blow. Fortunately there was Gianna whose first birthday was approaching and who was a light in our lives.

LUCAS FUEL INJECTION

Ingegner Alfieri, ever in search of new features and attentive to the evolution of fuelling technology, entered into a technical partnership with Lucas for the application of their fuel injection system to our 3500 GT and 5000 GT engines. In general, the system was fairly simple and composed of an electric pump that sent the fuel pressurised to around seven atmospheres to a keyed metering distributor actuated by the camshaft that rotating in phase with the engine delivered the fuel to the injectors on the intake manifold. The adjustment of the carburetion, dosed in identical quantities according to the demands of the sensors to the individual cylinders, determined the opening of the injectors. The control system that defined the quantity of fuel to send to the nozzles in relation to the quantity of air that was aspirated by the cylinders was regulated via rollers that determined the variation of the distribution shuttle stroke in the distributor rotor, which was also equipped with a datum adjuster to trim the fuel mixture in relation to atmospheric pressure. A Lucas engineer stayed in Modena for around a month to work on the tuning of the system along with Ingegner Pollio and Carlo Sitti, a lad who had recently been taken on and who was to become our injection system specialist. I participated in the completion of the project with a new intake manifold, a new fibreglass air filter and a new intake side cylinder head cover. Our 3500 GTI was the first Italian car to be fitted with the fuel injection system and benefitted from an increase in power from 220 to 235 hp. Ingegner Alfieri wanted me to follow the development of the new system alongside Ingegner Pollio in order to facilitate me in the drafting of the technical documentation destined for the workshops of our concessionaires. Similarly, the Lucas injection system was also applied to the V8 5000 GT engine and over the years was adopted by other manufacturers for Formula 1 and sports car engines.

THE GO-KART

In the October of 1960, a Bultaco 125 cc engine turned up in the Technical Office, brought home from Spain by Commendator Orsi after a business trip. It was probably a gift from the Bultaco firm with which he would have had contacts. A few days later, Roberto and Adolfino, Signor Omer's sons, came in to see the engine and asked me to design a go-kart for them. I told them that I couldn't without authorization from Ingegner Alfieri as it would be a long and complex job. I suggested that they should take the necessary steps to ensure that I was given permission. One morning, Ingegner Alfieri came into the office and said to me, "See if you can throw together four tubes for a chassis for that Bultaco engine." I told him that I'd first have to make a drawing of the engine and then study how to build a proper go-kart. He told me to proceed as I saw fit, but without neglecting the more urgent commitments in the office. I got hold of a few magazines about go-karts to get to know a little more about these new machines were attracting increasing numbers of enthusiasts. I found out that there were various categories, depending on the cylinder capacity, and that the new sport was attracting a lot of kids and also adults. Our four-speed 125 cc Bultaco engine was suitable for a Class C international go-kart and the chassis would therefore need a wheelbase of 1350 mm and front and rear tracks of 750 and 850 mm respectively, all information found in the magazine *Kart* from April 1961.

I couldn't work on it everyday because the updating of the parts lists for the 3500 GT and 5000 cars with the continual modifications and improvements that were made, required a constant and urgent commitment as both the purchasing department and the stores needed to be informed of every modification. Moreover, the Birdcage-type sports cars that we supplied to the Camoradi and Cunningham teams also demanded constant attention. Slowly, however, the go-kart was taking shape. Roberto and Adolfino would drop by every now and then to see how things were coming along. They had also obtained permission from Signor Omer for me to have the chassis built by Mario Boni once I'd finished the design work, while the kart would be assembled by Erio Mezzetti, a trusted mechanic from Pradella (a former Fiat concessionaire owned by the Orsi firm, Pradella being located in the area between Via Emilia and Viale Trento Trieste). Erio was responsible for the maintenance of Maserati's cars and trucks; a highly skilled veteran, he was easy going and ever willing to give advice to us youngsters. The Chassis Department eventually finished construction of the frame I'd designed and I passed it on to Erio to whom I'd already spoken about what needed to be done, checking what commercially available parts could be used for the steering assembly. Erio told me that his brother had a Fiat garage in the Crocetta quarter of Modena from which he would have obtained a series of Fiat 500 parts to use for our project if suitable. Finally, after around 10 months, the go-kart was ready, I tested and retested to set up the gear change and the pedals before one afternoon Roberto and Adolfino arrived with Signor Omer. The boys were eager to try it out, especially Adolfino who couldn't wait. He was already behind the wheel before his father told him to get out and said that he would like to see me take it for a spin around the flowerbeds in front of the building. Erio was also there and we completed a few laps before handing the go-kart over to the boys who, in their turn, did a few laps as they got to know the object of their desires. For many years, when school permitted, they would come with their friends and have fun with the go-kart, which fortunately never broke down because Erio always kept it well maintained.

THE REAR ENGINE

Even though our Tipo 60 and Tipo 61 sports cars, the Birdcages as the Americans called them, still had room for development, Ingegner Alfieri, always very attentive to technical innovations, in particular the new ideas being introduced to single-seaters by the English marques, decided to transfer the new engineering concepts to sports cars. This led to the birth of the Tipo 63 (the Tipo 62 was instead a V8 marine engine of around six litres). In the technical office I timidly (so as not to arouse criticism from certain quarters) tried to organize and establish a rule for the designation of new engines and cars. After an initial discussion, we all agreed to adopt the following numerals as internal designations: from 1 to 50 for single-seater engines and cars, from 51 to 100 for sports cars and engines, from 101 to 150 for GT cars and engines and from 151 to 200 for prototype cars and engines.

After some second and third thoughts, Ingegner Alfieri decided to fit the four-cylinder engine from the Tipo 61 to the Tipo 63, locating it in a central position and inclining around 60° to the right. As it was no longer possible to fit the 48 DCO carburettors, I helped adapt the vertical IDM carbs used on the V8 engines. In this way I resolved the delicate fuel feed problem and even provided a slight increase in power. This was the only contribution I made to the development of the rear engine configuration. Two four-cylinder cars were built before Ingegner Alfieri decided to fit the 12-cylinder engine derived from the Tipo 2 and enlarged to three litres in order to get more power, as the four-cylinder provided no more than 260 hp against the V12's over 310 hp. Despite the efforts of Ingegner Giampaolo Dallara, who had recently joined Maserati, the Tipo 63 failed to live up to its promise. Dallara was an excellent chassis designer, as he was to prove at Lamborghini and De Tomaso when he set up his own business, becoming a world-renowned specialist in the construction of carbon-fibre chassis for many car manufacturers.

For the Tipo 64, Ingegner Dallara completely revised the chassis, seeking to improve the weight distribution, shifting the cockpit and the engine further forwards, modifying the front suspension and completely redesigning the rear layout. Production of the Tipo 64 was restricted to just two cars that were actually modified Tipo 63s that had returned to Maserati in view of the 1962 season; one was built for the Cunningham team, the other for the Scuderia Serenissima of Count Giovanni Volpi di Misurata. As Maserati was unable to maintain the kind of constant commitment required to develop this kind of car, Ingegner Alfieri was reluctantly obliged to abandon the sports racing projects.

The commercial success of the 3500 GTI Touring, which had been flanked by the 5000 GT, the Spyder and the new Sebring, a Vignale-bodied coupé, brought a certain stability to the company in economic terms allowing the factory as a whole to be reorganized. Oerlikon had returned to Milan, leaving our buildings vacant and available for the immediate installation of the first series production line. This elevated facility allowed the cars to be worked on from above and below at the same time. Moreover, a further three sheds were constructed next to that of the heat treatment department and Erio Mezzetti's maintenance shop.

THE NEW DEPARTMENTAL ORGANIZATION

The Technical Office found a definitive home in a bright, spacious setting that was appropriate to its increasingly important role. It was located in one of the latest three sheds to be built, the first on the right. From the entrance you could reach Ingegner Alfieri's office, that of Ingegner Pollio and the draughtsmen's room. A staircase led to the upper floor that housed the Factory Manager's office and the Production Office. At the back of the Technical Office a door led through to the new Prototype Development Department and everything had been designed and produced to achieve optimum functionality. Space was found in the other buildings for the Client Services Department office and store, the Tool Room and the Chassis Department. The Post-Sales Office and Ingegner Bertocchi's Client Services Department was instead installed in the former Technical Office. With the new car assembly line installed in the former Racing Department, production rose to three or four cars a day, which in turn meant that the workforce had to be increased in both the Engine Assembly Department and the Testing Room, but above all the Client Services Department where increasing numbers of cars were arriving every day for repair or scheduled maintenance operations.

The Technical Office staff was also expanded as Ingegner Alfieri had a very intensive programme of work, regarding both the development of the 3500 GT engine and a new V8 engine for two new cars, a sports coupé and a saloon. Moreover, the new regulations for a category of prototypes in the championship reserved for GT cars immediately caught the eye of Ingegner Alfieri who was interested in the design and production of three cars on behalf of the Cunningham team and Maserati France, in the person of Colonel Simon, our French importer. This led to the birth of the Tipo 151, powered by a 4000 cc V8 derived from the 450S, fitted at the front of a tubular chassis with the transmission from the 450S, disc brakes and closed bodywork as the car was to take part in the Le Mans 24 Hours. Great attention was paid to the bodywork, above all in terms of aerodynamics. As soon as Carrozzeria Allegretti had finished the first short-tailed body, Ingegner Alfieri got me involved, as he was accustomed to do when certain tests had to be conducted. I attached to the bodywork with strong adhesive tape 15-centimetre lengths of wool on the flanks, the roof and especially on the tail. Then, with the aid of the Traffic Police from whom we had obtained permission to stop the traffic on the straight to Spilamberto for 10 minutes, while I drove the 1100, trying to stay alongside Bertocchi at the wheel of the Tipo 151 at 100 kph, Ingegner Alfieri took photographs as he muttered instructions to me, "A bit further forwards! Hang back a little!" Having thanked the two policemen, we returned to the factory, leaving the film to be developed urgently by a photographer. Ingegnere Alfieri was already satisfied with what he had been able to observe, the behaviour of the woollen threads confirming his intuitions regarding the shape of the new body. In the photographs we picked up the following morning the threads, particularly those on the tail, confirmed the favourable air flow. There were no wind tunnels for cars at that time and we tried to overcome their absence as best we could in our search to improve aerodynamics.

After Ingegner Dallara left another two engineers arrived: Severi, who worked on the development of the mechanical side and the prototypes, and Melchionda who instead focused on the bodywork. Three Tipo 151 prototypes participated unsuccessfully in the 1962 Le Mans 24 Hours. Two in the white with two blue stripes Cunningham livery and one in the red with blue stripes of Maserati France. However, the Technical Office was working above all on the production of new GT cars, as after four or five the Touring and Vignale models were beginning to show their age. The chassis group led by Giorgio Molinari was working on a sheet steel chassis, a novelty in that Maserati had never previously taken into consideration this type of structure. A tubular chassis was in fact ill-suited to the challenges presented by the large saloon that was being designed.

Our engine building group led by Ennio Ascari was instead working on a new 4200 cc V8 engine for this new saloon, while Ennio Golinelli's team of designers was working on the completion of the rolling chassis with a new type of independent rear suspension.

Together with Ingegner Pollio, we worked on preparing all the technical documentation for the homologations procedures for the new cars, as when we had an example of each type available we would be able to start all the tests required by Ingegner Verdi of the Bologna Department of Motor Vehicles. The bureaucracy required firstly the presentation of all the printed material and photographs of the various components. Moreover, I had to prepare the parts lists as the Purchasing Department would then have to begin to place orders for the various third-party items and the Production Office to process them internally. Put like that it may seem fairly simple, but organizing this kind of thing in a small, craft-based firm like ours where we had to keep a constant eye on economy was fairly demanding. Harmony, collaboration and, last but not least, a sense of belonging to a company with an important name brought us all together and encouraged us always to give our best. I was fully content with my job, I was satisfied with the role of *trait d'union* between the Technical Office and the other departments, principally the machining and assembly shops. I had heard indiscretions whereby Ingegner Alfieri had suggested that I played an indispensible role for the Technical Office.

When the pressed steel chassis for the new Quattroporte saloon, constructed externally by Forghieri of Maranello, arrived at Maserati it was immediately sent to Pietro Frua's studio in Turin, together with the other tubular chassis built in-house for the new coupé. There was a considerable commotion within the firm because the two new cars were due to be presented at the Turin Motor Show and there were only a few months to go. The new 4200 cc V8 engine I had helped Guerino Bertocchi fine-tune was giving excellent results, while the displacement of the six-cylinder was further expanded from 3700 to 4000 cc. The straight-six was therefore available with three different displacements to be fitted to the new 2+2 coupé before being phased out after over 10 years' service.

THE TURIN
MOTOR SHOW

Early in the last week of October 1963, Ingegner Alfieri called me into his office and said, "The day after tomorrow you're going to Turin with Setti in the transporter, to install the five cars on the Maserati stand." I was a little surprised and worried, "But Ingegnere, how should I arrange the cars? How can I do it by myself? I don't know anyone!" The Ingegnere replied, "Cozza, calm down! Our Turin dealer, Signor Bordese, will be there to give you a hand. He's booked you into a hotel nearby. Take what you need to stay away five or six days. Once you've unloaded the Sebring and the Spyder you'll take up from Modena, pick up the two new cars from Frua and arrange them with the car that Bordese will be bringing, more or less like this sketch", and passed me a sheet of paper on which he had scribbled five rectangles with the names of the cars. Then he added, "Signor Omer and I will arrive the day before the inauguration, I don't know anything about Commendator Orsi yet, but I think that he'll be there too on the 30th of October." I immediately went looking for Setti, one of the oldest but also most reliable truck drivers. He had a notoriously bad character but had always treated me well. We arranged to leave on October the 28th at 6 AM, so that we would be in Turin before noon.

The trip was monotonous, Setti spoke little and I occasionally told him something about my work. At about 10 AM I needed to go to the bathroom but daren't say so

213

because I knew from those of the Racing Department that when they left with Setti, if someone mentioned that they wanted to stop for certain needs, Setti would do everything he could not to do so. He was driving and he decided when and where to stop. Instead, shortly after taking the Milan-Turin motorway he stopped and said to me: "*Adèsa andam a tòr un capuccio e nà brioss, pò andàm in bagni e dàp, via drèt fin a Turein*" ("Now we'll go and get a cappuccino and a brioche, we'll go to the bathroom and then straight on to Turin"). I beamed and said, "Setti, if you don't mind, I'll go to the bathroom first." "*A'vegn anca me!*" ("I'm coming too!).

When we arrived at the Parco Valentino, the site of the Palazzo delle Esposizioni, Setti looked for a suitable place to put the ramps on and unload the two cars, while I ran into to see where the space reserved for Maserati was. I had no difficulty finding it, because over each stand were large signs with the names of the manufacturers and I saw ours in the distance, near the Lancia sign. There was a great deal of hustle and bustle given the number of exhibitors, with everyone arriving and setting up their cars. I looked for the most suitable route to take our cars inside and then went back to Setti who had already unloaded the Sebring. I led the way, with Setti following very slowly and very carefully and we put the first car on our stand. We then went to back for the Spyder, but not before Setti had stowed away the ramps as they were in the way of others who had to unload.

After setting up the Spyder and locking the cars, we set off again for Frua at Moncalieri to pick up the other two brand-new cars. Setti knew Turin as well as Nonantola, his home-town, so after a few kilometres we stopped at a trattoria for lunch. By two o'clock we were in front of the door of Frua's workshop. I had heard much about his skill and great affability. In fact, when I saw a large gentleman come to meet me, wearing a grey coat and a big smile, even before introducing myself, I had guessed that he was Commendator Frua. At that moment I never imagined that our friendship and esteem would last until the Eighties, through to his death. Setti was at home at Frua because he had been collecting his creations or delivering our chassis since the Fifties. Signor Frua, as he wanted to be called, told me that he and his workers had eaten a quick sandwich to finish and make the final touches. I was amazed when I saw the two-seater berlinetta coupé. Setti was in a hurry to load up, take me to the show with the two cars, unload and then leave for Modena.

While I was preparing to position the cars, as indicated in Ingegner Alfieri's sketch, our Turin dealer, Signor Bordese, arrived with two of his workers to bring the final car and help me with arranging the stand. I had noticed that the Lancia had placed its new car, the Fulvia Coupé, on a Persian carpet to give it more prominence. I pointed this out to Signor Bordese and told him that our new Quattroporte was also deserving of similar treatment. Bordese looked at the clock and said to me, "We can't do it in time now, but tomorrow morning I'll pick you up at 8:30 and we'll go to a large carpet shop in the city centre and see if we can rent one."

We arrived in Piazza Cavour just before nine o'clock. They were opening the shop at the request of Signor Bordese. A short, stocky gentleman, with an olive complexion, probably oriental, the owner of the large shop, informed us that he had a carpet of the dimensions that we needed, in as new condition, which we could rent for 100,000 Lire, paying a deposit of 400,000 Lire. I was of course concerned about the huge amount of money regarding which I would have to ask for approval from Maserati. I said I had to explore other options but that I would decide what to do before midday. Signor Bordese was instead more decisive and asked if he paid for the phone call, I could phone Modena. Another non-European gentleman took me to the back of another office and pointed out the telephone to me. When I had the Maserati doorman on the line, I asked him to pass Norma to me (Norma was the head of the Purchasing Department, with a strong, authoritarian character; she was very talented and blessed with an exceptional memory and I knew I had her respect). "Norma, I need permission for expenses of 100,000 Lire, with a deposit of 400,000 Lire for a carpet to be placed under the saloon." After a minute's silence, so much so that I thought the line had fallen, "What? What? 500 thousand lire for a carpet, you're mad!" "Norma, the actual expenditure is only 100,000 Lire. "Even if it were only 10,000 Lire, I wouldn't authorize you!" "Then put me on to Ingegner Alfieri! "He's already left with Signor Omer, ask them when they arrive this afternoon." "Norma, I have to decide immediately, otherwise I won't have time to set up the car." "I don't know what to say to you. Bye! No, wait! Commendator Orsi is coming, ask him". I passed the receiver over to Signor Bordese, telling him to talk to the Commendatore and I stepped to one side, irritated and mortified for not being able to convince Norma. Five minutes late a smiling Signor Bordese rejoined me, saying that he had explained my proposal to the Commendatore and that he had the green light for him to pay in advance and to proceed to put the Quattroporte on the carpet. The shopkeeper, with

Signor Bordese's cheque in his hand, promised us that the carpet would be delivered to the Maserati stand in the Parco Valentino Palazzo delle Esposizioni before midday.

Signor Bordese accompanied me back to the show telling me that he would return late in the afternoon to meet Signor Omer and Ingegner Alfieri. When I arrived at the stand, I marked the Quattroporte's position with a pencil on the white marble floor, and then moved it after moving the other two cars to make room to manoeuvre. I was anxious, I couldn't wait for them to arrive with the carpet. Finally two guys unrolled the carpet in the precise position indicated and very kindly helped me to place both the new saloon on the carpet and the other two cars I had to move. I was on my own and I should have waited for the lad from the concessionaire who was bringing more chairs and a coat stand. But I was too eager to see the effect and the final configuration of our display, so I worked hard. Getting in the car, starting the engine, moving half a metre, getting out, going to check the effect and so on is a gruelling if you're on your own. It was two o'clock when I went to eat a sandwich at the bar. I was exhausted, but I had the satisfaction of having been able to finish, half a day before the official opening, both the positioning of the cars and the arrangement of the stand the first time I had been entrusted with the task.

When Signor Omer arrived in the afternoon with Ingegner Alfieri, they caught be lying under the Quattroporte laying a sheet of transparent plastic sheet to protect the carpet below the sump. I heard the tapping of a shoe "What's going on down there?" I recognized the voice of Ingegner Alfieri and I stood up to explain everything I had done, while Signor Bordese also arrived and explained the matter of the carpet. Signor Omer congratulated me on the idea of the carpet and all the work I had done and then he handed me box saying, "Take it, you deserve it." I couldn't work out what it was and couldn't open the box I was so excited. I eventually found a gold Trident badge, the one that was usually given to drivers and important customers. I have to admit I had a tear in my eye, I didn't expect such gratitude, after all I had only done my best to complete the task I'd been given.

THE ULTIMA DEA

After the post-war success of our four- and six-cylinder engines in the nautical field, from 1958 the requests for Maserati engines to equip inboard powerboats did not catch the company unprepared. It had in fact already supplied the Guidottis with a 4500 cc V8, to all intents and purposes the engine from the 450S sports car.

The Tipo 59 engine, a 5600 cc V8 delivering 520 hp at 7000 rpm, was specifically designed for power boats and led in 1962 to the Tipo 62 engine, a V8 6400 cc producing 580 hp at 6000 rpm, which was used until 1968 in the 900 kg KD racers by various customers who established themselves in all the national and international championships. In the wake of this success, from 1962, Maserati engines were also sought-after to certain types of offshore powerboats. This type of engine required different characteristics and the Tipo 201 was developed to satisfy this demand, a 5400 cc V8 giving 420 hp at 5500 rpm, again with carburettors.

Maserati built three examples of the special Tipo 202 marine engine, a V8 of 5000 cc with Lucas fuel injection, producing 320 hp at 6000 rpm, which were to be fitted to Ultima Dea, the boat which the Anzio yard was completing for the Avvocato Gianni Agnelli. Amedeo Selmi, known as Mimmo, one of our talented mechanics, was sent to Anzio to assemble the three engines for the Ultima Dea. Selmi completed this demanding job, which lasted about two weeks, to the satisfaction of Avvocato Agnelli, who after trying the boat, sent it to the Isle of Wight to participate in the Torquay offshore race in the English Channel, with the number 19 (the author refers to the Cowes-Torquay of 1962, where Ultima Dea was sportingly retired by Avvocato Agnelli himself after the banal missing of a buoy, *ed*). We have no evidence of other placings or other races.

In the spring of 1964, Ingegner Alfieri received a request for an engineer from the Anzio boatyards as problems had been found with the carburetion on the engines of the Ultima Dea. As these were fuel-injected engines and Pollio's engineer had followed the development of the new system on the 3500 GT engines, we were assigned to go to Anzio to solve the problem and get the three engines running. Ingegner Pollio and I left early for Anzio in the company Fiat 1100 and during the trip we did nothing but talk about the issue and what might have caused it. There were many suppositions, but no certainties, as we had not yet materially identified the problem. When we reached the boatyard we were greeted by Signor Cerri, the man in charge of the Ultima Dea, who took us immediately to the boat, which had been laid up for six months, explaining that he had received an order from Avvocato Agnelli to prepare the boat because he wanted to use it. While the two side engines started without any problems, the central one only started reluctantly and then, after a while, stopped. We checked the system: the petrol was reaching the distributor, which was spinning and was not blocked, but the engine did not run as smoothly as the other two. It was a huge boat but below deck, where the engines were located, space was at a premium. I immediately set up the manometer on the distributor to check the pressure, Ingegner Pollio was above, at the helm, ready to power up the pump at my command and to start the engine. The pressure was regular at 7 atmospheres, but as soon as we started the engine the manometer needle vibrated. Ingegner Pollio gave me the instrument to measure the current voltage and the ammeter to check the fuel pump. I asked him to turn on the 12-volt current, which was regular, but the absorption of the pump was higher than 10 amperes, sometimes it went down to 5-6 but was not constant, so we decided to replace the fuel pump.

While I was busy replacing the pump, which was quite an easy operation, I heard voices on deck; I recognized that of Ingegner Pollio speaking to another person who was asking about when they would be able to leave. I called loudly for the ignition key to be turned and saw that the pump was now working properly, but the manometer continued to show irregular pressure. I asked the engineer to pass me a large container because I wanted to disconnect the fuel delivery pipe because in my opinion there was an air bubble. When I received the receptacle I placed it under the pipe, in the area of the junction between the rubber hose and the copper pipe. I then saw someone come below who asked, "Will this take long?" I recognized Avvocato Agnelli. "A few minutes, but please, stay above, don't come below or you're liable to get dirty." I shouted to the engineer to turn the key to switch on the pump but while I was detaching the fuel pipe, which at 7 atmospheres vibrated in my hands as I tried to drain the petrol into the container, it splashed everywhere, even on Avvocato Agnelli's trousers and shoes. I managed to connect the hose and tighten the clamp as I shouted to stop the pump. Then I leapt up on deck and breathlessly apologized to the Avvocato, who replied: "Don't worry, it's just petrol, the important thing is to solve the problem. Is the engine running now?" Ingegner Pollio replied, "In a minute, as soon as the boy has checked all the pipes, I'll start it up." I took the pressure gauge off the distributor and handed up all the tools and the container. While the engine was running, I adjusted the idle speed, which was too low. All three engines were now running smoothly and I went up on deck because the noise even at just 1000 rpm, was deafening. As Signor Cerri left the yard for a test run, we bid farewell to Avvocato Agnelli with further apologies for what had happened. As soon as we got the all clear from Signor Cerri, we set off back to Modena.

THE FIRST SERIES QUATTROPORTE

From the 1ˢᵗ of June 1964, I was promoted to the second level on the pay scale, with a relative salary adjustment. An almost unexpected satisfaction. The work I was doing in the Technical Office was increasingly interesting. I was working on the new parts catalogues for the new two-seater Berlinetta (later to be known as the Mistral) and the Quattroporte saloon, with the relevant use and maintenance manuals for which I had obtained approval for them to go to press. In the case of the 3500, however, they had been produced internally, with heliographic copies and the sheets collated and stapled into a folder. I was also involved in the homologation and certain technical issues with the prototypes from the new department that had been operational for a few months.

One afternoon, Ingegner Alfieri called and told me to get the sound level meter and go with him. I followed him and we picked up the AM107.004 saloon, the one we were using for type approval and various tests. He told me to sit in the back seat and measure the noise level we would hear on a fairly rough road. I directed him to a private street in the town, a side street off Via Nonantolana, where the refuse collection trucks went to unload. I didn't understand why he wanted to conduct that test, but when we began to drive down that potholed road at 50 kph, I detected 87/89 phon (around 90 decibels, *ed.*) and I immediately guessed the problem. Both Bertocchi and I, along with Ingegner Pollio, had always driven and tested the car on motorways or paved roads and no one had ever thought of testing it on a rough or unpaved surface because a luxurious saloon of that size was naturally designed only for fine roads. Ingegner Alfieri had also test-driven the prototype several times with Bertocchi and had never thought it appropriate to test the car under the conditions we encountered that afternoon.

When we returned to the workshop, the engineer told me that he had received a phone call from Signor Sonvico, the Swiss importer, who had picked up the third example of the Quattroporte to be built after our two on the 21st of July and delivered it to a customer a few days later. The client had a farm about a kilometre off the main road, along a cobbled lane and he had noticed that the rear seat passengers had to shout to make themselves heard at 30 km/h. I knew the car down to its smallest details, because I was working on the spare parts catalogue, so I told engineer Alfieri to replace the silentblock on the De Dion tube struts of the new independent rear suspension anchored to the chassis that being made of sheet metal transmitted the vibrations of the wheels, turning the back of the car into a sound box. Within a couple of hours two softer silentblocks were mounted on the struts and we returned to the same road only to discover that the noise level had decreased by just 2/3 phon to 85/86 phon, which was still too high. As it was already half past seven, I agreed with Ingegner Alfieri that the next day I would mount two even softer silentblocks.

The next morning, while Cleto Grandi was assembling the two new components, I was thinking about how to save time because between going out to test on that side road and coming back we wasted almost two hours and as the engineer had asked Molinari to design a different strut with dual silentblocks, I foresaw a lot of work if we were going to find a solution. I don't know why I had gone to an old store of obsolete parts and my gaze fell on a bundle of trapezoidal belts from our milling machines. They had a diameter of over a meter and were now hard and dry and no longer usable for their original purpose but right for what I was thinking of. I managed to create two 20/25 metre-long rows in the inner courtyard, sufficient to drive the car over and make the sound level measurements. With Cleto's assistance, we had also tried the third series of silentblocks without obtaining a satisfactory result. Late that afternoon, they gave us two new struts and I couldn't wait to try them, we had gained another 5/6 phon, but 76/78 phon was still not an acceptable level.

While Cleto went back to the department with the car, I had gone down to collect all the belts and met Commendator Orsi who asked me how the tests were going. Clearly, Ingegner Alfieri had talked about the problem with Signor Omer and perhaps with him too. I was tired and disheartened and answered that if you wanted to solve the problem you had to fit leaf-springs. The Commendator smiled at me and said, "We'll see".

Before going home I went to look for Ingegner Alfieri and told him how the test with the new silentblock had gone. Then, after talking to Molinari and others from the Technical Office about the handling and roadholding of the Quattroporte with that rear suspension, which both Bertocchi and Cesare Perdisa, our former Formula 1 and sports car driver and at that time a dealer in Bologna, thought was fantastic.

I suggested to Ingegner Alfieri that he should let me try fitting the 3500's leaf-spring rear axle, because in my opinion it was the only way to eliminate road noise on rough surfaces. After various discussions about the dimensions of the 3500 axle, with its track of 1360 mm against the 1403 mm of the saloon, I had to insist that two and a half centimetres per side were nothing, as long as the wheels turned and that we should have tried, even just to get some feedback. He told me that we would talk about it the next morning. The day after I was impatiently waiting for Ingegner Alfieri to arrive in order to get permission for my proposal. I had already informed Cleto Grandi who knew what to do and on my way back to the office I saw the engineer arriving, ran up to him and just as I was about to speak he cut me short by saying, "Try your idea with the leaf-springs, so at least we have two different results." Having placed the saloon on the reference plane and disassembled and removed all the rear suspension, we offered up the 3500 GTI axle complete with leaf-spring to see where we could weld the mounts. For those at the rear, it was quite easy, while for the front mounts the problem was more complicated and we had to cut away part of the wheel arch through to the side member to weld the pivot. The two chassis builders had understood the task and knew how to do it, so I left them under Cleto's supervision. When I returned from the lunch break I went to see how the work was proceeding only to find that it was going slowly. I was informed about the difficulties encountered and confirmed that the work was progressing, albeit slowly because we did not want to damage the interior of the car with welding under the leather upholstery and the carpeting. At around six o'clock that evening, before the welders went home,

I went back to see where we were at; Cleto was sure that the following afternoon we would have the car ready for the test. Ingegner Alfieri was dropped by, eager to see the work finished and wanted to be present at the test. Shortly before five o'clock the following afternoon, Cleto came to tell me that the car was on the ground; it was a bit high at the back, as was to be expected, but the important thing was that the wheels did not rub against anything! While Cleto went to look for Ingegner Alfieri, I positioned the belts and installed the sound level meter in the car. The engineer wanted to sit in the back, to read the instrument, while I got behind the wheel and made a first pass at low speed. The engineer didn't say anything, another pass at about 50 kph and the engineer told me: "58/60/59/61". By using the leaf-springs we had improved by over 20 phon! Of course, in that condition the car couldn't be driven on the road and was therefore returned to its original specification. Following construction of 260 examples of the Quattroporte with the De Dion axle, in June 1966, in concomitance with the restyling of the dual headlights and the interior, a leaf-spring axle was fitted and the 4700 cc engine was homologated. Moreover, the car was also fitted with ventilated brake discs.

VENTILATED DISC BRAKES

The introduction of disc brakes on the 3500 GT had brought a high level of reliability and we had never had braking problems with the Sebring and the Mistral either, cars with fully laden weights of 1500/1600 kg. The Quattroporte saloon instead weighed over 1900 kilos and at speeds of over 200 kph after braking two or three times the pedal tended to fade (that is, it became softer and went flat to the floor). The hydraulic fluid was in fact boiling due to the high temperatures and causing vapour to form in the circuit. Until the temperature fell below 300° there were no brakes. The saloon also featured in-board rear disc brakes, mounted either side of the differential where the cooling effect of the air flow was diminished with respect to the front discs.

Ingegner Alfieri told me that an engineer would be coming from Girling to conduct tests and study the problem. I was to help and assist him as he went about his work using our prototype car. Signor Cappa was from Milan and after having graduated from the Technical Institute, he had gone to work for Girling in England. After six or seven years there, the company had begun to send him around Europe to those companies that were using its products. We were immediately on the same wavelength and after a brief chat in which he explained what he intended to do, we began installing all the instrumentation required for the tests: four thermocouples on each disc with the relative panel in the cockpit, a decelerometer on the dashboard, a manometer to measure pedal force and lastly a pedal travel gauge. The first test involved driving on the motorway to measure the brake fade. Signor Cappa drove and I recorded the data we measured. After braking from 200 to 160 kph four times, the temperature of the rear discs was 450°, while those at the front were at 400°, with a deceleration of just under 0.5 G, while the pedal force and travel were within the norms. We repeated the test a number of times to confirm the validity of the data. We then returned to the workshop where Signor Cappa wanted to fit a different kind of brake pad and to talk to Ingegner Alfieri about our findings and to emphasise that the brake fluid boiled at 350°. The fluid had to be kept below this temperature to avoid fade. The next day we planned to conduct further tests with different pads, having four or five different types with diverse compounds. We tested them all so as to have a broad range of findings to compare. Otherwise we would have had to consider a new system with ventilated discs to dispose of the accumulated heat more quickly.

Ingegner Alfieri agreed that Signor Cappa should proceed with all the experiments he deemed necessary so that he could go back to Girling with as much information as possible and come up with suggestions on how to constructed the ventilated discs as soon as possible. The test measuring the performance of the different types of brake pad involved braking from 60 kph with the car in neutral, measuring the deceleration with a constant pedal pressure. We found that the S-5 pads were those that after a number of applications were those with the greatest friction and therefore those that Signor Cappa suggested we should use until the ventilated discs were available. The three days spent with Cappa allowed me to learn much about braking systems for cars that were becoming faster and faster and therefore required equally efficient means of coming to a rapid halt. This was all further experience to add to my technical baggage that I was enriching with new and diverse notions I could put at the disposition of the company as and when required.

About a month later we received the general layout drawings for the ventilated brake discs from Girling. General in the sense that they were also offered to our rivals and the sampling and the centres were different for every type of wheel used and size requested. We met Ingegner Alfieri and the draughtsman Golinelli to analyse the fairly complex engineering involved. In practice, Girling advised contructing the disc separately from the mounting hub to allow for expansion at different temperatures. I immediately expressed my doubts in that the disc, rotating by centrifugal inertia, expelled heat from the slots and did not influence the hubs and bearings. Ingegner Alfieri was of the same opinion but preferred to follow Girling's instructions and so the mounting hub had a series of notches where the disc, of a thickness of 33 millimetres for the front brakes and 27 mm for those at the rear, engaged. The assembly was secured by a ring with a series of small screws, thus allowing the disc to expand and contract freely.

The second series of the Quattroporte saloon, with the dual headlamps required for the US market, a restyling of the interior, a leaf-spring rear axle and the 4700 cc engine (the 4200 cc unit remained available on request), was fitted with the system of ventilated disc brakes. With the leaf-spring rear axle, the brake discs benefited from a greater flow of air as they were set within the wheels rather than at the centre of the car. The tests conducted with

Signor Cappa as soon as the new car was available gave particularly positive results. The temperature of the brake discs never exceeded 300° even under the most extreme conditions. We also conducted a test in the mountain, in our Apennines, where the brakes were subjected to greater stress. We descended from Sestola via the old serpentine road, using the brakes continuously and the temperature never rose; we also prepared a list of the brake pads to be used according to the driving styles of the various clients, thus providing an opportunity for drivers to choose softer or harder brakes as they preferred.

THE MASERATI MUSEUM

Perhaps it was just my impression, or perhaps I am doing my colleagues in the Technical Office a disservice, but they didn't seem at all interested in the things that Maserati had done in the past. The only one was Golinelli, who, being an enthusiastic photographer, sometimes printed photos of our cars or drivers. I think he would have given anything to get his hands on a box, guarded by Ingegner Pollio, containing numerous photographs of races and drivers. A number of my colleagues and I, especially the foremen or departmental managers, dealing with Bertocchi, were more interested, and also because we had cars, chassis and engines on which we had worked; in particular, I was interested in certain pre-war engines that I would have liked to put on display at some of the car shows. In any case, we found a supporter in Bertocchi as he was in charge of the workshop and was the one who had most contact with the customers. It was he who collected the used cars when he delivered the new ones, some of which remained in the company for some time, where they were parked in the central shed of the last three built. This space was empty and surely could have been put to better use rather than being a car park for used vehicles.

Late one afternoon, I made sure that when I embarked on one of these reflections, as Ingegnere Alfieri called them, not only Ingegner Bertocchi was present but also a number of colleagues from the workshop with whom I had agreed on the subject to be dealt with. We found the Ingegner Alfieri to be in agreement, even though he was not as enthusiastic as Bertocchi, about assembling a collection of everything in the workshop that had been made in the past. Ingegner Bertocchi assumed the responsibility for talking to the Commendatore and Signor Omer about our project for using the space we had agreed to be the most suitable for our project. The shed was paved with red stoneware tiles, the walls were white painted brick and the space we intended to use was about 500 square metres (15 metres wide and 35 metres long, up to the internal corridor). A few days later, Bertocchi informed me that he had obtained permission from the management to create our museum. This was in the middle of September 1965 and without neglecting our normal work we organized ourselves to collect everything that was no longer used by the Racing Department: flags, forklift trucks, funnels and tools temporarily gathered together with engines, gearboxes, chassis and cars that we then gradually arranged in chronological order. What was important at the time was to collect the items we were interested in from every store, every department, and bring them together; we would think about their display later.

I had always enjoyed a very good relationship with Bertocchi, there had always been a very good understanding, even though sometimes our ideas did not coincide and we ended up in rather animated discussions. When it came to the work on the museum we were instead in perfect harmony. I had a nice table with a few chairs brought along because once all the material was in place I expected to use the museum as a waiting room for customers. In fact, after a few days, I met *Bertocchino* who said to me: "I meant to tell you to provide a table and chairs but you're ahead of me." I had also put a register on the table for the signatures of future visitors.

The first was that of Juan Manuel Fangio who Mr. Omer brought to see what we were doing. Fangio wrote a beautiful dedication to us, although we were a little disappointed that the display had yet to be completed. Much still remained to be done and a tour for the automotive journalists had been scheduled for the 27th of October. By working a few Sunday mornings, without clocking in, we managed to complete everything we had hoped to.

On the 27th of October, the Maserati Museum was officially opened, with the compliments of numerous connoisseurs, whose signatures were followed by those of many clients, school parties and visitors.

COLLECTING AND RESTORATION

For some years now, colleagues from Moncalieri's Sales Office would occasionally call me to ask for technical or historical information to meet the requests of collectors, particularly those from abroad. Early in 1965, given that these requests were becoming ever more numerous, I decided to keep a record of everything: from the type of car to the chassis or engine number and the name of the enquirer or owner. I usually did the research to handle these enquiries at the end of the working day and it would sometimes be protracted, especially if I had to find information about pre-war cars. On more than one occasion, Ingegner Alfieri saw me poring over old drawings and asked me why and whether all the time spent replying to requests that he felt were unimportant might not have been put to better use. As I saw it instead, it could only be good for Maserati's reputation as I believed that if a collector successfully restored and displayed his Maserati it would be thanks to the helpfulness of the company. I therefore continued in this fashion, doing all I could to avoid giving Ingegner Alfieri cause for complaint.

From a single sheet of names, as the years passed, we progressed to two or three which became ever more numerous. On more than one occasion I came into contact with two collectors who were trying to reconstruct the same mechanical component and would give one a copy of the page with the name of the other with the same problem. With the sole aim of giving Maserati the prestige and publicity it deserved I was without knowing it piecing together the foundations of the Maserati Classiche department officially created in the 2000s.

tp.Vettura	N° mot. o telaio	Nominativo ed indirizzo
MASERATI AUTOMOBILI MODENA		Proprietari di vetture Maserati anteguerra da competizione e speciali - in Europa e USA. ① Date 5-65 Cozzz.
tp. 26 +	A6GCS	Sig. Maurizio Forleo via Panciatichi 11 ... 51100 Pistoia Italia
16 cil.	3003 V5 / 5003	Ing. Leto di Priolo Milano 20145 - via Monti 79 - Italia
16 cil.	4002 V4	Mr. John Howell Horley sussex ex - Pembley Green England
tp.34	3023	" Hampton Hall Nr. Malpas Cheshire England
8CM	calbc -mneo.	Sig. S. Pozzoli 36 Bld. Gouvion Saint Cyr Paris 17° Francia
6 C.	"	Mr. Vialard. M. Claude 25 bis Rue Duvivier Paris 7° Francia
4CL		Mr. Matti 33 Grand Ave 1180 Rolle/VD. Svizzera
4CL-4CM	26B. 250F	Mr. Fritz Schumj. 68 Mälmerspach Italia
✗✗✗✗	✗✗✗✗	✗✗✗✗✗✗✗✗✗✗✗✗✗✗
4C5	1124	Sig. Salomoni Mozzacane Verona Italia
4CL+200S	1564-240	C.W Drake 4 Wavel Mews London England
4CL	1505 calfa	Rob de la Riv box. Reben 22 - 5612 villmergen AG Svizzera
4CL	1584	Robert C.J. Wood - Temple wood Lang slough Bucks. England
4CLT	1606	Sig. Arvedi via Poloni 7 Verona Italia
A6G.1500	094	Sig. Fabrizio Castellani Viale Corso 57 a 100 Roma Italia
A6G-CS		Mr. C.S Gilbert 13 Cannamag. Road Farncombe Godalming Surrey England
A6G 2000	2020	Mr. Hambledon Gorey Way Reigate Surrey England
A6G CM	1505. 2005. 6C.	P.S Nicolson Forres LTD Italia
1505. 2005	2005 mot. altro	Sig. Procovic via Bordello 11 Milano Tel. 02/898341 Italia
A6 GCS		Sig. Guido Artom via Leopardi 20 - 6 20123 Milano Italia
2005I.		David Waston Studio De Lavrenti's Casella Postale 10x0 Roma Italia
250 F	2518	Bruno Picco Josef strasse 200 Zurigo S. Svizzera
1505.	+1-60-61	E. Bailey 19 North Street Bourne Lincs England
200 S.1	2413	Jean Guichet C.MR. 27a Chemin du Littoral Marseille Francia
4CL	1566	Sig. Giulio Dubbini via Euganea 21 35100 Padova Italia
A6 1500	089	"
A6GCS 2000	2097	"
200 S1	2416	"
4C5 1100	1126	K.P. Painter 40 Vineyard Drive Newport Salop. T.F.10 -70-E England
150.S.	1668	Mr. Rudolf Fancken D 5300 Bonn. P.o.B 177 Germani
200 S	3083	Mr. Robert Cooper - Bridge House - Gipsi'Lane Swindon England
Prototipo con 8V Fiat	Telaio mas-fj.	Mr. Bernus Gérard 61 Ave de Costantine 62 Calais Francia
6CM	1548	Uwe Hucke Automuseum - Nettelbstedt 4991 über Lübbecke Richemportrais West|Germania
A6GCS	2045 - 2092	M.Claude Pibarot. 7 Impasse du Pont Trily 55 Bar le Duc Francia
8VR1	4503	Paul Kyle 319 Cypress Drive Laguna Beach California 97651 USA
A6GCS	2006 (ex Musma)	72x81 Sig. Dubbini Via Euganea Padova Italia
4CM.	1119 (ex Ferri)	
250 S4 cil	008 (ex Dubbini)	Peter Van Rossen England
450 S	4508 - 4509	Richard Fellows Maserati Citroen stvg... England
150 S cil	1676	John. A.R. Curmi P.o Box 423 Guarena Palace Malta
6C tp.34	3029 2435	Jörg Klasen 433 Mülheim (Ruhr) Schultenhof straße 14 Germani
200S	2407	Mr. Claude Priez 5 Rue Sedaine Paris XI° Francia
450S	4504	Mr. Simeon R. Shoritham 1950 Wellington Street Massachusetts USA
A6G 2000	Spyder Frua	Ervin H. Dibbern 956 S.E -14th Terrace Deerfield Beach Florida US
200SL	2429	Orizio Eugenio via Sebino Provaglio d'Iseo Brescia Italia
A6G 2000	2189	oreste Pascualetti via Redi 2 56010 Madonna dell'Acqua PISA Itali
6C 1937	1537	Mr. Owe Haah Klövervagen 14 - 36 Broma Swede
6C	1538 - 1540	Mr. R. Fielding Bogton Place Forres Moray scotland Englan
60-61		Joel E Finn 6 Volino Drive Poughkeepsie New York 12602 US
✳ 250 F.	15116 venere + altre dell. BG. ecc.	Club. Maserati-Hunters Pot Aldbury Tring Herts England

COOPER-MASERATI

In the September of 1965, Maserati received by way of Signor Mario Condivi, our importer for Great Britain, and Roy Salvadori, one of our former sports car and single-seater drivers and at that time the sporting director of the Cooper team, a request for the supply of engines for the new three-litre Formula 1 regulations due to come into force in 1966. Ingegner Alfieri could hardly believe he would have the opportunity to dust off our Tipo 2 V12. The project was relatively straightforward and involved the development of the 3000 cc engine based on the bore and stroke of 70.4x64 mm already used in the Birdcage. This had the added advantage of limiting Maserati's investments and a contract was signed with Cooper for the supply of Maserati engines to be fitted to their T81 car.

When the first 2989 cc Tipo 9 F1/66 engine was mounted on the test bench in October to begin the fine tuning of the six Weber 38 IDM carburettors, Ingegner Alfieri asked me to work with the lads from Bertocchi's Testing Room and put at their disposition all the experience I had gained in 1957 when Reggiani and I had tuned the first 12-cylinder engine in Maserati's history. During the tests a number of valve springs broke and were replaced with others with a thicker diameter, but these too tended to fail. I immediately contacted the supplier as we had never had any problems with the valve springs back in 1957. Ingegner was unsure whether to change the diameter of the spring wire, not wanting to increase the friction on the cams and ordered a supply with the utmost urgency of springs with wire diameters of 3/3.5/ 4 millimetres. I saw that Alfieri was very worried about this problem and offered to test the new valve springs in the way Reggiani and I used to do in the Experimental Department in the 1950s. During the dismantling and move in 1958, the two electric motors from the dynamometers had been located in a small room alongside the testing room. This room also housed the test bench for the development of the Lucas fuel injection system.

This was on a Wednesday and so I would have plenty of time as the new springs would not have arrived until the Friday afternoon with the lorry from the Cagnola firm of Milan. With the help and assistance of Carlo Sitti, who occupied the injection system testing room, I set up a half cylinder head from the T9 engine attached to a support aligned with an electric motor that was in turn connected to a suitably modified section of a camshaft that allowed two needle valve springs to be run at a camshaft speed of around 5000 rpm, equating to an engine speed of 10,000 rpm. Ingegner Alfieri sent for me in the Technical Office at about six o'clock because the new springs had arrived. I immediately installed a series with a diameter of three millimetres and then started the cam lubrication pump and the electric motor. I had to take care a few drops of leaking oil but, despite the noise, everything was working well. Manfredini had something brought for me to eat, Ingegner Alfieri came back after nine o'clock to see how things were going. We agreed to test each type of spring, of the three different wire diameters, for six hours. At midnight I replaced the springs with others with a diameter of 3.5 mm along with the relative tappets. Every now and then I'd leave the room and sit down leaning my head on a bench to rest and recover from the noise.

At six o'clock on the Saturday morning I replaced the springs with 4mm diameter wire springs and new tappets. The evening before I had called home to ask someone to bring me a towel, soap and a clean T-shirt and a pair of fresh socks the next morning. At around half past seven my wife kindly brought everything to me in the gatehouse, along with breakfast. When Ingegner Alfieri arrived I was conducting the final test with the set of 4 mm springs that would finish at around one o'clock. Analysing the tappets and testing their hardness on the part where they came into contact with the cams, I noticed that the springs with the 4mm diameter wire were overloaded, while on the tappets used with the other types of springs there was no marking and the hardness was still 60 RWC. It was about one o'clock on the Saturday and I was quite exhausted after the all-nighter. As I prepared to go home Ingegner Alfieri came to thank me for all the work done. At home, after a nice shower and a good meal, I went to bed and slept until Sunday morning. When I got up, my ankles were unusually swollen. My wife was concerned and wanted to call the doctor, while my father was of the opinion that the cause was due to the many hours spent standing. When I took a new clean of socks from the dresser, I noticed that the nylon ones I never used because I didn't like them were missing: they were the ones that Giordana had brought to me at Maserati the day before and that I had slipped on without noticing. When I found the cause of the swelling, an allergy to the synthetic material, I spent a very pleasant Sunday with my family.

On the following Monday morning, Ingegner Alfieri told me that he had chosen to have the 3.5mm diameter wire springs fitted to the engine, which was to be prepared for testing at Goodwood. Ascari was already modifying the valve covers and other parts for the application of the induction system with piston flow control as we had already done in 1954 on the 250F. The ignition was also modified with the Lucas transistorised system being adopted.

In December 1965, the Tipo 9 F1/66 injection engine was approved and with its 360 hp and 10,000 rpm, was a match for the engines of the rival teams. I followed the evolution of this adventure as an observer despite being swamped with work. I was in fact compiling the spare parts catalogue and manual for the Mexico; together with Ingegner Pollio, I was following the homologation procedures for the second series Sebring 3700 cc and 4000 cc, while the Client Services Department also frequently called me in for updates or modifications to cars built earlier. With the start of the racing season in the spring of 1966 at Syracuse, the Cooper-Maserati was subjected to a series of tests, but it was the races themselves that allowed improvements to be made that led to the new T81B chassis, ahead of the Italian Grand Prix at Monza in September. Maserati was ready with engines with new cylinder heads.

One afternoon I met Ingegner Alfieri in the workshop, his eyes were downcast and by his expression it looked like he was suffering. I asked him if he felt unwell and whether he needed anything. "No! No! I'm just furious! The Cooper mechanics are out there waiting for the engine to be mounted in the car, but Guerino has tried it and found a leaking valve and now Bietolini has remove the head." I asked him if I could go and take a look. "You'd be doing me a great favour..." I arrived in the testing room to find the lads taking the engine off the test bench, they had already disconnected the exhaust manifolds on one side. I asked them to reassemble everything so that we could start it up again. They didn't take too kindly to that, saying that Guerino, their boss, had told them that the valve on the third cylinder was leaking. I repeated that Ingegner Alfieri carried more weight than Bertocchi and that he had instructed me to take a look and investigate the problem. Grumbling, they started the engine again and indeed the exhaust manifold of the third cylinder was cold. I asked if they had tried replacing the injector and they replied, "Guerino said that there's a leaking valve!" At that point I started giving orders, "Go to Sitti and get a new injector, you get me an inch wrench and you go to Bietolini and have him give you an injector spanner!" When the injector had been replaced the engine ran smoothly. I told them not to touch anything else and rushed over to the Technical Office to tell Ingegner Alfieri, who said with a big smile, "Thank you, I'm going over right away to tell them to give to the engine to the English lads."

Guerino was still the chief tester and head of the Testing Room; his team worked on everything except the final signing off and they called him in for the last test on any type of engine. Bertocchi was very good with carburettors but lacked experience with fuel injection systems and in this specific case he had blundered. When Ingegner Alfieri arrived the following morning he called me to his office, "Listen, I got something to ask you! I've been talking to Signor Omer, would you like to take over responsibility for the Testing Room?" "Aren't I doing well in the Technical Office? Have I done something wrong?" "No, no, I'd be creating a gap but I'd be closing a bigger one". After a pause and a deep breath, I replied, "Ingegnere, thank you, but I don't have the personality for certain power games, even knowing that I have your backing, I would always be caught between two stools." Another breath... "If you really order me! But I'd prefer to continue working here in the Technical Office". "Then I'll take different measures". A few months later, a lad from Maranello, my age, who trained at Ferrari and gained further experience at Lamborghini, joined Maserati.

After a year of intensive development, the Cooper-Maserati triumphed with John Surtees in the Mexican Grand Prix. The quarrels and the reasons for a possible divorce receded as Maserati had in the meantime developed the Tipo 10 Formula 1 engine with two intake and one exhaust valves per cylinder, triple ignition and guillotine intake trumpets that delivered 380 hp, while for its part Cooper had developed a new chassis, the T86. However, Pedro Rodríguez's victory in the South African Grand Prix on the 2nd of January 1967, however, did little to resolve the disputes between the English team and the Italian engine builders. In fact, after a few more races in Europe, the contract between the two was finally dissolved. A few Coopers entered by private teams were seen racing through to 1969, using the Tipo 9 F1/66 engine in the T81 chassis. ten years after its birth in 1967, and having been subjected to appropriate modifications and updates, our 12-cylinder engine was considered to be the most powerful engine in the new three-litre Formula 1 field.

GHIBLI AND GHIBLI SS

Penned by Giorgietto Giugiaro while he was still working at the Ghia coachworks, these cars were named after
the wild south-easterly wind that blows in Libya. A low
coupé with sleek, sporty lines. The engine was the 4700
cc V8 converted to dry sump lubrication with a scavenge
pump to allow it to be fitted into the shape of body. This
made it possible to reduce the height of the car and have a
low bonnet sloping down to a front end with retractable
headlights. It was shown at the 48th International Motor
Show in Turin in November 1966. One car was on display
at the Ghia stand in the coachbuilders' area, while I had
managed to place another metallic copper-coloured car on
the Maserati stand (I had been in charge of organising
exhibitions at the various shows for many years by that
time). There were five cars on display: the Sebring, Mistral,
Mexico, Quattroporte and the latest, the Ghibli, in the
foreground, which was a huge success with both the press
and the public.

Ingegner Bertocchi, who had been appointed commercial
director, had insisted that a Type 9/F1 engine be displayed
to honour John Surtees' win at the Mexican Grand Prix
in the Cooper-Maserati. Since I had to set up our stand, I
always arrived a few days before press preview, but inevitably some journalists managed to get in earlier, looking
for new cars and scoops for their publications. I consequently got to know and talk to many of them, and over
the years I had the honour of becoming their friend. When

they came to Modena to test one or other of our cars, it was my responsibility to accompany them, providing them with the necessary support and the technical information they needed. Up until the Eighties it was customary for car manufacturers to bring a few cars to international shows for their customers to try. For Maserati, this task could only be entrusted to Guerino Bertocchi, our chief test driver, who had an innate sensitivity for high-speed driving and, above all, a great deal of experience, gained over many years of work on both sports racing cars and single-seaters. One evening we went to a restaurant for dinner and met three Lancia test drivers, whom Guerino knew and who didn't want to go in, because one table was occupied by Alfa Romeo test drivers. Bertocchi managed to persuade them to go in by suggesting to them that we should sit in the middle to keep them apart. That's what rivalry means sometimes!

In 1969, the Ghibli Coupé was joined by a spider version with an optional hard-top. In 1970, in addition to these two versions, a more powerful 4930 cc engine was also available, with a displacement of nearly 5000 cc developing 320 hp at 6000 rpm. At the 1968 Turin Motor Show, in addition to the Ghibli V8, one of our classic engines was exhibited, the 1940 Type 8 CL, a thee-litre unit with four valves per cylinder and a double compressor, the last racing engine to have been designed by Ernesto Maserati. In a photo of the Maserati stand, behind this engine, four very famous people in the automotive field stand out: Count Giovanni Lurani, Signor Omer Orsi and the two great former racing drivers Piero Taruffi and Gigi Villoresi. Count Lurani asked me for some technical details. I promptly told him what he wanted to know, then he said to me, "Do you know what the Maserati brothers were secretly called?" I looked at him questioningly. "The Holy Trinity." "Of course they were!" added Villoresi. "Ernesto designed, Ettore built and Bindo organized everything." Motor shows were always very tiring but they were also occasions when you met people who you listened to open-mouthed.

At the time, speed tests were carried out on the Milan-Modena motorway by Bertocchi and Ingegner Pollio, who dealt with the timing, but by now the A1 motorway was so busy that it was no longer possible. When it came to the speed test for the Ghibli SS Ingegner Pollio was in the United States for the homologation process and I was instructed to go down the Bologna-Padua motorway with Guerino Bertocchi and time the flying kilometre, as all the speedometers always over-read by 2/3%. On the three occasions that it was possible to get an accurate reading the stopwatch clocked 12.4 seconds, equivalent to 283 kph. After a while the Bologna-Padova motorway also became too busy and more significantly a speed limit was also introduced, despite the fact that we at Maserati (but I think it was the same for the other companies) had permission to exceed it if we put two adhesive panels on the sides that allowed us to test our cars beyond the set limit. Later the Nardò track, built by the Department of Motor Vehicles for all homologation testing, assured greater safety and precision.

Maserati received a request from the Michelin tyre factory to purchase a Ghibli SS car, with the highest possible axle ratio, so that high speeds could be maintained, with an adequate hydraulic braking system, to test their tyres. As I had developed the ventilated brake disc system with Signor Cappa of Girling and had also tested various types of brake pads, Ingegner Alfieri asked me to see what could be done for this special car ordered by Michelin. I had a look around to see what materials were available. The calipers that were available were the 3Cs we used on the front and the 12/12 ones used on the rear. We could not ask Girling for larger calipers because Signor Cappa had told me that the 3Cs were the biggest they made. So I then asked Ingegner Alfieri to fit two 12/12 rear calipers on each front wheel. The engineer doubted that the one-inch pump would be able to actuate so many pistons because we had calculated that the sum of the various diameters was greater than that of the 3C calipers we usually used. I was very insistent about this very fact, as this configuration would give us greater pressure but above all a larger area of friction. I managed to persuade him and he told me to design the support according to the size of the two callipers within the space available inside the rim. I designed the support and supervised work on it carried out by Barani, with heat treatment by Montipò, and two days later I gave Cleto Grandi the double front calipers to fit to the Ghibli SS. After Ingegner Alfieri and Cleto Grandi had tried the car, they came and congratulated me because they had noticed a clear increase in friction. However, I never trusted other people's impressions and the next day I used all the instruments to check the pedal pressure and the amount of pedal travel, and above all I used the decelerometer to gave me a reading that I could compare with tests previously carried out on the Ghibli. The measured readings were in fact higher. The double caliper set up was later fitted to a number of other cars for special customers.

"AIR POLLUTION" AND "SAFETY"

From January the 1st 1968, new regulations on pollution and safety came into force in the United States. We at Maserati were therefore also working to modify our engines and cars for the American market. Above all because these regulations would come into force in Europe sooner or later. The most challenging problem was that of "air pollution", since the aim was to reduce the percentage of CO_2 at the exhaust to 3.5/4%, whereas at that time we had much higher values, almost double that. As regards to "safety" we had to fit seat belts, have a collapsible tube on the steering column and front and rear rubber bumpers; in addition, all the controls on the dashboard had to be flat switchgear rather than protruding levers. This was in September/October 1967 and the company was completely unprepared for these new demands. To regulate the exhaust gases, an air pump could be applied to the engine, driven by a belt connected to the crankshaft. The speed was regulated by an electromagnetic clutch, a diverter valve, two non-return valves and air injectors on the exhaust manifold to ensure more complete combustion. Fittings were inserted in the exhaust manifolds to make it possible to connect probe pipes that would record CO_2 emissions at tick over.

Naturally, all these devices were fitted at the expense of power and speed. Ingegner Pollio had gone to the relevant department in America to obtain information and instructions on how to conduct the American type approval tests. As usual, I was also involved. I was given the task of simulating a test on a 50-mile track (about 81 kilometres) at a top speed of 38 miles per hour (about 60 kph) with 7 stops, one every 5 kilometres, and to measure the exhaust emission values. I had laid out a route from the beginning of Via Panaria towards Bomporto, Nonantola, the Navicello bridge, placing signals every 5 kilometres, stopping to take the required measurements of gas emissions after each stop, for a specific time ranging from 5 to 10 minutes.

We had to perform these measurements on every single car, so I had been busy for a few days, when he had Norma, who was the head of the Purchasing Office, call me, "Listen, I know you're doing road tests near Bomporto and Nonantola and I need a big favour!" "If I can help, I'd be more than happy to." "I need to find out about a feature of the new test benches at the Borghi e Saveri company in San Giovanni Persiceto." "But... but... Norma, it's not on my route, I can't!" "Oh, come on, I don't know who else to ask and it's really urgent!" I could hardly say no! There had always been the utmost cooperation between colleagues and when it was necessary we helped each other out. So I went to the company in San Giovanni in Persiceto and Signor Borghi's son welcomed me as he already knew about the information that he had to give me. He asked me to follow him to the warehouse and while we were walking through one of the departments he showed me an engine, which looked like it belonged to a motorcycle, because it had a large finned head. "Do you know who that engine belongs to?" "Some motorcycle factory in Bologna, I imagine." "You're kidding! It's one of Ernesto Maserati's engines; he asked us if he could come and test it on one of our test benches. He's given it the name MA.ER. (Maserati Ernesto).

He's doing some research on the combustion chambers. There are two or three heads to try out with combustion chambers of different shapes and sizes." Signor Ernesto, who I knew was already quite old, certainly over seventy, still had the passion and the will to get things done!

Over the years, the maximum allowed percentage of CO_2 in emissions was steadily dropping and the industry was becoming increasingly committed to research. The regulations regarding safety were also gradually being standardized until the crash tests had to be carried out in specialized laboratories abroad, because in Italy they did not exist. It was a matter of placing a dummy in the driver's seat and propelling the car, placed on a sled, at 30 kph against a wall, in order to be able to detect any deformations in the bodywork and to find out what happened to the dummy when it came into contact with the airbag. It was then necessary to work on the front of the chassis and on the steering column. When other regulations were introduced it became necessary to reinforce the doors to pass the side impact tests. Then, over the next few years, we ended up fitting airbags to every part of the interior and introduced engines with increasingly sophisticated exhaust systems, with probes and filters, to reduce CO_2 emissions.

THE C.114 ENGINE

One evening in mid-October, Ingegner Alfieri told us to wait before we went home because Commendator Orsi wanted to talk to us although even he didn't know why. When the Commendatore came into in the Technical Office, we were all anxious to find out the reason for this unusual meeting. He informed us that he had received a request from the president of a major automotive company for a very compact 3000 cc engine for a front-wheel drive car. In his usual, very friendly manner, he asked us to help Ingegner Alfieri to make the engine as quickly as possible. The Ingegnere promised that work would begin the following day. The Commendatore thanked us, said goodbye and left. We gathered around Ingegner Alfieri who immediately told us about the idea he had had. "Our 4200 cc V8 has a unitary displacement of about 515 cc, so if we remove the two rear cylinders and make a slightly shorter crankshaft, we'd have an engine with a displacement of about three litres that we could have ready for testing in about ten days." We had been concentrating so hard that we hadn't noticed that it was already eight o'clock. The next morning, as soon as I got to the Technical Office, I picked up two right-hand and a left-hand cylinder heads from the warehouse along with a 107 crankcase and had them taken to Ingegner Alfieri's office. Shortly afterwards he summoned Barani, the head of machine tools. With Ascari, the engine designer, they explained to him where to cut the two cylinders and where to cut the cylinder heads. I was given the task of supervising the work and, after Barani had finished, sorting out the welding needed to seal off the oilways after milling and take care of the delivery and assembly of the engines. Ascari immediately began to design the new crankshaft and four camshafts, which were the parts that would need at least a week to be finished as they had to undergo various heat treatments, even though Montipò had been informed that we did not need for any undersizing of the crankshaft so that we could reduce the time needed for case hardening.

Around 10 days later, the engine, with a displacement of about 2800 cc, was in the testing room for the first tests. Encouraged by Ingegner Alfieri, Ascari had thrown himself headlong into designing the definitive engine, the C.114: the main thing that he had to bear in mind was that it was to be used for a front-wheel drive car, so the drive for the valvegear had to be moved to gain 10/12 centimetres of longitudinal space. All the designers had been instructed to work with Ascari on the detail. Grana, who was responsible for the casting of the models for the foundry, had the task of working with the supplier to obtain at least a couple of castings straight away in order to build the two engines as soon as the final drawings of the cylinder heads of the crankcase and all the other parts that could be made from castings were ready. After about a month, towards the beginning of December, Ciccio Montanari assembled the new C.114 engine with a displacement of 2675 cc and a bore and stroke of 87x75 mm, fuelled by three carburettors.

After an endless period of running-in, power and endurance tests began, resulting in about 180 hp at 6250 rpm. The engine was run for a whole day, alternating between low and high revs, without showing any sign of failure or any other problems. In the meantime, we had heard that the engine had been made for Citroën and that Ingegner Alfieri and Ciccio Montanari were going to go to Paris at the beginning of December to show our engine to the French engineers. On his return, Ingegner Alfieri told us that the engine had not received a very flattering reception, as the Citroën engineers had been a little surprised when they first saw the 90° V6 unit, but as Montanari dismantled the various parts, they began to appreciate it a little more. When they were confronted with the stripped-down crankcase measuring 420 millimeters in length, they fully approved the choice of a 90-degree V configuration.

On the 20th of December 1967, Citroën bought a 60% shareholding in Maserati from the Orsi family and our engine, fitted to their new car, underwent its first tests in the spring of 1968. At Maserati, thanks to everyone working together, we had managed to achieve a minor miracle. In less than two months Ingegner Alfieri had succeeded in his aim. Above all, this was a turning point for Maserati in the direction of industrialisation, which would open up greater possibilities and a greater safety margin to deal with all the regulations that the car industry would soon be required to satisfy.

CITROËN

By the 30th of June 1968, Citroën owned 75% of Maserati and at that time four French managers arrived in Modena to trigger a real internal revolution. After seeing and studying the location of the various departments and, above all, the space for the machining and production of the C.114 engine, Ingegner Guy Malleret, General Manager, assisted by Dr. Dominique Drieux, Administrative Manager, immediately moved the general warehouse into one of the buildings where the first workshop was located. At the same time they had a load-bearing platform built to halve the height of the building where we had moved to after the withdrawal from racing. The reception and the factory entrance were moved opposite the car park. The Customer Service department was moved out of the factory to an adjacent building.

This environmental renovation also included the construction of a new C.114 engine assembly building and a new test room. And of course they began to move staff around. Ardilio Manfredini was sent to Citroën in Paris, for a month's training, as he would have to manage the Personnel Office and recruit about 400 workers over the course of a year. Barani was involved in researching and purchasing all the new and used machine tooling to be used in the production of the C.114 engine. The shopfloor was managed by Ingegner Nicoletti, an Italo-Frenchman from Citroën, while Lecesne was in the Purchasing Office. Dr. Drieux was in charge of the administrative staff and all the offices needed new personnel. Renato Soli, who was acting workshop manager, was put in charge of the new Methods and Production Office, located on the floor above the Technical Office where I had made available all the drawings of the cars built in Bologna. I needed to consult them occasionally and I had put them, divided by type, into an old showcase where I also placed all the wooden models of the racing car castings.

One afternoon I got back from testing some new brake pads and while the doorman was raising the barrier to let me in he said to me: *"Guèrda chi vòdèn là sovra e tòta la tò ròba vecia i la matèn in dal rutàm!"* ("Look, they are chucking out everything up there and they're taking your old stuff to the rubbish dump"). I left the car in the middle of the courtyard and ran straight over to where they were throwing away all the packing material and all the rubbish. I saw all the models had been thrown into a heap, as two labourers came along with boxes full of rolls of drawings. I asked for an explanation and they told me that they had received an order from Ingegner Nicoletti to take everything away to make room for the new office. "Leave everything alone, don't touch anything else!" I was furious. I ran to look for Ingegner Nicoletti, whom I had already met and who had seemed to me to be a very reasonable person. I found him with Dr. Drieux and without hesitation I said: "Which fool gave the order to throw away all the old models and drawings?" I was very angry and Dr. Drieux said to me, "Calm down! Calm down!" I took a deep breath and explained that, never mind the models, but we absolutely had to keep the drawings. They were essential as we had so many cars spread around the world and sometimes collectors asked for information on how to make a part, and besides they represented Maserati's entire history and technical heritage. He said to me, "While we're on the subject, I'd like to inform you that we have to chuck out all that junk that you call the Museum." I stared at him and asked him to find a satisfactory solution to these issues. My eyes were shining with anger and apprehension but I think he listened to me. In fact, Ingegner Nicoletti was ordered to stop what he was doing and not move the old drawings.

The next day Ingegner Bertocchi summoned me to his office as he had heard about my outburst. He told me that he had contacted Signor Omer Orsi at Torrazzi, where he had been working for some time, after he had stopped working for Maserati. He had asked him and advised him to take away all the spare parts for the racing cars because, for reasons of space, but especially because they thought they couldn't be used, the new French management wanted to sell them as scrap metal to any company that would come and take away what was seen as manufacturing waste. At Torrazzi, the Orsi company had three sheds where they overhauled the Maserati milling machines and built exhaust systems for our cars. As soon as the load-bearing floor in the other building was finished, all the items from the Museum were piled up on temporary shelves as best we could so as to take up as little space as possible. I had better luck with the engines because they were put on proper shelves and everything was covered with a large tarpaulin until better times. I had at my disposal two wooden trunks for the old drawings that we also put near the engines so that they could be consulted easily.

The old building had been renovated and arranged to accommodate the new offices of Ingegner Malleret, Dr. Drieux and Ingegner Lecesne on the ground floor, the Accounting and Import Export Office on the first floor, and the provisional

Sales Office as this would soon be located in a new space in the first of the old buildings directly opposite the reception. The Personnel Office was placed in the former Technical Office next to the infirmary, while changing rooms and showers for the workers were built next to the canteen on the first floor of the other building, which could be accessed either via a large staircase or via a lift made specifically to bring up any cars or trolleys carrying materials. The whole factory had undergone changes and new configurations in view of a forthcoming sharp increase in the workforce for the construction of the C.114 engine. There was even a small room where trade union delegates could meet.

At the same time as new factory and office workers had been hired to strengthen the various departments, other managers had also arrived: two engineers in the Technical Office, Ingegner Burgio for international type approvals and Ingegner Mazzoli for type approvals in Italy. Ingegner Benedicti took his place on the shopfloor; the arrival of Dr. Torrusio, as the new sales director, created a situation that led to the resignation of Ingegner Bertocchi. When he called me to let me know what was happening, we both had tears in our eyes. We had had an extraordinary working relationship and shared a passion for Maserati history, and there had been those occasions that sometimes brought us together to work on the same problems, even though were employed in different sections. I have never really understood how the French managers could have made that mistake. Ingegner Bertocchi had a knowledge of our customers, dealers and the market that was without doubt superior to that of the newcomer, who knew nothing at all about Maserati. Perhaps they wanted to give the Sales Office a more international image.

31 October 1959, Turin Motor Show, the so-called "Shah of Persia" 5000 GT superbly bodied by Touring.

1964, Commendator Adolfo Orsi, CEO of the Officine Maserati, getting into the new Quattroporte saloon, a car that he was particularly keen to see in the Maserati GT range.

March 1962, the Tipo 151 Berlinetta being prepared for the Le Mans 24 Hours.

1963, the pits at the Reims circuit, the 2800 cc four-cylinder Maserati Birdcage Tipo 61 of the Franco-American Camoradi team, rebodied by Drogo.

1965, the author posing alongside the Mistral Spyder for a photo shoot organized at the Modena racing circuit.

27 October 1965, Officine A. Maserati, the factory museum inaugurated by Juan Manuel Fangio. A dream finally transformed into reality.

October 1966, Turin Motor Show; in the foreground, in the midst of the company's full range of the time, the new Maserati Ghibli with a 4700 cc V8 engine, bodied by Ghia to the designs of Giorgietto Giugiaro.

1966, Monza, John Surtees in the Cooper T81 with the Maserati Tipo 9 engine which he drove to victory in the Mexican Grand Prix that year.

1965, Ingegner Giulio Alfieri with Fausto Bietolini, the "white gloves" engineer, observing the (Tipo 9) 3000 cc V12 prepared for the British Cooper team. That engine was still fitted with carburettors, later replace with Lucas-type fuel injection.

5 November 1994, at the Ristorante Lauro in Via Ciro Menotti in Modena, I am with Ingegner Alfieri, telling him about the Formula 1 Veteran Mechanics Club.

The Maserati stand at the Barcelona Motor Show in 1973 with the Indy (left) and the Merak (right) in the foreground.

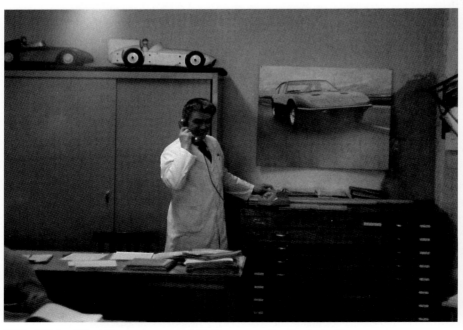

1968, Officine Alfieri Maserati, my new S.D. (Documentation Service) office.

1968, Officine Alfieri Maserati, the first 2675 cc V6 Tipo C111 engine that was to be built for Citroën.

1969, the new Citroën SM fitted with the C114 engine.

1972, the Turin Motor Show is the setting for the presentation of the Bora (at the centre of the stand), fitted with a 4700 cc mid-mounted V8 engine and bodied by Giugiaro. Accompanying it are on the left the Ghibli and on the right the Indy, partially concealing the Merak.

1976, Officine Alfieri Maserati, Gigi Villoresi, together with his old mechanic from the Forties and Fifties, Fausto Bietolini, talk to me about the Merak SS tests.

1976, the Turin Motor Show again. This time, the centre of attention on the Maserati stand is the Kyalami, officially presented that year.

1977, Officine Alfieri Maserati visited by the Maestro Luciano Pavarotti; turning away from the camera Mrs. Adua Pavarotti, Dr. Micheletti of the GEPI, me and Miss Lella Malagoli from the Import Export Office.

1977, Officine Alfieri Maserati, another shot from Luciano Pavarotti's visit (he was a great admirer of the Quattroporte and the Trident cars in general) to the Technical Office. I had the honour of showing the Maestro round.

1978, the new Quattroporte saloon designed by Giorgietto Giugiaro (Italdesign).

1979, the Quirinale Gardens in Rome, Mr. Alejandro de Tomaso talking to the commander of the Guards on the occasion of the presentation of the Quattroporte to the President of the Republic Sandro Pertini.

1982, the First International Maserati Car Rally. I am lifting the bonnet of a 250F from 1957 to show the engine to Mr. de Tomaso.

1981, dinner at the Ristorante Lauro, organized by our colleague Ciccio Montanari, head of the Engine Department, and the author. The photo features Emore Manni, Antonio Reggiani and Ardilio Manfredini.

1982, the First International Maserati Cars Rally. Mr. Hofer Jr., Franco Meloni, our concessionaire in Rome, myself and our former driver Sergio Mantovani.

14 December 1983, present at the Officine Alfieri Maserati are: Giuseppe Pellacani, Ardilio Manfredini, Don Sergio Mantovani "Don Ruspa", myself, Giulio Sala and Luciano Malagoli.

In the November of 1986, I am seen showing the new Sensitork differential from the Biturbo to Duke Amedeo d'Aosta who was visiting Maserati.

International Maserati Club Meeting in Austria, in the September of 1988. Left, Giulio Sala with his wife Anna, with Giordana and me on the right.

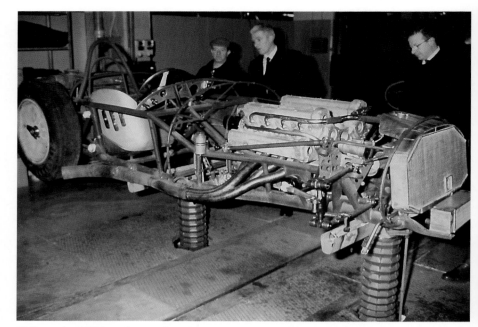

28 September 1987, on the occasion of the First International Maserati Meeting, I am accompanying the chief editor of the magazine *Oggi* to see the Eldorado in an advanced state of restoration.

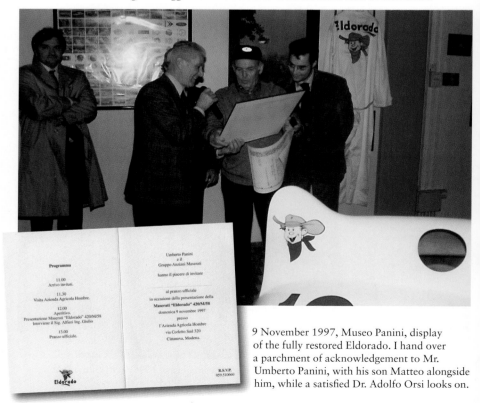

9 November 1997, Museo Panini, display of the fully restored Eldorado. I hand over a parchment of acknowledgement to Mr. Umberto Panini, with his son Matteo alongside him, while a satisfied Dr. Adolfo Orsi looks on.

20 February 1995, Vallelunga circuit, Rome. Presentation and race for the Trofeo Ghibli Open Cup. The Maserati "DNA": Primo Ragazzi, myself, Ingegner Eugenio Alzati, Ardilio Manfredini, Umberto Stradi, Emore Manni, Franco Barbieri, Giulio Sala, Rosario Camarda, Luciano Bonacini and Fausto Bietolini.

The then president of the Ferrari Club of Maranello, Alberto Beccari, presents a prize to the "Campionissimo" Juan Manuel Fangio. Alongside me is Giulio Borsari, while to the right of Fangio are Emer Vecchi and Pasquale Cassani of Ferrari.

4 June 1993, Castel d'Ario (MN), the Veteran Formula 1 Mechanics Club visit to the Tazio Nuvolari memorial, the great pre-war Scuderia Ferrari and Maserati driver.

October 1997, Officine Alfieri Maserati. Presentation of a plaque to Ingegner Eugenio Alzati who was retiring. From the left are Fausto Bietolini, Ardilio Manfredini, Alzati and me.

MASERATI INDY

At the Turin Motor Show in November 1968, two Maserati prototypes were on display on the Ghia and Vignale stands. One of the two would replace the Mexico, as both were four-seater coupés with more streamlined and modern styling. As I was strolling around the coachbuilders' area, after setting up the Maserati stand, as I had been doing for years, I stopped to look at the two prototypes, and behind me I heard a voice that I knew well say: "Which of them do you like most?" I turned around and found *Bertocchino*, or rather Ingegner Bertocchi; I knew he had been hired as general manager at De Tomaso, and we had not seen each other since he had left Maserati. I was delighted to see him again, even though we were now on opposite sides.

Of the two Maserati prototypes, I preferred the one with Vignale bodywork. The final version was presented at the Geneva Motor Show in March 1969 with the name Indy, commemorating the 8CTF's Indianapolis 500 victory 30 years earlier. The engine fitted in the first year of production was the 4200 cc V8 giving 260 hp at 5500 rpm for a top speed of 250 kph. It was also sold with a 4700 cc engine and from 1971 onwards the displacement of the engine was increased to 5 litres (4930.6 cc). The version with the 4700 cc engine, renamed Indy America, proved to be the most popular, as the internal restyling made it much more comfortable and elegant, with avant-garde seats featuring built-in headrests and new Borletti instruments giving the finishing touches to a completely new dashboard.

Ingegner Alfieri sent me to Milan, to the Borletti company, with the first Indy America for a photo shoot of the new car for advertising purposes with the instrumentation they produced there. I got to Borletti's, which was almost in the centre of Milan, at around three o'clock and the photographer was already set up with all his equipment: lights, reflectors and so on, because photographing the interior of a car is always very difficult. Some of the company's technicians had come to see their work and someone asked me about the petrol tank and the petrol gauge. I drew their attention to the fact that the car had two tanks located one on each side at the back of the car, accessible through two locked covers, which allowed access to the screw cap. In fact, as I was explaining this, I took the keys from the dashboard and opened one of the covers, while someone unscrewed the cap to have a look at the float which was in an area where it was impossible to see. Then he put the cap back on, locked it and gave me the key.

After the photo shoot, it started to rain and I left to go home at about 5. A thunderstorm began and at a busy junction the engine stopped, I couldn't get it started again and a furious policeman shouted at me because I had blocked the traffic. With the help of another policeman, we managed to push the car to the side of the road. I opened the bonnet and saw that the glass of the petrol filter was white instead of red. It was full of water. It was raining really hard, so I covered myself with the plastic cover from the passenger seat. I rummaged around in the boot to find the spark plug spanner and after removing all the plugs, I flicked the switch for the other tank, I emptied the filter bowl, turned on the ignition, petrol came through and I turned the engine over without the spark plugs, which I then tried to dry using my handkerchief and blowing on them as hard I could, in the torrential rain. I replaced the spark plugs hoping that some saint might help me, I turned the key again and after two or three attempts the engine coughed then started to run smoothly again. I shut the bonnet, took off my improvised cape, climbed in and set off for Modena, soaking wet.

I got to Maserati at eight o'clock. As I was walking through reception I met Signor Omer who was going home and he asked me where I had come from, I went down and showed him what a state I was in and then I told him about the experience I'd had. The next morning when we inspected the car we found the filler cap compartment full of water because the overflow pipe had been blocked when the underseal had been applied. The fuel cap that the technician had unscrewed had not been screwed up again completely – the water that had not drained out of the compartment had got into the tank and as it had a specific gravity higher than petrol had been sucked in immediately by the electric pump causing the problem, fortunately without damaging the engine, but leaving me a very wet memory of the Indy.

GREAT FAMILY NEWS

Gianna was growing up nicely, she was a beautiful, good and obedient child, but since Giordana had a lot of work to do with her tailoring atelier and the home, she was not able to help her with schoolwork so we decided to enroll her in the Dame Orsoline elementary school in Via Ganaceto. A bus used to come by every morning at 8.15 AM, to pick up other pupils as well, and brought them home at 5.00 PM. It was an expense we could afford, especially for the education and instruction of our daughter.

One Sunday afternoon, I was cycling past Reggiani's house, while Gianna was playing with his daughter, who was a few years older and I told him that my Fiat 600, which I had bought second-hand in 1961, was beginning to give me some trouble. Reggiani immediately said he could get me the car that I wanted with a good discount because he was an employee of the Fiat group, but he would only be able to sell it to me after six months, according to the rules. He bought me a white 850 with a red and blue interior. After about a month I called round to his house to settle the bill, since I didn't want him to be short of money because of the payment, but he didn't even want a deposit and at the same time he took me into the garage and showed me the car, which he kept under a cloth. He was so meticulous and precise in his behaviour that when he delivered the car to me, six months later, the odometer showed only 40 kilometres, that is, the journey from the Bologna dealer to Modena. In fact, after parking it in the garage, he had never moved it again.

My father, with the Accademia Militare, had always gone to prepare the barracks for the Cadets summer camp. For many years he went to San Candido, or Dobbiaco in the Dolomites, then when General Barbolini from Modena became camp commander, they began to go to the Apennines close to us, first to the Passo delle Radici and then to Montecreto. The summer following the year in which Dad retired, we rented an apartment in Montecreto, for the months of July and August, which was good for my father's chronic bronchitis and so that Gianna could be with him. Giordana and I went there on Saturdays or Sundays. During one of our walks we took a mule track and came to an area above the village where they had built two tennis courts and a football field with changing rooms. They had also built a road that, however, led to a dead end. On one side there was a chestnut grove and on the other a meadow with a few large chestnut trees to show where the boundary was. I told my father to ask the people he had met in the village, who the owner of that piece of land was, because one day I would like to build a house there. Dad ran into a conspiracy of silence, as sometimes happens in mountain communities and after three four weeks he still had not found out anything.

Giordana and I decided to leave early, one Saturday morning, so that I could go to the Town Hall in Montecreto, where I had the good fortune to find the surveyor who was in charge of roads, buildings and everything related to borders and property. He was a very talkative and helpful person and gave me the name and address of the owner of the land, telling me however that he had heard that someone

261

had already contacted the owner about buying it. In the afternoon, I went with my father and knocked on the door of an old house in Via Vaccari. An old woman opened the door and, after listening wide-eyed to my request, she answered us, in her mountain dialect that I had trouble understanding, that the land was indeed her property, but that her brother, who had a farm in Castelnuovo Rangone, took care of everything, because she was old and could barely read and write. I had finally made progress, but now we needed to find out how to get to talk to this brother. Luckily, on Sunday morning in the village I met the town surveyor again and asked him how to contact Signor Ballotti, the brother of the owner of the meadow. He replied that he often came to Montecreto, where all his friends were, and that they were the elders of the town. One morning my father found out from the deputy mayor (whom he knew from the days of the Cadet camps) that Signor Ballotti went to eat at the Ristorante del Gallo in Via Giardini every Monday morning, after market, at one o'clock.

So, one Monday, I took a day off work, otherwise I would never have got there on time, and at 1.30 I was in the restaurant. I asked the waiter to point out Signor Ballotti and I introduced myself. He was at table with two other people, elderly like him, and he asked me to sit down and told me that he already knew what I wanted to ask him and that other people had already been in touch with him about buying the plot of land. I asked him about the size of the plot and he replied that it was about 7000 square meters. I urged him to sell me at least 2000 meters, the area on higher ground. He told me that he would talk to his sister about it and that he would get back to me. I thought I had made a good impression on him. I had told him about my father, who used to go there to put up the barracks for the cadets and knew the village carpenter, the lady who cooked for all the people at the Academy, and the family who had rented the flat to us that summer. I urged him to give me an answer as soon as possible and left him a card with my address and phone number. In the last week of August my father met the surveyor from the town council in the street in Montecreto, who informed him that he had begun the process of dividing up the land. Dad rushed round to Via Vaccari to the house of the elderly owner and fortunately his brother, Signor Ballotti, was there too. He told him about my intentions and my interest in buying a piece of that land. My father was informed that the division of the land would be finalised in September/October. They shook hands with an understanding that the portion of land on the higher ground would be sold to us. When we went to pick up my father, Gianna and Aunt Argia at the end of August, I went to look for the town surveyor to get more information about the division of the land and any additional costs. He reassured me by telling me that another buyer from Livorno would be present when we signed the contract at the notary's office, and that we might be able to share expenses with him. I also asked about the cost of the land because we had never talked about money with the sellers, and the surveyor replied that land in the village cost about 500 thousand Lire per 1000 square meters. But he said that up there, outside the village, where there wasn't even a road, the land would cost less, just as I had hoped.

Towards the end of October, I received a phone call telling me that the sale had been fixed for Thursday of the following week. In the bill of sale the northern boundary of the property had been straightened, in fact, it conceded two triangles of land to a neighbouring property so that they would have access to the plot of land below ours. The other buyer was Ingegner Filippi from Livorno, a Maserati customer, whom I had met when he came to our workshop to have his Ghibli serviced.

The most important piece of news, however, was that Giordana was expecting a baby, who would be born around the beginning of August. We were all very happy, especially Gianna. When Giordana had an ultrasound scan that confirmed that it was a boy, my father was over the moon and Gianna said she couldn't wait to have a little brother. Gianluigi was born at the Policlinico on August the 14th 1969 at seven o'clock in the evening after a fairly short labour, weighing just over 3 kilograms. At home there was the usual hustle and bustle when a new born child comes along. The baby was quite well-behaved, he almost never cried and allowed us to sleep at night.

The news did not end there, however. In fact in early November I received a phone call from Geometra Magni, who had helped us to build our house in 1954. He informed me that a new law would be coming into force, which would change the land-use plan and if as planned as I wanted to build a second storey on our house, we would have to take immediate action otherwise it would no longer be possible. I spoke to my father, who immediately agreed, but I was worried about the expense. We had just bought the land in the mountains and so I didn't have much of my savings left. Dad told me not to worry, as he had some money set aside from the lump sum he had received when he retired, and it was right to invest the money in bricks and mortar. Giordana also still had some money from her dowry, so after calculating our overall expenses, we reckoned that we would be able to cover all our costs and in 1970 we started work on building another apartment.

This was a lucky coincidence because with the arrival of Gianluigi we would be needing another bedroom, added to which the beams of the old roof could be used for the house in the mountains, along with the boiler, the burner and the tank that we had had made specially. In October 1971 we were issued with a certificate of use and occupancy, Dad had his bedroom and bathroom in the new apartment, while the other rooms were left empty. Meanwhile, both Gianna and Gianluigi each had their own bedroom. Thanks to some considerable sacrifices the small house had become an elegant apartment block. While I was finishing assembling doors and fitting skirting boards I caught sight of my dad with tears in his eyes blowing his nose. I did not say anything, because I was also thinking about my mother, whom we really missed. And it was she who had made the suggestion many years before of maybe adding a second floor to the house. The premature death of my brother had left a deep scar on my parents and especially my mother.

FIRST CLASS
ADMINISTRATOR

Maserati had almost completed all the restructuring work and the new department, built and equipped with all the machine tools need for producing the new C.114 engine and those needed for our other cars, was divided into two areas: machining of castings and all the aluminium parts, and machining of steel parts, crankshafts, camshafts, connecting rods, cylinder liners and so on. The French management had selected several team leaders, chosen from among our best lathe-turners and milling machinists, and Barani, who did not agree with the changes, left Maserati to go and work for Alfasud in Naples. An assembly line for the C.114s was created in the Engine Assembly Department; our own engines were in fact assembled one by one as had long been the case. The department was entrusted to Ciccio Montanari with various team leaders, as Gino Bertocchi had asked to take his retirement. The car assembly department was entrusted to Rino Ragazzi, while the management wanted Oscar Gnoli, the multilingual motor engineer, to head the Experimental Department, which I often worked with, as he was the most experienced person in this area. All this had caused a bit of an upheaval as Cleto Grandi, who had always acted as head of that department, did not intend to give up his job.

One afternoon I was about to go out on with an Indy to which I had fitted the instrumentation used for brake testing. For some time now, in fact, Bertocchi had been complaining about a slight whistle on the Indy cars under light braking. Ingegner Alfieri had ordered other types of pads that he had instructed me to try out, believing that they were to blame for this annoying whistling noise. Personally, I thought it more likely that the cause was due to external factors such as humidity, but Ingegner Alfieri believed that the guilty party was the material used for the pads. The problem had become serious because even the new pads sometimes did the same thing, without making the brakes unsafe, because under heavy braking, with sustained pressure on the pedal, everything was fine, while with a very light touch on the brake pedal, you could hear this whistling noise that was really annoying. I was just getting into the car when Dr. Drieux asked me if he could come with me.

As we were driving along, he asked me about the tests, about my work in general and I explained to him about the connection I maintained between the Technical Office and the workshop. I apologized if he thought I was interfering in the problem of the Experimental Department, and said that Gnoli, in addition to being a good motor engineer, also spoke German and French, having been a prisoner of war, but that in my opinion he was not suitable to be in charge, while Grandi was indeed a very good test driver but also had the necessary determination to lead the department. He replied that he would keep my suggestions in mind, then asked me about my family and, while we were chatting, I measured the pedal pressure, the deceleration figures and the hourly speed, making a few stops to note down the various data. Dr. Drieux told me that he knew I was also organizing the Turin Motor Show, that I allowed journalists to try out the cars and that sometimes I invited customers or enthusiasts to visit the workshop. Then he told me that the majority of my work had more to do with what they did in the Commercial Office than the Technical Office. He therefore intended to set up a special office to monitor technical documentation. I outlined the difficulties I would be faced with if I worked outside the Technical Office. In fact, the information required for the owners' and maintenance manuals and the spare parts catalogues, which I used for the preparation of itemized lists, news and direct contacts with my fellow designers, would be missing. He reassured me that I would not have any difficulty as the Technical Office would have more staff and would give me all the necessary information. Furthermore, Manfredini, repèonsible for combing the workshop for some deserving youngsters for office assignments, had already been instructed to find four youngsters for the SD Office, the Documentation Service. When we got back Dr. Drieux complimented me on my driving style and said that he would call me into the office in a few days' time.

After handing over the car to the Experimental Department, I immediately went in search of Ingegner Alfieri, to inform him of what I had found out about my position and that I regretted I would no longer be working for him. He told me that he was already aware of this because he had attended the meeting about the organisational chart with Ingegner Malleret, Dr. Drieux and Ingegner Nicoletti. I realised that he was disappointed too, after fifteen years of mutual esteem and trust, but Maserati was becoming industrialized and he more than anyone else had to be aware of the new set-up of all the stages of the production process.

A few days later I was called to Dr. Drieux's office where he told me, in the presence of Ingegner Malleret, of my promotion to first-class administrator with a significant increase in salary. Shortly afterwards, Dr. Torrusio also came in. I had already met him, and he told me that my new office was waiting for me and that there would be a lot of work to do. However he assured me that, although I had a lot of skills to acquire and he was my direct superior as sales manager, I would still remain independent in my work looking after technical issues.

After leaving the Direzione Generale office, I followed Dr. Torrusio to our new offices. My new boss was a true gentleman and I imagined he had very high class origins. He was married but had no children, he spoke four languages and he was also quite talkative. I moved in with my desk, my drawing board and a cabinet with drawers for the drawings. I had asked Manfredini to allocate a lad to me who had recently started work in the Technical Office, who I knew to be very good at drawing in perspective, and who I needed so as not to have to rely on Signor Cavara who, being an outside freelancer, was not always available when he was needed. Manfredini told me that he would also give me a good lad from the Customer Relations Department. When I found out who he was, I agreed, as he could be used for the technical manuals, as he was a motor specialist. As for the other two I did not agree but there was nothing I could do about it, it was a waste of time complaining, in the end I had to accept them for a six-month trial period to see if they would fit in, otherwise they would be replaced. This wasn't necessary, as even the laziest of them, who they didn't know what to do with in the workshop, became responsible and very disciplined, so much so that even Manfredini asked me how I had managed to bring about the change in him. It was easier than I had imagined. I immediately gave a talk to all four of them about what we would have to do and how we would work together and help each other. The next day I took the one with the bad reputation to one side and asked him what he wanted to do when he was a grown-up. He was already 22 years old and it was time for him to realize that he was a man. I immediately made him responsible for some quite demanding jobs and after about a year he had become pretty good and much more responsible. He had a strong personality and wanted to show that he was worth as much as his other colleagues on the team.

I was surprised at how well things were going. Even the way the various advertising brochures were produced for our cars was no longer as makeshift as it used to be. In the early Sixties, Ingegner Bertocchi used to ask me to have our photographer make some colour slides of the new models of our cars. Everything was done on the cheap. During the homologation tests I used to go and pick up the photographer then, along the way, if we found a suitable place to use as a background, he would take some photos and always asked what I thought of them. Next the photos considered to be most suitable were chosen and one or two thousand copies were printed with the technical data. Since then I had earned a reputation as a choreographer for good taste in choosing the backgrounds of my photographs. Under the new management, Dr. Torrusio, wanting to do things in a more professional way, booked a photo agency, where I went with the car to be photographed, and then they thought about everything else, the choice of photos, the layout and format of the brochure.

Nothing was improvised within the company any more. We were no longer the craft workshop of the past, everything was planned at meetings and agreements were reached between the various managers. When the company canteen became operative, the times of the lunch break had also changed, from 12 to 1 for factory workers and from 1 to 2 for administrative staff. Personally, I only used the canteen a few times. I always preferred to go home, even though it was a bit of a race. But the two short kilometres from Maserati to my house meant that I could eat with my loved ones and see my son start to take his first steps.

MASERATI BORA

I was still in the Technical Office when I saw my draughtsman and chassis builder colleagues tackling the trend for placing the engine at the back of the car that was progressively establishing itself. After a good deal of discussion as to whether the side members should be used as fuel tanks (this idea was eventually discarded thanks to the emerging concerns over safety), a chassis in sheet metal was designed. A subframe in square-section tubes was attached to the back of the tub to carry the engine, gearbox and rear suspension. Giorgietto Giugiaro of Italdesign came up with innovative and very compact bodywork on a monocoque tub with an original roof panel in stainless steel, pop-up headlights, a capacious boot and a vertical rear screen dividing the cockpit from the engine bay enclosed by a large hatch. Initially it was fitted with the tried and trusted 4700 cc V8 delivering 290 hp and from 1975 with the 4930 cc unit providing 310 hp. As well as by its performance, the coupé was distinguished by excellent roadholding, agile handling and a well-soundproofed cabin. The exclusive features included a sliding pedal box (adjustable through 15 cm) and a tilting driver's seat, both hydraulically actuated via the high pressure Citroën system used for the brakes. The car was presented at the Geneva Motor Show in March 1971 with the name Bora after the strong north-easterly wind. In 1972, at the Turin Motor Show, Italdesign presented the Boomerang, an evolution of the Bora with a curvaceous external profile, a theme that many other coachbuilders were beginning to explore.

By the time the Bora went into production, Maserati was owned outright by Citroën. Commendator Orsi remained as Honourary President through to his death in November 1972. The Bora was also the first Maserati to use Citroën components, in particular the hydraulic system. When the French importer Jean Thépenier came to pick up his third Bora in March 1972, he had the opportunity to have it tested by a young driver on the Le Mans circuit. The lap times were so encouraging that it was only natural to think that if such results could be achieved with a production car, then a suitably prepared and tuned car could compete with the cars of other manufacturers. Thus it was that out of ordinary musings of Monsieur Thépenier was born a proposal for Ingegner Alfieri to prepare a Bora that met the regulations of the international Group 4 Prototypes class. Two cars were built, one with a 4700 cc engine the other with a 4900 cc unit, both specially prepared with a significant increase in power. The most important modifications concerned the bodywork that was lightened at every possible point, the overall dry weight dropping to under 1300 kilos. The two coupés, finished in silver grey with slightly wider tracks, flared wheel arches and no covers over the headlights, had an attractive, aggressive and sporty appearance.

Unfortunately, the powers that be at Maserati failed to react with sufficient energy to the protests of the CSI (International Sporting Committee) concerning the number of Boras produced to obtain homologation in Gr 4 (special GT cars). In 1975, the two cars were sold in the Middle East but returned to Europe in the Nineties where enthusiasts have driven them in classic car competitions. There follows the letter sent to the national and overseas press by the Maserati management.

OFFICINE ALFIERI MASERATI S.p.A. - MODENA

Gli Ets. Thepenier-Maserati, importatori in Francia delle vetture Maserati, avevano espresso il desiderio, nel febbraio 1973, di far correre due BORA nel gruppo 4 (vetture gran turismo speciali).

Le Officine Alfieri Maserati, tenendo conto:
- delle possibilità della vettura
- dell'effetto pubblicitario certo
- della qualità dei piloti interpellati
- dell'effettiva possibilità di omologazione nel gruppo 4, se si tenevano in considerazione i criteri adottati nell'omologazione di vetture simili,
avevano dato una risposta favorevole a questo progetto.
L'officina aveva quindi realizzato le due vetture entro un periodo assai breve e, in qualità di costruttore, aveva richiesto l'omologazione della vettura BORA.

Con la lettera del 13 settembre 1973 la C.S.A.I. (Commissione Sportiva Automobilistica Italiana) ci comunica ora, la decisione presa dalla C.S.I. (Commission Sportive Internationale), durante la riunione del 7 settembre 1973 a Milano:
"... la Sottocommissione, all'unanimità non ha ritenuto possibile accordare alla vettura in oggetto l'omologazione nel Gruppo 4, Gran Turismo Speciale, poichè la produzione in 12 mesi consecutivi risulta inferiore al minimo previsto all'art. 251 dell'Allegato J. ..."

Quando consegnammo la nostra richiesta di omologazione, sapevamo di non aver prodotto 500 BORA in 12 mesi consecutivi, del resto i dati ufficiali dell'A.N.F.I.A. (Associazione Nazionale Fra Industrie Automobilistiche) lo provano.
Ma sapevamo anche, che tempi addietro, erano state omologate delle vetture la cui produzione non aveva raggiunto il totale di 500 in un anno; anche questo lo si può constatare dai dati ufficiali.

Queste vetture di piccola serie, come le nostre, contribuiscono ad incrementare l'interesse per lo Sport Automobilistico e ad animare le competizioni. E' spiacevole che la C.S.I., in base ad un regolamento unico, usi un metodo particolare nel calcolare le produzioni, che non si rivela invece uguale per tutti.

Dobbiamo rendere omaggio al personale della Maserati che ha partecipato alla realizzazione delle due vetture, con ardore ed entusiasmo, sperando almeno che questo sforzo non sarà vano e che presto o tardi la BORA potrà allinearsi nelle competizioni, sotto i colori degli Ets. Thepenier-Maserati.

28 Settembre 1973   LA DIREZIONE GENERALE

CONCOURS D'ELEGANCE, MOTOR SHOWS ET AL

As a manufacturer, Maserati had always and only organised its stand at the Turin Motor Show, which I had been personally involved with since 1963. All the other international show stands were instead the responsibility of the various importers. Present at one of the first meetings held by the new Commercial Director, Dr. Torrusio, were the head of the Italian and Foreign Sales Office, the Spare Parts Office, me from the Documentation Service Office and the newcomer Ingegner Moretti of the After-Sales Office. Among other things, it was decided that it should be Maserati rather than the importers, which should be responsible for the firm's stands at the most important international shows such as Paris, Frankfurt and Geneva, and that it would be my job to deal with the matter. I was already rather concerned, but it proved to be easier than expected. Mr. Aldo Sonvico, the Swiss importer, had various documents sent from the management of the Geneva Motor Show that indicated on the basis of the size of the cars to be exhibited the area in square metres that would have to be reserved. The Marta Pallet company from Lodi, our supplier of materials for the Turin Motor Show and which also set up stands for other car brands abroad, was commissioned to build the stand.

Geneva 1971, produced in collaboration with Signor Basadonna, our Geneva dealer, this was my first show abroad. I drove to Geneva with Dr. Drieux and Dr. Torrusio. As it was already late they dropped me off me at my hotel and Dr. Drieux insisted on coming to pick me up the next morning; I told him that wouldn't be necessary as the show was still in the city centre at the time and I had checked on the map and found that it was not far from the hotel. I was already on the stand very early the next morning. Dr. Torrusio and Dr. Drieux were eager to see if everything had been arranged as planned. Ingegner Malleret and Ingegner Alfieri also turned up the following day. On that occasion, I met all the Swiss dealers, including Signor Sonvico, with whom I had only previously spoken on the telephone.

I met a few journalists that I knew, including the photo-journalist Bernard Cahier, who at the time was also Good-year's opinion leader, and who was with Peter Ustinov, the famous actor and owner of a Quattroporte he kept at his Geneva home. Ustinov asked me a lot of questions about how to keep it during the months when he was away on business and it was not used. I think I was sufficiently comprehensive in my advice because for several years meeting Peter Ustinov became a regular event on the first day of the Geneva Motor Show; in fact, Mr. Ustinov always visited me and spoke to me about his Maserati.

Dr. Drieux and Dr. Torrusio complimented me on the organisation of the stand, agreeing that, in the future too, cars of the same colour would be exhibited together, coordinated with the colour of the carpet. After three days in Geneva, I made the return trip with Ingegner Alfieri let me in on the secret that the C.114 engine, expanded to 3000 cc, would be fitted to our new model.

In the office we were already well advanced with the production of the Bora's use and maintenance manual and would have it ready for the first deliveries of the cars, scheduled for October/November 1971. Over the following months instead the relative spare parts catalogue would be published. The promotional material was put together with the assistance of Italdesign and consisted of an envelope containing several black and white photographs of the Bora with relative technical files in various languages while the commercial brochure was produced by the new agency in Bologna, to which I had taken the car to be photographed.

A Concours d'Elegance had been held in Sorrento in September for several years, organized by the Automobile Club d'Italia. Bertocchi had always attended but that year Dr. Torrusio asked me to go with a Bora. The event, which involved various marques, was held from Friday evening to Sunday afternoon and was attended by numerous journalists and various celebrities. On the outward journey, in the vicinity of Chianciano, I was doing over 200 kph when a van in the distance moved out of its lane to overtake. I raised the headlights and flashed; the van tucked back in and I crushed the accelerator again. The van driver then probably evaluating the distance but not my speed put his indicator on again and began overtaking. As I touched the brake pedal the car skidded, the nose touched the guardrail and sent me spinning three or four times. In a moment that seemed to me to be endless, I imagined myself in a hospital bed with all my loved ones around me, but then I stopped with the car facing in the opposite direction. Fortunately, I was unharmed but was left speechless with shock and perhaps the regret for having damaged the car which was no longer presentable. Having made the necessary notes, I left the scene to look for a telephone. At the first exit I found a bar and spoke to Dr. Torrusio, explaining the problem and the fact that I could no longer go to Sorrento because the car was damaged. He reassured me and told me to go on to Florence; he, in the meantime, would have telephoned Signor Buratti, asking him to have ready for me the Bora he had picked up a few days earlier. I'd known our dealer in Florence for some time; he was so fastidious that I was unsure how he would have taken such a request. When I arrived at the workshop I found a yellow Bora ready and waiting. I arrived in Sorrento too late to be able to participate in the inaugural dinner. I made my apologies to the organizer who in the meantime had shown me the location and the position where I was to park the car, which would be exhibited along with the others to be admired by the jury and the public.

Even though I was staying in a magnificent hotel and a beautiful room, I had had great trouble getting to sleep thinking about what had happened to me. On Saturday morning, I went straight to the car to clean off the midges and dust from the trip, but I found it already clean and shiny: a team of young people from the organization was detailing all the cars on display. At lunch and on Saturday evening, I met several sports journalists whom I had met at the Turin Motor Show and others from the general press. On Sunday afternoon, after driving onto the podium in front of the Concours d'Elegance jury, I returned to Modena with the first prize trophy.

The week after I met Monsieur Guy Ligier, a great French driver and manufacturer of the JS berlinetta, powered by a Cosworth engine that was abandoned in 1972 in favour of our C.114 engine for the new JS2. Dr. Drieux instructed me to go to Monza with Ligier to check the times of the three different engines, as Ligier had brought three cars, one with a 2700 cc engine, a Citroën SM with a 3200 cc engine and one with a 3000 cc fuel injected engine. The JS2 with the 3000 cc carburettor engine set the best times. The car recorded a top speed of over 240 kph, covering the standing start kilometre in 27 seconds. The JS2 with our engines enjoyed a very successful career. Ingegner Alfieri was very keen on this kind of collaboration and even produced a four-valve engine specifically for Ligier.

MERAK AND MERAK SS

The new French management chose the name of a star from the constellation of the Great Bear for the new mid-engined car. Everything was in place to make considerable savings, both in design and production, as we had the Bora's chassis and parts of its bodywork at our disposal. The engine was the C.114 that had been in production since 1970 for the Citroën SM, with the displacement increased to 2965 cc, the stroke remained unchanged at 75 mm while the bore was increased to 91.6 mm; in this form the engine delivered 190 horsepower at 6000 rpm. The more compact dimensions of this engine made it possible to create a coupé with a 2 + 2 cockpit, a modified tail, a flat engine cover and two buttresses linking the tail to the roof. Extensive use was made of Citroën SM components including the dashboard, instruments, steering wheel and high-pressure braking system. The Merak immediately attracted great attention when it was presented at the 1972 Paris Motor Show, thanks both to its lower price and the greater space it offered compared to the Bora, which was a strict two-seater. It was very easy to drive and extremely comfortable, equipped with the air-conditioning that was standard on all of our cars. It was also on a par with its main rivals from other marques in terms of performance.

The Merak was the model I did the most mileage in and the one I had the most adventures with compared to all the others I drove. On the outward journey to the 1973 Geneva Motor Show in the demonstration Merak, I left at two o'clock, expecting to arrive in Geneva at around eight. However, a trivial mistake made of those who had fitted the gasoline tank, meant I eventually arrived at two o'clock at night. Once beyond Aosta, in fact, I noticed that there seemed to be a problem with the fuel supply as the engine was stuttering even though I wasn't yet in reserve. I could hear that the pump working and thought it might be a clogged filter. I found a garage and had the filter removed but it proved to be clean; I set off again after filling up with fuel, but around 50 kilometers later I experienced the same problem. Having found another garage I asked if they had a replacement electric fuel pump, thinking that the one fitted was perhaps defective. With the engine at idling and with my ear close to the tank, could hear a rolling sound, as if it wasn't working properly. Fortunately they had an Alfa Romeo electric pump that I asked them to install. By the time I set off again it was gone eight o'clock and had begun to snow. When I reached the exit to the Mont Blanc tunnel at 11 o'clock it was snowing very hard and the French gendarmes stopped me and refused let me proceed due to the conditions. I showed them the bag with my snow chains, which fortunately I had stowed behind the seat, saying that I would fit them immediately. As the gendarmes left, the truck in front of me drew out and I tucked in behind. Travelling at 20 kph I arrived at the Swiss border just outside Geneva where the Swiss customs officer decided to open my suitcase and put on a pair of white gloves to rummage around inside. A yellow Merak at one o'clock at night in such weather conditions had probably made him suspicious. In the morning I left the car in our dealer's workshop where, after having removed the pump and filter and emptied the tank, they found a large flap of rubberized paper originally used to seal the tank aperture before the filler cap was fitted. It had probably had fallen inadvertently into the tank and was obstructing the fuel flow when the level dropped and when it surged from one side of the tank to the other in corners.

Another adventure I had with a Merak involved Oscar Gnoli, our polyglot technician, who toured our dealers abroad, training their mechanics, but this time the car wasn't at fault. We set out together for the Frankfurt Motor Show in a beautiful red Merak, which I was subsequently to have used as a demonstration car. As we passed through Munich we stopped off at our German importer's to leave a spare part for an Indy. Signor Walter, partner and director of the company, spent a lot of time with us and also wanted to take us to dinner, but I was looking forward to arriving in Frankfurt to see if our stand was finished and conformed to what had been agreed with the fitter. We had a sandwich in the bar in the dealer's showroom and by the time we set off again it was already eight o'clock, which meant we didn't reach Frankfurt until late. As we came off the autobahn we could see the Hotel Continental. It was dark but the sign could be seen glowing from a distance, which cheered us up. We thought we had arrived, but instead trapped in a labyrinth of junctions, flyovers and underpasses we simply could not find a way to get to the hotel. Time passed and it was almost midnight when we stopped to study the road map and we saw a car approaching.

Gnoli jumped out and managed to flag the car down and with his good German he asked how to get to the Hotel Continental, which we could actually see from there. The man did not understand, he wasn't German, but French, so Gnoli switched to his perfect French and once again asked how to get to the hotel. It turned out that our saviour was staying there too and we were able to follow him. Gnoli stayed with Dr. Torrusio for the entire duration of the show, while I returned by plane with the Ingegner Malleret and Dr. Drieux.

The sales department had recently appointed a new dealer in Benevento who, in addition to Maserati, also represented Alfa Romeo. He had been sent an Indy and a Bora to put on display in his showroom in view of a probable sale. A few days later their mechanic called to say that Bora's clutch was defective. One of our mechanics was sent to replace it and found the plates to be completely worn out. The following week Ingegner Moretti was asked to send me to Benevento with a Merak and a clutch for the Bora. I arrived there just as the inauguration of the dealership was being celebrated in the presence of the mayor and the other city authorities. Such ostentation for the opening of what after all was a car dealership, even it was a Maserati one, left me speechless, giving me the impression that it was more a matter of paying homage to the owner of the company than to the marque represented. I expressed my doubts to Dr. Torrusio, who told me that he head known Signor Muciaccia for a long time, that he had already sold two of our cars and was highly respected. I replied that this was not enough and that only in a year's time we would have confirmation or otherwise of the man's worth. In the afternoon I went to the workshop to check on the problem with the Bora's clutch. I had thought that the cause of the wear of the discs might have been a problem with the assembly and adjustment, instead the mechanic informed me that the problems had emerged on the return of Signor Muciaccia's two sons, after a few tours around the city. Suspecting of improper use of the clutch, I contacted the two sons, a 22-year-old and a 25-year-old, and discovered that they had been accelerating hard with the clutch depressed to attract attention. I think I probably offended them by suggesting that they had a lot to learn about driving a car. I referred the matter to Dr. Torrusio so that he could inform the father of the pair that Maserati cars were not toys and that you had to know how to drive them.

In the evening, Dr. Torrusio received a phone call from Dr. Drieux about the inauguration of the Rome-Cologne shuttle train and that the management of the State Railways asked for the participation of all Italian car manufacturers. I was asked to take the Merak to Rome where I would meet Baraldi of the Commercial Office with an Indy, with both cars to be loaded on the train along with all the others. On this occasion the train had dining and sleeper cars to accommodate the numerous journalists and government representatives. Once we were underway, Baraldi and I went to the dining car where we got to know the Ferrari and Lamborghini representatives who had also brought two cars, while Alfa Romeo and Fiat each had four cars brought by their dealers. We spent a nice evening dining and talking to various journalists. When we woke up the following morning, we were speeding across the Rhineland and we were scheduled to arrive in Cologne at noon. We would then be guests of the German Tourist Board following an itinerary in the cars that took in Cologne, Bonn, Koblenz, Wiesbaden and Frankfurt over the course of five day. During the trip we would host various participants who wanted to experience trips in the different cars. The best restaurants and the most luxurious hotels had been booked, with visits to the most evocative sights in the various cities. It was a pleasant holiday, even though we were representing Maserati and always had to be well turned out and willing to chat and give technical explanations to the numerous members of the group. At one o'clock after lunch in Frankfurt, those of us with cars headed for home by road, while all the others returned to Rome by express train.

EXECUTIVE

For the trip to Germany, Baraldi and I agreed to complete the travel form marking ten hours a day, even though the hours had been much longer; a few days later, Dr. Drieux's secretary called me at the office making an appointment for me to see him the next morning at 9 o'clock. I'd been absent for about ten days, my lads had kept on working but they needed me for some decisions, moreover the Ingegner Moretti had also instructed me to prepare a time sheet for the various maintenance operations in dealers' workshops and with one thing and another I forgot about the appointment. The secretary consequently called me saying, "Dr. Drieux's waiting for you". I arrived almost at a run, apologizing. Dr. Drieux kindly invited me to sit down and asked me about the trip to Germany, which is when I saw that he had my travel expenses sheet in his hand. He asked me if the hours marked weren't a little excessive, given the nature of the trip. In all the years I had been travelling for the company there had never been any dispute regarding my hours and expenses. I never made a profit on meals, never claiming anything if I had been a guest, contrary to certain characters who claimed reimbursements for everything. I naturally had no difficulty in answering him, reminding him that I had been away from home ten days between Benevento and Germany, on the road and away from my family, while my colleagues of the same category were at home. The doctor smiled at me saying that I was right, but to remedy these problems I would be promoted to an executive position with a contract that no longer provided for the counting of hours, that meant I would no longer have to clock in and out of the factory, and of course my monthly pay would also be raised.

Maserati had grown from what had been almost a craft workshop into a true factory with all the relative regulations and the bureaucracy of its parent company Citroën. All this certainly brought with it many benefits to almost a thousand employees (as we now numbered). However, many of these regulations went against the habits of our customers, who were used to visiting the factory, sometimes even to see their new car being finished. For safety reasons, it was decided that it was only possible to collect the car from the customer services department after repair or service once the correct invoice had been paid. Count Grandi came to withdraw his Bora, accompanied by his factor who had then immediately left. The Count was told by the head of department that he would not be able to take delivery of the car if he did not settle the bill beforehand. The rather surprised customer said he only had a few Lira and his driving license, but he would send the money immediately, as soon as he arrived home. Dr. Torrusio also spoke to Ingegner Malleret, but there was nothing he could do: "Rules are rules and must be respected". Count Grandi called a taxi and that afternoon sent his representative to pay the bill and collect his Bora, which he sold shortly afterwards. The owner of a immense estate between Albareto and Carpi, the Count was an important customer that we lost due to directives perhaps better suited to the sale of consumer cars. Numerous importers were replaced in various nations by Citroën companies. Since the Sixties I had maintained relations with customers and dealers and tried to explain to Dr. Torrusio and Ingegner Moretti, my direct superiors, of the errors and the inappropriate ways in which our cars were being marketed. When Guerino Bertocchi came into conflict with these new directives he left Maserati and went to De Tomaso, where his engineer son was already working. We had lost the Maserati figurehead, the oldest employee, the chief test driver whose innate sensitivity and skill in driving at high speeds was universally recognised and with whom, because of his character, I had sometimes quarrelled but then always made up; in fact, we shared a mutual esteem and our passion for Maserati.

In all these events my private life had also changed. Giordana had learned from one of her clients, who had high placed acquaintances, that expropriations had been made at Montecreto by the Comunità Montana to build a road reaching the sports center. One Sunday in September a few weeks later we went to see our land with our great chestnut tree, and we found, albeit still in an embryonic state, the route of the road traced out that would allow us to get to our land by car. We saw that a dismantled crane had been deposited on the land adjacent to ours, which the surveyor Ballotti had told me was the property of a certain Rubbiani who had an Alfa Romeo service garage on Via Bonacini. On Monday evening, on my way home from work, I stopped at the garage and introduced myself to Signor Rubbiani, whom I had already seen in Monte-creto. I found out that he had already received approval for the construction of a small house shared between him and his sister and that he had commissioned a certain Tintorri of Aquaria to do the building work. On Saturday afternoon, after lunch, my father and I met the Tintorris, the father and his two sons, who were assembling the crane; we introduced ourselves and asked them to build our own house as well, immediately showing the project I had been working on for some time, which only had to be signed off by a qualified surveyor. They had positioned the crane, but the boom wouldn't have reached us. We tried to persuade them, saying that it was a just small house 7 metres by 9 and then my father eventually convinced him thanks to the many acquaintances he had among the people of the village from the time of the Academy Cadets camp. In the end, the deal was done and we agreed on payments every two weeks as the work progressed. I still have the receipts from Signora Tintorri's restaurant-bar where I left the advance payments when I passed through Acquaria. That same Saturday, we visited the surveyor and left my project with him to be worked up into finished drawings for presentation to the local authorities and the land register. Another dream was coming true.

In December 1973, I obtained from the bank access to credit for holiday homes, after presenting photographs of the part-finished house complete with its roof. The loan, repayable in five years, allowed us to complete the construction of the house. Using the beams from the house in Modena, my father had made the beds and bedside tables in addition to panelling the ceiling in wood and used the largest to build the front porch. Being partly protected by a small hill on the north side, the balcony, accessed via steps made with railway sleepers and covered by the porch, gave it an attractive mountain hut appearance. As a family we couldn't wait to be able to use it and in Modena we had already started to put to one side numerous things to to be taken into the mountains. Dad was instrumental in the completion of the house and spent almost the entire summer of 1974, from June to September, in a pension in Montecreto, working every day with the local carpenter on doors, windows, closets and everything else that required woodworking.

NEW MODELS ON THE HORIZON

The Ghibli had been in production for five years now and despite its beautiful lines the time had come to replace it. Ingegner Alfieri, who always paid close attention to economic issues when drawing up new designs, decided to use the mechanical foundations from the Ghibli with the 4930 cc dry sump V8 engine and the same ZF S530 transmission. The new features were instead the load-bearing bodyshell rather than the tubular frame, the independent rear suspension, the high-pressure braking system and the steering rack with progressive servo assistance. The bodywork, designed by Gandini for Bertone, featured elegant 2 + 2 berlinetta styling with compact lines and an agile wedge-shaped profile, the truncated tail featuring a transparent glass panel. The new car was presented at the Paris Motor Show in October 1973 and named Khamsin, after the wind blowing in the Arabian Peninsula. The engine, delivering over 280 hp, allowed a speed of 275 km/h in complete safety with an extraordinary road holding. The first deliveries began in March 1974; personally, when I had the opportunity to drive the Khamsin, I was at first very disappointed. It had very light self-centring steering; this wasn't great for as I've always preferred fairly heavy steering. However, once I got out of the traffic and could increase my speed, the steering weighted up, giving me more and more security and after about fifty kilometres I began to appreciate the car's strengths.

I personally had confirmation of Khamsin's extraordinary talents when I went on a test with Peter Deatwyler, the 1957 European Mountain Champion with our 200S. This gentleman had already owned two Ghibli's, which he told me were great, but when he tried the Khamsin he was amazed at the handling and roadholding. However, he gave me quite the fright as he was drifting through every corner.

As the Quattroporte also needed rejuvenating, Ingegner Alfieri was almost obliged to adopt all the mechanicals and hydraulics of the Citroën SM, including the chassis with the modified wheelbase of 3050 millimetres and the three-litre C.114 engine that had long been fitted to the SM in place of the 2700 cc unit. At a technical meeting attended by the entire general, technical and commercial management staff, it was necessary to decide, among other things, whether to use Maserati or Citroën engine part codes in the spare parts catalogue. When it came to the C.114 for the new saloon, I was unable to keep my peace and expressed my opinion very energetically, so much so that Dr. Torrusio gave me a tap on the leg to make me understand that I should moderate my tone. I simply said that mounting a three-litre engine in a saloon weighing less than 2000 kilos was absurd, as the V8 was available in several different versions. Ingegner Malleret said he that agreed, but the Paris directives said otherwise. Ingegner Alfieri, eager to show that something new could be done while still paying attention to economic, had the idea of creating a new engine in the same way as we had done with the C.114 for which we started out by cutting two cylinders off our V8. He took two three-litre C.114 engines, one of which had the two front cylinders cut and the other the two rear cylinders cut. Welded the two together would have resulted in a V8 of almost 4000 cc

291

with over 250 horsepower; all you needed to do was build four new camshafts and the crankshaft; all the remaining parts, pistons, connecting rods, water and oil pumps, were the same as the C.114. The engine was fitted with some difficulty to Ingegner Alfieri's company SM, and he covered about ten thousand kilometres in it.

The Geneva Motor Show of March 1975 saw the presentation of the Merak SS: this new version had a 210-horsepower engine, the Bora dashboard and leather upholstery as standard. That year I was able to have the stand set up by a new company in Turin that was much more professional and experienced in the use of various materials for display purposes. On the podium, raised by eight centimeres and covered with burgundy carpet, I had placed an Indy 4900, a Bora, a Khamsin and a Merak, all finished in Ischia blue, while the Merak SS was red, emphasizing its novelty. The compliments of Ingegner Malleret and Dr. Drieux were fulsome and very welcome when they saw the new set-up.

Ingegner Alfieri was busy with Signor Frua, the well-known stylist, Dr. Drieux was occupied with the various European importers, and I had noticed a strange coming and going of our French executives to the Citroën stand and vice versa, to the extent that I pointed it out to Dr. Torrusio, who minimizing things said that it would be a normal exchange of information between compatriots, executives of the same company. At the Paris and Turin Salons, however, I had never noticed similar activity. Dr. Torrusio and Baraldi remained in Geneva while I returned with Ingegner Alfieri on the third day after the inauguration. He informed me that Signor Frua was building a new Quattroporte with Indy mechanics to offer to our dealers while waiting for the hybrid that Citroën had decided to put into production with the three-litre C.114 engine. I also mentioned to Ingegner Alfieri the strange movements I had seen between our stand and that of Citroën, which was unusual compared to Paris, Turin and Frankfurt. He too, felt that it was a matter of normal discussions between senior executives, but he also said that we had to expect big news.

THE COLLAPSE OF CITROËN

On the 22nd of May 1975, the Maserati management announced the liquidation of the factory in an official press release. The warning signs had been there to see in that Maserati, to a greater extent than other firms, was suffering from the oil crisis, speed limits and other restrictions imposed on large displacement luxury cars. However, no one could really have foreseen the collapse, not even the trade unions, who enjoyed a great deal of respect and consideration. The true reason, as was later known, was the transfer of control of Citroën from Michelin to Peugeot, which had given rise to the major PSA group, which required the closure of all subsidiaries with low profitability.

The company was too important for the city of Modena, for what it had given Italy, but above all for the more than 900 workers left without work. There was therefore a general mobilization, both on the part of the trade unions and also all the political forces of the city and beyond. Ingegner Alfieri and Dr. Torrusio immediately went to great lengths to find an industrialist or company interested in our factory. An ugly situation had been created, with the French executives fleeing in a hurry and a new director arriving from Paris with the task of leading the process of shutting down all relations with the various importers and dealers. For the employees, access to the wages guarantee fund was requested. The trade unions were on a war footing, organising parades through the city streets and meetings with political forces, in particular with the then mayor, Dr. Germano Bulgarelli. Ingegner Alfieri was very worried because no company was interested in Maserati, there were rumours that Dr. Torrusio had opened negotiations with Arab acquaintances but then that possibility too faded away. Meanwhile, the exodus of many workers to competing companies had also begun and, fortunately, over a hundred young people had found new jobs. Sadly, however, there were many older workers, who joined the firm in the Seventies, who would have struggled to find a new job. The trade unions worked hard to negotiate early retirement formulas so that, numerically, another hundred was removed from the total number of employees. To all intents and purposes, just a few more remained than those who had been working under the Orsi family management before the transfer to Citroën. All this turmoil went on during the period of the wages guarantee fund, between mid-June and November. Maserati was practically closed for more than four months; only a dozen or so people were still going into work, including employees from the sales and export department and workers in charge of preparing and shipping the last cars sold abroad. In the meantime, the internal union had set up a picket line in front of the factory, 24 hours a day, various demonstrations and meetings with the local community were called in the square in front of the factory and attended by many of the city authorities.

I took advantage of this period to go often to Montecreto, to lend a hand to my father who was up there from June. We wanted to finish the holiday home so that we could inaugurate it and spend August there. On the 22nd of June we obtained all the necessary permits and mains water. While we still had to complete the laying of the carpet on the upper floor, on the lower floor, the rooms were already finished both with salvaged furniture and other new pieces gradually brought up from Modena. Another dream was about to come true and in August all my family and my in-laws were in our new holiday home in the mountains. The perimeter wall, the gates and the paths were completed the following year. That August of 1975 I devoted most evenings to reading and correcting a volume of the book by Luigi Orsini and Franco Zagari, *Maserati. Una storia nella storia*, regarding which sponsorship had already been agreed with the previous management but it had not yet been allowed to go to print because of the problems that supervened. The authors were now searching for a publisher, which they eventually found in the Libreria dell'Automobile, which was willing to print the two volumes rapidly, in both Italian and English.

GEPI - DE TOMASO

Maserati avoided bankruptcy thanks to the interest of the then Minister of Labour Carlo Donat-Cattin, who set GEPI (the state company for industrial investments) in motion. The entire operation was conducted by Alejandro de Tomaso, who partnered GEPI in the take over of Officine Alfieri Maserati on the 12th of August 1975. For some years, de Tomaso, again under the aegis of the Italian State's involvement in the rescuing of companies in difficulty, had a controlling interest in Moto Benelli of Pesaro and Moto Guzzi of Mandello al Lario. It should be remembered that prior to the agreement with Citroën, de Tomaso had already been in contact with Commendator Orsi with a proposal to purchase Maserati on behalf of Ford, an offer that had, however, been rejected. Suspecting that Ingegner Alfieri, with whom there had never been any esteem or sympathy in the past, was behind this refusal, as soon he set foot in Maserati, de Tomaso's first move was to order the dismissal of Ingegner Alfieri and all the directors. He seemed determined to humiliate them and even obliged Ingegner Alfieri to leave his SM in the company and return home in a worker's Fiat 500. What remained of the Technical Office was transferred to De Tomaso Automobili, while Signor Omer Orsi was provisionally called in as general manager, assisted by Ingegner Bertocchi. The latter was responsible for the regrouping of the various importers and dealers.

I was called back to the factory by a phone call from Signor Omer early in September, because the usual formalities for the Geneva Motor Show had to be completed in various phases otherwise there was a risk of being excluded. When I met Bertocchi, we embraced and, as usual, he said to me, "*Voglia di lavoro, saltami adosso*" ("Come on then, get on with it"). He was the same volcanic leader of men I had always known, perhaps with even more desire to get things done given the joy of returning to Maserati, a company to which he was so attached and which he had had to leave due to misunderstandings with the Citroën executives. De Tomaso, in keeping with his reputation as an adventurer, immediately irritated many journalists. There were only a few newspaper editors to whom he was very attached, while he treated all the others very badly, especially those who questioned his pronouncements regarding the relaunch of Maserati. In addition, at the first meeting requested by the unions and the internal commission, he came into the office and before he down pulled out a gun and placed it on the table. I was later told that they were all shocked, but then the representative of the FIM CISL, coolly told him he could put away that thing because there were no criminals present. This climate of hostility was never extinguished; on the contrary, over time it generated increasing conflicts. In a move designed to demonstrate desire to diversify output, Signor de Tomaso stated that he planned to put Benelli-powered three-wheeler into production and within two or three weeks a vehicle had been put together that ran within the factory while waiting to be bodied. It was intended as an urban goods delivery vehicle.

One morning, on arriving at the factory, we found Professor Romano Prodi in the courtyard, who had been appointed as Maserati's CEO by GEPI. He was waiting for the new owner who was still in his office on the phone.

The professor was very talkative, he spoke with enthusiasm about the things that Signor de Tomaso was about to do and assured us that the company would recover. Meanwhile, the Chassis Department was working at full capacity, as all the Benelli and Guzzi metalworking work had been transferred to Maserati. I was on my own in the office, my two best lads had found other jobs: one at Lamborghini while the other had gone to assist Ingegner Casarini on the type approvals, as in order to generate immediate vitality and resume production, Signor de Tomaso had put a new car into development. He mated the chassis of the De Tomaso Longchamp, with our V8 engines of 4200 cc and 4900 cc, a ZF mechanical gearbox or on request a Chrysler automatic, independent four-wheel suspension with the original body designed by Tom Tjaarda and restyled by Frua. Unfortunately, nothing original ever comes out of this kind of manipulation. Frua created a classic three-box coupé, quite nicely balanced, for which the name Kyalami was chosen, as all the Maserati four-seaters were named after circuits at which our cars had won races. I immediately started work on the preparation of the spare parts catalogue and the use and maintenance manual. I was finalizing the tables for the catalogue when Ingegner Bertocchi turned up in the office and wanted me to go with him to Signor de Tomaso to show him the work that was almost ready to be sent out to be printed. Signor de Tomaso looked quickly at a few plates, nodding his head, and then said, "I've got someone at Benelli, so what". I was hardly expecting compliments, but neither an attitude of total disregard. Once we had left the office, Bertocchi told me not to worry as he was like that with everyone at Maserati, he liked to humiliate people. The Kyalami was presented at the Geneva Motor

Show in March 1976, displayed alongside the Merak SS, the Bora and the Khamsin.

I had gone to Geneva with the truck carrying the cars but we were late. I had only half an afternoon to position the cars and finish the stand, as the press preview was scheduled for the next day. The following morning I arrived in the salon early to make the final touches; shortly afterwards Ingegner Bertocchi arrived with Guerino from the De Tomaso stand came and then Signor de Tomaso also turned up and began to make a big fuss because he didn't like the wheels of the Kyalami: he had in fact ordered that those of Longchamp be fitted. Ingegner Bertocchi tried to explain why the situation had arisen, but all that achieved was to further enrage de Tomaso, who ordered the immediate replacement of the wheels. I ran to look for the lads from Bordi, the stand fitters, who were gathering up their things from the various stands they had finished, asking them to get me a board for the jack so as not to ruin the carpet. There were numerous journalists observing the scene as I, one wheel at a time, changed the four rims with my colleague from De Tomaso. I then asked Ingegner Bertocchi, who had assisted us, whether it was worth it and his answer was, "What can you do, he likes to show who's boss". When Signor Sonvico, our Swiss importer, and Signor Basadonna, the Geneva dealer arrived and I'd told them what we had had to do, they told me that they preferred the wheels that were fitted before. A question of taste. When Signor Frua arrived the next day, I also told him about what had happened and he complained about Signor de Tomaso's behaviour during the preparation of the prototype.

That year we didn't have any demonstration cars in Geneva and I had to stay for the entire 10 days of the Show, 11 rather, given that on the Monday I had to wait for the truck to load the cars and returned with Guerino Bertocchi who gave me a ride in the Longchamp that he was testing. At Maserati in the meantime, they had completed those 12 Quattroporte IIs with Citroën mechanicals and Bertone bodywork, to make the most of all the available components. The cars were then sold with no type approval certification in Arabia where no formalities were required. The three-wheeler project that had served to silence certain gossip mongers had already been completely abandoned.

HOTEL CANALGRANDE
HEADQUARTERS

Ever since he arrived in Modena in 1956 with his second wife, Isabelle Haskell, Alejandro de Tomaso had been living at the Hotel Real Fini in Largo Garibaldi. Around 1970 he had the opportunity to buy the newly refurbished Hotel Canalgrande, where he established his headquarters. Having to manage no less than six companies entrusted to him by GEPI, he needed a secretarial staff which he drew from Maserati and which he instructed to behave with his own arrogance towards those people he was not interested in, especially journalists asking for information. The De Tomaso factory, located in the Modena Nord area, where the Ford-engined Pantera, Deauville and Longchamp were built, was to all intents and purposes managed by Signora Isabelle. She created a Technical Design Office within the factory, integrating it with a number of the designers from Maserati and other factories under De Tomaso management. One of the hotel annexes was converted into the office of Signora Luisa Valdevit, Signor de Tomaso's new companion, who had placed in charge of New Callegari of Ravenna before returning in 1980 to Maserati to direct the press and public relations office. As a result, she also became my direct superior in terms of brochures, trade shows and external relations. Her son, Francesco Verganti, about twenty years old, had also joined Maserati with technical functions in the factory.

Unlike Santiago, one of de Tomaso's sons, who lived in Modena with his father, Francesco was uniquely polite and well-behaved a boy of his age. Santiago, his peer, instead tried all he could to resemble his father: he was rude, overbearing and unwilling to work.

In 1977-1978 Innocenti of Milan, then under the control of British Leyland, was abandoned by its British owners along with its workforce of around 3000 employees. GEPI then entered the scene and once again called in Signor de Tomaso to manage the Milan factory. In my humble opinion, I believe that the idea of Biturbo came to de Tomaso at that time due to the impellent need to keep the Innocenti workers occupied, given that in Milan there had been a long period of redundancy as production of Mini alone could not employ all the workers.

Late one afternoon, Bertocchi arrived in my office to tell me that Signor de Tomaso immediately wanted, for the following morning, a table detailing the technical specifications of all the two-litre engines in production around the world. I replied that such research took time, even though it was facilitated by the data published in the *Auto Revue* magazine. "Do as you please, but start right away and once you've finished, drop it off at the hotel on your way home so Signor de Tomaso can pick it up tomorrow morning from the reception desk. I'll let the gatehouse know you'll be working late, see you!" The first thing I did was to call home so they could bring me a couple of sandwiches and some fruit. I then immediately began consulting *Auto Revue* to get an idea of how many engines I would need to include on the list. I found about 40 units displacing between 1800 and 1999 cc produced by the various manufacturers. As I was about to start compiling the table I was called from the gatehouse because my children Gianna and Gianluigi had come to bring me the sandwiches. I was gone one o'clock at night by the time I had finished and I left the roll of paper at the Hotel Canalgrande at exactly 01:30 AM. The next morning, at around nine o'clock, Ingegner Bertocchi called and warned me that Signor de Tomaso was in the Technical Office to discuss the table. Many believe that the Biturbo engine is derived from the C.114 of the Merak but that's absolutely not true, it's completely different. All they have in common is the 90° V6 architecture.

NEW MODELS

Early in 1975, Frua was specifically commissioned to build two Quattroportes around the Indy mechanicals, but they remained at the prototype stage. Giugiaro's Italdesign had also used the Indy mechanicals as the basis of the Medici I and II, neither of which had been followed up and consequently remained merely concepts. With the approval and at the request of our two American importers, design work on a new saloon was started, as the Kyalami had not been homologated for the USA. Signor de Tomaso commissioned Giugiaro to design the third version of our four-door model. In a short order, Italdesign created a well-proportioned three-box car with sleek and slender lines, a characteristic trapezoidal grille with the Trident in the centre and dual rectangular headlights. A groove ran along the flanks from the nose, cutting across the front wheel arch and running across the top of the rear wheel arch to the tail. The interior was truly luxurious, upholstered in natural leather and finished with briarwood trim, and communicated an idea of great comfort. Rear-view mirrors, electrically controlled seats, central locking and an air-conditioned minibar for the rear seats completed an incredibly sophisticated means of transport. Powered by the 4200 cc V8 or on request the 260 or 290 hp, 4.9-litre the new Quattroporte could be had with either manual or automatic transmission and could achieve a top speed of between 230 and 240 kph. All-round independent suspension, servo-assisted ventilated disc brakes and power steering were mechanical features befitting the car's status. In November 1976 it caused a great stir on its presentation at the Turin Motor Show. With great difficulty I had managed to set up a reasonable stand, even though Signor de Tomaso found something to complain about regarding the floral decorations surrounding the cars. Some of the flowers were too tall and, according to him, obscured the grille a little, others were too low. The stand fitter had his work cut out but eventually the solution was found and finally, when he left, I could finish arranging the other four cars as per the agreed drawing. On the day of the press preview, the Maserati stand was invaded by journalists. Ingegner Bertocchi and I were not sure what to do or who to listen to, but then Signor de Tomaso arrived and dragged them all into the pressroom where he held his conference.

The oil crisis had raised the price of petrol, conditioning all companies and imposing many restrictions on the construction of new models. Moreover, in Italy, the energy crisis had a particular impact on taxes, as the VAT rate for cars powered by engines displacing over 2000 cc was 38%, compared with 19% for cars with smaller engines. To make up for the inevitable falls in sales, Maserati decided to reduce the capacity of the Merak engine to under 2000 cc, adopting bore and stroke dimensions of 80x66 mm to obtain a 1999 cc, 120 hp engine offering a top speed of 220 kph. The Merak was the only Maserati model that could be modified to comply with the new fiscal legislation. The Merak 2000 went into production in 1977 and was offered in two metallic colours, silver and light blue. It was distinguishable from its older sister thanks its black rather than chrome bumpers and black grille, conspicuous black trim along the flanks and an optional front spoiler.

Everything else was identical to the first series Merak 3000. The model remained in production through to 1983 as the SS Merak series 80.

In the meantime, a number of periodicals had begun to publish biting articles poking fun at the Quattroporte, which had been presented at the Turin Motor Show in 1976, but which had yet to go into production. Such was the resentment of certain journalists towards Signor de Tomaso that they chose to ignore the crisis affecting all flagship luxury cars and anything was fair game to attack a character who did nothing to make himself sympathetic.

Three years after its launch, the Quattroporte III finally went into production. At the 1979 Geneva Motor Show prices of 40 million Lire for the 4.2 and 42 million Lire for 4.9 were confirmed and deliveries began in May. The Maserati stand featured the four models in production: in addition to the new saloon, the Merak SS, the Kyalami and the Khamsin. Unfortunately, Signor de Tomaso's interference delayed proceedings. The organizers had assigned us a stand that was rather narrow and isolated compared to previous years. On the morning of the press preview, Signor Frua and Signor Bertocchi told me that we had to go and pick up Signor de Tomaso from the Hotel Richmond. I arrived in front of the hotel with the Merak SS I was testing and waited. After about ten minutes, Signor de Tomaso came out with his journalist friends Rancati and Evangelisti, who seeing me said, "Look, how kind, your Maserati guys have come to pick you up". But he refused to come with me and instead went with them. While trying to get back to the show I took the wrong exit and entered the car park under the lake. I had trouble getting out again and I arrived at the stand just as de Tomaso was screaming at Ingegner

Bertocchi because the stand was not in the main hall, as in previous years. Ingegner Bertocchi replied that it was his fault because he had kept all the registration documents on hold and only sent them after the due date. After that de Tomaso had nothing more to say and he left. To lighten the mood a little, I told the story of my adventure in the car park under the lake, which got a lot of laughs.

The next evening we were all invited to dinner by Signor Sonvico and Signor Frua arrived half an hour late, candidly apologizing and admitting that he too had taken a wrong turning and had ended up in the car park under the lake.

THE FIRST MASERATI RALLY, 1980

The complex industrial structure for the construction of the new car was being organized both at Innocenti in Milan, with regard to the chassis, bodywork, assembly and painting, and in Modena where an ultra-modern department for the machining of the cylinder block and heads was nearing completion in the first shed on the right. The structure was composed of 10 Olivetti machine tools, each carrying a drum of 50 numerically controlled tools, the boring machines were arranged so that a truck could run between them carrying and dropping of the piece to be worked and the finished component. All this was the work of Comau Robotics and was programmed automatically. The head of this new department was Francesco Verganti with three of our veteran workers.

As many periodicals continued to criticise the figure of Signor de Tomaso, Ingegner Bertocchi and I were tasked with organizing a Maserati rally with the aim of showing our clients and collectors the new facility to which the finishing touches were being put. Ingegner Bertocchi was given a very restricted budget and so we had to search for sponsorship, which we found thanks to Agip, a long-term supplier, and Marlboro, at the head of which was Baron Emmanuel de Graffenried, a former Maserati driver from the Fifties. Having set the dates for the 14th and 15th of June, we threw ourselves into the organization of the details for the two-day event. We were also assisted by the presentation of the first volume of Orsini and Zagari's book *Maserati. Una storia nella storia - Dalle orgini al 1945* (the second volume was completed in 1982). In the meantime, the cover of that first volume gave us the idea for a commemorative plaque for event with the same double Trident motif. From my lists, which I had kept updated since 1965, we drew the names of the various collectors, and eventually counted a total of over a hundred cars, although there was no guarantee they would all turn up; we had also invited the mechanics from the racing team and numerous celebrities. Unfortunately, a few weeks before the event we lost Signor Omer Orsi, a person both Ingegner Bertocchi and I were very close to. The news hit all those who had known him very hard.

On the Saturday morning around 70 Maseratis assembled in the car park in front of the factory. After a brief welcoming speech from Signor de Tomaso, there was a tour of the new department followed by a very abundant buffet and, in the afternoon, the presentation of the book on Maserati history. The first day concluded with dinner at the Hotel Canalgrande.

On the Sunday morning we met at the former Autodromo circuit where the cars were allowed to lap freely. Guerino Bertocchi and Gigi Villoresi had great fun driving our former Scuderia Camoradi Birdcage. We then convened at the Gatto Verde in San Venanzio at one o'clock for the farewell lunch and the presentation of the plaques to the owners of the cars. I'm sure there must have been some oversights on the part of the organizers, especially by those who were involved in an event of this kind for the first time. The few journalists invited nonetheless wrote kind words. They were particularly impressed by the advanced new department for the construction of the new

310

engine while our former drivers present attracted a great deal of attention, all eager to talk to Guerino Bertocchi, who sadly lost his life on the 13th of April 1981 aboard a De Tomaso car.

MASERATI BITURBO

By mid-October 1980, the new engine was on the test bench. The 90° V6 had bore and stroke dimensions of 92x63 mm, giving a displacement of 1999 cc, three valves per cylinder, a single camshaft per cylinder head, a Weber carburettor with two IHI compressors and electronic ignition: it was designed to deliver a power output of 180 hp at 6000 rpm. After a few days of running-in and tuning, Bertocchi called me while I was in the office and invited me to the final test. In the testing room, along with the De Tomaso men, were the designer, my friend, Ennio Ascari, Manfredini, the head of administration, and Ingegner Bertocchi. Shortly after my arrival, Signor de Tomaso also arrived, eyed me up from head to toe and in his usual authoritarian tone asked, "What are you doing here?" Bertocchi explained that he had invited me because I had considerable experience in the development of engines. His response was to say, "OK, OK... stay over there and learn how to build engines". After two or three sweeps at over 6000 rpm, both up and down, an output of 183 hp was recorded. When the engine was stopped there was a burst of applause. De Tomaso turned to me and said, "Did you see that power and how it revs?" I replied, "I have to congratulate you, it really is a nice engine with good power, but in my opinion the weather's quite cool now, when we're into June or July the two turbos will be sending too much hot air under carburettor dome and that'll cause problems". De Tomaso looked at me with contempt: "What are you talking about?

You don't know anything!" I shouted loudly enough for everyone to hear me, "I might not know anything, but we'll see who's right when the temperatures rise". I then said goodbye to everyone and went back to work. I knew that I'd shot myself in the foot, but I had been asked for an opinion and had expressed it, saying what I thought and what I thought was correct, namely that turbocharged engines with a carburettor won't work properly with temperatures of over 20°C. A fuel injected engine with turbocharging is instead unaffected by the ambient temperature.

Before leaving, Bertocchi called in to chat about what had gone on, telling me that I had been right to say what I thought and not to worry about the consequences. "You see, Ingegnere, they're all bootlickers and sycophants, they're all afraid to say what they think! De Tomaso isn't God!" Bertocchi then added that he would also have problems to solve as a fuel injection system would have greatly affected the price of the car: the only injection systems available on the market were produced by foreign companies and de Tomaso, out of respect for GEPI, only wanted Italian products and was waiting for Weber Marelli to be ready with its system. In the meantime, Pierangelo Andreani from the De Tomaso Styling Centre had completed the sleek and compact design for the bodywork, a coupé that echoed the style of the Quattroporte in the opulence of its interior that could accommodate five people. At the Innocenti plant in Milan, they were now ready for bodywork construction and general assembly.

For his part, Signor de Tomaso had chosen the 14th of December as the day for the car's presentation, indicated as the anniversary of the foundation of the Officine Maserati in 1914 although it was later ascertained that the correct date was the 1st of December. In any case, on the 14th of December 1981, a new car was presented to the press and to the many political authorities present in Modena. The Maserati factory was overflowing with people, all stunned by a three-box car of just 2 litres, with room for five and a top speed of over 215 kph. The interior fittings were of an extremely high standard, burr walnut, velour upholstery with air conditioning completed the equipment of the car, which benefitted from a VAT rate of 19% whereas its competitors with a similar technical specification attracted a rate twice as high. During the press conference held at the Hotel Canalgrande, Signor de Tomaso announced the list price of Biturbo, 16,700,000 Lire, leaving all those present amazed at what was a remarkably low figure. Unfortunately, given the ever-increasing inflation in Italy, by the end of spring 1982 the price had already risen to 19,000,000 Lire. The race to pre-order cars was incredible, with people even resorting to calling in favours. Despite that delays afflicting the first deliveries that slipped to December 1982, the price settled at around 22 million Lire.

In the meantime, Signor de Tomaso was vehemently criticised by the trade unions for the way he went about his business and his attitude towards them. In the first year of full production, 1983, more than 5000 Biturbos were built and the first reliability problems emerged (Might I have been right when I expressed my doubts?). Over the following years, a new, improved and enhanced version was presented every 14th of December. The original Biturbo spawned myriad versions and by the end of 1989 around 12,000 examples had been produced. The reliability issues with the engines, both the 2000 cc and 2500 cc version for foreign countries, were resolved with the introduction of Weber Marelli fuel injection from 1986. By then however, Maserati had lost a lot of customers, especially in the United States; reliability was improving but sales were dropping. Our fellow citizen, Maestro Luciano Pavarotti, had been adopted as our ambassador and when he arrived in America, Mr. George Garbutt, our agent, had a Quattroporte waiting for him that he used as his personal car, while when he returned to Italy, we brought another Quattroporte to his wife to use, which we then would then garage when he was away for months at a time. This was a way of promoting the marque, especially in the United States where Pavarotti was very famous. This arrangement lasted for a few years, through to 1990 when we had to withdraw from the American market due to the endless problems with the Biturbos.

JOYS AND SORROWS

At Maserati things weren't going as had been hoped and the De Tomaso management had brought chaos at every level. Personally, I was taken off the production of use and maintenance manuals and advertising brochures which was farmed out to Esseti of Bergamo, directed by Signor Cucchi, a lovely man with whom it was nonetheless a pleasure to work. In any case, I still had plenty on my plate, above all in the running of the after-sales service, together with Ingegner Meregalli of Innocenti and the secretary of the Hotel Canalgrande. There was an ever-increasing trade in our cars and I was having to devote more and more time to searching for data and information for our collectors.

Fortunately, I had my family to distract me from problems at work: Gianna had obtained a diploma as a nursery school teacher and had already been assigned her first supply teaching posts, while Gianluigi was attending middle school and was very close to my father, his Grandad Mario. Sadly, after a short illness my father passed away at 76 years of age on the 10th of March 1982, leaving a great void in the family and great pain. With his experience and wisdom he had helped me on may occasions throughout my daily life and the family as a whole lost a willing hand around the house and in the garden. Comforted by a saying that reminds us that in life things are never all good but at the same time never all bad, I put up with de Tomaso's many abuses as he had me supervised by his favourites from

Benelli or Moto Guzzi. However, what hurt me most of all was then I was unable to respond to one of his criticisms.

At the Geneva Motor Show in 1983 I had the Quattroporte test driven by a Swiss engineer who, a few months later, bought the car, telling me that in July he would be visiting Modena on the way to the seaside at Riccione with his wife and another couple of friends and that he would like to visit the Maserati factory. I went to meet him at the gatehouse; he was delighted with the car and had convinced his friend to buy one too. I apologised that I would be unable to show him around personally as I had people waiting for me in the office, but that I would have caught up with him later to say goodbye. I entrusted him to Silingardi, a good lad who they had recently given me as an assistant and whom I trusted because he really knew his job and knew how to treat people. While they were passing through the chassis department they me Signor de Tomaso who immediately called Manfredini to know who those people were. Manfredini explained that they were clients accompanied by Cozza's assistant. De Tomaso immediately had me called to go straight to his office. As soon as I arrived he started saying I had no authority to take clients into that department. I tried to defend myself but he wouldn't listen. He insisted on saying I wasn't authorised so I turned on my heels and left, saying as I went, "Well up yours... and all the louts like you!" I hurried back to my office and called Ingegner Bertocchi at De Tomaso and told him the whole story. He asked me whether I had received any instructions or ban regarding visits and I replied that he knew me, if there had been any rules I would have respected them. In any case, I told him that if I received any complaints or warnings I would have handed in my resignation. "Come on, don't do anything rash; if there are no rules then we'll have some fun. If he was just in a bad mood we'll soon change it." The following morning, as I had thought, the head of the personnel department arrived and handed me an envelope with a written warning to which I was to respond within three days. In my turn I handed him an envelope with my letter of resignation. After having read it he tore it up, so I tore up his. He then implored me, saying that he didn't know what to do with de Tomaso, to which I replied that I couldn't care less and "As you're a boot-licker you go and tell him I've no intention of justifying myself because I've done nothing wrong and caused no damage to the company, quite the contrary!" From then on I heard nothing more about the matter. I kept expecting to be called up, instead it was all forgotten.

In that period Gigi Villoresi, our former driver from the era of the Maserati brothers, a Maserati, Benelli and Guzzi dealer with his company Lambro Motori since 1976, had problems with the department of labour caused by his bookkeeper which led to a financial crisis. In order to avoid bankruptcy and possible imprisonment, he was obliged to sell all his property, with the exception of a small flat in Milan where he was living. In order to ensure he could earn a living, Signor de Tomaso took him on as our "opinion leader", frequently putting him up at the Canalgrande. We thus began attending the shows together and he would occasionally come to dinner at my home. On one such occasion I was able to tell him the story of my latest clash with Signor de Tomaso. They were friendly and would often dine together at the Canalgrande. Villoresi certainly had opportunities to bring the matter up with him and in fact, after a while, I began to notice a different attitude towards me.

THE MASERATI REGISTER

On the morning of the 6th of February 1985, a blanket of thick fog lay between Lodi and Milan and the Mini De Tomaso, driven by Corghi and carrying Ingegner Bertocchi and Barani, bound for Innocenti, crashed into a stationary lorry. Ingegner Bertocchi was killed instantly, a terrible tragedy. He left a wife and two daughters and also left the entire De Tomaso factory, of which he was general manager, in total despair. We at Maserati, who had worked together, lost a colleague, an untiring friend, a man with a great desire to get things done. I'd known him for over 30 years and had never seen him lose his temper. He had a wonderful temperament as well as an innate passion for work. During the De Tomaso period of management, whenever he visited Maserati, he never failed to come to see me; I spoke to him about the ever-growing interest in and requests for information regarding our classic cars and he always said to me, "Keep a note of everything, always write everything down, leave a trace in the files you consult, it'll come in useful one day."

In fact, as usual he was right and a few months after his death I was summoned to the Hotel Canalgrande for a meeting at which Count Giovanni Lurani, Signora Maria Teresa de Filippis and her husband, Ingegner Huschek, Gigi Villoresi and the notary Brancaccio were all present. They asked me about our collectors or owners of vintage cars and the number of cars built by 1960-1965, because Signor de Tomaso wanted to establish a Maserati Register with a statute and regulations. The notary, Dr. Brancaccio, had already prepared a draft statute, which he read out. He was interrupted several times and asked to make corrections, but in the end after various minor disputes, the statute of the Maserati Register was approved and launched. Gigi Villoresi was the President, with Signora de Filippis as his vice-president, Ingegner Teo Huschek the secretary, while the head of the technical commission was Ingegner Sergio Mantovani with Cozza and Sala.

19 June 2009, New Jersey (USA), in Mr. Auriana's showroom while I compliment him on his important collection of Maseratis, the largest in the United States and ranging from 1930 to 1965.

17 June 2009, Pocono (USA), talking to a group of Maserati collectors about the originality of this 8 CM single-seater that is currently a two-seater.

19 June 2009, New Jersey (USA), with Mr. Auriana alongside the ex-Giletti 1953 Mille Miglia A6GCS *2040*.

16 June 2009, Pocono (USA), observing one of the four A6GCS berlinettas bodied by Pinin Farina.

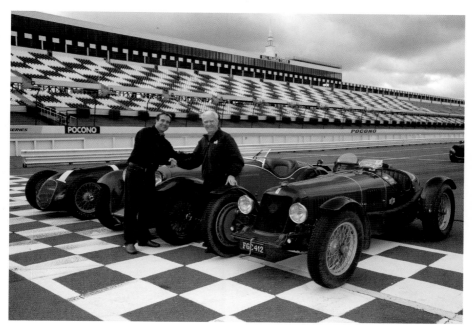

18 June 2009, Pocono (USA) circuit, Mr. Jeff Ehoodin of Maserati USA and I in front of three historic Maserati cars.

On that occasion, along with Joe Colasacco, one of Mr. Auriana's mechanics, I was testing the 1930 16-cylinder V4, bodied by Zagato.

The publication dedicated to my 60th anniversary at Maserati titled "Cozza 60" and published by the firm itself in 2011.

October 2001, Historical Challenge Ferrari-Maserati Monza, Borsari and I, Maserati officials, during scrutineering.

23 October 2001, the "Cozza 60" anniversary, at the table with me on that occasion were, on the left, Carlo Maserati (son of Ettore, one of the legendary brothers) and right, the grandson of Marquis Diego de Sterlich, the Maserati brothers' first patron, Alberto de Sterlich Aliprandi.

Another shot from a Historical Challenge Ferrari-Maserati. This time we are at the Mugello in 2005 and seen aboard Marc Davis's 200S is Maria Teresa de Filippis, the first woman in Formula 1 and a former Maserati driver.

15 June 2009, New Jersey (USA). Here we are in the Maserati USA headquarters with all the staff.

23 October 2011, the Maserati showroom, celebrating my 60th anniversary at Maserati.
In the photo below, from the left: George Mauro, Giovanni Perfetti, Dr. Marco Armillei,
Dr. Adolfo Orsi, me and Dr. Luca Dal Monte.

23 October 2011, the Maserati showroom. Cozza 60°. Me together with my family, my beloved children with their respective consorts, alongside a beautiful Maserati 3500 GT.

18 September 2014, Festa 100° Maserati, Piazza del Nettuno, Bologna.
I am with Fabio Collina alongside the Quattroporte from 1966.

Again on the occasion of the centenary, this time in Piazza Grande, Modena, here I am showing the splendid Pinin Farina-bodied A6GCS berlinetta to Maserati CEO Ingegner Harald Wester and the mayor of Modena Giancarlo Muzzarelli.

20 September 2014, Festa 100° Maserati, Piazza San Carlo, Turin. A moment during the Concours d'Elegance.

MASERATI

Modena, ottobre 2014

Gentile Signor Cozza,

il Maserati Centennial Gathering è stato un enorme successo e mi auguro che l'evento sia stato all'altezza delle sue aspettative. Più di 200 straordinarie Maserati, 500 appassionati provenienti da 30 paesi, splendide parate, meravigliose esposizioni, un Concours d'Elegance e una cena di gala in una maestosa reggia italiana: le celebrazioni del Centenario sono state tutto questo e molto altro ancora.

Naturalmente, nulla di tutto questo sarebbe stato possibile senza il supporto di appassionati come lei e vorremmo ringraziarla della sua gradita partecipazione condividendo con lei alcuni dei momenti salienti di questo evento irripetibile. In allegato le inviamo una chiavetta USB Maserati Centennial contenente un'ampia galleria di immagini raccolte durante gli indimenticabili tre giorni trascorsi insieme.

Saremo per sempre in debito e riconoscenti per la sua passione, che ha contribuito a rendere il Maserati Centennial Gathering così speciale, siamo certi che conserverà a lungo nel suo cuore i ricordi di un evento davvero unico e memorabile.

Cordiali saluti,

H.J. Wester

MASERATI S.p.A. Viale Ciro Menotti 322 - 41121 Modena - Italy - Tel. +39 059 590511 - Fax +39 059 226765 - www.maserati.com

October 2014, a letter from the Maserati CEO Ingegner Harald Wester paying compliments for the success of the Maserati centenary celebrations. Below, the jury of the Concours d'Elegance in Piazza San Carlo, Turin.

A number of books dedicated to the history of Maserati, including the company's official centenary book. Over the years, I made my contribution to them in terms of historical research and the provision of photos and other material.

In September 2009, at the Ristorante Lauro, the "Menù dei motori" dinner with my friend Franco Gozzi, the Drake's legendary secretary, in a reciprocal and light-hearted rivalry. Looking on is an amused Lauro Malavolti.

24 August 2014, at St. Moritz with Venanzio Fonte, a Maserati collector, who back in the day had made me promise to write this book.

I BECOME
A GRANDFATHER AND
"MAESTRO DEL LAVORO"

Gianna had obtained a permanent position as a teacher and was teaching outside Modena so I bought for her a used Fiat 500 to allow her to travel more easily. She had had a fiancée for a couple of years and Giordana and I were happy because she had found a good boy. The first floor apartment that had been occupied by Grandfather Mario before he passed away was now free and also semi-furnished, so Gianna and Franco decided to marry in July 1984, in the Church of Sant'Agnese where Giordana and I had married. The bride's car, needless to say, was a Maserati Quattroporte and the reception was held at the Gatto Verde in San Venanzio. Giordana had made a wonderful wedding dress for her daughter and was very happy with the compliments she received but above all she was happy for Gianna. Giordana was always very busy with her work and housekeeping and never had much free time. Fortunately, she could still count on the help of her mother, Grandma Silvia, who lived very close by and visited every day to lend her daughter a hand. When Giordana and I talked about what we had achieved together, we were satisfied. We had a nice family, our own house and a cottage in the mountains that had been completed some time ago. Many of our friends envied us, for which we were sorry, but if only they had known the sacrifices we had had to make. But it had all been worth it.

One Sunday in May, during lunch, Gianna and Franco told us that they were expecting a child. It was an indescribable joy. Giordana I and gazed at each other, our eyes shining. A few months later, one afternoon, I received a phone call at Maserati and the switchboard operator said to me, "Cozza, I'm putting you through to your wife, I can hear crying". I immediately thought the worst, but then, "Ermanno, Ermanno, Gianna is expecting twins". As she sobbed, Giordana told me that my daughter had gone for the ultrasound scan during which they had seen the twins. I asked her if there were any complications and Giordana said, "No, no, everything's fine." So I said to my wife, "Two's better than one, come on now, stop crying, it'll all work out." Gianna had a normal pregnancy and in September, at the beginning of the school year, she was transferred to the primary school in Via Vaciglio, right next to our house. On the 23rd of January 1986, Marco and Luca were born, two beautiful, healthy and robust boys. Gianna didn't have enough milk for both of them, so she had to resort to artificial milk with the addition of a few tablespoons of mature grana cheese, as per the midwife's instructions. Inevitably, the house was turned upside down, our first grandchildren had arrived and clearly for grandparents that is an infinite joy.

On the 1st of May 1986, I was invited to Bologna by the Ministry of Labour, as Maserati had nominated me as being worthy of the "Maestro del Lavoro" honour thanks to my impeccable performance during my 35 years of work during which I had trained and passed on my experience to new staff and above all I had curated and protected the Maserati historical archive. This was another great personal satisfaction. I was particularly happy that my children, who mean the world to me, could be proud of their father and be able to draw an example for their lives. Gianluigi was about to graduate as a bookkeeper and then if he wanted, he would go to university.

THE MASERATI REGISTER'S FIRST INTERNATIONAL RALLY

Sixty years of sporting tradition: the 25th of April 1926 saw the first victory for the Trident's first car, in reality a class win. The aim of the Maserati Registry's first International Rally was to bring together and display on the factory forecourt as many Maserati cars built since 1926 as possible. The foreign clubs, which had long been the finest custodians of our classic cars, especially the British Maserati Club, which also published a magazine, together with the presidents of the clubs in Austria, France, Germany and Switzerland, helped to ensure their members' participation. The event was scheduled for the weekend from the 25th to the 24th of September, starting from Viale Ceccarini in Riccione. 44 Italian cars alternated on the starting podium, followed by 27 Swiss cars, 8 from Germany, 12 from France and 7 from Great Britain, for a total of 98 cars. It was a dizzying parade that featured an alternation of GT cars from the Fifties and Sixties with sports racing cars from the Thirties, Forties and Fifties. In addition, a delegation of 23 American collectors was present. Naturally, the attention of participants was captured by the racing cars, true jewels, some of which I had personally helped restore by providing the various owners with the data and information they requested. A dozen Biturbo cars owned by Club Maserati members completed the line up. The inaugural event was held at the Peter Pan Club, a gala evening sponsored by Michelin, with romantic music for the elderly and wilder tunes for the young.

On Friday the 26th of September, everyone took to the track at the Santa Monica circuit in Misano, where Martinelli and I were very busy with the fine tuning and the adjustment of the carburettors of the racing cars. After a day at the track, with regularity trials and tests of skill, in which everyone enjoyed themselves, we returned to our various hotels to prepare for the second gala evening. Several coaches were waiting for us to take us to the Paradiso Club, one of the most beautiful venues in the area. The evening's sponsor was Martini & Rossi, who had an enormous beige and brown cake placed in the middle of the room, representing the logo of the Maserati Register with the inscription First International Rally. Signora Maria Teresa de Filippis, after a brief greeting to the more than 350 people present, cut the cake with the help of Ingegner Mario Murri, at that time Maserati's CEO. The evening continued happily into the small hours, but then it we had to get some rest because at 08.30 the next day, Saturday the 27th, the participants were scheduled to set off for Modena.

On the way, the crews were asked to answer quizzes on Maserati's history compiled by Dr. Chilò, the event's MC and assistant organizer. The caravan of cars that arrived in the Maserati forecourt was received the workers and by Signor de Tomaso and his friend Lee Iacocca, CEO of Chrysler. Another sponsor, Agip, offered a rich buffet and gave a briefcase containing car care products to all participants. The day continued with a tour of the factory, followed in the afternoon by a parade through the streets of the city to the Teatro Storchi for the photographic exhibition organized by Franco Zagari and sponsored by the Banca Nazionale del Lavoro. The evening ended at Hotel Canalgrande with the Maserati dinner in the Secchia Rapita restaurant, in the presence of the civic authorities. Dinner was followed by the prize-giving ceremony for the winners of the track events and short speeches by the presidents of the various Maserati Clubs. Gigi Villoresi, President of the Maserati Register, closed the evening by thanking all the participants, while Signora de Filippis mentioned the organizers and thanked Signor de Tomaso for supporting and promoting what had been a wonderful and significant event.

On Sunday morning, the 28th of September, everyone gathered at the Officine Alfieri Maserati to pick up their cars. The technical commission, chaired by Sergio Mantovani, a former Maserati driver, and completed by myself and Giulio Sala, finished examining and registering the cars that had applied to join the Register.

The foreign clubs were also very active, the first to organize a major international event being the Deutscher Maserati Club, chaired by Peter Kaus, a collector of no less than 125 Maserati cars. From the 14th to the 16th of August 1987, the Club invited all owners of Maserati "old timers" to Bad Neuenahr, near Koblenz. The Register was present with a healthy range of cars. I had gone with a Quattroporte, accompanying Gigi Villoresi, Ingegner Mantovani and his son. There were three days full of sporting, social and culinary engagements. On Thursday the 14th August, we drove to the old Nürburgring circuit, where a controlled speed test was awaiting us. I handed over the wheel to Villoresi, a far more experienced driver who had already raced on that very difficult circuit. After a trial run, he abandoned the idea of regularity, put his foot to the floor, making my hair stand on end with fear in the process. During the gala evening at the Kurhaus Barockhall, Kaus gave me a picture of my favourite Maserati, the 3500 GT Touring, to thank me for all my help in the restoration of his cars; the various prizes were then presented. The next day, the long caravan of cars drove to Aschaffenburg, near Frankfurt, to visit the Kaus museum-collection with its array of perfectly restored cars. After a short lunch we returned to Italy.

The following year, from the 22nd to the 25th of September 1988, it was the turn of the Austrian Club to organise the International Maserati Rally in Velden, which attracted more than 110 sports racing and GT cars, the numbers actually causing the organizers some difficulties. President Herwik Matschy invited me and Sala with our wives and we drove to the event taking turns at the wheel of the Quattroporte, followed by Villoresi driving a Biturbo. The participants assembled at the Park Hotel Velden, a charming tourist resort in Carinthia. The next day, there was a regularity hillclimb event to Mount Dobratsch, in which Signora de Filippis excelled with the firm's 3500 GT. Lunch was at the Landskron Fortress, which offered a spectacular view of the entire valley. Lunch was served in the medieval style in that it was to be consumed with the help of a single piece of cutlery, a knife. To the initial astonishment of the diners an excellent garlic soup arrived to be sipped from rough bowls, followed by various cuts of grilled meat. The ladies were having great difficulty using the knife to keep the meat on their plates rather than having it fly off onto the wooden table. I think that was one of the last times I saw Giordana laughing and having fun. Also present were Michael Miles, Mr. Wagner, Gunther Wulff and Hans Wulfers, respectively the presidents of the Maserati Clubs of Great Britain, Germany, Switzerland and France. We were up at dawn the next day, to make an early start for the Zeltweg circuit where, throughout the day, the participants thoroughly enjoyed themselves in regularity trials and speed tests. The event concluded on the Sunday morning on the Velden lakefront, with concours d'elegance and the emergence from the waters of the lake of the god Neptune, gripping his Trident. The next international event was to take place in France and each year one of the ten European countries before returning to Italy. Sadly, Giordana health was deteriorating and I was unable to leave home for very long, except on business rather than for fun and entertainment.

NEW DISPOSITIONS

Following the International Rally in September 1986, we began to receive increasing numbers of requests for information about our classic cars; a Maserati Club had been founded in America, and requests for help in the restoration of its members' cars, mostly GTs from the Sixties and Seventies, began to arrive from the United States too. The most demanding job was deal with the requests of the British and Germans regarding the pre-war cars. By taking the necessary time I always managed to answer every question. Until one Monday morning when Signor de Tomaso called me in to hear how I handled our dealings with the various collectors. I explained that for GT cars most of the enquiries were related to colour and year of construction, while for the racing cars, back in the days of Ingegner Bertocchi we would supply a copy of the drawing of the piece they had to rebuild after receipt of the chassis number and photographs of the car. He told me that from that moment on, these requests for drawings would have to pass through the executive offices over the past weekend he had been in Monte Carlo and had seen a number of reconstructed 250F cars. I explained to him that Cameron Miller, president of the British Maserati Club, had built at least five 250Fs using original spare parts, purchased from Maserati, and had numbered them MC 01-02-etcetera. The plaque on the dashboard was marked "Reconstruction by CM". He told me that they were making fakes abroad and from now on, therefore, his approval would be required before we handed out copies of the drawings.

Just a few days earlier I had sent a copy of the 450S number 4509 halfshaft drawing to an Englishman, who a few weeks later asked me for one of the 1933 8CM drawings. I replied asking him to send his request along with the frame number to the management offices. He called me back to tell me that the secretary had told him to speak to me. I asked him for the chassis number but he said that he couldn't remember it, so I once again I asked him to send his request in writing, to the Maserati management. The secretary then called to ask me why I was not dealing with the requests of that British gentleman, who kept calling her with the same enquiry. I explained to her that without the chassis number and without Signor de Tomaso's approval I could not handle any request. At nine o'clock one evening, I received a phone call at home from the gentleman in question with his usual requests. I spontaneously asked him if he were not by chance thinking of building a replica, he replied that he was ready to pay me to have the drawings he needed for an 8CM. I very politely made him understand that he was speaking to the wrong person and not to call me anymore. A few weeks later, I received requests from other collectors for copies of drawings to fabricate components and to complete various restorations. As I had been asked, I passed the enquiries on to the management office, which after a while sent them back to me with Signor de Tomaso's approval. One of these requests came from the same person: three or four months after the first request, the list contained many components that raised my suspicions. I sent the letter to Canalgrande for Signor de Tomaso's approval, but began to investigate by talking to various acquaintances about this gentleman's restoration. I came to know that it was not a restoration but rather the complete reconstruction of a 350S. About a month later, the secretary returned the letter to me saying that Signor de Tomaso wanted to speak to me. As I showed him the letter with its long list of parts to be fabricated, he said, "What does this guy want? Tell him that if he wants the components, we'll make them for him in the time it takes". I replied that I had learned that it was not a restoration but a complete reconstruction. Looking at me in surprise and anger, he ordered me not to provide anything else at all and not even to answer.

Six months passed and one afternoon the switchboard called me and told meet Signor de Tomaso in the Technical Office. He came to meet me handing me a sheet of paper, a sheet of paper, "What's this?" I read it and found it was a letter from Chrysler signed by Lee Iacocca, asking his friend Alejandro why we were no longer helping our collectors with the restoration of their cars. Between the lines I also read the name of that English gentleman who wanted the drawings of the 8CM. I explained the matter, from top to toe, including the phone calls to his secretary and the phone call received at home, where I was offered money to get drawings for a replica. "Ah yes, ah yes! He tried to buy you, now I'll tell Iacocca why we're not helping certain people!" After that, I had no further interference from de Tomaso in dealing with this kind of request. I went back to how I had always handled things before and never had any problem. I was, in fact, always very cautious as I realized that with the increase in the value of classic cars, more and more people were being attracted to that world and not all of them stood out for their honesty. I received offers of up to 20 million Lire to pass on the chassis number of a wrecked car, so that a replica could be made and passed off as an original. More than once I found banknotes in a handshake, which I always refused. Mindful of those chats with Reggiani, I've always thought it's better to be remembered as an "honest ass" than a "dishonest wise guy". Certainly by now I could have a bank account with a lot more zeros, but just as surely I wouldn't be able to boast the esteem of many and this for me is worth so much more.

RESIGNATION

I could see same very menacing dark clouds on the horizon. Giordana had fallen into a worrying depression. She had always been a very timid woman, she worried about everything, but now more than ever she always seemed to be unhappy, I never saw her smile as she once did. I spoke to our family doctor who urged me to be patient, it could simply have been the menopause.

Articles in the newspapers about possible changes to the statutory retirement age led me to think about the fact that I had 36 years of service, one more than was required to retire at the time. If we went on like this, with the rumours that flying around, those 36 years might no longer have been enough. I didn't want to stop working, I could never have managed, but I did think that if I retired I would have so much more time to dedicate to the family, to Gianna with her twins and to Giordana who wasn't well. I also knew of colleagues who had retired at more or less at my age (I was 54), and who had found part-time jobs. So I decided and in October I handed in the letter that would terminate my employment with Maserati. I had to give three months' notice, which I had to respect by law. In the meantime, I was sent to the Paris Motor Show, where a few days later I saw our dealer from Modena arrive, on his way back from England, where he had been testing at Lotus. He immediately told me that he'd heard I was retiring and that he would need me because as an importer of foreign cars, he had to complete the type approval process in Italy. I was the right man for him person, because he knew that I had worked on type approval issues in the Sixties.

Once back from the Paris Motor Show, every week the personnel director would drop in, trying to convince me to stay, even suggesting salary increases. At first time I told him that he should have given me the increase months earlier, when I was given responsibility for the Spare Parts Store. I never mentioned the on-going conflict I had with the CEO, because I knew that he would tell him because it was clear that it was de Tomaso who was sending him to convince me to stay. Speaking of disputes, the last and rather lively one had taken place the previous summer. Signor de Tomaso had had me called up to his office. As soon as I entered, he began shouting because the Biturbo bumpers that Garbutt was waiting for so urgently had not been sent to the MAI firm in Baltimore. I answered that Ingegner Meregalli, of Innocenti, had not sent them to me yet, I had the boxes with the other spare parts ready, I was just waiting for the bumpers from Milan to close and ship them. He began with his usual somewhat offensive way *"Tute bale! Tute Bale!"* ("Balls, all balls!") I asked him if he had finished shouting, placed my hands on the desk, looked him in the eyes 20 centimetres from his face and said to him very calmly, "Signor de Tomaso, I'm a professional, I'm not accustomed to talking 'balls', to use your own term." I turned on my heels and left the office, slamming the door. The next morning when I arrived the switchboard operator told me not to move as she had de Tomaso on the line for me. "Cozza, Ingegner Meregalli's sending the bumpers to you with the truck this afternoon, don't forget!" So I hadn't been talking *"bale"* yesterday, I replied. "Yesterday you lost your temper", only he was allowed to get angry! He was accustomed to treating many managers very badly, even insulting them sometimes, but with me he restricted himself, because he knew how I would react.

The 30th of January 1987 eventually came round, my last day. I was a little blue but tried not to show it. At six o'clock I invited my closest colleagues for a drink. When the phone rang in another office, someone went to answer and came back saying they were looking for Cozza. When I picked up the handset I heard someone saying, "You're having a party, I can hear voices". I replied, "Signor de Tomaso, it's gone six o'clock, I'm not damaging Maserati, I'm just saluting my colleagues". All he said in reply was, "Well, tomorrow morning I'll be waiting for you in my office at 9 o'clock. I want to salute you too".

The next day was the 31st of January, which in Modena is the feast of the city's patron saint. I had promised Giordana that we would have a walk round the fair at 11 o'clock. As usual, I arrived at Maserati ten minutes head of the appointment. On the way in I met Signora Valdevit, my head of department; she never wanted me to say she was my superior or my boss. We entered Signor de Tomaso's office together and found him with the head of administration, Dr. Micheletti of GEPI. To whom he began to say, "You see, someone still young who's retiring when he's still able to work." I tried to explain that my family needed me, that there were two one-year-old twins, that my wife had health problems and couldn't help her daughter as she would have like to and so on. Signora Valdevit addressed de Tomaso, complaining that without me she would never have known how to deal with the collectors' archive. Signor de Tomaso had in his hand a memo he had asked for, with a list of all my responsibilities. "So you take care of all these things?

Now what are we going to do?" I tried to explain how to divide certain tasks between the various offices and in the end only the archive of drawings and photographs remained. I explained to Signora Valdevit that whenever she needed me I would have been willing to go in to Maserati to lend a hand. She said that after all the problems we had with the unions regarding Ciccio Montanari, the head of the engine assembly, who had retired but had occasionally been called in, it was no longer possible, things needed to be on an official footing. They began to argue amongst themselves, Signora Valdevit insisting that it had been a mistake not to have flanked me with someone to whom I could have gradually passed the baton over the years and that with my departure a void really had been created that no one could fill. I had always had a very good personal and professional relationship with Signora Valdevit and she had frequently expressed her esteem and trust. Seeing her so disheartened, I crumbled and said, "I could get a VAT number like others have done and come in in the afternoon." Signora Valdevit's face lit up with a beaming smile as she embraced me; Signor de Tomaso stood up said he agreed and shook my hand. In the meantime, the accountant Rosi had arrived and de Tomaso had told to him to officialise the economic question as per my request. Following the instructions of my close colleague Erio Grana, an expert on castings and models, who after retiring had worked as a consultant for more than a year at Maserati, I completed all the bureaucratic formalities, obtained a VAT number and also sought the help of an accountant to look after my books.

About a month later, I started going in to Maserati every afternoon, from two o'clock to seven o'clock. Now that

I had been relieved of so many responsibilities and all the concerns over the Biturbo customers' complaints, I was even more serene. My office had also been changed, due to the need to install two more machines near the Olivetti line. The whole Sales Office and I had been transferred near the Technical Office, which was half empty as more than half of the staff had gone to De Tomaso.

BUSIER THAN EVER

Signor Omer Orsi's youngest son Adolfino was now a gentleman of over thirty years old, a graduate in law with a passion for automotive history and classic cars. He had already restored a 4CM and an A6GCS in the Torrazzi workshop, projects on which I had also worked along with others from Maserati. On behalf of Finarte, an important auction house in Milan, Dr. Orsi was now organizing an auction at the Hotel Raffaello of objects, photos, brochures and around 30 historic cars. He telephoned me to ask me whether now that I was retired I would have time to lend him a hand, a few days before, to arrange the cars and then during the auction, which would take place on June the 11th 1988. I told him I was willing to do all I could and after the event he asked me to consider myself commissioned for the next auction that he'd be organizing in December, again at the Hotel Raffaello.

Dr. Orsi went on to organize two auctions a year through to December 1991, the last at the Hotel Fini, and I continued to contribute to them. As I would be away from Maserati for the duration, I informed Signora Valdevit of the reason, because knowing about the issues between de Tomaso and Dr. Orsi, I didn't want to be the cause of any further problems, it would be much better if they all knew the reason for my absences. In addition, this new commitment was related to the work I was now doing almost full time at Maserati with our classic cars and collectors. Assisting at those auctions introduced me to numerous people and a whole world about which I'd had little idea. My naivety gave way to diffidence and experience taught me to handle certain situations with more caution. Unfortunately, I occasionally had to deal with people who were unprofessional or even dishonest.

I also caught up a friend, an old colleague from the Maserati Racing Department, Giulio Borsari, who was about eight years older than me. After our official retirement from racing, he had spent a few years with Mimmo Dei at the Scuderia Centro Sud, before ending up at Ferrari and becoming the chief mechanic of numerous drivers. With a 35-year career under his belt he was a very well-known figure at all the racing circuits. He had been retired for some time but his undiminished passion for the world of motor racing led him to nearby Imola. At the circuit he met Baron Emmanuel de Graffenried, the former Maserati driver from the Forties and Fifities and now a Marlboro manager, who asked him why didn't organise a mechanics' club along the lines of the Anciens Pilotes Club, of which the Baron himself was the current president. Giulio told me about the idea, asking me to help him out as he considered me suitable for the running of the administrative side. We met up again and began to note down, in addition to the names of the Alfa Romeo, Ferrari and Maserati mechanics, ideas for regulations, positions and so on, whatever came to mind. I had my doubts regarding the Ferrari mechanics, as it was well known that some of them felt they were better than any of the others; however, I was sure that the very precise and impartial Giulio, with his Maserati heart, would tip the balance. We decided on the positions to be assigned: Giulio Borsari, president, Antonio Reggiani, vice-president, Pasquale Cassani, treasurer, Ermanno Cozza, secretary.

On the 14th of July 1988, we went to the notary, Ramacciotti, to officialise the deed of association and the Formula 1 Veteran Mechanics Club was born. We had also registered the document with the Registry Office in order to have a fiscal code, which we would require if we were to obtain sponsorship. After a few dinners in a neutral area between Maranello and Modena that would maintain the equilibrium and keep everyone happy, the official baptism took place on Saturday, September the 10th 1988 at the Monza circuit in the large Marlboro marquee where we enjoyed a lunch together with the Club Anciens Pilotes. It was a historic meeting and in a sense moving too, as you saw after years people who had shared joys and disappointments, all the same protagonists in the history of motor racing.

THE MASERATI CLUB

After the founding some years earlier of the Maserati Register for our classic cars, an institution to which its president Gigi Villoresi and his deputy Maria Teresa de Filippis always devoted great commitment and enthusiasm, the Club Maserati was created in the summer of 1988 to give us the opportunity of establishing closer contacts with our customers given that there were more than 20,000 modern Maserati cars in circulation around the world. The artificer and promoter of the initiative was Signora Luisa Valdevit, the head of public relations and the Maserati press office. With the help of Signor Cucchi from Esseti, our supplier of brochures and manuals, a bi-annual periodical, *Il Tridente*, was launched and I was asked to contribute a number of technical articles, as well as being part of the organisation.

All Maserati car owners were eligible to join the Club, and it was to operate in parallel with the Maserati Register to create and promote initiatives of social, cultural and recreational interest to its members. Signora Valdevit was also involved in creating a series of Maserati gadgets and accessories to be included in the package of benefits reserved for members of the Club. Of course, all the dealers were also asked to promote the Maserati Club and to involve all establish and new customers by offering membership. A couple of convivial meetings were organised at the Secchia Rapita to allow the Club's members to get to know one another. Among their number were some particularly friendly individuals and proved to be good company and to share the same passion for the Trident.

The first meeting of the Club Maserati was scheduled for the 15th and 16th of April 1989 at Varano, Modena and Imola. On the 15th of April, a sunny Saturday morning, 54 Maserati cars assembled at the Riccardo Paletti circuit in Varano; the meeting was open to all Maseratis, with no age limits. Among the cars participating there were various Mistrals, Ghibli Coupés and Spyders, Mexicos, Indys, Quattroportes I and III, Khamsins and Meraks, all the variations on the Biturbo theme, Biturbo I and SI, 420, Spyder, 228 and 222. Almost all the participants had to undergo a medical examination to be issued with an amateur license that would allow them to drive on the racing circuit; fortunately Dr. Tosoni was present, a member of the club with a Biturbo S, who, assisted by an official of the Automobile Club of Parma, patiently compiled all the licenses in a very short time so as to allow everyone to take to the track. Following the skill tests and lunch at the circuit's restaurant, we all drove to Via Ciro Menotti in Modena, for a tour of the Officine Maserati, then two coaches shuttled all the participants to the Hotel Canalgrande where the various standings were published. Dinner was at the Secchia Rapita restaurant and was attended by the president of the club Signor de Tomaso with Gigi Villoresi and Sergio Mantovani. Signora Luisa Valdevit presented a memorial plaque to all participants. Everyone reconvened on the Sunday morning at Imola on the forecourt of the Mulino Rosso restaurant where we met members of the Club Citroën Maserati with over twenty SMs. It wasn't possible to have the cars parade around the circuit due to the concomitant tests for the Formula 1 San Marino

Grand Prix on the following Sunday. The final regularity trials were therefore held at the Tre Monti circuit not far away. Following refreshments in the splendid town hall of Imola, the event drew to a close with the prizes for the various tests and the Maserati cups being presented by the members of the jury who expressed their sincere hope that we would meet again soon to spend more days like these.

THE RESTORATION OF THE CARS IN OUR MUSEUM

With the exception of about ten engines, which were on display in various parts of the factory or in certain offices and which were sometimes used during motor shows or other such events, all the remaining materials (chassis, bodyshells, panels and complete cars) from the museum had been stacked on the mezzanine floor, next to the canteen, covered with tarpaulins and left there forgotten ever since the Citroën era. I agreed with my colleague, the head of the chassis department, that whenever he had time he would build a series of supports for those engines of particular interest. I had two assembled crankshafts designed by Signor Ernesto Maserati and used on the 4CL engine. I sent the most complete one still featuring its connecting rods to the woodworking department to make a support so as to be able to put it on display.

When Signor de Tomaso was touring the various departments one day with the new importer for Switzerland he arrived in the chassis department and he saw the crankshaft already mounted on its support. He asked the head of the department about it and was told that it was a piece from the museum, brought in by Cozza so that they could build the support. He immediately sent someone to call me and I rushed over thinking there would be another of his usual rants. Instead he asked me which engine it was from and the year in which it was made and after the necessary explanations I dared to say that I thought the piece was particularly interesting and I had thought it appropriate to put it on display. He surprised me by saying to the importer, "Look at the fantastic roller bearing technology used on the connecting rods, a Maserati brothers masterpiece". I spoke up, telling him that we had a lot more material stored away and reminding him of an old saying about "splashing out" every so often. The Swiss gentleman, who knew me, stepped in to say, "Cozza, if there's anything interesting, I'll buy it myself." To which Signor de Tomaso replied, "No, no! You're not selling anything!" I naturally said that it wasn't my property and I couldn't decide what to do with it. "Then I'll decide", he answered. He told me there and then that he'd give me an annual budget, starting immediately, to restore all of the museum's cars; the next day the accountant would have made available the first 10 million Lire.

I immediately informed Manfredini of this because as workshop manager, he would be able to advise me on a place, at the back of the car assembly department, where I could establish an area in which to work. The personnel manager found me two men to work with, but I didn't agree with his choice. I indicated the people I wanted and after brief negotiations, and the threat of bringing in Signor de Tomaso to decide, they gave me Giancarlo Martinelli, former head of the car assembly department, and one of his assistants. Good mechanics that I knew I could trust and who knew how to do their jobs without me always having to be present. We started with the restoration of those vehicles requiring the least work so that we would immediately have a group of road-worthy cars.

After a prolonged inspection of all the cars, Martinelli and I put together a plan of work that included those jobs that were to be sent out such as painting or interior renovations. We began with a Mistral Spyder, formerly owned by the King of Morocco, and an A6G/54 Allemano. The Spyder required little mechanical work, but the interior needed reupholstering as the leather was in terrible condition and everything had been ruined.

The Allemano instead required lengthy mechanical work, including the stripping down of the engine; we saved the interior but then had to repaint the body. We had agreed with the company accounts department that every time we started working on a different car we would open a new order, so that at the end of the restoration we would have a record of the hours employed and the costs of the work done externally for each car. One particularly demanding restoration concerned the refurbishment of a Ghibli coupé that had served as the basis and prototype test car for the Khamsin. We transformed a coupé into a Ghibli Spyder, using the existing spare parts we had in stock, and built a brand-new Bora from scratch. However, I had a dream, that of restoring the A6GCS Pininfarina berlinetta, one of the four built in 1954, brought back to the factory by its owner, Count Gravina of Catania, following an accident in 1955. It was originally supposed to be scrapped, but thanks to my whole team of colleagues, given the importance of the car, we had always made sure we kept it, complete with the damage to the left front wing and stripped of all its mechanicals. After around forty years of being shuffled from one part of the factory to the other, it was finally time for its restoration. I had Onorio Campana come in to Maserati and took him up to see the berlinetta. I had always had an excellent relationship with Onorio and in all modesty it was down to me that his coachworks had been working with Maserati for years. I therefore asked him for a written estimate, both for the repair and the remodelling of the nose and the front wing and for the repainting of the whole body, as cheaply as possible, of course. Onorio told me it was going to be a demanding job that he would have to do himself; jokingly, he told me that he would cost more than his workers. A few days later he brought me the estimate: 30 million Lire. Even though after a couple of years my annual budget had been increased from 10 million to 20 million Lire, for this project I needed a considerable increase otherwise we would be grossly overspending. I spoke about the matter to the accountant in the Maserati administration department who, knowing nothing about the classic car movement, began to rail against me as soon as he saw the sum I was asking for: "Thirty million for that heap, you'll see, I'll be telling Signor de Tomaso how you spend his money", and so on and so forth. The following week I bumped into Signor de Tomaso in the factory and he told me what the accountant had said to him. He asked me whether I had gone mad to be spending such a sum. After explaining the matter and describing the kind of car we were talking about, he said that he wanted me to show him the wreck and then he'd decide what to do. I had the bodyshell taken down to the department where we worked, but the weeks passed and I couldn't get Signor de Tomaso to see the car.

One afternoon, he called me to say that two gentlemen would be coming in, uncle and nephew, and to take them up, upstairs, to view the museum collection. I refused, saying that we had always said that the area was unpresentable and that no one should be taken there. "Do as I say, and I'll explain later!" Two or three days layer, the Artoms arrived, Guido and his nephew Gabriele. Once they had spoken to Signor de Tomaso, he handed them over to me, saying that he would join us in the department. When we got upstairs I apologized for the clutter and the stacking of the bodyshells and cars one on top of the other but noticed that Signor Gabriele seemed very interested in the former Scuderia Camoradi

Tipo 63 Birdcage, which lacked all its mechanicals but had an intact chassis and body.

Signor Gabriele was a very enthusiastic young man of about 30. He told me that his father and uncle had been collecting cars since the Fifties. In addition to Ferrari and Mercedes, they also had two Maseratis, a 6CM from 1936 and an A6GCS from 1955. I told him about what Signor de Tomaso wanted to do and the annual budget devoted the gradual restoration of the museum's cars that had been stored here since the Citroën era, so that they would not be lost. I took them to the back of the department to show them where my two mechanics were working on the on-going restorations; at that time they were finishing the Bora mechanicals while next to it, we had put the Pininfarina berlinetta on the stands.

When Signor de Tomaso joined us, he talked to them about me, my age and the fact that I had already retired, that I was coming in the afternoons on a consultancy basis, that I had a budget, that I was spending a lot of money, that now I was asking him 30 million Lire for the restoration of a wreck that he had yet to see, and so on… I pointed out with great enthusiasm that we were right in front of the wreck in question. Signor Guido Artom asked Signor de Tomaso whether he knew he owned one of the four famous Pininfarina berlinettas; his nephew explained to him that their A6GCS barchetta was originally a berlinetta, from which the body had been removed and renumbered. They told him more or less what I had told him, exalting the beauty of the lines of the bodywork, the proportions of the three volumes, to the extent that I noticed Signor de Tomaso looking at them then looking at the berlinetta before finally, he turned to me and asked for Campana's estimate. I hurried to the office, came back panting and handed the sheet of paper to him, which he placed on the car and signed, saying to me, "You're ruining me." The Artoms winked at me and there was an immediate feeling of complicity between me and Signor Gabriele.

When we returned to the office, they told me that they would like to exchange their Maserati 6CM for our Tipo 63 and that Signor de Tomaso would be happy to have a Bologna-built Maserati for the collection. I was in agreement as we already had a Birdcage Tipo 61, and a 6CM would have sat nicely alongside the 6C 34 that we were to restore a few years later. I said farewell to the Artoms with the promise that we would meet again as soon as they had defined the exchange contract with Signor de Tomaso. Then I went over to the office to inform the team that they had been given the green light for the restoration of the berlinetta.

All it took was a phone call and half an hour later the "wreck" was on the chassis builder's reference plane to straighten and repair the damage to the crossmember. Once we had thoroughly checked the frame, cleaned and repainted it in its original grey finish, the following morning Campana came in to pick it up and begin the reconstruction of the left-hand side. In anticipation of this work, at the Geneva Motor Show the year before, I had asked Leonardo Fioravanti, Pininfarina's chief designer, if any silhouettes or templates had been preserved. He knew the history of the four berlinettas and was aware that they had been built at the behest of Signor Mimmo Dei, our concessionaire in Rome, given that Pininfarina, having established a close working relationship with Ferrari, had interrupted all direct contacts with Maserati. Fioravanti had yet to join Pininfarina in 1954, but said he was enthusiastic about the restoration project, promising me that he would find out whether any drawings or templates relating to the design existed in their archives. A few weeks later he called me to say that he was sorry but he had found nothing that would be of help to me. After having straightened all the dents and cut away at the points where he would have to insert the reconstructed panels, Campana therefore had to stop as he was unable to make further progress.

In the meantime I had contacted Signor Lucchini of Brescia, whom I knew owned the PF A6GCS berlinetta *2059*, and who after some initial reluctance allowed me to go one Saturday morning with Campana to use his car to create the templates we needed. Campana was able to reconstruct the missing part of the front end and the wing. Unfortunately, Onorio was unable to reconstruct the oval of the radiator grille exactly like the original, but a true Pinin Farina connoisseur would ever notice this. On the mechanical side, instead, we had no problems as we had everything we needed. After more than forty years of accumulating dust and six months work, we finally managed to get the berlinetta running. I took a tour of the factory courtyard, under the admiring gaze of all my colleagues on the team who had contributed to the restoration of this magnificent car and prevented it being scrapped. In the meantime, after a good deal of toing an froing, as was always the case with Signor de Tomaso, the exchange of cars with the Artoms was completed. When the 6CM arrived at Maserati, I found it very difficult to get hold of the benzol and methyl alcohol to make 10 litres of the correct fuel mixture so that it could be started, checked and tuned. The restoration work continued on the Tipo 63, which we had to complete for Signor Gabriele Artom, and we had also begun the restoration of the Eldorado, about which Signor de Tomaso had known as a GEPI manager (the state company had in fact provided financial aid to the ice-cream manufacturer, our sponsor in the construction of the car back in 1958).

NOT JUST NEW MODELS

On the occasion of the company's anniversary celebrations on the 14th, 15th and 16th of December 1990 (the exact anniversary is and will always be the 1st of December), Maserati presented three new models. Beneath the large marquee set up in the factory courtyard that year were the Shamal, a 2 + 2 coupé with a 32-valve V8 engine displacing 3000 cc, presented in static form the year before and now ready for delivery; the Racing, a new two-litre coupé with 285 hp and four valves per cylinder, which with its 141.76 hp per litre was the most powerful production car in the world and finally, the surprise of the event, which stunned everyone present, from journalists to politicians, to the numerous celebrities and through to the members of the club, the Chubasco. This completely new car was quite different to rest of the current range and perhaps provided an ideal link to our sports cars of the past, thanks in part to the choice of the name of a wind. It was a two-seater coupé with a 3000 cc mid-mounted engine and longitudinal girder chassis, for which Marcello Gandini had designed a futuristic body. The doors were pivoted at the front and lifted forward, the roof sliding towards the rear above the engine bay to permit top-down driving. A full-width spoiler designed specifically to provide all the necessary aerodynamic benefits characterized the lines of the car from any angle you looked at it. The wooden mock-up, perfectly painted in classic Italian red, was so well finished in every detail that it looked like a prototype but was, and unfortunately was to remain, only a static model. It was to become part of Signor Panini's collection in 1996.

Some years previously, with the introduction of the four-valve engines and to put the Biturbo experience behind us, Signor de Tomaso had ordered that the names of the new models should correspond to numbers. Hence the 222, 222 4V and 222 SR were coupés and the 420, 422, 424v, 430 and 430 4V saloons. For tax reasons, the engines for the cars sold in Italy were still two-litre units, while for those intended for foreign markets were to displace 2800 cc.

The Turin Motor Show had also changed its venue and date. No longer held in November at the Parco Valentino, which was by now inadequate, but in May at the Lingotto, which was larger and more spacious. The change of date was dictated above all by the desire to distance the event from the Bologna Motor Show held at the beginning of December. The Bologna event, which had grown quietly, year by year, had expanded to the extent that it had become an international happening capable of replacing the Turin Motor Show from 1995.

Club Maserati's activities were also expanding: Signora Valdevit and Signor Antonello Cucchi were tireless organizers of magnificent events held every year in a characteristic location somewhere throughout our beautiful Italy. From Venice to Civita di Bagnoregio, from Spoleto to Lake Bracciano, from the Chianti hills to the Maremma. Not to mention the racing circuits of Varano, Misano, Imola and Monza, where the most demanding members could show off their passion for speed. Unfortunately, the health of everyone's favourite, our very own Gigi Villoresi, was failing. He had had heart problems and then suffered a fall in which he broke his hip, he was admitted to the Trivulzio

Hospital in Milan and when I visited him I was shocked by the standard of the facilities. Fortunately, as he recovered, a close friend of his took him to San Pellegrino Terme, to a home for the elderly where he stayed for a few months.

Meanwhile, on the outskirts of Modena in an area called Bruciata, a warehouse for Maserati's Spare Parts Centre had been built on land partly occupied by the De Tomaso factory. All of our employees, headed by a certain Signor Squassoni from Innocenti, had been transferred there. Squassoni was a former lieutenant of the Carabinieri, a Tuscan blow-hard. He never bought into the Maserati spirit. His boss, Ingegner Barazzi of Innocenti, had spoken to me about him as being an expert and capable person, but very touchy. He could never understand why our colleagues Monari or Cattabriga would sometimes, as they left in the evening, take urgently needed spare parts to the Modena Nord motorway exit where someone from the Bologna or Piacenza workshop or others would pick them up. It was a way of getting a 24-hour head start, the service workshop satisfied the customer and Maserati would benefit indirectly. This happened only occasionally, at most once or twice a month, but Signor Squassoni was not happy with it. Signor de Tomaso had him in his sights and sent me to check up on him, as had happened when he sent Signor Neri of Moto Guzzi or the other one from Benelli, Signor Sanchioni, to check what I was doing at Maserati in the early Eighties. The difference was that I had had a positive attitude towards my supervisors which then turned into friendship and respect, while Squassoni had, from the beginning, almost a hatred, which became evident when I went to visit my old colleagues and friends, so much so that I once told him to his face that he was a blow-hard, saying that he had understood nothing of the spirit of initiative that animated his staff.

In the meantime, the 222, 224V and 422, 424, 430 models and the Spyder were about to be discontinued. Signor de Tomaso was to dust off the name Ghibli for a new model, which would make its debut at the Turin Motor Show in 1992 and put on sale the following June. Without doubt the choice of name had a basis in superstition, as the Ghibli had marked a major turning point in the history of the Officine Alfieri Maserati in 1966. The new three-box coupé had little in common with the car created by Giugiaro but thanks to its soft and compact lines, it expressed and contained new aerodynamic concepts, such as the roof without drip rails designed to eliminate annoying air noise, the low front end with the large bumpers incorporating the sidelights, the fog lamps and the air intakes for the intercoolers, the extremely clean rear end with the rounded boot lid and the wraparound rear lighting clusters. The cabin was everything a customer could hope for, the high quality leather and the burr walnut confirming the Maserati tradition of fine interiors. There were two engines: 2000 cc for the Italian market and 2800 cc for the foreign one. The 24-valve V6 engine featured electronic ignition and fuel injection, constant overboost, two three-way catalysers with Lambda probes, two water-cooled turbochargers. The two-litre version was good for 306 hp at 6500 rpm, while the six-speed mechanical gearbox provided a top speed of 260 kph. A number of our loyal customers who came to greet me at the show whispered in my ear in disappointment: they had expected something more akin to the old Ghibli.

THE RACING BARCHETTA

During that journey of reconciliation, a round trip on his personal plane from Bologna to Rome in the mid-Eighties, Signor de Tomaso had already talked to me about his idea of building a racing barchetta and creating a championship for gentlemen drivers. On the 14th of December 1991, on the occasion of the day on which for ten years we had celebrated somewhat inaccurately the anniversary of the birth of Officine Alfieri Maserati, the press, the authorities, dealers, Club Maserati members and friends were invited to admire the prototype of the new racing Barchetta, in addition to the recent production cars. The bodywork was designed by Carlo Gaiano of the Synthesis Design studio in Milan: the strict two-seater was a remarkably low at just 850 mm, with a large air intake on the bonnet and an independent and removable wing on the rear engine cover. The central cockpit cell was rigidly connected to the load-bearing structure as per aeronautical technology. Composite materials and carbonfibre were used to create a three-part body that was manufactured in accordance with CSAI standards and incorporated the safety features required by the FIA. The supporting structure was composed of a longitudinal aluminium and composite girder, inside which the petrol tank was located. At the front an aluminium subframe carrying the suspension was attached to the girder, while the engine was rigidly mounted via another subframe that also carried the rear suspension. The six-speed gearbox was mounted on the rear of the engine. Ingegner Caliri had drawn inspiration from Formula 1 technology when designing the suspension. The mid-mounted 90° 2000 cc V6 engine delivered 315 hp at 7000 rpm, giving a speed of 300 kph, while the car had a dry weight of 775 kg. The alloy wheels were shod with 235/45 RZ-17 front tyres and 285/35 RR 3-17 MXX-TL rear covers.

Maserati celebrated its return to the track with a truly exceptional car that was easy and great fun to drive and capable of satisfying all those who entered the Gran Trofeo Monomarca Barchetta Maserati that scheduled to begin in July 1992. Six rounds were to be held at the Misano, Monza, Mugello, Varano, Imola and Vallelunga circuits. The sporting regulations were to be drafted by an expert in the field and in this regard I had been asked to contact my good friend Romolo Tavoni to ask him to be the sporting director. Sadly, for health reasons he was unable to accept our invitation. However, he did tell me about a former colleague of his from when he was at Monza, who Signora Valdevit then invited to Modena for preliminary talks. As usual, the day at Maserati would conclude with a visit to the factory, where guests would also be able to admire a Tipo 63 Birdcage from 1961 at an advanced stage of restoration.

Unfortunately, construction of the Barchettas was severely delayed due among other things to problems with the supply of the bodywork. In fact, while all the mechanical parts were ready according to the pre-established production schedule, at least ten of the cars were waiting to be bodied for a good six months. All the assembly work had been organized at the De Tomaso factory where, once the 25 cars had been built, all the repair and maintenance work after the various races would also be done.

THE BARCHETTA ON TRACK

A Maserati Day for the long-awaited presentation of the Barchetta was organised for Sunday the 6th of September 1992 at the Monza circuit. Eleven cars were lined up in front of the pits, waiting to be driven by potential customers. Numerous guests, sports journalists from the leading publications, Italian dealers, foreign importers and Maserati Club and Maserati Register members were all present. Twenty brand new Ghiblis had also been brought to Monza, along with three Shamals and two Spyders, for those who wanted to take them for a test drive. About a hundred members had arrived with 35 classic and contemporary cars and would complete the day with their regularity trial on one of the world's most iconic circuits. Signor de Tomaso received the guests and introduced them to the new car that would be used in a dedicated series of races. Once the static presentation was over, the eleven Barchettas, driven by De Tomaso and Maserati testers, covered several laps of the Junior circuit, creating a great impression among the spectators.

We had also invited Michele Alboreto to give his opinion as an experienced Formula 1 driver on the handling of our new racing car. When he arrived late in that morning, he was literally mobbed by journalists. After a careful inspection of the car he slipped on his suit and helmet and took to the track, completing the first few laps at moderate speed, and then as he became more confident increasing the pace lap by lap, eventually recording some impressive lap times. At the end of the test he gave his impressions to

357

the journalists, saying that he hadn't imagined finding a car that was so easy to drive and such fun, with excellent power and acceleration, exceptional braking, and that he immediately felt at home behind the wheel.

Carlo Facetti took over from Alboreto and having already tested the car at Varano months before he had a certain familiarity with it and began to push hard, with no thought of sparing the mechanicals, thrilling the spectators with spectacular braking. As indicated in the sporting regulations, the Gran Trofeo Barchetta was scheduled to be disputed over six races that year, but due to the delay with which it would begin, only three races would take place over the next three months, before the end of 1992.

In the afternoon, before the scheduled regularity trial for the cars of the Club and the Register members, there were many who wanted to try the new Ghibli that, alternating with the Shamal and the two Spyders, completed lap after lap. In the paddock area, a special course had been prepared for the first test of the Club and Register members. Divided into classes, the cars also had to complete a few laps of the track in order to draw up a classification that rewarded the top six in each category. Signor Silecchia, the Grand Trophy sporting director, had his hands full that day, having to manage at the same time the tests of the Barchettas, the new Ghibli and Shamal cars and, above all, the classic and modern cars belonging to the members of the Club and the Registry. The day ended with a splendid prize-giving ceremony and an ovation for Luisa Valdevit and her staff (of which I was also a member) for organising this spectacular and challenging Maserati Day.

While the first orders were coming in for the Barchetta, there weren't many, in part because it entailed a considerable investment; in fact, with participation in the Gran Trofeo Monomarca Maserati, the Barchetta had a list price of over 110 million Lire; with an additional million for registration in the Championship, plus of course the travel and accommodation expenses for the scheduled races that were to be paid in advance. Any off-track excursions and the consequent repairs also had to be factored in. The list of entrants to the first race was as follows: Thomas Bscher from Germany, Christian Lo Buono, Carlo Facetti, Luigi Menegatto, John Nielsen, Beppe Schenetti and Peter Sundberg from Sweden. The official sponsors for Maserati were Selenia, TNT-Traco, Magneti Marelli and Michelin, but each competitor was allowed to find their own sponsors. Separate technical and sporting regulations governed proceedings, with the latter providing for the assignment of points for each race, the sum of which determined the final standings and the prizes. The winner was presented with a Shamal car, 40 million Lire for second, 30 million for third, 25 million for fourth and so on.

As mentioned previously, due to the delay in the production of the Barchettas, the calendar of dates and venues had had to be completely revised. The first race took place on October the 11th at the Varano circuit, the second on November the 8th at Vallelunga, then the third two weeks later at the Levante di Binetto circuit near Bari, and the fourth in Sicily at the Pergusa circuit on November the 29th. Two further competitors had registered for the fifth race on the 6th of December: the German, Hubert Hahne and the Belgian, Julien Appels. We were back at the Varano circuit, where Signor de Tomaso had asked me to invite a number owners of classic Maserati sports cars to embellish the Gran Trofeo Barchetta race. Despite being so late in the year, Varano de' Melegari gave us a wonderful sunny day that contributed so much to the success of the event.

The first to arrive at the Riccardo Paletti circuit was Casoli with his 450S, which he drove on the road directly from home given that he lived so close to the circuit. Then, all the others began to turn up after varying delays due to the bad weather they had encountered when setting out from the various places of departure that had hardly encouraged them to bring out the family jewels. They turned up in the following order: Comelli with the A6GCS from Brescia, Alberoni with the 200S from Bologna, Pedersoli with the 200 SI from Carpi, Vitali with the A6GCS and Grazzi from Ferrara. The latter, instead of bringing his A6GCS, came with the 350S. As I crossed the garage area to go and meet them and supervise the unloading of the cars, I met Signor de Tomaso who was with his guests, Ingegner Mantovani, Signor Tomasi, Signora de Filippis and Ingegner Huschek, and he asked me if the classic cars had arrived. I told him that they were unloading the 350S from the trailer and I had to rush to ask the owner not to bother because instead of coming with the A6GCS, he had showed up with a car that he had rebuilt and that was not original. Signor de Tomaso told me, "Cozza, let it go, you know and I know that the car is a fake; let him participate but tell him never to show up again." After I had told Grazzi what Signor de Tomaso had to say, I inspected the car and found that it had no rear brakes and was unpainted, but it was complete with all the badges. The owner had some difficulty starting it, so I removed the bonnet to check the carburettors and noticed the plate on the bulkhead, *3501*. I couldn't help telling him that he was irresponsible to come and drive a car with front brakes only. He told me that his daughter would be driving and that she would go very slowly; she would just be testing it to see whether all the mechanical assemblies were running well. With the excuse of warming up the engines, Alberoni, immediately followed by the other participants, gave us an acoustic performance that flooded the Fornovo valley. The various tests and the races with the new Barchettas all went off smoothly and the drivers of the classic cars, while not actually, drove lap after lap, having fun and putting on a show of the first order.

THE LAMBRATE PLANT
CLOSES

Despite the fact that we had been in a general recession for some years, particularly in the automotive industry, on the 14ᵗʰ of December 1992, the road-going Barchetta Stradale was presented at the usual annual festival. Derived from the track version, with the elimination of the rear spoiler and the fitting of headlights and sidelights, the car was powered by a two-litre catalyzed engine giving 306 hp. The engine and gearbox were the same those fitted to the new Ghibli. Unfortunately, the car failed to pass the homologation tests, despite the fact that engineer Casarini had tried everything he knew to make all the requested and necessary changes to the front of the chassis. The construction of the 25 racing barchettas was also restricted to just 17, including the prototype used to develop the Stradale version, one destroyed in the crash tests and another scrapped after an accident. To date, 14 are still scattered around the world, plus a reconstruction, a forgery fraudulently obtained from the remains of the crash test car. Signor de Tomaso instructed me to prepare a price list for the racing Barchetta, as the accounts department had to invoice for repairs and did not know how to deal with spare parts. The most difficult part was to find and define the prices of the suspension elements as in the case of the engine and the gearbox there were already the price lists for the production cars we could use as starting points. De Tomaso's son Santiago should have helped me, but he told me to work it out as he didn't have time and to tell his father that his contribution had been decisive. Ingegner Bertocchi would have said, "pull your finger out".

It was well known that for some years now 51% of the Milan plant had been owned by Fiat, while in Modena Fiat had a shareholding of 40%. Signor de Tomaso's long-standing friendship with Dr. Romiti had allowed him to establish relationships involving Fiat in his affairs. Not everyone was aware, in fact, that at the 14th of December parties, Dr. Romiti used to visit, accompanied by Signor de Tomaso, once everyone else had gone home, to see the cars that were presented each year. I had already prepared the price list for Barchetta spare parts, I only needed the approval of Signor de Tomaso to pass it on to accounting. However, he was so caught up in the negotiations for the closure of Innocenti, with the consequent sale of the occupied area, that he was always travelling between Rome, Milan and Modena and I was unable to catch up with him. When finally, one afternoon in early January, I did manage to meet him, we began a discussion about the price list that just went on and on. For him, some prices were too low and I had to explain that these were parts already priced in the lists of the production cars; others were too high, so I had to explain to him that I started out by costing the materials and then analysing the production process and that Santiago had assisted me and had seen everything. Then, finally convinced, he said that he trusted me and gave his approval for the documentation to be passed on to accounting.

For some months a Fiat manager, a certain Signor Bongiorno, had been gravitating around Maserati, travelling between Innocenti in Milan and Modena. Knowing that they were dismantling Innocenti, I asked him to make sure that the production documents for the Biturbo were not lost, because they would be needed in the future. We agreed that I would go with him to salvage and then take to Modena everything I thought might be useful. In addition to thirty drawers with all the production files relating the various Biturbos, I found all the binders with invoices sent to the various dealers in which all the data regarding the individual cars were recorded: type of car, chassis and engine number, internal and external colour, there were about 60, divided by year and month, accounting for all the production output from around 1982 to 1990. Maserati Classiche would today have no hope of dealing with the many requests for information had I not taken care to rescue these documents. In addition to some office furniture, I also managed to bring to Modena the record-breaking Lambretta and a ASA 1000 car, a prototype that was to have been built by Innocenti with a 1000 cc Ferrari engine. That day I was particularly lucky thanks also to the help of Signor Bongiorno.

Signor de Tomaso was less fortunate as after dinner on the 31st of January 1993, he suffered a stroke that left him in a coma for some weeks, followed by rehabilitation and finally life in a wheelchair. The after-effects of the disease left him with sight in one eye only, while his mouth was twisted and he had great difficulty speaking; he barely managed to make himself understood. Sadly, he was never to leave the wheelchair again, even though he recovered his authoritarian and combative nature, to the extent that his company at the Bruciata continued to work on new initiatives and projects, the last one being the construction of an off-road vehicle, powered by an engine from a Soviet company. This project remained only on paper because of his deteriorating state of health that no longer permitted him the necessary lucidity to live. He died at 73 years of age on the 22nd of May 2003. Fiat acquired full ownership of Maserati, informing us that Ingegner Eugenio Alzati, a former director of Lancia, Ferrari, Alfa Romeo and at that time at Fiat Brazil, would be taking over.

THE ARRIVAL
OF INGEGNER ALZATI

The Geneva International Motor Show was held from the 4th to the 14th of March 1993 in the magnificent complex opened a few years earlier near the airport. The Maserati stand featured the Spyder 90, the Shamal, the Barchetta stradale and the Ghibli Gran Turismo, the new 2.8-litre coupé for the European market. The stand was set up by Sida, our Swiss importer's company. My colleague, the accountant Manicardi from the Sales Office, and I, had arrived in Geneva with a new Ghibli the day before the press preview; Signora Valdevit and the notary, Brancaccio, would be arriving the next day. For us, the most important novelty was not so much the new car, but the meeting with the new general manager, who was travelling from Brazil, where he managed the Fiat plant, specifically to get to know all our importers and to make his initial contacts with the Maserati world before definitively arriving in Modena the following month. While I was intent on presenting our new car to a group of journalists who were asking me for explanations, I saw him arrive. I realized that it was him because Brancaccio went to meet him and went into the office where they stopped to talk with the accountant Manicardi and Signora Valdevit for more than an hour. I knew that the meeting with importers had been scheduled for 11 o'clock that morning in a room at the Palazzo delle Esposizioni booked by Maserati and that at four o'clock he had a flight back to Brazil.

I had just finished talking to Peter Ustinov, the popular actor and an important client, when I turned around and saw that a gentleman was coming up me and smiling, "I'm Alzati, the new director of Maserati", he held out a hand which I shook. "They tell me that you're one of the oldest veterans, still with the company as a consultant." I replied that unfortunately the veterans at Maserati were not very well regarded. I told him that the day before I left, while I was preparing my car for the trip, I had met an old colleague of mine, an excellent engineer, and I had reminded him that when I got back I would be bringing him a classic engine that needed to be overhauled. He'd told me that it was his last day at work as he clocked off with his overalls under his arm, just like any other day.

"Impossible!" Ingegner Alzati said, "Unbelievable!" I replied that this was unfortunately the case. "When I'm in Modena, if you help me out, I'd like to bring together all the veterans with 18/20 years of work experience and make them feel part of the company in which they've worked." Increasingly surprised by this show of humanity, I told him that when he arrived in Modena he would find a colleague of mine at Maserati, Ardilio Manfredini, with greater seniority, who would be very happy to contribute to this project. As he bid farewell, he said to me, "I can't wait to get back to Modena where I have many friends." I didn't know what he meant at the time, but Manicardi subsequently explained that Alzati had lived in Modena for the seven years he had been managing director of Ferrari. He had also got to know the Ingegner Bertocchi and on Sundays they would take long rides into the mountains on racing bikes. He knew all those who frequented the Circolo della Biella and enjoyed fishing and hunting.

On my return, numerous colleagues came to look for me to find out what I thought about the new manager. I had no difficulty in reassuring them of the excellent impact he had made and told immediately Manfredini about Ingegner Alzati's plan to bring together all the Maserati veterans and make them feel a part to the company where they had spent all their working lives.

The following month, when Ingegner Eugenio Alzati arrived in Maserati, after an endless tour through the entire factory, accompanied by the factory manager Signor Bongiorno and Manfredini, he took his seat in an office located in a compartment of the Technical Office, where both the Sales Office and my office had converged and immediately realized the need for a more suitable arrangement as with the return of the draughtsmen from De Tomaso, the space was insufficient. Dr. Poggi had also arrived from Turin, as director of the Sales Office that was moved to Signor de Tomaso's office, along with Signor Condivi, our former importer to England who for three years, since he had sold his business, had been employed as a consultant for the right-hand drive market: Australia, South Africa and Great Britain. When Ingegner Alzati was presented with the opportunity, he immediately started renovating a building, that had formerly housed a transport firm and which had been acquired several years previously, adjacent to and at the corner of Maserati's entrance. On the ground floor of the new building there was a meeting room and a showroom; the first floor housed the Sales Office and the Public Relations Office while on the second floor were the offices of the Ingegner Alzati, the sales manager and the secretaries. The attic was to house the Historical Archive.

In the immense reorganization project that Ingegner Alzati had to undertake, given that we were also launching new cars, Ingegner Giacomo Caliri was appointed as the new technical director, with the consequent departure of Ingegner Casarini, who had been responsible for type approval and who had had an eye on that position.

In the meantime, in order to clear up any doubts over the Shamal V8 engine to be used in the new models, the former Ferrari technical director was brought in to inspect the design of the new engine, in relation to which nothing of note was found other than a need to enlarge an oilway to the cylinder heads as a further guarantee. Manfredini and I were in charge of bringing together our retired colleagues with at least twenty years of service at Maserati to create the Veterans Group. Dr. Massimo Burzio from Fiat, had been appointed as the new editor of the Club Maserati's *Il Tridente* magazine replacing Signora Valdevit. Ingegner Alzati wanted to transform the magazine from a club publication into an official house organ, the editorial board of which was composed of Ingegner Alzati as President and Dr. Poggi as Vice President. Signor Cucchi was editor and secretary while Ingegner Mantovani, Gigi Villoresi, the club member Walter Gualdrini and I were advisors.

Regarding Villoresi, Signora Valdevit had had him come to Modena to Don Sergio Mantovani's home for the elderly, the Casa della Gioia e del Sole. He had recovered physically, even though he had still problems with his legs and had a range of one hundred metres, which meant that he had to use a wheelchair. As he had no friends in San Pellegrino Terme, he was always alone, with only one close friend visiting him two or three times a week; he suffered from the solitude and was missing someone to talk to about cars. As it was Maserati that was dealing with his maintenance, a decision taken some time previously by Signor de Tomaso, Signora Valdevit rightly decided to bring him to Modena and we in the Veteran Formula 1 Mechanics Clubs organized ourselves so that someone would visit him every afternoon from four to six o'clock. Together with Pasquale Cassani of Ferrari, his co-pilot when he won the Mille Miglia in 1951, and our president Giulio Borsari, we decided to compile a calendar for the afternoon visit shifts; every Sunday Cassani would pick him up and take him home for lunch. I naturally had to inform Ingegner Alzati of the matter and spoke to him about it him a few weeks after his arrival, as previously he had had too many far more urgent things to deal with.

Firstly we spoke about my own situation as a consultant and then of that of Villoresi. I had no written contract for my consultancy work, my agreement with Signor de Tomaso having been sealed with a handshake. Ingegner Alzati got up from his chair and stretched out his hand saying, "Here's the new contract!" With regard to Villoresi's position, it was immediately agreed that we should continue as before: Maserati would cover his living expenses until Villoresi was able to benefit from the Bacchelli law (promulgated in 1985, the law established a fund for illustrious citizens who were in particular need, *ed*). Ingegner Alzati asked me to accompany him as he would like to visit Villoresi as soon as he had a quiet afternoon. Before leaving, Ingegner Alzati mentioned the cars in the Maserati Museum. They had not been included in the transfer contract with Fiat and belonged to OAM, a personal company owned by Signor de Tomaso. Nobody knew anything about it, only the administrator, the accountant Rosi, had been ordered to bill my expenses and those of the two mechanics employed on the restoration work to a different company; as a result, the cars had become personal property, no longer belonging to Maserati. Ingegner Alzati asked me to prepare two folders with photographs and descriptions of each car to take with him when he went to Turin to meet the Fiat managers and to try to convince them to buy them.

One Friday afternoon, after the normal working hours, I went to visit Villoresi together with Ingegner Alzati; I gave Don Sergio forewarning so that he would be there because he wanted to meet the new director. As I expected, they got on very well and it was if they had known one another for years, so much so that Ingegner Alzati accepted Don Sergio's invitation to stay for dinner. Naturally, I also introduced Ingegner Alzati to the world of the Maserati Register. At the Christmas lunch on the 12th of December 1993, held at the La Ghisiola estate in Bologna owned by our members the Zamboni family, the over one hundred members present appointed Ingegner Alzati as an honorary member, together with Ingegner Carlo Maserati and Dr. Adolfo Orsi. When Signora de Filippis and her husband Teo Huschek mentioned Maserati's eightieth anniversary the following year, they immediately received approval for the organization of a meeting in September that would also involve the Club Maserati.

MASERATI: FACING UP TO THE NEW CHALLENGE

Eugenio Alzati

1993 was a year of great change at Maserati. External causes, such as the severe global recession afflicting the automotive market and internal situations, such as the closure of the Lambrate factory and the serious illness that has struck Signor Alejandro de Tomaso, have led to period of difficulty, giving the impression that the future of the company was in danger. When last year [this article appeared in the magazine Il Tridente, in April 1994, *ed.*]*, Fiat Auto, acquiring the entire Maserati shareholding, asked me to deal with of the future of this prestigious brand, I accepted the assignment as yet another career challenge, one that I was ready to face with absolute commitment and great confidence. It took me just a few hours in Modena to recognised the degree of professionalism and passion animating those working here and how everyone wanted to show that it was possible to turn a difficult situation into positive events. With the transfer of all production and management activities to the single Modena site, Maserati has today rediscovered itself. The independence and individuality of the brand will always be my most important goal, both in the choice of products and in the commercial strategy adopted. Designing and manufacturing Maseratis means knowing how to interpret the wishes of customers who want to experience the car in an intense, almost passionate fashion. We therefore need to* *be able to merge, within the enthralling automotive object, a world of emotions originating from memories of glorious sporting victories with a technological and stylistic reality projected towards the future. I hope to be able to convey to everyone this message of stubborn desire for rebirth: the prestigious Trident marque and its customers deserve our very best efforts.*

THE MASERATI
VETERANS GROUP

When Manfredini and I checked the registers of the Personnel Office we found 182 names of colleagues who had spent at least 20 years working at Maserati as requested by Ingegner Alzati. On the 26th of February 1994, a Saturday morning with the fog cloaking the Officine Alfieri Maserati, the former Maserati workers gathered to receive a diploma and celebrate, in the present of the Archbishop Monsignor Santo Quadri, the first day of the Trident Veterans Group. Along with the diploma which read "For having contributed with his labour to the continuation of the legend of the Trident", everyone was given a gold badge which had been commissioned from the goldsmiths of Valenza Po, a simple object but one rich in meaning. Everyone was enthusiastic about this initiative and Ingegner Alfieri was greeted with an ovation when he called up the 85-year-old Pareschi to receive his scroll and gold badge. A blue banner carrying a large Maserati badge had been specially made with the following motto: "L'emozione di continuare nella leggenda" ("The emotion of continuing in the legend"). Ingegner Alzati wanted the 65-year-old Ardilio Manfredini, who had only recently, retired to preside over this group, while I, at 61 years old of which 43 spent at Maserati, would be the Vice President with Fausto Bietolini, Ennio Golinelli and Ezio Medici as counsellors, all of whom had spent over 35 years with the company. The closing address on that magnificent morning brought a tear to many eyes when

Ingegner Alzati said, "These people, for various reasons, have perhaps been forgotten, I was determined to allow them to feel once again close to the marque that accompanied them throughout their working lives."

THE TRADITION CONTINUES

With overwhelming enthusiasm, Ingegner Alzati, after a year at Maserati, introduced two new models, the Ghibli MY 94 and the new Quattroporte saloon. On its debut at the Turin International Motor Show in April 1994, the Quattroporte was well received by the specialist press and admired by visitors to the show. It was a success that had been sought and created employing the full breadth of Maserati technology. The bodywork had been designed by Marcello Gandini, it was a 4.55-metre-long saloon with taut, wedge-shaped lines rendering the car elegant, aggressive and aerodynamic. With a wheelbase of 2.65 metres, it provided a high degree of stability and also increased interior space, especially for rear-seat passengers. In the best Maserati traditions the interiors offered great comfort with Connolly leather upholstery, automatic air conditioning, airbags and seatbelt pre-tensioners. A great deal of care was taken with the security systems, with the doors being equipped with anti-intrusion bars. The Maserati Quattroporte was offered with two engines displacing 2 and 2.8 litres, the latter mainly for export. The modern V6 power unit featured all-aluminium construction, two camshafts per bank, two turbochargers with double intercoolers, a direct static ignition system with electronic fuel injection management, an exhaust system with double catalyst and double lambda probe, a six-speed gearbox and for the 2.8 an option four-speed automatic gearbox. The two-litre delivered 287 hp at 6500 rpm and a top speed of 260 kph, while the 2.8 topped out at 255 kph. This new Maserati was part of a very special market segment, in which the world's most elegant and exclusive cars were represented.

MASERATI'S 80ᵀᴴ ANNIVERSARY

Cortina d'Ampezzo, Riccione, Imola, Modena, from the 14ᵗʰ to the 18ᵗʰ of September 1994: the organizing committee, chaired by Signora de Filippis and consisting of Marcello Grigorov, Ingegner Teo Huschek, myself and the secretary Giovanna Romeo, with the direct involvement of Maserati and the managing director and general manager Ingegner Alzati, always particularly attentive to the realization of such events, had established these locations and these dates for the celebration of Maserati's eightieth anniversary. 138 cars were registered, together with more than 290 people from 13 different countries, which gives an immediate idea of how widespread attachment to our marque is among collectors and owners of cars (historic and otherwise).

The arrival in Cortina was not the happiest, the Pearl of the Dolomites welcomed us under driving rain and snow and the following day the town was actually isolated due to a number of landslides. With check-in completed as best we could, I accompanied Grigorov to scout the state of the roads that had in the meantime become impassable. We then returned to the hotel for the welcoming ceremony, having been prevented by the bad weather from staging the usual parade with all the cars driving along the streets of the town. At the hotel we listened to Sergio Mantovani talking about the Coppa delle Dolomiti he had won in 1954 with the A6GCS. Gigi Villoresi, President of the Maserati Register, captured the attention of us all by talking about the Maserati brothers and Adolfo Orsi, honorary member of the Register, recalled his grandfather. Then everyone dressed in their heaviest clothes, having to reach the Faloria refuge by chairlift for a typical local dinner, where, after Signora de Filippis presented the silver bowls of the Maserati Register engraved with the name of each participant, a band played for the dancers, creating a friendly and relaxed atmosphere that allowed us to put aside the disappointment of a Dolomites tour suspended because of the bad weather. During the descent in the chairlift late at night, a fortuitous gap in the clouds allowed us to admire Cortina from above, illuminated in all its beauty.

At half past nine precisely on the morning of September the 15th we departed for La Villa, after the illusion of a pale, timid sun and a snowy passage over the Valparola Pass. Ingegner Alzati had put two new Quattroportes at the disposition of the organizers, one for Signora de Filippis carrying Villoresi and the Englishman Roy Salvadori, our former driver, the other for Ingegner Huschek and Emmanuel de Graffenried; I was instead at the wheel of a new Ghibli with Ingegner Mantovani; the mechanics Martinelli and Sitti completed our caravan in the service van. We returned to Cortina for lunch, finally outdoors, with the pressure of alarming and discordant news about the situation of the roads interrupted by landslides. At around two o'clock we left for Riccione where we arrived after a fairly quiet journey. After the handing out the new roadbooks, we went to our hotel for dinner. Each of the three hotels occupied by the Maseratisti had prepared their own Maserati cake, a gesture much appreciated especially by the foreigners.

At eight o'clock on Friday, September the 16th, everyone was ready to drive to the Imola circuit. The caravan stopped at the Tamburello corner where Signora de Filippis, along with Villoresi and all the other former drivers, laid a bouquet of flowers at the point where Ayrton Senna had lost his life. We then moved on a hundred metres to the point where, the same weekend, another driver, Ronald Ratzenberger, had also lost his life. Fortunately, the programme that followed was able to disperse the melancholic shadow cast by those tragedies. The participants let themselves go in free practice, while at the same time the owners of the modern cars participated in the gymkhana in the paddock. At 12:30 PM everyone took advantage of the buffet at the circuit restaurant, a short break before the skill tests and another free practice session that no one wanted to miss. Among other things, I was under particular pressure from an architect from Bologna, a member of the Maserati Club, who had cornered me in Cortina about a recently purchased A6GCS barchetta. When he told me the chassis number, *2038*, I replied that it couldn't be a sports car, as I knew that number too well, it belonged to a single-seater A6GCM formerly owned by Baron de Graffenried. I couldn't get rid of him and he took every opportunity to talk about this car. At about six o'clock that evening, even the most hardened fans of the track were on their way back to Riccione; we had to prepare for the Maserati Register's gala evening. A number of coaches picked up the participants and took them to Il Mulino in Misano, a venue where the authorities of the ACI of Bologna and Sagis, manager of the Imola circuit were also present. The magnificent restaurant had extensive illuminated grounds and provided us with a very suggestive atmosphere and an excellent dinner. At nine o'clock on the Saturday morning we departed on a free run to Modena, where the caravan reconvened in front of the Officine Alfieri Maserati where Ingegner Eugenio Alzati, managing director of the company, was waiting, surrounded by executives, former mechanics and civic dignitaries, for a day that would be all-Maserati and all-Modena. To the delight of the many who had never entered the factory, a magnificent buffet had been set up under a large tent in the courtyard that after a visit to the workshop was literally mobbed. At half past two we staged a parade of all the cars through the city centre. A police car and two motorbikes from the city police cleared the way for the Quattroporte of Ingegner Alzati with Villoresi, de Graffenried and Salvadori, followed by de Filippis with Signora Emma Alzati, Valenzano and Munarón, then, one by one, the entire caravan of 139 cars that were to complete the tour of the city in Piazza Roma, where I had set up the grandstand for the judges of the concours d'elegance, Ingegner Giulio Alfieri, Dr. Adolfo Orsi, the journalist Rob de la Rive Box and myself. A very experienced speaker, the journalist Elvio Deganello, described to the many present the features of each car. Hans Wulfers of Monte Carlo, a member of the Registry, won first prize in the competition with his 1951 A6G Frua coupé. The gala evening had been planned for some time, as had the menu, at Villa Cesi, which I had visited some time previously with Giovanna Romeo and Signora Emma Alzati to organize every detail, given that it meant so much to Ingegner Alzati: he wanted to leave an indelible impression of Maserati, especially on the foreign guests. All the participants were taken by coach to Villa Cesi, where they joined the other guests, from the Mayor of Modena, Signora Mariangela Bastico, to the Chief Magistrate, the Police Commissioner, the Commander of the Military Academy and the Commander of the Traffic Police. After the welcoming speech by Ingegner Alzati, Gigi Villoresi, the President of the Maserati Register, apologised for not being able to attend the entire meeting for health reasons and thanked Maria Teresa de Filippis and the entire organizational staff. After an exquisite dinner, which ended with a fantastic Maserati cake greeted with applause, we moved to the conference room for the prize-giving ceremony, where before the meal a film about Maserati had been shown. Displayed on a table were the many beautiful blue enamel cups with the Maserati logo presented by the company together with the silver plaques depicting the logo of the Trident's 80th anniversary rally. I was called to present the plaques to the former drivers: Villoresi, de Filippis, de Graffenried, Salvadori, Mantovani and Munarón. Ingegner Alzati instead presented the plaques to Ingegner Alfieri and Dr. Adolfo Orsi. Then came the actual prize-giving ceremony, preceded by thanks to Marcello and Anna Grigorov for their hard work in compiling the standings. The overall winners were the British couple Henny and Arthur Kelly, while Giuseppe Bellanca from the Club Maserati Italia took the prize for the modern cars with his 224V. In the concours d'elegance, first prize went to Hans Wulfers with his A6G Frua coupé followed by Antony Hartley of the British Club with his 8CT26 from 1930, in third place was the German Rolf Schiemenz with his Quattroporte 123. The prize for the competitor who came from furthest away went to the Californian Greg Kiriakoff with his spider Frua A6G 54, who had come all the way from Los Angeles; the Michelin Cup was awarded to Stefan Enhoering of the Swedish Club who drove by road from Stockholm in his Mexico. Finally, there was even a cup for the most unfortunate participant, the president of the Austrian Maserati Club, Herwik Matschy, who only managed to get his Indy running after the end of the tests at Imola. Watches from the Maserati Register were presented to Giancarlo Martinelli and Carlo Sitti, our two mechanics who had provided assistance throughout the event. We returned to our respective hotels at two o'clock that night, while I was up on the Sunday morning examining the historic cars for homologation in the Maserati Register. We then said our farewells and looked forward to Maserati's 90th anniversary in 2004.

ASI COMMISSIONER
FOR MASERATI CARS

The Automotoclub Storico Italiano, in the person of
its President, Avvocato Roberto Loi, often calls me for
information regarding the originality of classic Maserati
cars. Not that the ASI lacks experts, even experts in Maserati cars, but what they certainly don't have is access to
the archival documents and cannot know the full history
of a car possibly built many years ago, now restored and
ready to be presented by the owner for registration with
the ASI. Since the world of classic car collecting, even in
Italy, is evolving rapidly, when you are faced with cars of
particular historical interest and a certain value, you have
to be very careful not to declare a car to be original when
it is in fact a stunning example of good counterfeiting.
The ASI, with its structure of numerous federated clubs
and thousands of members, organizes verification sessions
in different regions each month so as to cover all of Italy
during the course of a year. The Technical Commission for
Automobiles is composed of twelve regional coordinators
who oversee around fifty experienced marque or model
commissioners.

In the spring of 1995, Avvocato Loi asked me to take part
in a verification session near Bologna, as a Maserati A6GCS
car from 1950 had been registered. I asked for the chassis
number to check the history of the car and any owners that
may have been mentioned in the archive and I prepared a
copy of the chassis drawing and all the photographs of the

model. When I arrived at the workshop where the checks were being carried out, I was impressed by the profession- alism with which the various commissioners were working. While outside the chatter of the various owners could be heard, inside groups of three or four people stood around each of the three cars, discussing in low voices, taking notes and walked around the vehicles. One was on the lift and it was being examined from below. A gentleman came up to me and told me that I wasn't allowed to enter and I couldn't stay in the verification area. I introduced myself saying that Avvocato Loi had asked me to be present at the inspection of the Maserati. At that point he stretched out his hand to me smiling, it was Maurizio Tabucchi, from Pistoia, the ASI's Emilia and Tuscany coordinator and a great Alfa Romeo, Ferrari, Maserati, Cisitalia, De Tomaso, Osca and Bugatti expert. He told me that he knew me by reputation thanks to the numerous pieces of information I had already sent to ASI in previous years. Once the ver- ification of an Alfa 1900 from 1946 had been completed, he called up the Maserati, regarding which I had doubts over the chassis. Tabucchi introduced me to the other com- missioners who were with him, immediately putting me at my ease. They were all people of my generation in their fifties or sixties, all car enthusiasts, who did their job with care, attention and passion. The Maserati was brought in and placed on the lift. Signor Tabucchi wanted to check the chassis against the drawing, as the front end had been rebuilt. The diameter of the tubes corresponded, the welds were well made, only the colour was not Maserati grey, they had used a non-original hammered light blue. Having resolved all Signor Tabucchi's doubts, we put the car on the ground and started to check the body, finding problems with the shape of the radiator grille. The meticulousness with which I saw all the bodywork parts checked against the photographs I had brought with me, confirmed the professionalism of the commissioners. Apart from the engine, which was not the original unit (at the time of construction they had mounted a similar one with another number), the rest of the mechanical specification corresponded to the type of car.

Sitting around a table, while Mr Tabucchi was writing up his report, each of us offered our own considerations. Once the report was complete, we all signed it. While they were telling me about verifications conducted on cars of dubious originality, I told them about how I had been buttonholed for four solid days regarding an A6GCS *2038* at Cortina, during the Maserati 80th Anniversary meeting. In my opinion that was the number of a single-seater A6GCM, as I knew the vehicle belonged to Baron de Graffenried. The owner would be coming in to Maserati to show us an original document confirming his claims. I was both anxious and curious to see this document. I didn't have to wait long; in fact, a couple of weeks later he turned up at Maserati and showed me a series of photographs of the car with numbers stamped on the engine and on the chassis crossmember. Then he gave me a folded A3 sheet of paper. When I opened it I found that it was the technical report on the assembly of the car. The paper was original Maserati, identical, in all respects, to the pages of the twenty volumes of technical reports used until 1970. But there was one detail that made me smile and I very politely and regretfully told him that that sheet could have been used for another purpose. I pointed out to him that the handwriting was different to all the other archived reports. Every the report in the 20 volumes had been written by Signor Manfredini. I also explained to him that someone must have gone to the San Cesario paper mill, where in 1968, during the Citroën period reorganization, all the copies of the drawings of the racing cars form the Production Office had been taken to be pulped and that probably there had been a number of blank sheets, used for the reports which would then have been bound. While the paper was being dumped into the water and started to soak, it could hardly have seemed true to someone I think I knew personally to find original blank sheets of paper that he could fill out as he saw fit. I also explained that the engine No. 2038, with the pistons replaced so that it could run on petrol and the camshafts swapped to provide timing better suited to car to be used on the road, had been installed in a rebuilt chassis and passed off as an A6GCS of which only the engine was original. I warned the three commissioners who were listening to me very carefully that, if they were to check this A6GCS *2038* one day, they would already know what it was going on. Signor Tabucchi, thanking me for my contribution to the verification session, took me under my arm as we went to a table full of sandwiches and drinks to get something to eat because it was already one o'clock, and said to me, "The ASI could do with a man like you, an expert in Maserati cars, so I'll be asking the president to send you the official nomination as a marque commissioner, hoping that you'll accept." I thanked him and confirmed that I would be happy to be part of ASI.

The Maserati Register organised its 1996 Christmas lunch at the Panini Museum, with a table stretching the length of the building flanked by all the Maserati that fortunately had returned from London Signor Umberto Panini.

Among the guests was Avvocato Loi of the ASI who took me to one side to ask me to help convince Ingegner Giulio Alfieri to take over as Chairman of the Automobile Technical Commission. Signora de Filippis, President of the Register and organiser of the lunch, having been tipped off by Avvocato Loi, had arranged for Ingegner Alfieri, Avvocato Loi and myself to sitting close together. During lunch, between one speech and another by the various figures present, Avvocato Loi was therefore able to speak directly to Ingegner Alfieri, asking him to join the ASI. I also contributed by saying that the chairman of the Technical Commission should be capable, knowledgeable figure to which Ingegner Alfieri replied that now he was retired, he would have some time to devote to the ASI.

GHIBLI OPEN CUP

After the Ghibli Model Year 94 had been presented at the Geneva Motor Show in March 1994, the Ghibli range was completed with two new versions that would be presented at the Bologna Motor Show the following December. The KS (sports kit), which was the result of a specific development of the standard version, put greater emphasis on the sporting characteristics, without detracting from the car's elegance and comfort. The Ghibli Open Cup was instead a racing version: in 1995, Maserati promoted a one-make championship disputed over eight races which Ingegner Alzati presented at Vallelunga on the 26th of February. In addition to the many gentlemen drivers eager to try the car and the specialist press, the Maserati Veterans Group was also present in full. The Ghibli Open Cup was to be built in a limited series of 25 examples ready to race at a price of 120 million Lire, including 19% VAT. At the end of the championship season, the car could be transformed into a street-legal road car. The technical characteristics of the Open Cup were: 320 hp at 7000 rpm a two-litre turned engine with a "Ball-Bearings" turbo, oversized intercoolers, brake cooling, modified suspension with different dampers, springs and anti-roll bars, a new ZF limited slip differential and clutch, a short final drive ratio of 1:3.45, perforated brake discs, 8 x 17 front and 9 x 17 rear OZ Futura modular rims and 20/62 x 17 front and 24/62 x 17 rear Michelin slick tyres. The interior was partially stripped and adapted for racing with an integral roll-bar, a Sparco driver's seat and an automatic fire extinguishing system. Maserati entrusted the entire organisation, management and promotion of the Selenia Ghibli Open Cup to Historica Selecta, a company run by Adolfo Orsi that was also responsible for the technical and sporting regulations. In the Selenia Ghibli Open Cup calendar, five of the eight races would be held in conjunction with the DTM, the German Touring Car Championship, and one with a Formula 1 Grand Prix. The calendar was as follows:

29 April	Imola (Formula 1 San Marino GP)
21 and 28 May	Mugello (DTM)
4 June	Helsinki, Finland (DTM)
11 June	Nürburgring, Germany
25 June	Zandvoort, Holland
9 July	Donington, Great Britain (DTM)
6 August	Magny-Cours, France (DTM)
3 September	Estoril, Portugal (DTM)

The line up of drivers featured a number of leading names: Arturo Merzario, Markku Alén, Nanni Galli, Giovanni Lavaggi, Giorgio Pianta, Mauro Nesti, Tim Coronel, Tiff Needell, Beppe Schenetti, Federico D'Amore, Denny Zardo, Mauro Bompani, Gianni Giudici, Renzo Raimondi, Ermanno Martinelli, Luigi Menegatto, Massimo Biasion, Maurizio Ambrogetti, Jon Targett, Canti Muller, Jari Nurminen, Juha Varyosari and John Augenholz. They all brought prestige to this one-make championship, having fun while ensuring its success. The early season favourite was Arturo Merzario, but then the young Denny Zardo from Treviso, who initially no one had considered to be one of the possible protagonists, began to emerge with an impressive series of results that took him to first place in the final standings. Roberto Argenti, press officer of the Selenia Open Cup, told me that Zardo had started the season with little in the way of financial resources. He was a mechanic in the workshop run by his father who acted as his mechanic and logistics expert and asked for hospitality from race to race under the tent of one of the competing teams. The championship was a great success at circuits all over Europe, once again rewarding Ingegner Alzati, who had conceived and fought for it. Unfortunately, however, the Selenia Ghibli Open Cup trophy was abruptly interrupted after the second or third race of the 1996 edition. The powers that be at Fiat, in the person of the engineer Paolo Cantarella, intervened to oblige Ingegner Alzati to cease any competition activity, despite the fact that economically it was at no cost to the company and indeed brought only benefits to the marque in terms of image. In all probability, as Maserati and Fiat Auto were working together on new models that were already under development, Ingegner Roberto Testore, the Fiat CEO, was unwilling to divert resources and energy away from the mass production lines. Ingegner Giancarlo Spelta and Dr. Luigi Maglione had in fact arrived from Turin as general manager and commercial manager respectively.

WEDDING BELLS

After graduating with a diploma in accountancy and an initial brief work experience at a company producing lubricating oils, my son Gianluigi had been employed for some years at Banca Popolare dell'Emilia Romagna and for years had been going out with a girl he had met at the Institute of Accountancy. Giordana and I weren't surprised threfore when he told us one Sunday at lunch that they were going to get married. My wife's only objection was that perhaps they could wait a few more years as he was only 25 years old. I realised that she was saying this because of her mother's fear of losing her male child. We knew Francesca, she was a good girl, employed at a company trading in building materials. She came from a family like ours that had made sacrifices to buy their own home and had raised their children at well. Luigi asked me if I could help him because he intended to buy an apartment; they had already been to see several but for various reasons (location, traffic), they did not satisfy me. Then they took me to see an apartment that I liked immediately; it had a favourable southeast exposition and overlooked a closed street so it was quiet. It was an old apartment that needed renovating, but the kids would be able to transform it into what they wanted. They were convinced and Luigi went ahead with the purchase. They immediately began to work on it, removing the tiles from the floors. One Saturday afternoon Giordana and I went to see what they were doing and found them both dusty and sweaty, labouring with hammer and chisel, paying a price for their inexperience but showing no lack of will to work. The apartment in front of them had also been sold and the new owners had already commissioned a company to start the renovation work. Knowing some of the bricklayers, it was easy to agree on the restoration of Luigi's apartment as well. The wedding date was set for June 1994, the apartment was delivered finished, as the kids had hoped, in mid-December of the previous year, so they had plenty of time to furnish it at their leisure. My wife, on the other hand, was already in turmoil because she was supposed to make the wedding dress.

June 11, 1994 was the date set for the ceremony and Maserati provided a Quattroporte saloon to accompany the bride to the church of Sant'Agnese and then take the happy couple to Villa Tusini in San Prospero for the reception. The day started off perfectly with plenty of sunshine, but then in the afternoon it clouded over and as we arrived in San Prospero it began to pour with rain through to the next morning. The old Italian proverb "wet spouses are lucky spouses" was heard several times.

THE MASERATI MUSEUM CARS

The Eldorado rolling chassis was now complete and in running order, on display with three other classic cars in the atrium of the new office building. The bodywork had been sent to the Campana coachworks because I had decided to restore the vehicle to its original condition, with the rear fin and the all-white livery. In 1959, when it was prepared for the Indianapolis 500, the fin had been removed and the car painted red. However, the enthusiasts, the experts, knew the first version of the Eldorado and so I thought it was more appropriate to take the body back to its original form. When in May 1993 Fiat acquired 100% of Maserati SpA from the De Tomaso group, ownership of the museum unfortunately remained with OAM, even if all the cars continued to be exhibited within the company despite no longer being owned by it. The Eldorado's bodywork therefore remained at the Campana coachworks for over three years, until all the cars in the museum had found a new owner.

In June 1996, I received a phone call from the secretary of Signor de Tomaso, who said that he was passing me over to his boss, "Cozza, tell your director that I want the money or the cars!" "I'll tell him Signor de Tomaso, pass me Mafalda!" I asked the secretary if I had understood correctly, because due to the after-effects of the illness that had struck him, Signor de Tomaso was struggling to make himself understood. After confirmation that I had in fact understood correctly, I went to Ingegner Alzati to give him the bad news. "Tell him to come and pick up the cars... unfortunately I wasn't able to convince anyone in Turin to buy them." A week later a De Tomaso truck turned up and went to and fro for days, carrying all the cars to a warehouse near their factory. In the meantime, I began to stir up a fuss regarding the 15 engines. I pulled out of the archive various photographs showing our engines on display at various motor shows together with famous people. I shouted that all of the engines had been mounted on their supports before de Tomaso arrived. Moreover, there had never been any expenses billed for their restoration and they could not therefore be owned by OAM. Such was the commotion that I created that, I don't know how, Ingegner Alzati conducted negotiations with two lawyers who came specifically from Turin and in the end, at least the 15 engines remained at Maserati.

Professor Franco Lombardi from Genoa, a Maserati collector and great expert on Maserati history, had been travelling on business in England when he learned that the English auction house Brooks was preparing the catalogue for an auction of all the cars from the Maserati Museum, due to take place on the 2nd of December. On his return to Italy, he sent a fax to the Mayor of Modena and one to the *Gazzetta di Modena* informing them of the matter. The morning after, on the 18th of October 1996, the local newspaper gave ample coverage to the news, so much so that Signor de Tomaso's men had all the cars transported to England that very morning, in three huge trucks.

That same morning, Signor Umberto Panini went to Stanguellini, a well-known Fiat dealer, to have his Croma serviced. Signor Francesco Stanguellini, aware of Panini's passion for mechanics and knowing that on his farm he had also set up a collection of tractors, motorcycles and cars, told him about the news regarding the auction of Maserati

₴ROOKS PRESS INFORMATION

November 14, 1996

For immediate release

SAVED FOR THEIR NATION
Brooks helps negotiate sale of Maserati collection to Italian syndicate and prepares for the biggest sale in its history

The magnificent former collection of *'Officine Alfieri Maserati'* - that of Maserati's own factory - has been saved for the Italian nation prior to the cars' much-awaited sale at *Brooks* Olympia on December 2.

In a special arrangement with *Brooks Europe* and Notaio G Brancaccio of Modena, the cars have been acquired by a lavishly-financed new enthusiast syndicate to be preserved in a brand-new museum in their home city of Modena.

The Collection comprises a representative cross-section of racing Maseratis from the 1930s to the 1980s, and includes several unique Motor Show 'dream cars' alongside rare factory production development prototypes.

In a major coup for the newly-formed *Brooks Europe*, the syndicate's offer has been accepted by the owners of the Collection, following close consultation with *Brooks Europe* Chairman, Robert Brooks, and its Managing Director, Simon Kidston.

The owners had selected *Brooks* to launch their Collection upon the world stage, and the auction house's high-profile media campaign has proved instrumental in triggering a major Italian effort - orchestrated by the enthusiast *Registro Maserati* - to find a home buyer.

Said Robert Brooks, " From the moment we were entrusted with this important Collection, we were confident we could find good homes for every car. As enthusiasts as well as auctioneers, we appreciated that to secure one home for them all would be the ideal. The opportunity now offered to preserve the Collection intact in its native city was too compelling to ignore, and we advised the owners accordingly."

"We are confident that collectors' car enthusiasts worldwide will applaud this outcome, the logic of which echoes our success in negotiating the sale to the nation of part of the Peter Hampton Collection in lieu of death duties - the first time such an arrangement had ever been made involving a car."

Issued by Gordon Bruce Associates, 29 The High Street, Marlow, Bucks SL7 1AU, UK   Tel: +44 (0)1628 890505   Fax: +44 (0)1628 890525

396

Apprendiamo con dispiacere e con sconcerto che la Collezione
di automobili del Museo Maserati — un insieme di 19 vetture
comprendenti esemplari di insostituibile valore storico —
verrebbe dispersa in un'asta organizzata da Brooks il 2
Dicembre a Londra.
Ci auguriamo che gli sforzi attualmente in corso per
raggiungere un'intesa con la proprietà, riconducibili ad un
generoso intervento di forze imprenditoriali e di istituzioni
locali promosso dal Sindaco di Modena Giuliano Barbolini,
abbiano successo ed esprimiamo il pieno sostegno a tale
iniziativa.
Ribadiamo la nostra più viva contrarietà ad ogni soluzione
che preveda la dispersione del patrimonio storico,
progettuale e sportivo dalla Maserati, che, integro, deve
rimanere a Modena, dove è rimasto esposto negli ultimi 31
anni.

Giulio Alfieri
Angelo Tito Anselmi
Nino Balestra
Nuccio Bertone
Carlo Felice Bianchi Anderloni
Karl Bloechle
Griffith Borgeson
Thomas Bscher
Dean Butler
Bernard Cahier
Gianni Cancellieri
Adriano Cimarosti   ppis
Sandro Colombo
Valerio Colotti
Neil Corner
Nigel Corner
Ermanno Cozza
Cesare de Agostini
John de Boer
Maria Teresa de Fil
Toulo de Graffenrie
Fiorenzo Fantuzzi
Leonardo Fioravanti
Mauro Forghieri
Greg Garrison
Giorgetto Giugiaro
Winston Goodfellow   i
Graham Gauld
Franco Gozzi
Lukas Hüni
Hartmut Ibing

DOTT. ADOLFO ORSI

Spettabile Associazione
Club Meccanici Anziani F1
c/o Giulio Borsari
Viale degli Esposti 1
41050 MONTALE RANGONE

Caro Borsari,

ho il piacere di informarLa che le vetture della Collezione Maserati
non verranno più disperse all'asta.

L'offerta dell'imprenditore modenese Umberto Panini è stata accolta
anche grazie alla pubblicazione della lettera aperta da Lei sottoscritta,
che ha sostenuto l'impegno comune degli appassionati Maserati in Italia
e nel mondo, del Sindaco di Modena e delle altre istituzioni locali.

Le Maserati torneranno dunque nella loro città di origine, per essere
esposte in un costituendo "Centro dell'automobile modenese di ieri, oggi
e domani".

Nell'esprimere il compiacimento per questa soluzione ed il ringraziamento
più vivo di tutti coloro che si sono adoperati in tal senso, e in primo
luogo ad Umberto Panini, Le allego l'elenco delle firme a tutt'oggi
pervenute a Franco Lombardi, al Registro Maserati e a chi scrive, oltre
al comunicato stampa di Brooks.

Modena, 15 Novembre 1996

cars, but met with only lukewarm interest. In the meantime, the news spread to a great many personalities from the Maserati Register and city authorities, who thought of petitioning the Minister of Cultural Heritage, as the collection was an asset of the city of Modena, the fruit of the labours of men from Modena. Unfortunately, however, the cars were now abroad and the relevant authorities no longer had the opportunity to intervene. Francesco Stanguellini, after leaving Signor Umberto Panini, phoned his friend Dr. Adolfo Orsi, whose grandfather and his father, Signor Omer, had permitted the creation of the Maserati Museum in the Sixties, where he himself, as a boy, had often gone to browse. He told him about the conversation with Signor Panini, saying that his client had been not entirely disinterested in the news. They therefore decided to go that same evening to the Hombre farm to talk to Signor Umberto. It's not known whether it was Dr. Orsi's description of the cars or whether Signor Panini had been mulling over Stanguellini's words from that morning. I was told that at some point in the conversation he said, "If my poor brother Joseph were here, who in addition to creating the production of the stickers was a true lover of all things Modenese, this matter would surely have interested him, so I'll buy out the entire West company, the owner of the 19 cars." On the 14th of November 1996, the Brooks auction house announced that it was withdrawing the Maserati cars from sale because Signor Panini had contacted the notary Brancaccio, who was managing the West company on behalf of Signor de Tomaso; he had formalised the purchase and that the evening, following the Orsi-Stanguellini meeting, he had set in motion the formalities to bring all 19 cars from the Maserati Museum back to Italy, to his Hombre farm in Modena.

BLACK CLOUDS
ON THE HORIZON

Giordana hadn't been well for over a year, she just wasn't herself anymore. She would put things away in the kitchen in different places and then get angry because she could no longer find them. She often had a headache and she was always dispirited and melancholic. According to our family doctor it was depression, menopause, age; he told me to be patient, to avoid drawing attention to the problems and so on. Personally, I had serious doubts and was sure that is was something else altogether. I was at the barbers one day and while I was waiting for my turn, browsing through a magazine, I found myself reading an article about Alzheimer's, about the terrible disease and the association for the families of people suffering from it. There was also the telephone number of the doctor who chaired this association in Milan. I called her for more information and learned that Professor Neri at the Estense hospital in Modena was an expert on the disease. I went to the Estense to talk to the professor, explaining my doubts to him. He asked me what our doctor had diagnosed and I told him that for more than a year he'd been telling me that it was depression. I asked him to schedule an examination because personally I thought it was Alzheimer's disease. He made an appointment with me and two days later I accompanied Giordana to the professor, who showed us into in studio and asked various things about the family, our jobs and other things. He then he asked me very kindly to step outside because he wanted to talk with my wife alone. After ten seemingly endless minutes, she opened the door and called me back in. I heard the professor say, "We're probably faced with what you feared! Unfortunately, no medicine is yet available, we only have one experimental drug, that is not yet on the market. If you agree to start the treatment you'll have to sign a release and we'll begin tomorrow". I did so immediately, hoping to find relief but hardly imagining what awaited us.

Fortunately, life reserved joy as well as adversity for us. In fact, three years after the wedding my son's own first son Cesare was born, a beautiful baby weighing almost three kilos. In the meantime, I had got myself organized: in the morning, in addition to doing the shopping and preparing food, I took care of Giordana. In the afternoon I had a lady coming in as a carer while I went into Maserati. Sadly, my mother-in-law, who had always been so close to her daughter, was also suffering from senile dementia at the age of 87 and also needed a permanent carer. We could no longer count on her help. Once a week, Giordana and I went to the Estense Hospital where Dr. De Vreese would measure her blood pressure and take a sample drop from a fingertip to check the effect of the experimental drug she had been taking for several months. One morning at the end of June after we had gone in for the usual checks, Professor Neri called me into his study to tell me that the drug Aricep had finally been put on the market in Italy. He gave me some sample boxes, which would be enough for a couple of months, but then I would have to buy it at quite a high price as it was not yet available on the national health. He told me that the drug cost significantly less abroad, knowing that through my job I had numerous contacts abroad. He advised me to look into in finding a way to purchasing it perhaps 50% cheaper with a prescription. I immediately thought of Ciro Basadonna in Geneva, then Franco Meloni of Rome came to mind, from whom I had learned that the Vatican pharmacist was one of his Alfa Romeo clients. I phoned him straight away to find out how much the drug cost in the Vatican City. After confirming the lower price, I made arrangements with Meloni; I sent him the prescription via fax and he sent me two boxes by courier, after which I would reimburse him.

The Centro 9 Gennaio, a facility built specifically for people suffering from dementia and Alzheimer's, one of the first in Italy, had been operational for two years. I had applied via the social worker in my neighbourhood for a day hospital place but unfortunately, this kind of service was not yet available. I was told to be patient and that as soon as the day ward had been opened, Giordana would be the first to use it. We went on this way for another year, with a carer in the afternoon, while I spent the mornings with Giordana doing the shopping and the household chores. Giordana was wonderful and did everything I said, but we had reached the point where she could never be left alone. She tried to help me by busying herself, but became angry when she couldn't get things done. My daughter had picked up some books about Alzheimer's and we learned everything we could about how to care for these patients and we knew that as time passed the commitment would be increasingly exhausting. Finally, I received a call from Dr. De Vreese, Professor Neri's assistant, who summoned me to the Centro Gennaio 9, because for some months he had been the director of the structure and the opening of day care was imminent. He told me that the drug Aricep was finally available free on the national health, but after a review of the case – a this point Giordana could not even eat alone – the doctor told me that at this stage of the disease the drug was no longer of any benefit. Having completed all the bureaucratic formalities to establish the fees to be paid, based on my income and those of my children, Giordana began to attend day care at the Center where there were five patients and two assistants. I took her in at eight o'clock in the morning and went to pick her up at about seven o'clock when I left Maserati.

THE MENÙ DEI MOTORI

Lauro Malavolti was the waiter at the Cantoni restaurant in Via Emilia, in the Ponte della Pradella area, where all the drivers and celebrities who frequented Ferrari and Maserati gravitated. In the Seventies, Lauro decided to set up his own business, opening the Ristorante Lauro in Via Ciro Menotti. Within a few years it had become the restaurant par excellence for all those involved in the automotive world. The food is excellent, Lauro knows his stuff and on the walls there are motor racing photographs and posters, of which Lauro is a true collector. Dinners, openings, round tables and seminars are therefore always held in his restaurant. I have had the honour and the pleasure of visiting him often, both with the Maserati Register and Club and with the Veteran Formula 1 Mechanics Association, meetings to which we always invite our former drivers.

Fabrizio Ferrari, a well-known designer from Parma who would later become Professor of Styling at the Department of Engineering of the University of Modena, decided to organize a dinner together at Lauro's on the 7th of November 1996 for all the craftsmen and restorers of historic cars in the region and a similar number of people from the various car manufacturers.

The evening became known as "Il Menù dei Motori" or "The Menù of Engines" and on that occasion Fabrizio Ferrari also presented the first issue of the magazine of the same name. Given the success and the large number of participants, the evening has been repeated every year, always followed by the publication of the magazine in which Fabrizio, showing his skills, publishes countless photographs of the various events and new cars presented during the year by the car manufacturers of the Emilia region.

At the third annual dinner, again held at the Ristorante Lauro, the diner to my right was Giulio Alfieri, who had been my direct superior for 18 years at Maserati and now was my boss on the ASI technical commission. The conversation was naturally focused on historic cars and in particular on the last verification session that he had attended in Vicenza. He spoke to me about the Maserati A6GCS *2097*, as he was unconvinced about the car's originality. I assured him that I knew the former Bellucci car, which had belonged to Ingegner Monti of Treviso from 1968 to 1997. Reggiani had overhauled the carburettors in 1990 and Monti sold it to Signor Berton of Vicenza who'd had it restored in the Cognolato coachworks, which also polished the brake fluid reservoir. The car looked like it had just left the factory. Among other things, the opportunity was too good not to get a few things off my chest and I asked, "Ingegnere, remember when you asked me if it was time well spent, while I was looking for technical data and drawings to deal with the requests of collectors!" A smiling Ingegner Alfieri replied, "Only now do I understand the importance of that job you did with such care! It's never too late to change one's opinions!" At least I've had the satisfaction, after so long, of knowing that the work that I started almost unnoticed is now widely appreciated.

QUATTROPORTE IV SERIES
AND PRIMATIST

Despite the limited financial resources available, Ingegner Alzati did his best to ensure that Maserati progressed, drawing on all his enthusiasm and commitment to do so, even considering the construction of a new Quattroporte saloon. Unfortunately, only the Biturbo platform was available, providing a 2650 mm wheelbase against the 2800 mm of the previous Quattroporte models from the Sixties and Seventies. Rear seat space would therefore have been rather limited, but despite this handicap Ingegner Alzati turned to Marcello Gandini for the bodywork, the designer's talent producing lines of undeniable elegance. Two versions of the car were offered, a 2.0-litre for the domestic market that avoided punitive Italian taxation and a 2.8-litre for the foreign markets. The turbocharged V6 engine with electronic fuel injection delivered 287 hp at 6000 rpm in two-litre form, with the 2.8 giving 284 hp at 6000 rpm, outputs that allowed the car to reach 260 kph.

It was presented at the Turin Motor Show in 1994 and achieved unexpected success, so much so that in 1996 the range was extended with a version powered by the 3200 cc V8 engine producing 335 hp at 6400 rpm for a top speed of 270 kph.

In the spring of 1996, Ingegner Alzati undertook a joint venture with Bruno Abate, the owner of boatyards, for the supply of a 2000 cc engine with twin turbochargers good for over 360 hp to power a carbonfibre catamaran, which the multiple championship winner Guido Cappellini intended to use to make attempts on two major world records on water in the up to 3000 cc class: those of speed and endurance.

For Maserati, this marked a return to a tradition in the powerboat racing sector with roots in the Thirties. In recognition of the powerboat record set on the 4th of November at Campione d'Italia at a speed of over 216 kph with the Abate boat, a special edition car named the Primatist finished in blue inside and out was produced in a limited series of about 60 examples.

ALL CHANGE AT MASERATI

When we heard the news, a number of my colleagues from the Fifties and I were shocked, we could hardly believe it! Experiencing a mix of astonishment and scepticism we simply couldn't believe such a thing was possible. And yet it was all true: from the 1st of July 1997, Ferrari had acquired a 50% holding in Maserati. Our historic competitor, our close neighbour with whom we had enjoyed remarkable rivalry at a World Championship level from the Thirties to the Fifties, would be dictating terms at Via Ciro Menotti 322!

We felt betrayed and offended, it all seemed beyond a joke. However, once we had had the opportunity to talk to Ingegner Alzati, we realized that there was simply no alternative. We just had to be content that finally an opportunity had presented itself that would allow us to put all the uncertainties behind us once and for all and to secure a brighter future. For some time, in fact, we veterans had realised that the managers from Turin, which Fiat had sent to work alongside Ingegner Alzati, lacked the mentality and experience required at Maserati. Only the other company in the group, Ferrari, had the possibility, the experience and the capacity to make a definitive difference at Maserati.

Initially, Ingegner Alzati asked two engine designers from Maranello to check all the drawings of our 3200 cc V8 engine, in view of its use in a new car then in the design phase. Almost as if they had to find something wrong with our engine, an oilway to the cylinder heads was widened by half a millimetre, but they did pass on their congratulations for a well-designed engine.

In 1998, all three versions of the Quattroporte were thoroughly revised with the modification of several components; the new ownership was thus able to add the Evolution tag to the Quattroporte models.

On a Friday afternoon in October 1997 the employees and heads of department were all summoned to the meeting room in the presence of Avvocato Luca Cordero di Montezemolo, the Ferrari CEO. Without beating about the bush, he informed us of the retirement of Ingegner Eugenio Alzati, having reached the age limit. For us veterans it was another cold shower. We knew that Fiat was retiring its executives at 65, but we could imagine they would be so precise, especially with a person who occupied and had occupied the role of managing director in several of the group's companies. In all likelihood, the corporate manoeuvring would also have affected others at the top.

For us, Ingegner Alzati had proved to be an exceptional person, who in addition to having hauled Maserati out of the abyss, had during the almost five years in which he had been at Maserati succeeded in instilling through his enthusiasm, humanity and wisdom, a new sense of belonging in all those Maserati veterans who had pensioned off without so much as a farewell. With the help of Manfredini and myself, he had created the Veterans Group that, thanks to him, is still united and operational.

When, on his last day, we presented him with a memorial plaque, we all had a tear in our eyes. If not a monument, at least a bust of him would have been an appropriate memorial in the midst of the many trophies around the factory, as he was one of the few executives to have truly left an indelible memory with all of us.

About mid-November, I was called by Dr. Antonio Ghini, Director of Communications and the Ferrari Press Office, for information on Maserati history as he was preparing a press release. He also informed me that, in a few days, Giovanni Perfetti, a trusted colleague of his, would be arriving to run the Maserati Press Office. The next day Dr. Ghini called me again from Maranello, to tell me that he had heard that I was not an employee and that I was to consider myself engaged as a consultant by the new management too. I was honoured and flattered, so much so that I committed myself to Maserati's new direction with the same passion I had always brought to my work.

THE "ELDORADO" PARTY

Having brought all the cars from the Maserati Museum back to his Hombre company, Signor Umberto Panini finally brought a conclusion to the long story involving Carrozzeria Campana, which over four years previously had completed the restoration of the Eldorado, bringing its back to the white livery of the original version from 1958 with the tail fin. As soon as the car was ready, Signor Panini told me that he would like to start it up in the presence of all those who had taken part in its construction at Maserati.

I therefore advised Ardilio Manfredini, in his capacity as president of the Maserati Veterans Group, to prepare a list of all those who contributed the work, through to Ingegner Alfieri, and to inform them that on the morning of Saturday the 9th of November 1997, we were invited to the Panini Museum for the "Eldorado" party. Naturally, I also brought Tonino Reggiani, my maestro, who even though he was working at Weber at the time had come in to help me set up the carburettors. In addition to us from Maserati, Mr. Panini had also invited many other figures: from Dr. Orsi to Signor Francesco Stanguellini, to the maestro Nello Ugolini, our former sporting director, and many of his friends. There were more than a hundred of us.

Signor Umberto had given me the honour of the controlling the accelerator lever, while his son Matteo had the task of pushing the starter motor button after flipping the magneto switch. After two or three tries the engine was struggling to start, I looked at Matteo and showed him two fingers, he immediately sensed that he had to give the switch two flicks and as soon as he actuated the starter motor, the engine burst into life; I allowed it to idle for three or four minutes, before letting rip with the accelerator to great applause.

After I had presented on behalf of Maserati a memorial scroll to Signor Panini, he had boxes distributed to all the participants containing a commemorative medal with the script "1958-1998 Eldorado" and the figure of a cowboy.

REBIRTH

In planning for the future of Maserati, Avvocato Montezemolo, the Ferrari CEO, began an energetic restructuring
of the entire plant in addition to consideration of the production of the new car that had already existed on paper for
some time. Production was temporarily halted, the various
departments emptied and equipped with new machinery;
an ultra-modern assembly line for new models came on
stream in just over six months while some of the employees,
who had been moved to Maranello, returned to Via Ciro
Menotti in Modena where production of the new Maserati
began. The Giugiaro-designed 3200 GT was a sophisticated
sporting coupé with space for four comfortable seats in a
refined and elegant interior. The mechanical specification
was the area that was most affected by the company's new
direction. The whole front end, from the suspension to the
engine, was supported on a subframe that was assembled
off-line and then mounted on the bodyshell from below and
rigidly fixed with eight pins. The same system was used at
the rear. The car was fitted as standard with a Getrag six-
speed gearbox, but an optional four-speed automatic 'box
was also available. The engine was the turbocharged 3.2
with two Marelli with twin turbos and integrated injection
and ignition, for a power output of 370 hp at 6250 rpm
and a top speed of 280 kph.

The car was presented at the Paris Motor Show and at
the same time at the Foro Boario in Modena, an ancient
historical building adjacent to Piazza d'Armi, built at the

end of the eighteenth century by the Este family, the lords of Modena. It is now the home of the University of Modena's Faculty of Economics.

On the 24th of September 1998, an exhibition of all the Maserati models built in the past, brought together from all over the world, was the setting for the christening of the new 3200 GT. At the entrance to the exhibition, the eyes of the many journalists and guests were drawn to the historic cars: from the Type 26/B of 1927 to the 8CM of 1933 and the 8CTF brought over from the USA, the winner of the Indianapolis 500 in 1939 and 1940. Then, one by one, all the racing cars of the Fifties and Sixties, the 250F with which Fangio won his fifth World Drivers' Championship title and finally the front-engined Birdcage, the Tipo 63 with the rear-mounted 12-cylinder engine and the Types 151 and 65 prototypes. Then came the road cars: from the 3500 GT to a rare 5000 GT Shah of Persia and the Aga Khan's Quattroporte. We also displayed all the engines from our former Maserati Museum between one car and another.

Before reaching the new car, visitors were obliged to pass through four areas where the various parts of the car were exhibited: gearbox, suspension, chassis, and the cockpit and the body, expertly lit via a system designed to set them off to best effect. A wall with the samples of body colours and swatches of cockpit upholstery leather completed the presentation.

This major promotional exhibition was the fruit of the work of Dr. Ghini of Ferrari with whom I had worked on the tracing and loan of all the historic cars. He had also involved me in a project by Avvocato Montezemolo, who wanted to present the many journalists and personalities this original and important event with a souvenir. The idea came from our archive, which I had visited a few months earlier with Dr. Ghini, who was surprised to find so much material, with all the drawings and documents so well archived and preserved. A file was created, a large 40x50 cm folder, containing copies of the most important documents, drawings and brochures from 1898 to 1998. Published by Giorgio Nada in 1998 numbered copies, it was entitled *Archivio Maserati*. Dr. Orsi, Ingegner Giulio Alfieri, Signor Balestra, Manfredini, Carlo Maserati, Matteo Panini and myself all participated in the important selection of the many documents. The introduction was written by Avvocato Montezemolo who, underlining Maserati's prescience in preserving so many documents and drawings, protected in less tranquil, hoped this collection would arouse new emotions in those leafing through it.

THE OLD IRON WAREHOUSE

As the modernization and restructuring project set in motion by Avvocato Montezemolo proceeded methodically it eventually reached the two-storey shed where we had stacked all the cars from the museum. Having to completely empty the whole floor, they found an area of about seventy square meters enclosed by a metal cage with a padlocked door. This was my "old iron warehouse", so to speak, because with the help of all my colleagues I had gathered there all the individual parts of engines or cars that were found around the factory or that over the years had become unusable.

We had started in the Seventies to put aside various incomplete engines, crankcases, cylinder heads, gearboxes, a number of racing car chassis and some bodywork panels, petrol and oil tanks; the radiators were the bulkiest items. Then came the guts of the engines: the various types of connecting rods, pistons, crankshafts, camshafts, intake and exhaust manifolds, numerous pipes and boxes of nuts and bolts. Finally, miscellaneous parts such as springs, shock absorbers, leaf springs, dashboard instruments including rev counter and odometers, even a case with all the special wrenches and tools made for racing cars and engines; there were even injection pumps for 250F engines.

Fortunately, a few years earlier, under the management of Ingegner Alzati, Dr. Adolfo Orsi (son of Signor Omer, affectionately known as "Adolfino" to distinguish him from his grandfather) had advised the engineer to catalogue all this material, above all to produce a detailed list. For a couple of weeks, Dr. Orsi and one of his partners Raffaele Gazzi, with the help of a few workers, tagged each piece with a reference number and recorded the name of the piece so as to create a precise list of everything. So when I was asked for the key to that "pile of scrap" I asked to speak to the new plant manager. He was a young engineer from Fiat, who had recently spent time at Ferrari, to whom I explained that there were various offers from third parties to take everything away. I informed him that, a few months earlier, I had sold 12 pistons and the same number of connecting rods for the Tipo 9 12-cylinder engine for the Cooper in England, earning Maserati a considerable profit. There was also the possibility, with the existing material, of assembling at least four cars: a 6C 34, a 150S, a 250F and a Tipo 63 Birdcage. I could have managed the whole thing through industrial accounting. I tried to make him understand what we were talking about by explaining the material value of those objects. At the end of the interview he told me that he would let me know. I left very saddened and disappointed because it had seemed to me that I had been talking to an inexperienced person ill-suited to making that kind of decision.

A few days later the engineer, whose name I do not recall, came to my office to inform me that it had been decided to pass everything on to Signor Umberto Panini. I replied that it was the right thing to do, as he had saved and brought back to Modena all the cars that were about to be sold at auction in England. I informed him about the economic value I had calculated for the majority of the mechanical parts, suggesting that a clause be inserted in the contract whereby, after having completed with the various parts the possible four cars, Maserati would be given the opportunity to use them for advertising purposes.

I later learned that Signor Panini had come to withdraw all the material on several occasions, paying a figure that was much, much lower than my estimate. The clause was never discussed, as Maserati undertook the negotiations with Panini in an atmosphere of mutual friendship. I was also involved in the completion of the cars mentioned above. With Signor Umberto, an extraordinary person to say the least, and with his sons Giovanni, Marco and Matteo, who are equally capable and always generous, to the extent that even today, after sixteen years, they occasionally make available to us not only their Maserati cars for exhibitions and shows, but also the museum itself, which we use for conventions or meetings with the staff of our foreign importers.

REVIVING THE 16-CYLINDER
V4 AND V5 FROM 1929-1930

For the Foro Boario exhibition in September 1998, I borrowed a 16-cylinder Maserati engine, one of the two V5s built for Count Rossi di Montelera's racing power-boat. The owner was Alberto Procovio, a great admirer of the Maserati brothers and a collector of our products. Our friendship and collaboration began with help with an engine support for a 150S he owned and then continued after he had purchased, at an auction organized by Dr. Orsi in the late Nineties, of this extraordinary 16-cylinder engine displacing 5000 cc.

When I phoned him at the end of the exhibition to arrange for its return, he asked me to keep it at Maserati until he had finished restoring his garages. I told him that we would be happy to keep the engine, even forever should he be willing to sell it. He replied that it was something we could talk about. I immediately went to discuss the matter with Signor Giovanni Perfetti, my new Ferrari contact, acting as the Press and Communications Officer, who told me he would bring the matter up with with Dr. Ghini and others and get back to me in a couple of days. In the meantime, I also talked about it with Signor Igor Zanisi, another collector of ours and my assistant on the Club Maserati technical committee. The latter immediately showed great interest and asked me to keep him informed of the fate of this engine and whether or not it was to be purchased by Maserati. A few days later Perfetti informed me that, for the moment, Maserati could not proceed with the purchase of the engine. I immediately gave the floor to Signor Zanisi who asked me to put him in contact with Signor Procovio, who then telephoned me for information about Signor Zanisi intentions.

A week later I received a letter authorizing me to deliver the engine to Zanisi. After another week Perfetti passed on to me another letter from Zanisi to put on file in which he informed Maserati of his intention to rebuild the 16-cylinder V5 car destroyed in Tripoli in 1933, declaring that he had the original Maserati engine, gearbox and differential available. The chassis was therefore to have been stamped *Z. 01* to avoid any disputes over originality, given that this was a reconstruction assembled with the knowledge of the manufacturer and above all with considerable technical and economic commitments.

A few months later I received a fax from the USA, from Signor Auriana, who informed me that he had bought the V4 car with chassis *4001* from Lord J. Howell in England and that he needed the drawings of the pistons, connecting rods and camshafts to restore the engine. This was the first time that under the new Ferrari-Maserati management I had been asked to copy drawings and so I went to ask Signor Perfetti for permission to process the request. He informed me that Ferrari never provided drawings for the reconstruction of parts for restorations. Disappointed at not having the opportunity, to help the owners of our old cars as had always been my policy, I put the fax aside.

In the meantime, I learned that the new synergies with Ferrari would lead to the use of an engine built at Maranello, a 4000 cc 90° V8 mounted in the new Spyder that would go into production in 2001. Leaving aside any personal prejudice, if the relaunch of Maserati was to be a success, this too was necessary; in addition, these Ferrari engines mounted on Maserati cars, would have been adapted to give a less overtly sporting character more appropriate to our cars.

When I was tidying my desk I came across the fax sent by Signor Auriana to which it was only polite to send a reply. As I thought about what to write, I decided to make another attempt. I went back to Perfetti and told him that I knew about our new Spyder. I explained that Signor Auriana needed the drawings for the restoration of a 1929 Zagato-bodied Maserati spider, the car used by Borzacchini for the world 10-kilometre record of over 246 kph at Cremona in 1929. The car had then been sold to Professor Galeazzi of Rome who had it rebodied for road use by Zagato. After various transfers of ownership, it ended up in the United States and sixty years one it was finally being restored and if we lent a hand there would be more chance of it being available for the launch of the new Spyder in the United States Perfetti looked at me and said, "You're really determined I have to admit, I'll let you know tomorrow!"

When I got the okay to make copies of the three drawings, I immediately sent them to England, to the restorer of all the mechanical assemblies and the engine, Mr. Sean Danaher. As for the bodywork, Dr. Orsi, who was supervising the restoration, entrusted it to Cognolato who took it back to its original two-tone green livery. The car was then taken back to the United States by its owner and made available to Maserati for the launch of our new Spyder in the United States.

THE FERRARI-MASERATI HISTORIC CHALLENGE

At Maserati, work on the production of the 3200 GT had been in full swing for several months. The production director from Turin was Cavalier Alberto Caponera, who had trained and gained his initial experience at Lancia and was a close friend of Ingegner Alzati. He was extremely talented and he too possessed that gift of humanity so useful in getting the best out of his subordinates. Dr. Marcello Pochettino arrived as general manager and with whom we immediately got on very well as he was a great lover of historic cars. As soon as he met me he asked me about the important items we had at Maserati and when he heard that the Tipo 26 engine number *001* had been lent to a private individual, he became very angry with me because he felt I should have ignored the orders of a Ferrari manager to allow such an important piece out of the factory. He asked me to take immediate action to get the engine back and to make sure it was not lent out again without his permission.

In early December 1999, Ferrari had had a 100% shareholding in Maserati for a month when one afternoon Dr. Pochettino called me to introduce me to Dr. Luca Matteoni, a Ferrari manager who was organising the historic Shell Ferrari Challenge and asked me to give my full collaboration in contacting the collectors owning Maserati racing cars in order to unite the two marques in a Historic Challenge, to be held at the same time as the Ferrari F430 Mono-marque

Championship. As we came down to my office I told Dr. Matteoni that Maserati racing cars were mostly abroad, in England and Germany. In particular England because at Goodwood, at the festival that held every year in September, there are never less than 30 or 40 Maserati sports and single-seater cars to mark the history of the circuit and arouse the enthusiasm of the many fans.

I was told that the organization would be the responsibility of the French company Peter Auto based in Paris and that initially the Historic Challenge would take place on four or five circuits: Nürburgring, Spa, Silverstone, Montlhéry and Monza. Then, if the number of participants had increased, the series could be expanded to include Hockenheim, Paul Ricard, Le Mans and Mugello. While I was handing over copies of the names and addresses of the various owners, I also attached contact details for the various Maserati Clubs, as I thought it likely that I was not aware of all the Maserati racing cars still in existence and of their owners. Dr. Matteoni informed me that once the "Maseratisti" had joined, I would be asked to attend with his guys from Ferrari, Angelo Amadesi and Riccardo Andreoni, the events at the circuits to verify the originality of each Maserati car and their correspondence with the period of construction. I replied that regretfully I would be unable to participate because I had a daily commitment to take my wife to the Via 9 Gennaio Day Centre, a facility for Alzheimer's patients; I was very sorry but I simply couldn't leave Modena. I could tell the Dr. Matteoni was worried, he told me that it was essential to verify every car so as to avoid any later complaints. I suggested that the organisers could send me the details of every Maserati entered for the races, then, having checked the data in the archive,

I would have accepted or rejected the entry. This wasn't acceptable for Matteoni as he felt some one had to be on site to check the cars thoroughly as they could have been modified over time. I then suggested contacting my friend Giulio Borsari, who had worked in the Maserati Racing Department for over ten years and then another twenty at Ferrari; he was retired but had a thorough knowledge of both the sports and single-seater Maseratis. A relieved Dr. Matteoni immediately agreed to send me the details of the Maserati cars and that after I had checked them I would pass them on to Borsari before each trip. When I called Borsari to ask him if he would accept the assignment, I could hardly have imagined how enthusiastic he would have been. On his return from every trip, Borsari brought me the greetings of many Maseratisti with whom I had worked over the years to keep their cars efficient, as well as reporting on the outcomes of the various races.

Since 2004, the entire Challenge organisation has been managed by Ferrari, as it is increasingly demanding given the ever-greater number of cars taking part. Signor Vaglietti and myself were added to the team of scrutineers for Ferrari and Maserati respectively. In the meantime Giordana's condition had worsened and as we were no longer able to take car of her within the family, permanent hospitalization was necessary. My daughter would sometimes go in the evening to assist her at dinner, giving me the opportunity to go away every now and then, four or five days, the travelling helping to distract me and relieve the tension caused by caring for an Alzheimer's patient.

The Historic Challenge was divided into three categories, A, B and C. Category A was open to cars built before war and single-seaters, category B was for sports cars with drum brakes and category C sports cars with disc brakes. Many members, having several cars availability, could participate in more than one category. The races were held over two heats lasting between 10 and 15 laps, depending on the length of the circuit. A few minutes after the end of each race, the timings and the standings for each category were immediately available from the Race Managers. Naturally, there was also a podium presentation allowing the mechanics responsible for the maintenance of the cars and the many spectators a chance to celebrate. The organization was perfect, in addition to providing the timings of the various grids for the races, breaks were also scheduled. Moreover, there was always some one ready to take charge of the parking of the various transporters, organizing pit passes for the various teams. There were special facilities for the single-marque races given the large number of participants and there was a large tent accessible to members on presentation of the special coupon issued by the Race Managers that offered a good and plentiful self-service lunch.

The atmosphere was always friendly and cordial and we commissioners never had any major problems. A customer with a single headlight Maserati A6GCS once asked me for written permission to fit a twin rather than a single camshaft engine. Having verified that the last three cars of 1952 the modification had already been made by Maserati, Borsari and I agreed to the switch. We had the carburettors replaced on a 200S because Weber 48 DCOEs were mounted instead of Weber 45 DCOEs, these were little tricks to get a few more horsepower, but they altered the originality of the car with respect to when it was built. I would certainly have liked to have been able to check the engines of a couple of A6GCS/53 cars internally, which were far too strong compared to the 300S. We knew that in Germany they had assembled some new A6GCS engines and Borsari asked me, "What do you think they've done to make them so fast?" They had certainly kept the correct displacement at 2000 cc but the valves, the timings and the cams had certainly been modified. In addition, new engines were pushed far harder which meant that cars with smaller displacements could place better than others with original engines that were more delicate and treated with greater respect.

The Ferrari-Maserati Challenge was one of the many victims of the economic crisis of. It was, in fact, a not inconsiderable expense even for those with deep pockets. Gradually the number of participants dwindled more and more until it became clear that a racing series that had allowed so many gentlemen drivers to have fun showing off their family treasures had run its course.

THE MYSTERY
OF NUVOLARI'S 8CM AT SPA

When Gianni Perfetti returned to Ferrari he was replaced as head of communications by Dr. Antonio Ferreira de Almeida, a friendly, open and very talkative Portuguese man. He became my new contact at Maserati, even though I spent most of my time dealing with the enquiries of the ever-growing number of GT customers from the Sixties and Seventies. In particular, they would ask me about a year of construction, external or internal colour and where to find certain components that had worn out with the use of the car: mainly clutches, the discs or the ratings of the suspension coil and leaf springs.

One day I received a fax from the United States asking for historical information about a pre-war car, an 8C from 1933 chassis number *3004*. I have to point out there was no technical data sheet for this number at Maserati and neither does the number *3004* appear in the list in Orsini and Zagari's book, which jumps from 3003 to 3005; the data in this list came from Maserati sources as we had contributed to the drafting of the book.

A few years before, while I was looking through the drawings of the 8CM cars for the drawing of the intake manifold to make a copy for a German customer of the 8CM *3020*, I had found a list where the number *3004* did appear. This list included all the numbers along with the drivers and the races disputed. Considering that this list was in the midst of the drawings that had arrived from Bologna with the Maserati brothers, it was impossible for it to have been compiled later because I had had these drawings since the Sixties. I therefore learned that 8CM *3004* was the car that Tazio Nuvolari had driven to victory in the Grand Prix of Spa and the Montenero Grand Prix in Livorno in 1933. Contrary to what was reported by Orsini and Zagari who indicated as the winner chassis No. *3001* carrying the registration number BO 9754, *3001* is a two-seater 8C, the one driven by Giuseppe Campari when he won the French Grand Prix, so I thought there must be an error; it is beyond doubt that it must be No. *3007*, which was then sold to Goffredo Zehender so this cannot be true either. In any case, this uncertainty remains whenever any historian writes about the car driven by Nuvolari in the Belgian Grand Prix. Even recently, a great historian such as Nigel Trow, in his two-volume history of Maserati racing cars, attributes *3001* to Nuvolari, even mentioning a manuscript by Signor Ernesto Maserati as a contract to supply Nuvolari with *3001* for the Belgian Grand Prix. In my opinion it could well be true that it was number *3001* because the customs documents used for Campari's 8C when he went to France were already ready. The archive contains many examples of documents relating to export files with chassis numbers used previously and temporarily reused for other trips. At a later stage, the car was given its final and original chassis number when it returned to the factory before being sold. Considering the list I had found to be reliable, I told the American collector that the Maserati with the chassis number *3004* was the car used by Tazio Nuvolari. What a mistake! Every week I received a fax with questions of all kinds about the history of his car. The matter then blew over very quickly. A few months later, in fact, when I went to California, I found myself looking at a two-seater car with headlights and mudguards similar in all respects to the Tipo 8C, while it should have been a single-seater Tipo 8CM. The engine and chassis were stamped with the number *3004*; unfortunately there was something amiss. The owner was disappointed with my objections, but I was unshakable in declaring the car a reconstruction. I then had everything confirmed thanks to Signor Igor Zanisi who gave me a copy of an article taken from an English magazine in which it was written that a certain Mr. Peter Shaw had rebuilt a chassis and a body as a Tipo 8C, as it was a car more marketable than a single-seater, with the engine, gearbox and differential from the wreckage of the 8CM *3004*, consequently stamping the chassis with the same number as the engine.

MONTEREY, LAGUNA SECA, PEBBLE BEACH

In 2000, I was brought in by Dr. Ghini together with Dr. Ferreira to assist in the organization of a major event in California, which would take place in and around Monterey in the week of from the 8th to the 16th of August. Maserati had been officially absent from the American market for ten years and a special event was needed to renew the interest of the many fans of our marque, in anticipation of the arrival and marketing in the United States of our new products. I was asked to contact our American collectors and source as many cars as possible.

At Monterey, a canopy was to be erected to host a preview of no less than twenty of the most significant cars in Maserati's history, in addition to a display of our latest creation. The exposition was to be completed with giant photographs and illustrations by the artist Alberto Ponno. Maserati's official participation as the marque of the year was planned for the Laguna Seca circuit, with the presence of numerous driver-collectors, for a series of races featuring sports cars and single-seaters from the Thirties through to the Eldorado driven by Matteo Panini. The event would then end on the greens of the Carmel and Pebble Beach golf courses for the Concours d'Elegance, in which Signor Gabriele Artom with Tipo 63 and Matteo Panini with the Giugiaro prototype of the Maserati Tipo 124 were also expected to take part. All the greatest American collectors, custodians of fine Maserati cars, took part. We had also planned for arrival of the two 3200 GTs taking part in the "Canada 10,000", a 10,000-mile trip covered in around a month with the aim of verifying the cars' mechanical reliability in conditions that were far more demanding than usual. Everything was organized so that 20 pilots, journalists, and photographers from ten different countries would alternate with one another, travelling through the eight regions of Canada and on to Monterey by the 14th of August.

Dr. Ghini informed me that Dr. Matteoni would be in Monterey two weeks earlier to check on the assembly of the marquee and to receive all the cars and prepare the interior. Dr. Pochettino, Mr. Corradi, Cavalier Caponera, Dr. Ferreira and I were due to leave on the 8th of August, arriving in Monterey two days later. I pointed out to Dr. Ghini that I could not travel as was still taking my wife to the facility for Alzheimer's patients every day. He insisted that I absolutely had to be present and if necessary he would have arranged for one or two carers for the ten days of my absence. I tried to make it clear that the problem was not one of carers, but was much more serious and more delicate. I took some time and told him that I would be able to give him confirmation in a couple of days.

I went to see Dr. De Vreese, the director of the Centro 9 Gennaio, and I explained my problem to him, asking his advice as to whether if I could be absent for 10/12 days. He didn't see it as a problem as in the evening at seven o'clock Giordana would be taken to the hospital for dinner and to sleep while in the morning, after breakfast, they would take her back to the Day Centre. She would be fine for two weeks. My children told me I should to go to relieve some of the tension. My daughter would go in the evening to make sure her mother ate and to see to all the other things she needed.

When I confirmed to Dr. Ghini that I would be able to participate in the trip to the United States he informed me that two girls from his staff would also be part of the group and that they would provide me with all the information regarding departure times and travel plans. The organization also included the presence of Signora de Filippis and Signora Gabriela, Dr. Ghini's wife, a well-known photo-journalist, as well as five or six journalists from leading Italian newspapers or news agencies to make sure the event received ample coverage in Europe, underlining the importance of Maserati's return to America.

Dr. Matteoni came to pick us up at the small airport of Monterey where we had landed in a small plane following the intercontinental flight to Los Angeles. When I arrived in the area of the large white marquee with a two-metre-high Maserati script, I saw a Maserati road car from the Thirties with mudguards and headlights of a type I didn't remember from my lists of cars in the United States. When I approached with my Maserati Staff pass around my neck with my name, the owner introduced himself: it was the collector to whom I had written that the 8CM *3004* was Tazio Nuvolari's car. I couldn't hide my surprise as this car was a two-seater 8C, while *3004* was an 8CM single-seater. We started to talk and he showed me the stamping of the engine and chassis numbers, the characters of the numbers corresponded in size and shape to those I knew to be original. Nonetheless, I was immovable, Dr. Ghini also helped me out because he spoke English much better than me and assured the customer of my experience with Maserati cars, while we pushed the car onto a lift so

431

that we could examine it from below and check whether the gearbox and the differential were manufactured by Maserati. All the parts were original, I had no doubts, but I was sure I was faced with a body that did not correspond to the number stamped. I reassured the client that I would make the appropriate enquiries and would let him know as soon as I found anything out.

All the other cars on display were perfectly original and well-preserved. The next day I took a look round the pits at the Laguna Seca track, a short distance from the exhibition, where I was truly surprised to find so many different examples of our cars and in particular to meet the many owners, who after learning who I was, wanted to talk about their cars, thank me for the help given in the restoration and for advice on certain technical adjustments to the mechanical parts. I was surprised to find such a welcome and consideration for me.

Ahead of Sunday's races our general manager, Dr. Marcello Pochettino, took to the track for a parade of Maserati cars with the two 3200 GTs at the head as the "pace cars", the 250F driven by Stirling Moss, followed by Carroll Shelby with the 450S, then Maurice Trintignant with the 150S, Jack Brabham with the 300S, Maria Teresa de Filippis with the A6GCS, Augie Pabst in the Birdcage Tipo 63, followed by the Maserati 8CTF that won the Indianapolis 500 for two consecutive years, the Eldorado driven by its owner Matteo Panini, the other Birdcage Tipo 63 of Gabriele Artom and over a hundred sports and GT cars. The roar of the engines of all these splendid cars echoed round the natural bowl surrounded by the hills of the circuit.

The Maserati Club America was also present and Dr. Ferreira and I were invited by their president, Mr. Seymour

Pond, to a dinner where many other GT car owners would be present as well as racing car owners, who had come from all over the United States to participate in the event. The evening was also attended by Signora de Filippis, as the President of the Maserati Club Italia, and Dr. Adolfo Orsi, who was at home at Pebble Beach as he was a member of the jury of the Concours d'Elegance every year. There were also Fiorenzo Fantuzzi, the son of the famous coachbuilder who bodied all our racing cars, and Mr. Grossman, our former importer of the Sixties, who, when he saw me, ran to embrace me remembering our first GT cars imported into the USA.

I started out by saying that after so many years at Maserati I had contracted a virus, harmless but very contagious, and from which it is difficult to recover, called "Tridentitis". While Dr. Ferreira was translating, some diners made as if to leave the table while others approached to shake my hand saying: "I'm infected, I'm infected too." There was endless applause, in an atmosphere brought together so many people sharing a passion for Maserati. Another evening was spent with the journalists and all the other members of the party from Modena, during which as Dr. Ghini, Dr. Matteoni and other Ferrari people were present there were inevitable comments on the rivalry between the two car manufacturers.

On the 15th of August we were driven by bus to Pebble Beach to attend the Concours d'Elegance, in which Maserati distinguished itself with various models from different eras, in three categories, Grand Touring cars, Sports Racing cars and single-seaters. The field crowded with so many historic cars was framed by numerous white tents where the most diverse objects relating to the automotive world were on sale. The celebration of the 50th Concours d'Elegance saw the arrival at Pebble Beach of a myriad of cars of many different marque; enough to make the mouth water for lovers of classic machinery. In the special classes, in Maserati's honour, the winner was the A6GCS Pinin Farina berlinetta, one of the four built in 1953, second place went to the the Farina-bodied 5000 GT, formerly owned by Avvocato Gianni Agnelli, with third going to the A6G spider Frua, in the Sport class the 300S in first place was followed by the Tipo 63 Birdcage and an A6GCS/53 barchetta.

The Californian event concluded for Maserati with the applause of many of our fans and with numerous articles in the press that exalted the elegance and aesthetics of our cars and reporting the official announcement of the imminent arrival on the U.S. market of the new Spyder and the new coupé that would be followed, two years later, by the new Quattroporte saloon. On the morning of the 16th of August, we set off to San Francisco to catch our plane and return home. I was aware from the requests for information from the United States of the prestige that our brand enjoyed in North America and the work of the Maserati Club, whose American members have grown over the years, but only after a few days in California did I have the certainty of the extent to the respect in which the Trident was held. Above all, I could never have imagined that I too would enjoy such consideration. The emotions I experienced during that trip repaid all the work I had done.

SPYDER AND 4200 GT COUPÉ

With the acquisition of an area of approximately 7000 square metres adjacent to the Maserati plant in Viale Ciro Menotti, work began on the construction of a new office building and a showroom for the display of cars, as well as a multi-storey garage for the parking of employees' cars and a ten-storey office block.

At the same period in 2001, the new Spyder was presented at the Frankfurt International Motor Show. The name Spyder has always been written with a Y at Maserati, to the dismay of Italian linguists. This was a new car based on the chassis of the 3200 GT with the wheelbase shortened by 22 centimetres for which Giugiaro created a beautiful, low and compact body with clean lines and a very elegant two-seater cockpit with two fixed, body-coloured roll-bars behind the seats upholstered on the front in leather identical to that of the interior. The canvas roof opened automatically in just 25 seconds. A sophisticated car that would surely have opened the door to international markets. The most revolutionary aspect was the mechanical specification that did have some people turning up their noses; in my opinion, however, given the situation, it was absolutely necessary and positive move. Avvocato Montezemolo had once again recognised Maserati's need to develop further and while giving Ferrari a broader economic foundation. The twin-turbine turbocharged engine that had been in use for years was abandoned in favour of a naturally

435

aspirated 4200 cc Ferrari V8 engine, as fitted to the 360 Modena, naturally adapted for more tranquil use by limiting power but improving torque, as befits a GT car. The engine's specification also featured by four valves per cylinder actuated by two overhead camshafts per bank, while the gearbox mounted in unit with the differential was a six-speed manual or, on request, a Formula 1-style automatic 'box. The car boasted a power output of 390 hp at 7000 rpm and a top speed of 280 kph.

Unfortunately, the presentation in Frankfurt took place on a day that has gone down in history for events of a far more serious nature: the 11th of September 2001, the day of the attack on the twin towers of the World Trade Center in New York.

When the many international journalists arrived in Modena and tried it over the roads where Ferrari and Maserati had tested their racing cars for years, the Spyder passed with flying colours all the tests it was subjected to. A few Italian journalists whom I'd known for a long time did ask me about the Ferrari engine, making slightly ironic allusions to the never dormant rivalry. I took the opportunity to remind that we were in the new millennium and that the era was long gone in which so as not to pronounce the name Maserati Commendatore Ferrari would ask his men, "C'sa fani quì là in fànda?" ("What are those lot down the road doing?"), the road of course being Via Ciro Menotti. Once when I accompanied an American journalist from *Road and Track* magazine to Maranello in a Maserati Mistral the concierge wouldn't let me in and once, when the President of the Republic Sandro Pertini visited Ferrari in the official Maserati Quattroporte the agreed protocol was that Commendator Ferrari would open the door to the President, but Maresciallo Funetta told me that Ferrari, at the sight of Maserati, stood stock still and refused to move. There were about thirty seconds in which no one knew what to do, then Funetta leapt to the door that Pertini had already opened himself, but that was all ancient history.

Synergies with our great rival had already begun with the arrival of Ingegner Alzati in 1993 and now that the management was 100% Ferrari, the engine castings and the painting were done for us in their factory. At Maranello they had the opportunity to expand eastwards and create new departments, in particular the Nuova Meccanica, while we in Modena were almost in the town centre and we had no room for expansion. Our workshops were consequently dedicated to the assembly and finishing of the cars.

The new Spyder had already been on sale in Europe since October and was due to arrive in the US in the spring of 2002. The Ferrari-Maserati North America branch in New York rented a strategic space of 10 square metres in Manhattan's coveted Times Square where our open car was on display for five months from November; television stations from all over the world were constantly filing in this iconic location and the indirect exposure for Maserati had a very strong effect, especially in view of the forthcoming Detroit Motor Show, where the new 4200 GT coupé would be presented. The engine was the same as that of the Spyder, as was the electrohydraulic transmission, equipped with the steering wheel paddles as used on Formula 1 cars. The bodyork was that of the 3200 GT, with only minor modifications. Giugiaro had redesigned the rear lighting clusters to adapt them to American standards as the boomerang lights of the 3200 GT were not homologated in the USA. An evolution of this latest model was to give rise to a model named the CambioCorsa, intended for customers participating in the Trofeo Monomarca Maserati.

NOTICE OF INVESTIGATION

When I arrived at Maserati on Wednesday the 15ᵗʰ of
November 2001, I found Lieutenant Spatola and two finance police officers from Florence waiting for me. I was
very surprised and when I asked what they wanted, they
asked me for an identity document and the fax number
of my office and its location. As we went upstairs to the
fax machine, I heard that the Lieutenant was repeating
my name and the fax number I had given him on his cell
phone. I still had no idea what this was all about and at my
insistence he replied that I'd soon find out. A few minutes
later in fact a fax arrived which they handed to me: it was
an official notice from the court of Cuneo that I was under
investigation for the alleged crimes referred to in articles
416, 473, 474, 517 and 623 of the Penal Code. I was at a
loss for a moment; I just couldn't understand why, I didn't
know the specifics of the articles of which I was accused
and I reacted instinctively by saying, in a voice altered by
anger, that I was an honest man and that I had never done
anything against the law in my life. When they demanded
that I sign the copy of the notice in acknowledgement of
receipt, I refused and continued to protest. In the meantime,
the Ferrari administration's accountant Cappi had arrived
in the office. Alarmed by the presence of the men from
the Guardia di Finanza he called Maranello. Half an hour
later, while the officers were informing me that it was an
investigation regarding classic Maserati cars that had been
reconstructed or falsified, Avvocato Scortichini with two

young lawyers from the Ferrari Legal Department. After having read the notice of investigation, they reassured me by telling me that these were formalities and not to worry, because in due time the proceedings against me would be dropped. Meanwhile, the officers asked to see the lists of cars in the Maserati Register and also wanted to see the archive where all the documents relating to the historic cars were kept. They showed me a sheet listing five of our sports car models: the A6GCS, 200S, 300S, 450S and 151. I pointed them to the shelf where the boxes containing all the folders divided into files with the progressive chassis number of the individual cars. After having examined some of them, Lieutenant Spatola informed me that they would have to sequester them all in order to inspect them one by one. I protested, explaining that I needed them every day to process requests for information from all over the world. He promised me he would get everything back to me in a week. They formalized the seizure of the files divided into two boxes in writing, saluted me and left after asking for the telephone number of the office for any further information they may have needed. I went to thank the accountant Cappi for his promptness in bringing in Avvocato Scortichini from Maranello and at the same time he told me to not to worry because even Ferrari had had problems with counterfeit cars in the past, again in the province of Cuneo.

Late that the afternoon I was called by my friend Igor Zanisi of Brescia to inform me that at six o'clock in the morning his home had been searched by the Guardia di Finanza who had created such a fuss that they had woken up his two children of three and five years of age, who had been crying, and that he had to sign an acknowledgement of receipt of the notice of investigation. Having heard that

I was in the same boat and that I and that the lists of the Maserati Register and Club and all the files regarding five types of car had been seized, he informed me of the whole matter. He too had been worried by the incident and had telephoned Avvocato Nicola Sculco of Milan, a Maserati collector and a member of the Club Maserati, board who, in addition to reassuring him, had explained to him of how the Guardia di Finanza had had out names. During a tax investigation relating to a famous collector from Florence who had sold four Maserati cars for over five billion lire, they had discovered his dealings with a workshop in the province of Cuneo specializing in the restoration and reconstruction of historic Alfa Romeos, Ferraris and Maseratis. When the investigators found files, documents and correspondence relating to Maserati cars in this workshop, they had started looking into who else was involved. They had found some of my faxes and drawings of details and components from our cars that I had naturally sent in response to legitimate requests indicating the type of car and the chassis number to be restored. In Signor Zanisi's case they had found invoices for work on two absolutely original Maserati cars. Further notices of investigation were issued against three craftsmen from Modena who had built engine components or gearboxes for Maserati cars which the Cuneo workshop had then restored.

After ten days and two telephone reminders to the Guardia di Finanza in Florence, Lieutenant Spatola returned the two boxes containing all the folders I had taken away from Maserati by the officers from Modena. Exactly one year later I learned of the seizure by the Guardia di Finanze of Florence of ten or so Maserati sports cars from the Fifties, some of the racing models. They were all returned to their owners except two: an A6GCS chassis number *2085* and a 350S chassis number *3501*, which were withheld and then examined by a court expert. In the meantime, on the 28th of September 2005, the Public Prosecutor's Office of Cuneo requested that the notices investigation filed against me and all the other parties I have mentioned be dropped with no further action to be taken.

THE NEW QUATTROPORTE

As planned, Maserati's new headquarters were completed in 2003 with the office building featuring the large showroom on the ground floor, the commercial offices on the first floor and the boardroom and executive offices on the second. There was also a new multi-storey car park for employees and a tower carrying the Trident logo.

Dr. Antonello Perricone joined the management team in place of Dr. Pochettino, Dr. Silvio Vigato replaced Dr. Ferreira at the head of the Communications Department and Dr. Andrea Cittadini joined the Press Office from Maranello and was placed with me in an office located in the first building in the attic of which I had had installed the entire Maserati archive. Dr. Cittadini was young enough to have been my son and we immediately established a good relationship. By the way he talked I could tell he was a great *Ferrarista*, but I was pleased when he asked me about the history of Maserati and I tried to infect him with the "Tridentitis" virus.

When the fourth generation Maserati saloon, which had been christened in 1963 at the behest of Commendator Adolfo Orsi, left the stage in 2001, the fifth generation that shared only a name with its predecessors was already under development. The platform was designed by Ingegner Corradi, the head of the Technical Office, with characteristics that would allow it to be used for the marque's future models. The new Quattroporte was equipped with the 4200cc V8 engine from the Spyder and Coupé, suitably adapted for use in a saloon, but still producing 400 hp at 7000 rpm and fitted with a six-speed sequential gearbox. The chassis had a wheelbase of 3.63 metres in the interests of interior space and was clothed with bodywork designed once again, half a century later, by Pininfarina. The lines were both sleek and softly harmonious, with a length of 5.052 metres and a dry weight of 1,930 kilos. The interior boasted the ultimate in luxury, finish and functionality. Personally, I found only the sequential gearshift with steering wheel paddle controls to be wrong for a saloon. I had the opportunity to point this out to Avvocato Montezemolo, Maserati's CEO, who replied that we had to offer something different with respect to our competitors, but that in the future a six-speed ZF automatic transmission would certainly also be offered.

The exclusive Pebble Beach Golf Club in California was chosen for the world premiere in mid-August, in front of an audience composed not only of American clients and collectors, but also the editors of the American specialist magazines. Sergio Pininfarina flew out to California with Stradivari's famous 1715 violin, as a symbol of the craftsmanship and beauty of form that had inspired him in designing the Quattroporte. The official launch took place the following month at the Frankfurt International Motor Show. The President of the Italian Republic, Carlo Azeglio Ciampi, chose the new Maserati Quattroporte finished in Pertini blue as his official car, continuing a fine tradition. Avvocato Montezemolo presented him with the car during Ciampi's official visit to Maserati as head of state before the summer of 2004. This car won 57 international awards in the various versions and trim variants that have followed. In 2008, it underwent a restyling and a 4700 cc 440 hp engine was fitted to the GTS version. Between 2003 and 2012 24,000 examples of this saloon were built, levels never previously achieved by a Maserati. It even took to the track in the 2011 Superstars Series in which the talented Andrea Bertolini won four of the twelve scheduled races.

CERTIFICATIONS

In order not to interfere with production and given that there was no suitable space Maserati, the management of the 3200 GT cars participating in the single-marque trophy series and in view of further racing activities in the future race, a number of warehouses with office facilities were rented in Via delle Nazioni, on the northern outskirts of Modena. This structure was named Maserati Corse. It was directed by Claudio Berro from Ferrari, who had the idea of bringing together the Ferrari and Maserati Historical Archives under one roof. The aim was to create two working teams that would certify all of the two marques' historic racing cars, their history and above all the originality of the cars owned by the various collectors. Naturally, this would have a cost that would vary depending on the difficulties and the time taken in searching for data or verifying the car.

My colleagues at Ferrari, Angelo Amadesi and Riccardo Andreoni, who were also involved with the Challenge series, moved to Modena and were those who actually worked on the documents and prepared all the papers for the certification of the Ferrari cars that would then be countersigned by Signor Piero Ferrari and Signor Zagni, people with more than thirty years of experience and knowledge of their cars.

As far as Maserati was concerned, I was summoned by Dr. Perricone and asked to organize the transfer of our archive to Maserati Corse and to put together a team for Maserati like Ferrari had done. Dr. Berro would have assisted me.

I replied that, as I travelled in to Maserati, I would have no problem continuing for three or four kilometres to reach Via delle Nazioni, but it would be appropriate for the Maserati archive to remain where it was. I had bent over backwards to save it from the French, and even though its location was inconvenient, it was tidy and well organized. "Dr. Perricone, try to get me to me help, because if anything should happen me, nobody would know where anything was." Dr. Perricone looked at me rather perplexed and I could tell that he was surprised at my refusal to move the archive. So as to buy time, I asked him who at Maserati would be responsible for certifying the originality of one of our cars. He replied that one would have to be me, another would be Dr. Berro, then a certain Dr. Maurizio Bruno from Marketing and Dr. George Mauro, head of the After-Sales Service. I tried to explain that they were all people who knew nothing about Maserati, that all the responsibility would have fallen on one person and that I didn't want to take on this burden, it was too risky. We left with the understanding that I would talk to Dr. Berro about what could be done with regard to the certification of Maserati cars.

Amadesi and Andreoni came to visit me to see my archive and were surprised to see so much material. They had scanned or microfilmed almost everything, but while we at Maserati had had a lot of quotes for the work over the years but we had never done anything because the costs were too high. I also went to visit Maserati Corse to see how they had arranged things and, above all, to talk to Dr. Berro.

I explained to him the reasons behind my refusal to move the Maserati archive and also my concern about the certification process. He agreed with me about the archive, but regarding the certification he said that it was something we would have to try. However, I insisted that Maserati didn't have an appropriate structure and that what was needed was to put the matter in the hands of a professional, I had a name in mind but kept it to myself for the time being.

In the meantime, I had a problem with a German gentleman who had bought a Maserati A6GCS. I had expressed a negative opinion regarding the car as I believed that it was not original. The gentleman had gone ahead and bought it anyway and now wanted to take part in the Ferrari-Maserati Challenge. When I received the list of cars for the race and found the A6GCS belonging to the German client, I made a note not to accept the entry because the car was not original. I also sent a memo to Dr. Berro in which I explained in detail the full history of the car. Not only did Dr. Berro fail to respond to my memo, he actually accepted the registration of the car for the event. When Giulio Borsari stopped by on the Monday to tell me how the races had gone, I learned that the A6GCS I had expressly noted should be reject had actually participated in the race. I immediately went to Maserati Corse, ran up the stairs and entered Dr. Berro's office without knocking. What I then calmly told him doesn't bear reporting here. Borsari, who arrived shortly after the me, could only heard the finale, but he pointed out that although I was perfectly right to be angry, I had raised the tone of the protest a little too much. Berro justified himself by saying that he had been forced to accept the car because of the fuss the German had also made at Ferrari.

I had no opportunity to explain to Dr. Perricone what had happened because he had recently been replaced by the engineer Martin Leach as General Manager of Maserati. In anticipation of the Fiat parent company retaking 100% control of Maserati, all the equipment and Ferrari men who had come to Modena had returned to Maranello, where they had also set up a special department for the restoration of historic cars, increasing the number of certifications. Although I had the support of Dr. Ghini himself, who when he knew that I was running the historical archive alone, had taken me to Dr. Garello of Human Resources, as they now call the Personnel Office, to point out that additional staff was urgently required in the archive, it all ended with the usual fine words and promises that were never kept. As always, I continued to run the historical archive alone and to follow the Challenge series. Even though I was overburdened with work, I was able to handle the requests and process the correspondence within a reasonable time, despite only going to Maserati in the afternoons. The work, even if tiring, provided me with some distraction from burden of taking care of my wife. Even though Giordana was hospitalized, I could hardly abandon her there and every evening I went to feed her because she was no longer able to eat on her own.

MC12

47 years on, Maserati's official return to racing was an epochal event and took place at the Imola circuit in the fourth last race of the International FIA GT 2014 Championship. The Maserati Corse car was equipped with a rear-mounted V12 engine of almost 6000 cc that produced 630 hp at 7500 rpm, and a mechanical gearbox offering six speeds plus reverse mounted in a carbonfibre and composite materials chassis. The aerodynamic configuration of the two-seater targa bodywork, designed by Giugiaro, and a weight of just 1335 kilos allowed the car to reach a top speed of 300 kph.

On its debut it finished second and third with the Bertolini-Salo and Herbert-De Simoni crews. The second race in Germany coincided with the 90th anniversary of the company, which we were celebrating at Modena, the Mugello and Rome. The car recorded its first victory in the hands of the Sassuolo-born driver Andrea Bertolini and Mika Salo. Homologation in the FIA GT category required the construction of 25 cars in 2004 and the same number in 2005, they all were highly sought after and sold to enthusiastic gentleman drivers.

The MC12 was a winning car from the word go. I can be said that no other Maserati racing car recorded as many international victories. Between 2004 and 2010 it won 24 races and two Constructors' titles, while its drivers won the World Championship title five times. The Spa 24 Hours was won no less than three times. Despite the variations to the regulations and the recourse made to ballast to render our MC12 less effective and the races more competitive for the other cars participating in the Championship, Maserati continued to dominate. Derived from the MC12 Stradale, but never homologated for racing and built in just 15 examples between 2006 and 2007, the MC12 Corsa was fitted with an engine delivering 755 hp at 8000 rpm and the same bodywork with the addition of a rear spoiler. Weighing in at 1150 kg, this version had a top speed of 330 kph. Every example was sold in a flash for one million Euros each.

FAMILY AFFAIRS

When my son Gianluigi came to see me one Sunday in September 1997 to get me to repair a puncture on his bike, I was anxious to know how Francesca, his wife, was as she was pregnant (Cesare was to born around November in fact); for now everything was going well. At the same time Gianluigi told me that he would be going to Urbino on Monday; I imagined that he would be going for work but he told me that he was actually taking an exam at the university. I looked at him shaking my head, "You didn't want to go there when it was time and now you're working with a child on the way!" He told me that he'd decided to give it a try, he knew that it would be five hard years but he wanted to have a go. With perseverance and a great deal of determination he always managed to keep pace with the exams. In the meantime, my daughter Gianna's twins, Luca and Marco, graduated with full marks, one from the Corni Technological Institute and the other from the Fermi Institute. Luca then enrolled at university in the Faculty of Engineering Management, while Marco enrolled in Electronic Engineering. I was only sorry that Giordana was not able to understand and rejoice in this wonderful news.

In October 2002, Gianluigi called to ask me if I wanted to go with them to Urbino to attend the discussion of his degree thesis. Over these years his family had increased in number, in addition to the five-year-old Cesare there was now Emanuele, who was two. We left the day before so to be at university early in the morning well rested. We saw the thesis presentations by a dozen graduates, then we were invited to go out until the Commission had finished its evaluation work. We took the children to a small park nearby and went back to the hall at around noon. When they called Gianluigi Cozza all the members of the commission stood up and Gianluigi was proclaimed a Doctor of Political Science with a grade 110 cum laude, my daughter-in-law began to cry from the emotion and seeing her the children began to cry too. I then picked up the little one and took the hand of his brother and we hurried out so as not to cause a disturbance. Shortly afterwards, Gialuigi joined us and we went for lunch in a nearby restaurant. There we met the members of the university commission who, seeing us, came to congratulate the beautiful family and my son for his brilliant performance, despite his work and family commitments.

In preparing his degree thesis on the development of banking activities in the Este Duchy in the seventeenth and eighteenth centuries, had had to study certain documents deposited in the State Archives, among which he was lucky to find the a deed, relating to the workshop of Mario Cozza located in Modena in the street in front of the Cathedral, dated 1683, thus discovering the roots of our surname in Modena.

90TH ANNIVERSARY

From the window of my office I saw Ardilio Manfredini, who had his own office in the other building, arriving in the distance. He had been the first of that team of boys Ingegner Bellentani had formed in the early Fifties. Only the two of us had were still working; after holding various management positions, he was now the president of the GAM, the Maserati Veterans Group, and often came to see me to talk about the group's activities, trips to be organized and places to be visited. He was sorry that I could not participate in the various activities due to my wife's illness. For some time he had also living with a serious illness, and knowing the difficulties he had had lately in walking, I went to meet him so that he wouldn't have to climb the stairs. I thought about the kilometres he must have covered in the factory, walking from one department to another, in his over fifty-year career.

When I told him that I'd heard that Maserati would be celebrating its 90th anniversary in September with an impressive event, I saw him delighted and enthusiastic, he just said that he hoped would still be able, as in the past, to contribute to the success of the event. Unfortunately, on the 11th of March he died, leaving an unbridgeable void with the company and in all those who had had the good fortune to know him.

Dr. Ghini's staff, with whom I had been called to collaborate on organization of Maserati's 90th anniversary, chose the dates from the 17th to the 19th of September

2004. The programme was devised by Dr. Ghini himself and was divided into two parts: in the first, entitled "90 Years in History", 90 Maserati 3200 GT Coupés and Spyders would leave from Milan. An easily removable 3M film would be applied to each one to protect the bodywork and to decorate the bonnets and sides with images of the important historical event, celebrated every year for 90 years. In effect, the cars represented 90 mobile pictures of history and technology. The cars assembled in Piazza Duomo for the Pirelli evening at the Loggia dei Mercanti. On Saturday the 18th they departed for Modena and the city centre parade, factory tour and lunch. In the afternoon they set out again for Rome and the Grand Gala dinner at Villa Miani.

The second part, the "Classic Tour", was scheduled for Friday the 17th with the arrival in Modena's Piazza Roma of 120 historic Maserati cars, a parade through the streets of the city and then back to Maserati where the production manager, Cavalier Caponera, did his best to organize the more than two hundred people in various groups to visit the factory. After lunch, the caravan left for the Mugello circuit and a gala dinner.

I'd already been contacted by various members of the Maserati Register who wanted me as co-driver, but I had already been committed for some time, and with great pleasure, to accompanying Igor Zanisi in his 1948 Maserati A6 Pinin Farina. During the trip from Modena, Zanisi had mentioned a surprise at Mugello, but I could never have imagined what it might actually be. When we arrived, we met Gianni Torelli, a famous restorer of cars from the pre- and post-war periods, who had supervised the reconstruction of the Maserati V5 16-cylinder Grand Prix car, which was now ready to receive its track baptism. It really was a huge surprise for me.

Maserati had been informed by Zanisi of his intention to install the 16-cylinder engine (formerly owned by Procovio) in a chassis rebuilt some years previously, but I never imagined I would find myself in front of a car that was so well built, down to the smallest detail. Among the many participants in the Trofeo Novantesimo who gathered around the V5 some purists will certainly have turned up their noses in disapproval. I am instead of the opinion that for an engine of particular technical and historical interest, rather than seeing it displayed on a static support, it is better to have it in a reconstruction so as to be able to hear it running.

The Trofeo Novantesimo regularity trials on the track were divided into various classes, from A to E: class A for cars built pre-war and up to the Fifties featured the Cupellini's Tipo 26/B from 1927, the Zanisi V5, Zivieri's monofaro from 1950 and Mauro Bompani's A6 from 1948, all widely admired along with those of class B, the Fifties cars, including five A6GCS, two 150S, Sculco's 200S, who then lent it to our managing director Martin Leach for the entry into Rome, the Pinin Farina A6GCS berlinetta and the 450S of Professor Lombardi, Signor Adamoli with the Maserati brothers' Osca and then all the other cars and categories from the Sixties, Seventies and Eighties. Cars from all over Europe and characters who also came from overseas such as Seymour Pond who drove the Simun prototype from the Panini collection. The regularity trials were great fun and were followed the publication by the impeccable organizers of its rankings, which was followed, as usual, by endless discussions in an atmosphere of warm friendship. Then the whole caravan of historic cars left for the capital, where everyone found their hotels before meeting up with the first part of the event, "90 Years in History", at the Grand Gala at Villa Miani, where Audemars Piguet had organized the dinner. The marque's CEO, Martin Leach, thanked everyone for taking part in Maserati's 90th anniversary celebrations in such numbers with all the models of in its history being represented and went on to mention the growth of the company and its future.

Sunday the 19th saw a parade through the capital, where modern and historic cars followed two different paths before finally gathering in Piazza del Colosseo after being admired and warmly applauded in the streets of Rome. Dr. Antonio Ghini had organized an event whose success was widely reported in the press as an opportunity for us to see so many cars that in terms of their sporting character and elegance have always enjoyed such success around the world.

The celebrations for Maserati's 90th anniversary continued on Friday the 15th of October at the Stanguellini Museum in the presence of Ingegner Carlo Maserati, son of Ettore, one of the famous brothers, where proceedings were conducted by Dr. Adolfo Orsi, a veteran of the official event. The historical journalists Gianni Cancellieri and Cesare De Agostini and the author Nunzia Manicardi were present. The ninety years of Maserati's history were retraced with new and interesting ideas emerging. The evening concluded with the inaugural dinner of the "Pianeta Modena" Yearbook. The Menù dei Motori was the official spokesman for the great Maserati Novantesimo celebrations and that evening was attended by craftsmen and collaborators, as well as many historical figures such as Sergio Scaglietti, Franco Gozzi, Francesco Stanguellini and Lauro Malavolti.

THE RETURN OF FIAT

On the 1ˢᵗ of April 2005, Fiat regained 100% control of Maserati. The new managing director and general manager, Ingegner Karl-Heinz Kalbfell, had the important task of managing the post-Ferrari transition. Having experienced certain events first-hand I can say that Avvocato Montezemolo had been the true protagonist behind Maserati's rebirth over the previous eight years. Even though my pride in belonging to Maserati is very strong, I must admit that Ferrari was the trailblazer for Maserati's relaunch around the world.

There were rumours of certain synergies with Alfa Romeo, another historic manufacturer within the Fiat group. Maserati would certainly now have to prove that it could continue to maintain its position on the international market on its own.

In order to expand certain offices and create new ones for different purposes, the Press and Communications Office was moved to the third floor of the tower block. Dr. Cittadini and I therefore had to move. Dr. Luca Dal Monte was brought in from Ferrari Maserati North America to direct the Communications Office and occupied the middle room, the smaller one became Cittadini's office while I needed at least three cabinets for all my documents and so occupied the larger room with the two secretaries. Knowing that Dr. Dal Monte was from Cremona, I spoke to him about Gino Rancati, the journalist at the RAI in Turin, who was also from Cremona and who often came to Maserati and was a great friend of Signor de Tomaso. We immediately established a good relationship and he told me that he would certainly have much need of my help regarding the history, people and everything else about Maserati. I felt an enthusiasm and a will to work that I had not seen in those who had preceded him and hoped he would stay for many years to run the office. I settled in quickly and had all the space I needed for my documents and my things. The only inconvenience concerned the archive of drawings and the folders on the individual cars that had remained in the building I had just left. For consultations or other matters I would have to take the lift down and cross the internal courtyard, nothing too difficult and after all, a little physical activity at a certain age can only be a good thing!

When I went up to the archives at about two o'clock I found two young engineers from Technical Services department engineers on their lunch break. They had seen me passing by several times and knew who I was and where I was going. One day, they timidly introduced themselve: "We're Cristian Bolzoni and Fabio Collina, could we come with you to see the archive? Would it be possible? Are we bothering you?" I told them that I was delighted that there were young people who were passionate about history and old things. When they came in and saw the all the numerous wooden models of our racing cars, the posters and photographs, a few paintings, all the boxes stacked on the long shelf, the chest of drawers with the drawings and so on, they were stunned. While I was looking for what I needed I explained to them how the archive had been organized: according to the year and the type of car from 1926 through to the present day. As I was in a hurry, I told them to back again and I'd show them some engine drawings.

One day Silvia Orrù, Ingegner Kalbfell's secretary, called me to say that the engineer wanted to talk to me. I asked if she knew why, and she replied that the engineer had received a letter in German and when he had finished reading it, he exclaimed, "Who is this Cozza! You don't treat customers like that!" The secretary apparently told him, "That's odd, because he's always so highly regarded by all the collectors". The appointment was postponed a couple of times due to the boss's commitments. I was curious to know who it was who had been complaining about me; I did have a vague idea and it turned out I was right. It was the German gentleman with the A6GCS who after having been permitted to participate in the Historical Challenge once and in exceptional circumstances, was demanding that he should continue to be permitted to do so despite me having declared that his car was a non-original reconstruction. In fact, during the meeting with Ingegner Kalbfell, he mentioned the letter he had received in which I was accused of being a poor consultant, of having caused economic damage to an upstanding citizen and so on and so forth. Kalbfell had immediately imagined there was something odd about the matter and I briefly explained to him how things really stood at which he smiled said to me, "These things happen in the world of motorcycles too, I'll reply to him saying that I agree with your findings". The engineer had a classic motorcycle in his office and told me that as a young man he had raced bikes and that he would have liked to buy a Maserati Bora; I warned him to let me know the chassis number before proceeding with the purchase so as to check the originality of the external colour, the interior and the year of construction. As he was clearly a fan of classic engineering, I asked him if I bring a single cylinder engine used as a pattern for our 1956 12-cylinder engine to his office as I didn't know where to put it. He immediately accepted with pleasure, telling me that the office was big and there was even room for a complete engine.

Unfortunately, his stay in Maserati lasted just over a year; it was a shame because he was a good person, an executive who knew his job. He was replaced by Dr. Roberto Ronchi from Turin, who had already been worked at Maserati as sales director for a few years before being called to Fiat. He already knew the environment and the people well and was therefore facilitated in his new position as managing director.

I was called in for an interview by the new head of Human Resources, Dr. Marco Armillei, who suggested that I should replace Ardilio Manfredini at the head of the Maserati Veterans Group. I told him about my family situation, how my part-time commitment at the company only allowed me time to manage the archive and collectors and that as vice president and co-founder of the GAM I would have liked to take on the role of president, but I would not have been able to reconcile the two role. I then took the opportunity to ask for an assistant to work alongside me. He told me, as his predecessors had already done, "We'll look into that! However, I urgently need you to find someone among the veterans to run the group". Finding someone to replace Manfredini was impossible, his charisma, his skill in dealing with people, having also been the head of the Personnel Office, his "Modenesity" (he would always close every newsletter after a trip with a disquisition on the animal, the pig, whose meat has always enlivened our dinners). While browsing the list of potential candidates to find someone with at least thirty years at the company who was also familiar with office work, it occurred to me that the ideal figure could well be a woman. There were, for example, the Bortolotti sisters: Teresita had been in charge of the Purchasing Office and Anna the Italian Sales Office, I made a mark and continued my search. In the end I found six veterans, all with over 35 years service. I knew them all personally and was sure they would all do a fine job, but the accountant Giorgio Manicardi, the former head of the Foreign Sales Office, seemed to be the most suitable. I phoned him, we met at Maserati and I put the proposal to him; he immediately told me that he didn't feel it was right for him. I tried to convince him and he replied that he would have to think about it and that he would get back to me within a few days. Two days later he phoned to tell me that he would give it a try. I accompanied him to Dr. Armillei and introduced him as the only man who could carry on with the Maserati Veterans Group.

The other members of the board gave him their full support. His office was on the ground floor of the tower and at the annual membership renewal meeting at the end of February he already had a programme of visits organized, along with a proposal for a three-day trip. My intuition had served me well, Manicardi was perfect for the job, he was running the group with increasing confidence and proposing interesting initiatives.

462

MASERATI CLUBS
AROUND THE WORLD

Maserati collectors and fans are scattered throughout the world and since the early Sixties, I have received enquiries about our historic pre-war cars; moreover, I had also received a brochure on the life of the Maserati Club in Great Britain. I therefore believe that the British, with their tradition of automotive clubs, who founded the first of the many Maserati clubs that have been created all over the world. The last to be born in Europe was in the Netherlands in 1989, while Maserati Clubs had already been operational in the other European countries since the early Eighties. Overseas, Francis Mandarano founded the Maserati Club International in 1976, which was mostly an association for business purposes: the owner created it not only as a club but also to sell spare parts. The Maserati Club of America, on the other hand, has since 1985 brought together all the American Clubs scattered throughout the various states; its president, Mr. Seymour Pond, did an excellent job and I received daily requests for information on our cars from him. There are even two Maserati Clubs operating in Australia.

In 1993, two Maserati Clubs were founded in the Far East, in Taiwan and Japan. In Japan in particular, in addition to contemporary Maseratis, our classic cars are particularly highly appreciated: the president of the Club, Shinichi Ekko, owns a Maserati Bora and a 430. Over time I have established a relationship almost of friendship with this gentleman. On his European business trips he never fails to drop in to Maserati to bring us their magazine and pick up information regarding his members' cars. After more than twenty years, when he arrives at Maserati it always seems like the very first time, with his concern about not disturbing us, with that air of being a little in awe of his surroundings. For some years now, Mr. Ekko has been publishing a kind of episodic tale of Maserati's history in the most important Japanese magazine. He has interviewed me on several occasions, with the assistance of one of his compatriots living in Modena, married to an Italian. He is so precise and methodical that he asked me to set up other meetings for him with other people from Maserati, company managers and, in particular, members of our Veterans Group.

Another character, a former president of the German Club, is Rolf Schiemenz of Bonn, the owner of a number of classic Maseratis as well as the whole series of Biturbo cars. He never misses a Club Italia event.

Given my position, I have had the pleasure of meeting both personally and through correspondence, all the Maserati Club presidents and secretaries who have succeeded one another over the years. Almost all of these clubs are constantly active and have developed over time as their membership has expanded. Most have also published an annual magazine or calendar.

France and the Principality of Monte Carlo were very active in the Eighties before waning, but lately the French club has been revived thanks to Monsieur Bernard Guenant, a great collector and restorer as well as a Maserati dealer.

Some nationals clubs, such as those in Spain and Belgium, have had difficulties in terms of continuity, but representatives of both never fail to participate in the international gathering organized every year in a different European nation. The first International Rally organised by the Maserati Register in 1986 was without doubt responsible for establishing this remarkable tradition. After the loss in 1997 of our beloved Gigi Villoresi, President of the Maserati Register from its foundation, Signora Maria Teresa de Filippis, formerly his deputy (and who later founded the Club Maserati Italia in 2004), was elected to the position on the occasion of Maserati's 90th anniversary.

This was made necessary by the unification of the Register and the Club managed by Antonello Cucchi into a single association of collectors of both historic and modern cars. Avvocato Nicola Sculco, a former member of the Register committee, was appointed Vice President, while Ingegner Teo Huschek became the coordinator of the foreign clubs.

In 2006, Dr. Ronchi, Maserati's new CEO, decided that the Club's secretariat should be located and supervised directly in-house. A unifying logo creating a certain image was specially designed to be adopted by all clubs. The secretary, Maurizio Bruno, was in charge of dealing with members, promoting enrolment and attending to the administrative work. Signor Igor Zanisi and I managed the technical commission, while the committee was composed of the members Lello Montorsi, Matteo Panini, Stefano Chiminelli, Dino Dini and Dr. Claudio Ivaldi. The latter, despite his youth, had accumulated a great knowledge of the Biturbo cars, as his dentist father was another who had owned every model. He was consequently aware of all the various versions and was already a long-term sufferer of "Tridentitis" as well as the proud owner of a 3500 GT spider Vignale and a Ghibli 95.

For reasons I am unsure about, Signora de Filippis resigned as president of the Maserati Club along with her husband Teo Huschek, but remained honorary president. Avvocato Nicola Sculco provisionally took over the position, while looking for a more important and more prestigious figure in the Maserati world. The name of Ingegner Carlo Maserati, Ettore's son, was put forward but unfortunately he declined the invitation. I then suggested another name that I thought might be of interest and appropriate for the role, but proved not to be to Avvocato Sculco's liking.

With the resignation of Dr. Ronchi in 2008, Ingegner Harald Wester came in to direct Maserati, but Avvocato Sculco struggled to establish same dialogue and relationship he had enjoyed with Dr. Ronchi. Ingegner Wester was very busy because, in addition to directing Maserati, he was also a director of Alfa Romeo and had other duties within the Fiat group. Avvocato Sculco wanted a more direct relationship with the upper echelons, rather than with Signora Roberta Bicocchi, Ingegner Wester's secretary, who in the meantime had been appointed to keep in touch with the various foreign Maserati Clubs in place of Ingegner Huschek. Other rather opaque issues then arose that affected me, as a result of which I had occasion to point out to Avvocato Sculco that his behaviour was not, in my opinion, becoming with the professional ethics of his role. Since then, he hasn't spoken to me! Despite my attempts at pacification, that same day Avvocato Scortichini of Maserati, dissolved the Maserati Club Italia committee, starting from the secretariat that would no longer be managed in-house at Maserati. Avvocato Scortichini also took charge of and guaranteed the transfer of the new Maserati Club Italia executive committee that was to be composed as follows: Chairman Luigi Santoro, who had already been a member of the previous board, Vice-Chairman and Secretary Claudio Ivaldi; these two gentlemen were responsible for the hand-over that permitted the definitive continuity of the Maserati Club Italia, whose current Board is made up of Vice-Chairman Giovanni Niccolini Serragli and Councillors Giuseppe Andreatta, Antonio Mariani, Fabio Moscato, Raffaello Poggiana, Roberto Ricciardello, Antonello Salvi, Antonio Vivenzio and Davide Volpe. The Honorary President, in my opinion undeservedly, being the undersigned.

Eighteen years later, as I write these lines, the Maserati Club of Italy is alive and more active than ever. Its magazine, edited by Dr. Claudio Ivaldi, has announced that the Maserati International Rally is to be held in Italy andorganised for the first time by the Maserati Club Italia, from the 21st to the 24th of September 2017, at Saturnia and the surrounding area.

FROM THE GTS AND GT SPORT TO THE GRANCABRIO

The new GranTurismo S coupé was unveiled at the Geneva Motor Show in March 2007. It featured a 4700 cc V8 engine producing over 440 hp at 7000 rpm mounted in a chassis derived from the floorpan of the 4200 GT, while the gearbox was ZF a 6-speed + R with on request robotized DuoSelect shifting, for a top speed of over 285 kph. The sleek 2 + 2 coupé bodywork was designed by Pininfarina with a wedge-shaped profile and the C-pillar running softly into the boot. In 2008 it was also produced in the Gran Turismo Sport version, with a 4700 cc V8 engine delivering 460 hp and a top speed of 300 kph.

The press launch was scheduled from the 9th of July to the 1st of August on the passes of the Dolomites between Bolzano and Moena. Dr. Luca Dal Monte, Head of Communications, brought in 200 journalists from all 28 countries in which Maserati is present, divided into 12 groups with photographers and cameramen, who for three weeks would have ten Maserati GranTurismo cars at their disposal, with support from our test drivers who were ready to provide all kinds of technical explanations. The Maserati managers were to take turns attending the various evening press conferences organised by Dr. Dal Monte. The press coverage all over the world was quite exceptional repercussion with a very significant return in terms of both image and especially sales.

Our new Head of Communications, Dal Monte, had already demonstrated his ability to organise events and get people talking about Maserati. This had been the case, for example, in June, on the occasion of the Military Academy of Modena's Mak Pi 100, a ceremony held to celebrate the hundred days remaining until the end of the two-year course after which the young officers are appointed as sub-lieutenants. Dal Monte had come to an agreement with the commanding General that two Maserati Quattroportes would also be present at the ceremony. The Academy's ceremonial courtyard welcomed over sixty debutantes dressed in white, while slowly a blue Quattroporte rolled to the centre of the courtyard and a bridesmaid emerged; she was welcomed by the Cadet Commander of the Course, ready together with her to open the dances. In the words of the evening's master of ceremonies, "Once the debutantes arrived in coaches, now they arrive in Maseratis." Dr. Luca Dal Monte's ability to devise and find ever-new situation and locations to excite even the most obstinate of journalists was unsurpassed. On one memorable occasion more than 150 international journalists were invited to Modena for the GranTurismo S Automatic road test. For eight different evenings over three weeks, between April and May 2009, following road test sessions in the hills between Bologna and Modena, at 19, Signora Nicoletta Pavarotti, wife of the great Modenese tenor "Big Luciano", as he was called by the Americans, hosted the press conference in her home, while at 20:30 dinner was served in the large hall on the ground floor. In the middle of the evening, two of Maestro Pavarotti's students, accompanied at the piano by another student, performed songs that sent everyone into raptures. I had the pleasure and the honour of attending one of these evenings, reminding Signora Pavarotti of when she would call me to bring her the series III Quattroporte for the Maestro when he was back from his long tours. A heard a few old journalistic acquaintances say, "In addition to the tests of extraordinary cars, Luca's able to come up with a put you in places that leave you with indelible memories for life". The girls from the Communications Office, Claudia Casarini and Silvia Saporetti, told me that Japanese journalists could hardly stop applauding so ecstatic were they about the music and their surroundings.

The GranCabrio completed the Maserati production range, exactly two years after the presentation of the Gran Turismo, when it was launched at the Frankfurt International Motor Show in September 2009. Photographs had appeared in the press two hours after our Communication and Press Office had issued several shots on the 24th of August. This just goes to show the degree of expectation there was for this new car. After two four-seater Maserati spiders had been bodied in Great Britain in 1930 on the Tipo 26/M rolling chassis, Maserati had always built two-seater spiders: the A6G Spider Frua in 1950, the 3500 Vignale Spyder in 1960, the Mistral Spyder in 1965, the Ghibli Spyder in 1968, the Spyder Biturbo in 1985 and the Spyder in 2001. The GranCabrio was therefore not only a novelty, but also a synthesis of Maserati's open-top cars. The mechanical specification was the same as that of the GranTurismo; only the floorpan was revised in order to guarantee the rigidity and flexibility required for the transformation of the bodyshell. The lines of the bodywork, designed by the Maserati Style Centre, were slender, concealing a length of almost five metres. The multi-layered canvas roof was electrically foldable in less than thirty seconds. The car provided space for four with the same luxurious trim as the coupé.

It was exported to the United States under the name of Maserati GranTurismo Convertibile, Cabrio being a term to which that market was unaccustomed. The Maserati Communications Office, headed by Dr. Luca Dal Monte, has continued to devise, on the occasion of press conferences and road tests of our new models around the world, locations that are guaranteed to amaze the participants, combining art, cuisine and sites in Modena and the surrounding are that the world envies. For example, when he had Beppe Zagaglia, the most Modenese of the Modenesi, accompany the journalists to Modena Cathedral where, in the background, the Ave Maria sung by Pavarotti could be heard. Zagaglia then took them to the Doge's Palace for dinner with the Commander of the Military Academy with the presence in turn of our historic drivers: from Nino Vaccarella to "Dino" Govoni, Maria Teresa de Filippis, Stirling Moss and John Surtees. And then on to the next event, six months later, visiting the birthplace of Giuseppe Verdi at Roncole di Busseto with dinner at the home of the children of Giovannino Guareschi, the creator of Peppone and Don Camillo.

SUPPORTERS AND CRITICS

I am honoured to have the friendship and esteem of so many people, some of whom I do not even know, but unfortunately there are also the critics, who fortunately I think can be counted on the fingers of one hand. It's a shame, but you can't have everything in life. There are two types of detractors, the shady ones who will gossip about you behind your back and the wicked and idle ones who openly and publicly bury you in mud, in an attempt to prove at all costs their good faith while disguising their misdemeanours.

Those two Maserati sport cars that had been seized by the Florence Finance Police in 2001 were submitted to inspection by the Court of Ferrara because they were considered to be counterfeit. The expert appointed by the Court, after examining the vehicles and gathering all the necessary information, presented two extensive dossiers in which he presented the evidence confirming that they both were non-original cars, practically two replicas. In March 2006, the judge ordered the destruction of the two vehicles, which were taken to the scrapyard by the carabinieri and crushed. This was the first such conviction in the world of historic cars. I have no intention expressing any opinion regarding the judge's decision and it's simply not my place to do so. Between June 2006 and July 2010, every six months, the owners of the two cars destroyed took turns to make sure that articles were published in the monthly magazine *Auto d'epoca* and elsewhere regarding the destruction of what they claimed to be original cars due to an inexperienced expert and Ermanno Cozza who had presented false information. I replied in the same magazine presenting my case and explaining the facts, but then I let it go as each time, with the complicity of their peers, they would always bring new arguments, absurd and inexplicable theses, alleging that chaos reigned in the Maserati archive, that the chassis number plates were made of tin and that Maserati moved them from one car to another. My fault consisted in leaving, as was my custom, in the two files on the cars that were destroyed, notes regarding my doubts over the originality of each. When the two boxes containing the files on our A6GCS and 200S cars were seized at Maserati, at the bottom of the 300S files were also the three folders regarding the 350S, 450S and 151 models. The Finance Police examined them one by one and when they arrived at the A6GCS *2085*, they found the first letter, an enquiry about where to find the spare parts to restore the car, which had been the property of the family for over twenty years, and a second letter in which the author explained that he had met an expert who would help with the restoration and asked for a copy of the production sheet. After checking the relevant folder in the archive and considering that we had sent spare parts to Germany more than thirty years earlier, I found it plausible that the car had returned to Sicily from where it had been sold in 1954 and sent in good faith a copy of the document as requested, adding the chassis number and the names in my lists. A year later I received a phone call from a friend who had seen the number *2085* in a copy of my documentation and informed me that the car was in Germany. After some time, Igor Zanisi called me to confirm that number *2085* was in Peter Kaus' Bianco

Rossa collection in Frankfurt. When Ingegner Huschek asked me about this car, I sent a fax saying that I believed the car in Germany to be original on the basis of the information I had received. When Lieutenant Spatula of the Finance Police read these notes it was sufficient for him to have the Sicilian car inspected.

The case of the 350S it was simpler, as among the documents that I used to leave for future reference, as Ingegner Bertocchi always told me, "Write, write everything, every movement", was the report that I had made to Signor de Tomaso, when he had told me not to provide any more information about the 350S *3501* as he'd learnt that it was a reconstruction.

Among other things, there were a number of notes in which I advised the gentleman not to use that chassis number as it no longer existed in Maserati; a V8 4500 cc engine had been installed in the car and consequently the chassis had been renumbered *4501*. My advice remained unheeded and a car was assembled complete with stamping and a 350S *3501* plate that was easy to establish as a replica.

The court-appointed expert, increasingly called into question by the articles in the specialist press containing insults and denigration of his work, eventually sued the two gentlemen. A few years later I was called as a witness by the expert at the trial that took place over several sessions. On each occasion the plaintiffs presented themselves with different individuals ready to plead their causes. I in turn found myself accused of false testimony. When my case went to trial shortly afterwards, my lawyer told me that my presence in court would not be required, as the written defence he had advised me to prepare would be sufficient. I was acquitted because as there was insufficient evidence to support the accusation. The process initiated by the court expert is still on-going and it is not known when the judgment will arrive. After appealing to the Supreme Court in 2010, the owner of the 350S did manage to have the confiscation revoked, but unfortunately the two cars had already been scrapped.

I often pass by the Candini workshop where historic Maserati cars arrive from all over the world for restoration. Giuseppe is currently struggling with a 1948 Maserati A6 1500 Pinin Farina. The car had been owned for several years by our friend Dr. Bernardo Favero, who had imported it from Argentina, a country he often visited on business; this car is said to have been owned by Evita Perón. Dr. Favero, a friend of Guerino Bertocchi, and of course of Fangio and González as well as other drivers, had had over the years the opportunity to participate over in many rallies with this car, which had always been kept in its original state and never restored. Now owned by the Nicolis Museum of Verona, the car now really needed a complete restoration. Dr. Favero had already visited Maserati early in 2000 with our former driver, Froilán González and after a tour of the factory we had met with Ardilio Manfredini to talk about the races of the Fifties. They returned in 2004 to say hello as they were on their way to Ferrari. I looked for a factory manager to make the visit official and introduced González and Dr. Favero to the head of Maserati's after-sales service, Dr. George Mauro, who entertained them by explaining Maserati's plans and the arrival of new models. González told a few anecdotes abut our racing cars, but then as they had an appointment to go to they saluted us with a promise to come back when they had more time available. Sadly, González then suffered heart problems that no longer allowed him to travel by plane.

FAMILY TRAGEDY

Only those who have seen a relative of their own suffering from Alzheimer's can understand just I have been through over the last ten years. Certainly, it was painful for my children to see their mother in that condition, but it was I who suffered the most. I did my utmost to remain close to her in every possible way and if I didn't collapse I owe it in a way to Maserati, because those four or five hours I spent working every afternoon gave me some respite from my problems. I was asked so often by my closest friends how I managed to keep going, how I found the strength to always be close to her. One day even Don Sergio said he was amazed at how I coped. I replied that she was the mother of my children, the person I had loved most; he embraced me and told me that he would pray for me and for Giordana. I had become cynical, I didn't believe in anything anymore, let alone in prayers. I knew there was no prospect of improvement, but I had to go on hoping that, if there really was someone up there, they would come to my aid.

My daughter and her husband Franco had decided to celebrate their twenty-fifth wedding anniversary with a trip, but Gianna was unsure and told me she had a bad feeling about going away. I told them not to think about certain things and that they should leave; they due back after about ten days.

Three days before their return, it was July the 6th, 2008, the telephone rang at seven o'clock in the morning. It was the head nurse at Villa Regina who told me that Giordana was not responding as she had always done in the past. I dressed quickly, without even washing my face, jumped on my bicycle and in less than ten minutes I was at Giordana's bedside and with tears in my eyes I watched her take her last breath.

I immediately called my son Gianluigi and together we decided to wait for Gianna's return for the funeral and to announce Giordana's death only once the funeral had taken place. Giordana was to remain for three days in the chapel of rest at the Policlinico. Gianna had agreed to meet her children at Bologna airport and when she saw me there instead, she knew right away what had happened.

Although we had already lost her many years previously, it was terribly painful to lose her once and for all.

THE PLEASURE OF TELLING STORIES

The head of the After-Sales Service, Dr. George Mauro, had so enjoyed the meeting with Froilán González that when we met, he never failed to ask me questions about our company's past. One day he told me that he was going to send his young engineers talk to me for half an hour every day so that I could tell them a bit of Maserati history. In this way, when they visited our foreign importers as inspectors, they would have a more solid grounding in Maserati culture as far as the cars built in the past were concerned.

For a few weeks, on arriving at the office, I would find four young men who, at the end of their lunch break, had come to listen to my stories. Then there were only three and after a month just two; they were the ones who had asked me, a long time previously, if they could see the archive. They were in fact particularly interested in the history of the Maserati brothers and said that listening to me telling the stories was more exciting than reading it in books. There were also occasions when young people from various offices asked me to tell them about certain events or about certain cars of the past. In particular, Luca Giraldi, Fausto Novelli, Filippo Ghialamberti and especially the girls in the office where I have my desk: Claudia Casarini, Ilaria Ciccotti, Silvia Pini, Silvia Saporetti and Arpita Pandya who have alternated over the years. And many more... I have a pleasant memory of their interest in learning about Maserati's history.

Early in June 2009, Dr. Luca Dal Monte informed me that Mr. Joe Corbacio, one of our American collectors, was organizing a gathering for a Concours d'Elegance "The Beautiful Cars of Italy", in the hills of eastern Pennsylvania and would like me to be there. Although very honoured by the invitation I was equally concerned about travelling so far away by myself at my age. Dr. Dal Monte told me not to worry because he would organize everything so that I would have no problems. Having already had proof of his organizational skills in the past, I agreed to go.

At six o'clock in the morning on Wednesday the 16th of June, I found a car in front of my home waiting to take me to Malpensa airport where Maurizio Baietta, a Maserati colleague, was waiting for me. He was in Milan on business and accompanied me through to check in. At JFK airport in New York, I was met by a gentleman carrying a Maserati sign: this was Renato Zacchia, whom I knew by name as he is the official photographer of the Ferrari Maserati North America headquarters. Renato kindly accompanied me for all five days of my stay in the United States. For a small town man like me, the impact with the Big Apple was not very exciting, especially when I looked out the window of the 22nd floor of the hotel where I spent the first two nights. Among other things, I discovered that the owner of the chain of hotels I stayed in was the owner of one of the four A6GCS Pinin Farina berlinettas from 1954. The next day, Renato met me at the hotel for a tour of the city and a pleasant walk in Central Park, timing our arrival at the Maserati headquarters in New Jersey for lunchtime. I can hardly describe the welcome I received; I barely had time to nibble something from the buffet they had prepared as all the staff members wanted to exchange a few words with me. In the afternoon, Mr. Jeff Ehoodin of Maserati North America, Renato Zacchia and I set off in a Maserati Quattroporte for Pennsylvania and the Pocono circuit area, a journey of about 150 miles. We were put up in a magnificent hotel, a very old building that stood in the middle of an endless golf course. The following morning, I was to have been part of the jury for the Concours d'Elegance with the cars lined up on the lawn in front. Over dinner I got to know the various owners of the magnificent Maserati cars entered for the concours, people I knew only by name having sent them information about their cars in the past. I was so busy listening to everyone that I stayed up until the small hours. In the morning, we woke to rain and a heavy blanket of fog that forced all the owners of the cars to cover them with large plastic sheets. Everyone was upset because nothing like this had ever been seen before in the area in June. I was eager to record the chassis numbers of the Maserati sports racing cars, in particular. So I put on my yellow folding raincoat and started to tour the lawn among the middle of the cars with my notebook in my hand. Suddenly I saw a horde of open umbrellas coming towards me; given the adverse weather conditions nobody had expected me to examine every car. Fortunately, when we went to the Pocono circuit the next day the weather had turned fine and everyone had a chance to lap the track and let the roar of their engines be heard.

The previous evening I had told Joe Colasacco, responsible for the great collection of Italian cars of Mr. Larry Auriana, the owner of the Zagato bodied 16-cylinder V4, that I had driven the reconstruction of Igor Zanisi's 16-cylinder car at Mugello and he was eager to hear my opinion on the high speed handling of their car. After a few laps of

480

the track at over 160-180 kilometres per hour I reassured him that the vibration at high speeds was completely normal for cars from the Thirties. It was impossible to turn down the opportunity of further drives in different cars and the emotions I experienced in a single day were indescribable and unforgettable. Also present was our 8CTF that won the Indianapolis 500 Miles in 1939 and 1940.

Mr. Corbacio had introduced me by phone to Mr. Onofrio Triarsi, our new dealer in the United States who had been unable to be present at the event due to prior commitments, but who wanted at all costs for me to stay with him as his guest for a few days. However, as my trip had been carefully scheduled through to the return flight, I unfortunately had to pass up the invitation.

I was instead reluctant to miss a chance to visit Mr. Auriana's collection, which I knew to be particularly interesting. As I had agreed with his man at Pocono, on my return, while Renato Zacchia was accompanying me to the airport, we just had time to spend a couple of hours in Connecticut.

When we arrived at the address we had been given, a large gate opened and we entered an immense park before drawing up in front of a large white villa where Mr. Auriana was waiting for us with his brother, whom I knew only by name having exchanged a few faxes when he was preparing to restore the V4 16-cylinder. Dr. Orsi, his consultant, had informed me of the importance of the collection. When he opened the door of the immense space, I was left speechless. From the 26M of Arcangeli with which he won the Trofeo della Lupa in the Rome Grand Prix of 1930, still on show at Maserati, to the A6GCS that won its class in the 1953 Mille Miglia, to the 300S driven by Fangio and through to historic motorcycles, three Alfa Romeo cars and a number from other marques. In the restoration area, where we spent more time, they were working on two Maseratis: a Tipo 63 and the only remaining example of the Tipo 151, about which they asked me a lot of technical questions. I would have liked to have been able to stay longer, Mr. Auriana was a very knowledgeable and competent person and it was really very pleasant to get to know him.

Renato Zacchia then took me to the airport and waited for me to check in. We then said goodbye and I thanked him warmly for all his care over the past five days. I think, however, that he too had enjoyed having the opportunity to photograph cars that can only be seen on certain occasions. When I arrived back in Milan I found a car waiting for me that finally brought me back home.

The next day, when I arrived at the office, I rushed over to Dr. Luca Dal Monte, first of all to thank him because there hadn't been a single snag throughout the trip and also to give him a full account of the reception I had received and the passion for the Trident I had found among our American collectors.

MASERATI CLASSICHE

At the end of June 2009, I was summoned by Dr. Armillei, head of the Human Resources Department, who informed me that he had received pressure to find a young man to work alongside me. I could hardly believe my ears and thought I must be mistaken. He asked me again to give him the name of a lad I thought might be suitable to manage the archive with me. I had been asking for help for years and had witnessed growing interest and dealings in of historic cars. I certainly wasn't getting any younger and asked myself should happen to me and I was no longer go in to Maserati who would take care of and manage all the material that I had accumulated, put in order and conserved for so many years? No one is indispensable in life and an ancient proverb says "when a Pope dies another takes his place", but there would be consequences. Last but not least, I would have been very sad to see the problems Maserati would have found itself in. Finally, a long-held dream was about to come true. I had recently met a number of young people within the company who were particularly interested in Maserati history and who were passionate about cars. I was reminded of those two lads from the Technical Assistance Department who sometimes asked me to come with me when I went to the archive. So I submitted the names of Bolzoni and Collina. I avoided taking about the matter with anyone for fear that it would not happen. A week later, Dr. George Mauro called me, telling me that for a few months Ingegner Fabio Collina would be coming to help me and get to know the workings of the archive. For the moment it would be in the afternoons only so that in the morning he would, in his turn, have time to instruct and initiate another colleague who would replace him in the Technical Assistance Department where he had been working for ten years. He also told me that he felt Collina would one day be a suitable replacement for me, because he was a hard-working and willing young man.

For over seven months, five afternoons a week, Fabio Collina was my shadow. He would be with me when I went to find the documentation to deal with the requests of our collectors, he listened to my telephone conversations on technical topics related to restorations with workshops and mechanics, I showed him where to find the tables to insert the types of bushings, the machining dimensions, the tolerances and everything regarding our engines. Fabio had a great advantage over me in that he had professional computer skills, something which given my age, I have always had a problematic relationship. He therefore started working on digitalizing data and tables. I liked the boy, I saw the he was interested in the work and I treated him as if he were a son. In addition to explaining the various practical aspects of the job to him, I never failed to talk about professional ethics, about how to deal with certain people. The position he was to occupy would mean that he would have to manage certain situations that might have compromised Maserati as well as damaging his personal reputation. He was already suffering from the "Tridentitis" disease and as I was sure of his sense of belonging and the passion he put into his work, I began to give him the necessary space to acquire independence. I had already spoken to Dr. Dal Monte about my move, he was sorry I would be leaving the Communications Department where a climate of mutual understanding had been created for some time. However, with Fabio's own move confirmed, the space available was insufficient. My new office was on the first floor of the new building, next to and communicating with that of our boss, Dr. George Mauro.

He is without doubt to be credited with having understood the importance that the creation of Maserati Classiche would have as in terms of image and prestige, a structure that, once up and running would also have brought the company an economic return. This was all made official March 2010 in the office of the managing director Harald Wester, who had wanted to meet us and wish us good luck. I will never be able to thank the Maserati management enough for having valorized my work to such an extent over the years.

"COZZA 60": 1951-2011

Maserati Classiche was erected on foundations I'd been laying since 1965 without ever imagining the importance that work would have had in the future, a process that had started quietly and had sometimes received little consideration from my superiors. Now, together with Ingegner Fabio Collina and the full collaboration of the After-Sales Service directed by Dr. George Mauro, we are tasked with promoting and supporting various initiatives that have found renewed impetus from the creation of the official website, *www.maserati.com*, to requests for spare parts and other activities. Since this department was founded, we have made available copies on parchment paper, historical information regarding the cars, certificates of origin, technical and styling specifications of the cars, facsimiles of the original test sheets and shipping notices. By writing to the e-mail address *maserati.classiche@maserati.com* you could and can have information regarding the prices of historical documents and their availability. After so many years of indecision and with the guarantee of a modest annual budget, we have finally started work on the digital scanning of the drawings from the whole archive. This is a vitally important, very long and delicate process, which will only be completed in a few years' time. Maserati Classiche has also created a merchandising line for all collectors and enthusiasts of our brand, and will in the future be present with its own stand at the specialist historic car shows.

An unexpected dream had come true. My first sixty years at Maserati came to an end on the 23rd of October 2011 and I felt that the time was right to end my collaboration, a decision that provoked quite a reaction. I had come to this conclusion having seen that Fabio Collina no longer needed me around and above all I wanted to close my VAT number that was more trouble than it was worth. Also, the 78 years under my belt were not to be underestimated. In order to silence the many comments, I promised that every Wednesday afternoon I would in any case spend some time at Maserati dealing with a few matters and advising my replacement on certain matters of particular importance, promising that I would be around whenever needed. The umbilical cord that tied me to Maserati was too strong to be severed completely and I never have been able to. As the 23rd of October 2011 was a Sunday, I had planned to take a pair of magnums in on Monday the 24th to celebrate with about twenty colleagues after work. I'd also purchased two dozen plastic goblets for appearances sake rather than paper cups. The office mini-bar was too small to hold the two huge bottles, so I took them to the company in my portable icebox. The agreement was to meet at six o'clock in the Press and Communications Office, which was large enough to accommodate about twenty people. At five o'clock Fabio handed me a document asking for my advice on how best to deal the matter so as to keep me busy and told me that Claudia Casarini had problems accommodating us in the office us because she had received a delivery of parcels that were taking up too much space. He asked me to take a close look at the document while he was trying to find another location for us to meet. When he came back he told me that everything was ok, the meeting room of the

Commercial Department was available, but not to go over and not to take anything there yet because there was nearly six o'clock and we'd go over together.

I was impatient, I had tidied up my desk with a little regret, even though I knew that I would be sat at it again every Wednesday over the following weeks. I headed for the meeting room, but Collina told me that the location had been changed again and took me to the showroom. He opened the door to me because I had both hands full and I was welcomed by a burst of applause; the wave of emotion was so strong that I stood stock still and my eyes were clouded with a few tears. I caught a glimpse of my family, all those in the Veterans Group, my current colleagues, managers, Dr. Adolfo Orsi, Don Sergio Mantovani. Dr. Santoro and Dr. Ivaldi, president and secretary of the Maserati Club, presented me with me a miniature 250F in silver, sculpted by Alessandro Rasponi; Dr. George Mauro gave me a painting of the 6C 34 with Nuvolari at the wheel. In the meantime, a special edition of the in-house magazine *Idee in Linea* was circulating dedicated to "Cozza 60". Behind all this there could only be one person: Dr. Luca Dal Monte, who had forgotten nothing, not even Signora Laura from the restaurant who had prepared a delicious buffet, and the official photographer who was there to immortalize the event. After speeches by the various personalities, when was given the microphone I thanked the management of the company for the magnificent and unexpected party and then I showed the copy of the dynamometer test of the 250F engine signed by Giulio Alfieri and dated 25 December 1953 and a number of pay slips of the time that recorded 307, 312, 310 hours work per month, proof of the reality of what I had told Dr. Armillei of the Personnel Department.

It was 19:30 and after innumerable hugs and handshakes and greetings the party ended. My daughter asked me if she could drive with me, while Franco and the boys went straight home, because she had to go call in to the Biblioteca Delfini. I later discovered that that was an excuse to waste time as we were supposed to arrive in Piazza Sant'Agostino at the Trattoria del Museo after the arrival of the other guests. Another surprise and further emotions! I was welcomed by Carlo Maserati, Dr. Adolfo Orsi, my friend Giulio Borsari, the grandson of Marquis Diego de Sterlich, patron of the Maserati brothers, whom I knew only by telephone and who brought me a ceramic plate depicting a Maserati car painted in front of his grandfather's palace in Penne. Keeping to the theme, Matteo Panini presented me with the accelerator pedal of the Tipo 60 Birdcage mounted on a wooden plaque. The other guests included Dr. George Mauro, Dr. Marco Armillei, Dr. Fiorentina, head of administration, who in her way also gave me a gift by increasing the budget for 2012 and informing my deputy Fabio Collina directly. In addition, my entire family was present.

Dr. Dal Monte's final surprise was the souvenir menu card. Only a press and public relations director like him could have thought of combining food, wine and ingredients with the entire geographical area of Maserati. Aperitif with wine from the Oltrepò Pavese area, around Voghera, the city where the Maserati family originated; tagliatelle alla Bolognese in memory of the original location of the Alfieri Maserati workshop; tortellini and fillet of beef with balsamic vinegar in honour of the city of Modena. All washed down with the red wine of the Abruzzo vineyards, dear to the Marquis de Sterlich, the brothers' first patron. Finally, the dessert stuffed with pine nuts from Balcarce in Argentina in memory of the great Fangio. A few days later I also had the honour of being invited to lunch by the managing director Ingegner Harald Wester in his office.

The satisfaction and emotions I felt in these days amply repaid me for all the sacrifices made in sixty years of work at Maserati. It has been a hard life but also a wonderful one. I have learned from many Trident masters how to take work seriously, how to learn, how to listen and how to help others. I have enjoyed the esteem and friendship of all. Sadly, after 15 troubled years I lost my wife but I still have two wonderful children: Giovanna and Gianluigi who each gave me two beautiful grandchildren.

As I write these last few lines about my life at Maserati, I have 83 notches on my belt, my memory is still quite clear and I enjoy good general health, although of course I shall never really recover from the disease of "Tridentitis".

A CENTURY OF HISTORY: THE MASERATI CENTENARY

In 2014, it was my great pleasure to participate in Maserati's Centenary aboard our 1968 Quattroporte. I had always hoped that I would be able to take part in this event in view of my age. The celebrations got underway on Wednesday the 29th of January 2014, with the presentation in the company's showroom of the official book *Maserati. A century of history*, published by Giorgio Nada Editore, and closed on Monday the 1st of December with the unveiling of a plaque at number 1 Via de' Pepoli in Bologna, where the first Alfieri Maserati workshop had been founded, in the presence of the heirs to the legendary brothers, Ingegner Carlo, son of Ettore, and Ingegner Alfieri, son of Ernesto, the managing director Harald Wester and many other personalities.

Further events celebrating Maserati's 100th anniversary were held in Modena on the 4th of April at the Marco Biagi Foundation Auditorium with the theme "Maserati in Modena and around the world", organised by the City and Province of Modena. The municipal authorities and the University of Modena were present, and speeches were made by Harald Wester and Ingegner Alfieri Maserati. An exhibition at the MEF (Museo Enzo Ferrari) was inaugurated on Thursday the 19th of June and was to remain open through to the 1st of December. The exhibition curator, Dr. Adolfo Orsi, succeeded in bringing together in Modena from all over the world the most beautiful and glorious cars ever built by Maserati. In addition to the marque's top management, the opening was attended by the President of Ferrari Avvocato Montezemolo, former drivers Stirling Moss, Maria Teresa de Filippis, Emilio Giletti, and "Dino" Govoni, the heirs of the founder, Ingegner Carlo and Ingegner Alfieri, the mayor of Modena, Gian Carlo Muzzarelli, and naturally Dr. Adolfo Orsi.

The Maserati Centennial Gathering was held in Modena, Cremona and Turin from the 18th to the 20th of September. On Thursday the 18th of September, more than two hundred Maserati cars of all kinds and from all over the world were exhibited in Piazza Grande and Piazza XX Settembre to be admired by the citizens of Modena after driving in from Bologna, where they had passed under the statue of Neptune. The gala dinner was held at the factory, between the production lines, in an unusual and evocative atmosphere that was much appreciated by all the guests. The evening also saw the performance of four singers from the Luciano Pavarotti Foundation, testifying to the bond between Maserati and the Maestro. On Friday the 19th, the cars left for Cremona to take part in a regularity trial on the track before arriving in Turin for the Grand Gala at the Reggia di Venaria, where in the great courtyard the A6GCS Pinin Farina berlinetta and the Alfieri prototype, the coupé of the future, were on display under spotlights. Maserati's CEO Sergio Marchionne and Fiat CEO John Elkann, the evening's host, were welcomed by Harald Wester. On the morning of Saturday the 20th of September, there was a visit to the new Giovanni Agnelli plant in Grugliasco, where 150 cars, Quattroportes and the new Ghiblis, are produced every day. The Concours d'Elegance held in the afternoon in the evocative setting of Piazza San Carlo, crowded with spectators, brought the three-day carousel to a close. In the hope that we will still be around, if only as spectators, for the 110th anniversary celebrations.

WHY

by Gianluigi Cozza

There might appear to be something presumptuous about writing a book of memoirs, but as I see it that's not really true. Above all it's a legacy, principally for loved ones, children, grandchildren, friends and mere acquaintances. An account of a life, of experiences and passions that have the power to inspire and teach through their actions and their individual and social ethics. Moreover, such memoirs are extremely important testimony and an example of "history from the bottom up".

According to the British historian Peter Burke, who was the first to use this definition in the early Sixties, the study of so-called minor episodes, of ordinary people, of peripheral movements represents a wealth of memories enclosed in the minds of many unsung heroes that would be lost without individual initiatives, focussing knowledge solely and exclusively on facts, thoughts and actions of history's protagonists.

History from the bottom up has instead allowed us to explore the thinking, the aspirations and the facts that have distinguished many men and women who through their actions have determined the destiny of those who have gone on to play leading roles.

For example, we might mention how out of the letters of the French soldiers of the Grand Armée emerges an unconventional vision of Napoleon Bonaparte, how the letters sent by Italian soldiers from the trenches of the First World War reveal a vision of a young, unified Italian state that is different to the one propagated by the central powers and again how the letters of our fellow Italians who emigrated in past decades abroad to other regions of Italy, describe aspects of domestic and social life that are crucial to an understanding of the true conditions of life at that time.

My father's book may itself be seen as an historical analysis from the bottom up in that it is a vision of life within the Maserati company from a perspective different to the conventional portrait of a business focussing on the actions of the founder/s. The analysis departs, in fact from the bottom, from the perspective of the workforce, the employees and engineers, frequently mute players but nonetheless of vital importance in the success of an enterprise.

If we think of the histories of other important car manufacturers, first and foremost Ferrari, it is absolutely normal for the story of the company to revolve around the figure of the Drake (this is also true of Fiat and the Agnelli family and the Ford Motor Company and its founder Henry).

And so it is with Maserati, the genesis of which runs from its foundation and early triumphs with the legendary Maserati brothers passes to the Orsi family, responsible for further victories and industrial consolidation and then to Citroën, GEPI, Alejandro de Tomaso and finally to Fiat, Ferrari and FCA.

A difference is, however, apparent from these few lines: while for the other successful carmakers, the pairing of owner/key figure and company was destined to last for years, this was not the case with Maserati. In fact, in its over one hundred-year history, the company has changed hands no less than seven times and that dualism was at least in part broken. A third party instead came on the scene, the workforce, which with their commitment and dedication succeeded in overcoming the vicissitudes of the business and keep the reputation of the firm flying high even in the darker times.

My father's story focuses on this specific aspect, on the story of a young school leaver who at 18 years of age (in 1951) entered a factory for the first time (a large firm, at least in the eyes of a boy from the countryside of Collegarola, on extreme outskirts of Modena) and who still today, 65 years later, looks with the same eyes at that factory at the bottom of Viale Ciro Menotti on which the Trident proudly rises, the symbol of the story of "his" firm.

In the early Fifties, Modena had only recently emerged from the war, people were still going hungry and a factory job would undoubtedly have been a great help to a family planning to build a new house.

This was not the aspiration of an individual but the desire of many, many people. It was within this desire to construct and to grow that in the Fifties the seeds of the Italian wellbeing of the years to come began to germinate. In Modena in those years the foundations were laid for the construction of the mechanical engineering district that has made it famous throughout the world and the students graduating from the Istituto Tecnico Fermo Corni had two preferential career paths: with Ferrari or with Maserati.

Fate led my father to Maserati even though at the very beginning of his career Carlo Benzi, the Drake's historic accountant, did make a number of attempts to take him to Ferrari.

Italy is a nation of "campanili" or bell towers, with the population divided into factions around the myriad churches. While not quite on the level of the Guelphs and the Ghibellines, in those years Modena was also split between Ferraristi and Maseratisti, with the youngsters eager to elicit the secrets of the other camp, something my family was hardly immune to. In fact, when my father visited my mother when they were engaged he would meet her sister's fiancée (who then became my uncle) who was working at Ferrari and it was naturally difficult not to talk about work on those occasions.

As I have already mentioned, in those years, following the privations of the war, it was the ambition of all to improve their standard of living and therefore with his first wages my father put to one side his bicycle and bought the Lambretta with which he would take Giordana (my mother) to dance. The family had in the meantime left their rented accommodation in Collegarola and had built a house on the outskirts of Modena.

The family had been shocked by the premature death of my father's brother who drowned in the Panaro river at just 15 years of age. Life went on, however, and the house had to be raised by a storey when my father married Giordana; the new family needed its own apartment.

Here we really are talking about history, about images in black and white, photos of my sister and I with smocks (unthinkable today) and shorts. My father's professional history proceeded at the same pace in a sequence of different experiences: workshop, racing department, design, sales and post-sales.

My childhood memories of Maserati are concentrated in two images; the first is a red Merak parked in the courtyard which the day after my father would drive to the Geneva Motor Show and the second my mother crying because she had received an anonymous threatening letter; this was in the early Seventies and there was a hostile atmosphere in the factories. My father, who refuted all ideologies and concentrated only on his work, had perhaps been identified by some one as a scab.

What does a child think about his father's job? Certainly not about the fact that it allows you to live well or that, thanks to the sacrifices of both parents, you also had a little house in the Apennines where you could spend your holidays. All this is secondary to the memories associated with the stories of when my father delivered a car (a 5000 GT for the record) to Avvocato Agnelli who gave him what was an astronomical tip for the standards of the day, or when he met Peter Ustinov or Luciano Pavarotti. Undoubtedly, the figure of one's father and his job take on an almost mythical aspect when he meets people who are being talked about on TV.

As an adult instead, the idea of my father's job is more associated with the sense of belonging that emerges from his every story. My father is truly affected by "Tridentitis", a neologism he coined to describe the "illness" that strikes all Maserati enthusiasts. You should have seen his face when, in 2011, the company threw a surprise party for him to celebrate his 60 years in the job – he looked like a kid who'd just been taken on full time.

He has been fortunate enough to do what he loves and this has nourished that sense of belonging to the extent that it overshadows every adversity (and we all know how many things can go wrong every day at work and elsewhere). Passion mitigates all fatigue and avoids all recriminations while giving you an understanding that you are an active part of the success and the prospects of "your" company.

Sociologically speaking, we might say that this sense of belonging is typical of my father's generation, of people who created prosperity for themselves and for their families with sweat and determination, people who struggled to improve their style of life and the quality of their own work and that of their colleagues, people who, though silent, made a concrete contribution to the fortunes of the company in which they worked.

Today it is perhaps difficult to recreate such situations; young people struggle to find stimuli, there are barriers that are difficult to overcome and access to the world of work is more difficult and jobs are certainly not as stable as in the past. Similarly, professional mobility is very rapid and therefore it is more difficult for that sense of belonging to take root and for employees to feel they are actively contributing to the life of the company. What remains is the example of the "veterans" like my father, for whom the world may collapse around them but the company and their job are always there and to be done, done well because it is by the way that you do your job that you will be judged. This has always been my father's approach to work: commitment and a job done well. For the record, it has to be said that it was always him who determined the level of "well" a job had to be done to; I, for example, never managed to mend a punctured bicycle tyre, because I didn't do the job "well".

To give an idea of the my father's sense of belonging to the company I think about when my mother was sick with Alzheimer's Disease and my father said he was grateful to Maserati because the company allowed him to go to work and keep his mind sharp rather than fall ill himself, or when, a few years ago, Fiat paid after a number of months and he had to pay the VAT on a number of consultancy invoices and I would tease him about spending his own money to go to work and in reply he would say he only had to thank the company.

An example is set through gestures and behaviour, but also orally, through stories, and my father has always been really good at telling stories (let's just say that, like me, once you get him started it's hard to get him to stop); for example, his stories about the years of the Second World War, seen through the eyes of a little boy, anecdotes that always fascinated me, or the episodes associated with the motor races, such as the one about his boss Reggiani (who was then working for Ferrari) who flew hundreds of kilometres in Mexico, at night, to pick up the spares for a car participating in the Carrera Mexico that had to restart the next morning.

An example can, however, be transmitted in written form and this is, as I see it, the WHY of this book.

A book that I have read and reread time over because naturally my father wrote it... by hand and I helped him bring it into the 21st century by typing it up on the computer. A handwritten book that is nothing more and nothing less than his life, which for me has always been an example.

NOTES

NOTES

NOTES

NOTES

Printed by D'Auria Printing, Ascoli Piceno (Italy)
in May 2018